Democratisation and Constitutional Reforms in Kazakhstan

Democratisation and Constitutional Reforms in Kazakhstan

Mukesh Kumar Mishra

PENTAGON PRESS

Democratisation and Constitutional Reforms in Kazakhstan
by Mukesh Kumar Mishra

ISBN 978-81-8274-767-8

First Published in 2014

Published by
PENTAGON PRESS
206, Peacock Lane, Shahpur Jat,
New Delhi-110049
Phones: 011-64706243, 26491568
Telefax: 011-26490600
email: rajan@pentagonpress.in
website: www.pentagonpress.in

Branch:
Prime Arcade
Office #11
1154 Saifee Street
Opp. M.G.Road, Camp
Pune-411001
Email: pentagonpresspune@gmail.com

Printed at Avantika Printers Private Limited, New Delhi.

Dedicated to
My Beloved Wife
APARAJITA

Contents

APPENDICES

Preface

The Republic of Kazakhstan is situated in Central Asia between the Ural river and the lower courses of the Volga river to the West, the Altai mountains to the east, the west-Siberian plateau to the north and the Tien Shan mountain chain to the south. The territory of the Republic stretches 1,600 kilometers north to south and more than 2,800 kilometers, west to east occupying an area of 2,717,00 sq. kilometers. In terms of area, the Republic is the 9th largest country in the world and until December 1991 it was the second largest of the former Soviet Republics. Kazakhstan is bordered to the north, northwest and west by Russia, to the southeast by China and to the south and southwest by Kyrgyzstan, Uzbekistan and Turkmenistan. Kazakhstan shares a long border of 6447 km in the north with the Russian Federation and a coastline of 2,320 km on the Caspian Sea in the southwest. It also borders with the People's Republic of China (1,460 km), Kyrgyzstan (980 km), Turkmenistan (380 km) and Uzbekistan (2,300 km).

Kazakhstan is politically divided into 14 oblasts and five economic regions. They are, Aktybinsk, Atyrau, western Kazakhstan and Mangistan oblasts in western Kazakhstan, Kostanai, Northern Kazakhastan oblasts in Northern Kazakhstan, Akmola, Karaganda oblasts in Central Kazakhstan, Almaty, Zhambyl, Kyzylorda and Southern Kazakhstan oblasts in Southern Kazakhstan and Eastern Kazakhstan and Pavlodar oblasts in Eastern Kazakhstan. There are 82 cities and town in the Republic. The largest are; Almaty, Chimkent, Karaganda, Zhambyl, Semipalatinsk, Pavlodar, Ustkamenogorsk, Astana, Uralsk and Aktyubinsk. On December 10, 1997 the city of Astana was declared to be the new capital of Kazakhstan replacing Almaty (Alma Ata). Despite its vast territory, the population of Kazakhstan is only 14.953 million people (1999 census). Population density is as law as 6 persons per square kilometer. Kazakhs, Russians, Germans, Ukrainians, Tatars, Uzbeks, Byelorussians and Uighurs comprise the majority of the population. Numerically speaking Kazakhs constitute 39 per cent Russians, Germans 5.8 per cent and Ukrainians 5.4 per cent, with smaller ethnic groups comprising the rest. The predominant religion is Islam, most ethnic Kazakhs being Sunni Muslims of the Hanafischool.

Mikhail Gorbachev's accession to power in 1985 and his subsequent anti-corruption campaign, as well as the new policy of *Glasnost* (openness), had its impact on Kazakhstan as well. In December 1986, the Kazakhs protested in Almata (now Almaty), the then capital of Kazakhstan, against the appointment of GennadiKolbin, an ethnic Russian as First Secretary of the Communist Party of Kazakhstan. The Almata riots of 1986, reflected the growing assertion of ethnic Kazakhs in Kazakhstan's civil, political and cultural domains. In September 1989 the Kazakh Supreme Soviet (Parliament) adopted a legislation declaring Kazakh as the official language of the Republic, while Russian remained the language of inter-ethnic communication, though the new law was opposed by many non-Kazakh residents.

On 25 October 1990, the Kazakh Supreme Soviet declared its sovereignty, asserting republican control over natural resources and the economy. Although this declaration emphasized ethnic equality, there were protests in the predominantly Slav-populated city of Ust-Kamenogorsk. Kazakhstan participated in the referendum on the future of the USSR conducted in nine Soviet republics in March 1991. Almost 90 per cent of the electorate voted in Kazakhstan, of whom 94 per cent endorsed the proposal to preserve the USSR as a 'Union of Sovereign' states with equal rights. In June 1991 the Kazakh Supreme Soviet voted in principle to adopt a draft Union Treaty, although Nazarbaev expressed reservations about certain aspects of the proposed federation.

In October 1991 Kazakhstan signed alongwith seven other Republics, a treaty to establish an economic community, and in November 1991 it agreed to the draft treaty of the new Union of sovereign states. These accords were largely nullified by the proposed Commonwealth of Independent States agreed to by the leaders of the three Slavic Republics (Russia, Ukraine, Belarus) in December 1991. Kazakhstan (despite initial reluctance) and the other Central Asian Republics agreed to join the new Commonwealth. On 16 December 1991 Kazakhstan became the last of the Republics to declare independence from the USSR, and was redesignated as the Republic of Kazakhstan. The country was formally recognized as a co-founder of the CIS at the Almaty meeting on 21 December 1991. The constitution adopted in January 1993, invoked the law of 1989 (denoting Kazakh as the state language with Russian as a language of inter-ethnic communication).

Kazakhstan is an area with little tradition of either constitutionalism or democratic politics during the Soviet period. However, the constitution making experience of the former Soviet Union did provide some basis. The governing structures which Lenin's Bolsheviks created were guided by the euphoria of 1917 revolution. The Russian Federation was presented as the territorial successor to the Russian Empire. In 1922 the Russian Federation joined the Belarusian, Ukrainian and Transcaucasian republics as constitutionally equal partners in a Union of Soviet Socialist Republics (USSR) and institutions of the RSFSR were re-formed as institutions of the new Union. The Russian Federation, in common with the other republics, experienced hardship as a result of the collectivisation campaign of the early 1930s and the widespread repression under Stalin. Shortly after the death of Stalin in March 1953, Nikita Khrushchev took over the post of First Secretary of the communist party of the Soviet Union. He ended the most brutal aspects of the Stalinist regime. He was replaced by Leonid Brezhnev who stayed till 1982 and brought a thaw in the two superpowers relationship.

But the far reaching changes, in the form of '*glasnost*' and '*perestroika*', were introduced by Mikhail Gorbachev. His policies were totally contrary to the centralizing tendencies of the past. His era came to an end with the end of the USSR itself. The constitutional apparatus during the whole period of USSR was highly centralized. Democratic centralism was the guiding spirit of constitutional space. 'Party' was the all powerful tool to capture and control the state. 'Party', 'Politburo' and 'ideology' were the three main pillars of the Soviet state. All soviet constitutions reflect the clear influence of this tripod. In the 1977 constitution of the USSR there was a clear-cut continuity of the ideas of the 1918 constitution of the RSFSR, the 1924 and 1936 constitution, which established the principles for demarcating jurisdiction between the organs of the USSR and of the Union Republics.

However, Kazakhstan embarked on its constitution making exercise, when constitutional commission headed by President Nursultan Nazarbayev was created in December 1990, but little was published regarding its early meetings. Alongside this, work on a draft was carried out by a parliamentary group headed by the commission member and Deputy Chairman of the Supreme Soviet, Zinaida Fedotova. In May 1991 a round table discussion involving commission members, deputies and parliamentarians from other Soviet Republics debated the proposed draft, and in October 1991 the revised draft was submitted to a group of academics for comments. Addressing the Kazakhstan parliament in early June 1992, Nazarbayev noted the extensive discussions that had already taken place and outlined the main features of the draft constitution. In particular he emphasized what he described as the separation of executive, legislative, and judicial powers. He argued for strong presidential powers which would enable the President to overcome the problems of a transition period during which Kazakhstan would have to carry out substantial economic restructuring and maintain the unity of this large multi-ethnic state.

When one looks at the developments in the five former Republics of Soviet Central Asia, one observes that in all of them constitutional evolution was preceded by elements of constitutional change during the last days of the USSR. Nonetheless, there were differences in various processes the discussion was perhaps more extensive in Kazakhstan and Kyrgyzstan. In May 1995 Nazarbayev ordered the establishment of a special council to prepare (under his guidance) a new constitution. The new constitution preserved the extensive executive powers of the President and also abolished the post of Vice-President. The Supreme *Kenges* was replaced by a bi-cameral parliament, comprising a 47 member senate (the upper chamber – with 40 members elected by Kazakhstan's regional administrative bodies and seven being appointed by the President) and a directly elected, 67 members *Majlis* (Assembly). The Constitutional Court was replaced by a constitutional council, the rulings of which would be subject to a Presidential right of Veto.

In June 1996 a joint session of Parliament approved a motion of confidence in the government tabled by *Kazhegeldin*, following rejection by the *Majlis* of his administration's controversial draft pensions legislation (the main provision of which was the gradual raising of the retirement age) from 60 to 63 years for men and from 55 to 58 years for women. It stated that the President of the Republic shall be the symbol and guarantor of the unity of the people and the state power, inviolability of the constitution, rights and freedoms of an individual and citizen. He would be elected by universal, equal and direct suffrage under a secret ballot for a seven-year term in accordance with the constitutional law by the citizens of the Republic who have come of age.

In November 1997, the new capital was officially inaugurated by Nazarbayev, and a joint session of both chambers of Parliament was held for the first time in Akmola in the following month. Nazarbayev undertook several far reaching measures to structure and rationalize the state administration in March 1997. Nazarbayev continued the reform process, by reducing the number of administrative regions from 19 to 14. Further, in September 1998, in his annual address to Parliament, Nazarbayev outlined proposals for political reforms including amendments to electoral procedures and enhanced powers for the legislature. Moreover, the session subsequently voted overwhelmingly in favour of a parliamentary amendment whereby the presidential election would take place before the expiry to Nazarbayev's extended mandate in 2000. Further in May 2010 Parliament made legislative changes that bestowed new powers on President Nazarbayev. In addition to granting Nazarbayev the title of "leader of the nation," he now gained the right to intervene in politics after he officially retires from the presidency and would enjoy enhanced immunity from prosecution.

Nazarbayev's nation-building scheme has had at its core a policy of 'Kazakhisation'; reviving the Kazakh language, restoring traditional names to cities and landmarks, revising history to reflect a Kazakh national perspective, and observing Kazakh and Islamic holidays. The constitution provides an even more direct preventative measure. One clause expressly forbids the establishment of any social organisation which seeks to forcibly change the constitutional order, undermine state security, violate territorial integrity, or promote social, racial, national, religious, class or tribal discord. In addition, parliament of the Republic of Kazakhstan is the highest representative body performing legislative functions. The powers of parliament may be prematurely terminated in cases and according to the procedure stipulated by the constitution. Parliament consists of two chambers acting on permanent basis; the senate and the *Majlis*. Term of the senate deputies is six years, while that of *Majlis* deputies is five years.

The Government exercises the executive power of the Republic and is responsible to the President. The Government drafts the main areas of the state's socio-economic policy, defence capability, security and public order, and orders their implementation; presents to parliament the Republican budget and reports of its implementation, and insures that the budget is implemented; submits draft legislation to the *Majilis* and provides for the implementation of laws, organises the management of the state property; formulates measures; pursues Kazakhstan's foreign policy; directs the activity of Ministries, State committees and other central and local executive bodies.

Local state administration is exercised by local representative and executive bodies, which are responsible for the state of affairs on their territory. The local representative bodies – the councils (*Maslikhat*) express the will of the population of the corresponding administrative territorial units and bearing in mind the overall state interest, define the measures necessary to realize this will and monitor the ways in which these are implemented. Councils are elected for a four year term by a secret ballot of the public on the basic of general, equal and direct suffrage. The local executive bodies are part of the unified system of executive bodies of Kazakhstan. Each local executive body is headed by the *Akim* of the corresponding administrative – territorial unit, who is the representative of the President and the government of the Republic.

Electoral system has been reformed in Kazakhstan. The people have the chance to vote either according to party membership or according to the party's ideas and views. Earlier the citizens of Kazakhstan did not have the opportunity to select their chief executive in a democratic freely contested election. In December 1991, official election results confirmed Nazarbayev the winner in an uncontested race, with 98 percent of the vote, in which 80 percent of the electorate was said to have participated. His only potential opponent reportedly failed to collect the 100,000 signatures required to appear on the ballot. One month after the disbanding of Parliament in April 1995, a popular referendum was organized to ratify President Nazarbaev's proposal to do away with the scheduled 1996 Presidential election and allow him to remain President until the year 2000. The government claimed that 91 percent of the citizens participated in this poll and 95 percent approved the measures.

In March 1994, Kazakhstan held a parliamentary election that created the first post-independence national parliament. Until that election, the Republican Supreme Soviet deputies elected in 1989, despite its disbanding, remained in office. Seventy-two of the new 177 member lower house were directly tied to the President, whose Union of Popular Unity (SNEK) won 30 seats, while candidates from a Presidential list filled forty-two of the seats. OSCE observers called the elections unfair, noting inflated voter turnout reports. August 1995 produced a result in which 89 percent of voters allegedly supported a draft constitution vastly expanding Presidential powers. Nazarbayev gained the authority to dissolve the parliament for, among other things, its failure to approve the President's nomination for Prime Minister. The new constitution removed a significant potential barrier to complete Presidential rule, the Constitutional Court, to consultative body, enabling Nazarbayev to effect any constitutional changes unchallenged.

Civil society in Kazakhstan, in particular, NGOs, media have to face burdensome regulations which involve lengthy registration period and high fees. Furthermore, the arbitrary rejection of certain NGOs puts obstacles in the functioning of NGOs. Freedom of press in Kazakhstan is promoted with the active support of the local civil society organisations. NGOs advocating freedom of speech by their activities and publications play a substantial role in protecting rights and interests of mass media. The Kazakhstan civil society has proven to be an important player in building open society through establishment of open objective and progressive journalism in everyday life of the country. Among the most active, well-known and progressive civil society organisations promoting media rights in the country are, Association of Independent Electronic Mass Media of the countries of Central Asia, *Azia Dauysy* (Free Tribune of Journalists), *Birlesu*, Eurasia Foundation Kazakhstan, International Journalism Centre, Kazakhstan Press Club, National Press Club, Soros Foundation Kazakhstan, Kazakhstan Broadcasting Association. This shows that some measures for democratic development of the media have been taken in Kazakhstan. Consequently, democratisation process in the Republic is developing in compliance with several principal directions, i.e., legal reform to consolidate the independence judicial system, expansion of authority of representative government bodies (such as *Maslikhats*), extension and improvement of the election legislation (autumn 2001) etc.

It is against this background that the **introductory chapter** analyses the geography, demography and history of the Republic of Kazakhstan in detail. The process by which Kazakhs have become a nation involving a long term and complicated historical ethno-genesis is being discussed into three historical phases: the pre-Turkic (18th century BC to 4th century A.D.), The Turkic (4th century AD to 13th century) and the Turk-Mongolian period (13th century till 15th century). The **second chapter** discusses the distinct geo-cultural and ethno-religious mosaic of Kazakhstan, which has conditioned the legal and political process in independent Kazakhstan. It has located the statehood of Kazakhstan in the Soviet experience of constitutionalism in the former Soviet Republic of Kazakhstan. The process of political transformation in Kazakhstan took place in the 1990s, when a flurry of activities, aimed at the setting up of the institutions of modern democracy, was unfolded.

The **third chapter** discusses the constitutional developments in the independent Kazakhstan and contextualizes it in the wider process of political transformation in Central Asia. It enumerates the landmark events in the pre and post independence period in Kazakhstan and discusses them in the light of its existing constitutional set up. This chapter also discusses the challenges that Kazakhstan has faced in establishing the present constitutional set up. The **fourth chapter** examines the working of democracy on the ground, i.e. especially the process of elections in Kazakhstan. It has, recognized a number of issues relating to the electoral process of Kazakhstan namely its emergence, manner of functioning, consolidation and its impact on the democratic process at large. The **fifth chapter** focuses on the constitutional powers and role of President in independent Kazakhstan, who has been assigned with the enormous powers in the present constitutional framework. This chapter explores the centrality of the role, which the President has assumed in the process of democratisation in Kazakhstan.

The key issues such as status of civil society and its components like media, NGOs, think tanks etc. in Kazakhstan have been addressed in the **sixth chapter** which conceptualizes civil society as an institution within the larger context of Central Asian regime which is undergoing the process of democratic transformation. Besides, it also analyses the evolution of civil society institution in Kazakhstan as a slow but concrete process especially in the post-USSR period. This chapter also highlights the fact that while the newly evolving Kazakh civil society has its interface with western democratic regimes as well as transnational actors, it also faces challenges from the domestic political regime which is formally democratic but still having dictatorial legacy manifested through its pattern of interaction with non-state democratic entities. Thus, civil society like any other democratic institution in Kazakhstan is in the stage of making, and is yet to reach the optimum level of its potential.

Mukesh Kumar Mishra

Acknowledgements

While completing this book in the present form I would like to acknowledge the help and support rendered by numerous people at various stages. First of all, I am greatly indebted to Prof. K. Warikoo, under whose supervision I did my M.Phil and PhD. It was through his encouragement and help that this work saw the light of the day. From the bottom of my heart I am also thankful to Prof. Devendra Kaushik, the doyen of Central Asian Studies in India, whose guidance, support and encouragement in several ways helped me improve the quality of this work. I would also like to express my gratitude to numerous people who helped me during my research trip in Kazakhstan to obtain necessary materials. They include Mr. Daulat O. Kunyshev Ambassador of the Republic of Kazakhstan to India as well as Mr. Dmitri and Mr. Timur. I would also like to express my gratitude to Prof. Dzhunusova Zhanylzhan, teaching at Department of Public Administration under President of the Republic of Kazakhstan.

I am also thankful to Mr. Kairat E. Umarov, the former Ambassador of the Republic of Kazakhstan to India as well as Mr. Nurgali Arystanov; Prof. Kuralay Baizakova, and Dr. Fatima Kukeyeva and Ailuna Utegenova, Al-Farabi Kazakh National University, Almaty. Dr. Alia Akataeva, Her friendship was invaluable to get familiarity with an alien country. My sincere gratitude goes to the people who helped me to collect materials and provided other academic requirements. Prof. Kenes Khodjahmetuly who teaches at the Department of History Kazakh National University; Prof. Abishev Ali Azhimovich, (Rector) Ministry of Education and Science, Republic of Kazakhstan; T. Ryskulov of the Kazakh Economic University; Dr. Askar K. Nursha, Head of Department, Kazakhstan Institute for Strategic Studies; John Leonard, Director, Center for Research and Development Kazakhstan Institute of Management, Economics and Strategic Research; Alma Nurshaikhova of the United Nation Development Programme at Almaty and Dr. Leila Muzaparova, Deputy Director, Institute of World Economy and Policy at the First Kazakhstan President Foundation—are the people whose cooperation in Kazakhstan was invaluable. I am grateful to Taskyn Rakhimbekova (President) and Serik Jaxylkov (Executive Director) of Republican Network of Independent Monitor, Almaty, for allowing me to take their interviews at Almaty.

The help provided by Prof. Ramadhikari Kumar, former Rector of JNU in guiding me how to deal with Russian sources has been valuable and I express my gratefulness to him. Prof. Ganganath Jha, Dr. Sharad K. Soni and Dr. Sanjay

Bharadwaj, all from School of International Studies, JNU, have been very helpful at different stages of the preparation of this book. My elder brother Vijay and sister in law Snehal provided invaluable support to me. I also thanks to Dr. Anurag and Sajjan for cooperation.

It is really symbolic that I am acknowledging the person at last who actually stood with me to see the completion of a rather long tumultuous journey with many ups and downs. Her indomitable will, stamina and 'never say die attitude' is indeed infectious and it is she who always restored my self-confidence. I can never express enough thanks which would be proportionate to her contribution form the day one to the completion of this book. Indeed this book belongs to my beloved wife Aparajita equally as it belongs to me.

Mukesh Kumar Mishra

1

Introduction

The Republic of Kazakhstan, which is situated at the heart of Eurasia, has established itself as an important country in Central Asia. Being the largest republic in terms of area in Central Asia, it has emerged from a nascent state to a major force in the region, with a growing economy and stable political order. Against this backdrop, the introductory chapter focuses on the geography, demography and history of the Republic of Kazakhstan.

GEOGRAPHICAL PERSPECTIVE

Kazakhstan is situated in Central Asia between the Ural River and the lower courses of the Volga River to the west, the Alatau mountains to the east, the West-Siberian plateau to the north and the Tien Shan mountain chain to the South.[1] The territory of the Republic stretches 1,600 kilometers north to south and more than 2,800 kilometers, west to east, covering an area of 2,724,900 square kilometers.[2] In terms of area, the Republic is the 9th largest country and the second in the CIS after Russia in terms of territory, and is one of the world's richest countries in terms of natural resources; it is considered to be the most stable of the former Soviet states,[3] in the world. Some 47,500 kilometers of the total area is occupied by water bodies.[4] Until December 1991, Kazakhstan was the second largest of the former Soviet Republics.[5] The independent republic of Kazakhstan is bordered to the north, northwest and west by Russia, to the southeast by China and to the south and southwest by Kyrgyzstan (980 kms), Turkmenistan (380 kms) and Uzbekistan (2,300 kms). There is a long border in the north with the Russian Federation (644 kms) and a coastline of 2,320 kms on the Caspian Sea in the southwest. It shares a border of 1,460 kms with the People's Republic of China. Kazakhstan has caught the world's attention in the last two decades due to its successes in the creation of institutions of statehood, the implementation of market reforms in the economy and the formation of a tolerant, multi-dimensional and multiethnic society. Kazakhstan's contribution to the global stability and nuclear security, along with its role as an initiator and active player in the sphere of disarmament and the creation of a collective system of security has earned it respectability in the comity of nations.[6]

Kazakhstan is located on the junction of two continents—Europe and Asia, between 45 and 87 degrees east longitude, 40 and 55 degrees northern breadth. The geographical center of the European-Asian subcontinent is in Kazakhstan (on an intersection 78 meridians with 50 parallel)—in epicenter of former Semipalatinsk Nuclear Zone. The northern most point in Kazakhstan is 55″26″ NL and it corresponds to the southern latitude of the central part of the East-European plain and to the southern part of the British Isles. The southernmost point is 40″56″ NL. It corresponds to the latitudes of the Trans-Caucasus and the Mediterranean countries of Southern Europe.[7] Most of the area of Kazakhstan is flat and low lying. In central Kazakhstan, vast plains give way to the isolated low mountainous range of Saryarka, to the south and southeast they melt into the mountainous systems of Altai, Sauyr-Tarbagatai, Dzhungarski Alatau and Tien Shan. Steppes occupy some 26 per cent of the territory of Kazakhstan. Deserts cover 44 per cent of the territory and 14 percent of the surface is covered with semi-deserts. Forests occupy 21,000,000 hectares.[8]

Some 9.4 per cent of Kazakstan's land is mixed prairie and forest or treeless prairie, primarily in the north or in the basin of the Ural river in the west. More than three-quarters of the country, including the entire west and most of the south, is either semidesert (33.2 per cent) or desert (44 per cent). The terrain in these regions is bare, eroded, broken uplands, with sand dunes in the Qizilqum (red sand; in the Russian form, Kyzylkum) and Moyunqum (in the Russian form, MoinKum) deserts, which occupy south-central Kazakstan. Most of the country lies at between 200 and 300 meters above sea level, but Kazakstan's Caspian shore includes some of the lowest elevations on Earth. The highest elevation, Khan Tengri Mountain, on the Kyrgyz border in the Tien Shan range, is 7,010 meters; the lowest point, at Karagiye, in the Caspian Depression in the west, is 132 meters below sea level. Only 12.4 per cent of Kazakstan is mountainous, with most of the mountains located in the Altay and Tien Shan ranges of the east and northeast, although the Ural Mountains extend southward from Russia into the northern part of west-central Kazakstan. Many of the peaks of the Altay and Tian Shan ranges are snow covered year-round, and their run-off is the source for most of Kazakstan's rivers and streams.

Nearly all rivers of Kazakhstan pour out into the Caspian Sea and the Arabian Seas or the Balkhash. Alakol and Tengriz lakes except for the rivers Irtysh, Ishim and Tobo, which flow into the Kara Sea. The biggest river is the Irtysh which stretches for 1,700 km within the area of Republic.[9] The largest rivers of Kazakhstan are: Irtysh (total length: 4248 kms, 1,700 kms of length is referred to Kazakhstan), Ishim (2,450 and 1,400 kms accordingly), Ural (2,428 and 1,082 kms), Syr-Daria (2,219 and 1,400 kms), Ili (1,001 and 815 kms), Chu (1,186 and 800 kms), Tobol (1,191 and 800 kms), Mura (all 978 kms in the republic's territory). Except for the Tobol, Ishim, and Irtysh rivers (the Kazakh names for which are, respectively, Tobyl, Esil and Ertis), portions of which flow through

Kazakstan, all of Kazakstan's rivers and streams are part of landlocked systems. They either flow into isolated bodies of water such as the Caspian Sea or simply disappear into the steppes and deserts of central and southern Kazakstan. Many rivers, streams, and lakes are seasonal, evaporating in summer. The three largest bodies of water are Lake Balkhash, a partially fresh, partially saline lake in the east, near Almaty, and the Caspian and Aral seas, both of which lie partially within Kazakhstan.

The climate of the Republic is deeply continental and extremely dry. It is severely influenced by the Arctic region and Eastern Siberia. The absence of any natural barriers in the north of the Republic enables cold arctic winds and arctic air masses to come from this direction without restraint. Conversely, the high mountains walling the east and the southeast of Kazakhstan act as a barrier to the air masses from the south. This accounts for the rather unsparing winters over the greater part of the area of the Republic. In Kazakhstan, summers are hot and dry with hot winds.

Demographic Setting

Official figures indicate that in the first half of 1994 some 220,400 people left, compared with 149,800 in the same period of 1993. In 1992 and 1993, the number of Russian emigrants was estimated at 100,000 to 300,000. Such out-migration has not been uniform. Some regions, such as Qaraghandy, have lost as much as 10 percent of their total population, resulting in shortages of technicians and skilled specialists in that heavily industrial area.[10] To some extent, the outflow has been offset by in-migration, which has been of two types. Kazakstan's government has actively encouraged the return of Kazaks from erstwhile Soviet Union and from China and Mongolia. Unlike other ethnic groups, ethnic Kazaks are granted automatic citizenship. More than 60,000 Kazaks emigrated from Mongolia in 1991-94, their settlement—or resettlement was smoothed by government assistance. Most were moved to the Northern provinces, where the majority of Kazakstan's Russian population lives. Because these "Mongol Kazaks" generally do not know Russian and continue to pursue traditional nomadic lifestyles, the impact of their resettlement has been disproportionate to their actual numbers.

The other major source of in-migration has been non-Kazaks arriving from other parts of Central Asia to avoid inhospitable conditions; most of these people also have settled in northern Kazakhstan. Although officially forbidden and actively discouraged, this in-migration has continued. In a further attempt to control in-migration, President Nazarbayev decreed that no more than 5,000 families would be permitted to take up residence in the republic in 1996.[11] Negative demographic and migration trends remain a challenge for Kazakhstan. As noted earlier, following the collapse of the Soviet Union, the county's population declined to 15 million

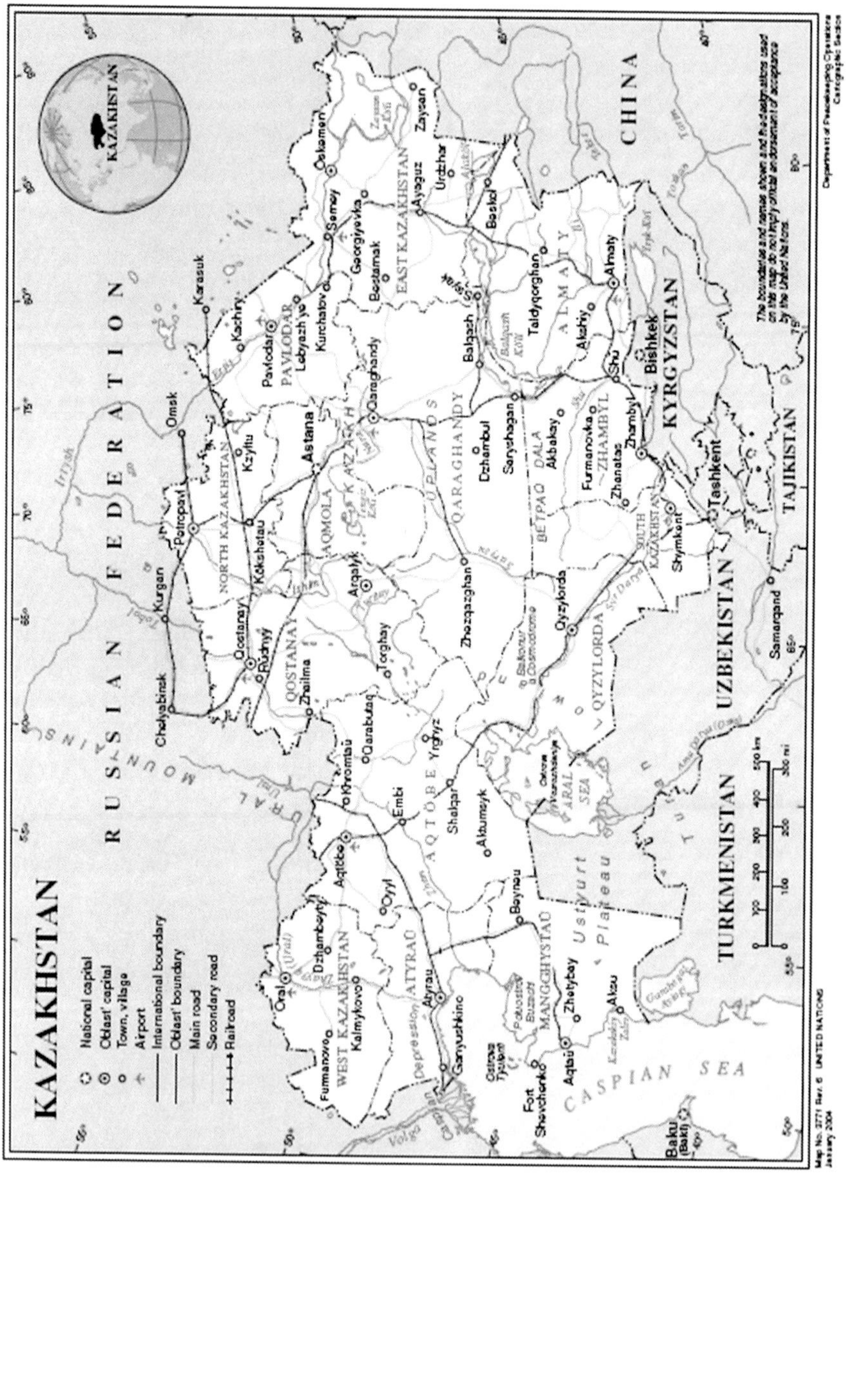

Source: Kazakhstan: http://i.infoplease.com/images/mkazakh.gif

people and was insufficient to support industrial sector growth. In an attempt to reverse this trend, Kazakhstan launched a repatriation program directed at the Kazakh diaspora. According to some estimates, China, Uzbekistan, and Russia alone are home to approximately 4 million ethnic Kazakhs.

However, it was in 2000 that the Kazakh government launched a programming to stimulate the birth rate and attract working age migrants from among former residents of Kazakhstan. By 2001, domestic economic growth and political stability reversed the population outflow, with the number of people applying for Kazakhstani citizenship 2.5 times higher than those wishing to give it up.[12] In 2004, Kazakhstan reached a positive migration balance and the country has now become a net recipient of migrants,[13] and an attractive place for labor from such areas as the Caucasus, Central Asia, China, India and Turkey. According to the World Bank, it has become one of the top countries receiving immigration. As of July 1, 2005, over 110,000 Kazakh families had returned to Kazakhstan.[14] At the same time, the growing labor migration into Kazakhstan has led to two additional concerns among the Kazakh authorities. First, the number of unregistered immigrants in the country is growing. Secondly, there are occasional conflicts between the Turkish, Chinese, and Kazakh workers in large enterprises. Nevertheless, despite these issues, in the final analysis, the foreign labor force plays an important role, filling in gaps in the country's demographic makeup. It also facilitates the development of the construction sector, the oil and gas industries, as well as the trade and service sectors.

Moreover, in the last 20 plus years, the Kazakhstan's population has witnessed significant urbanisation. In his 2006 address to the Assembly of Peoples of Kazakhstan, Nazarbayev commented on the demographic shift in the country when he said:

> All of us remember the social fabric of the Kazakhstan cities. With the exception of small group of party officials and intelligentsia, the vast majority of Kazakhs were engaged in low-paid and non-prestigious work. Today, the urban ethnic Kazakh population is well represented in all areas of business, management, IT, and other most prestigious fields. This shift is fundamental for understanding the current societal processes. The Kazakhs' level of national status and national self-esteem became correspondent to the status of a state-building nation.[15]

Thus, the small and medium entrepreneurs and the middle class provide the social basis for the relatively stable Kazakh society leading to an overall amelioration in the living standard of the people. According to a 2007 poll conducted in seven CIS countries by the Russian Centre for the Study of Public Opinion, Kazakhstan among Central Asia has the highest proportion (73 percent) of respondents satisfied with their lives. Half of the respondents also were optimistic and confident that within a year their lives would be better.[16] A prosperous symbol of this new country and new life is the new capital of Astana.

	Total population		*In 2009 as %*	*Urban population*		*In 2009 is %*	*Including Rural population*		*In 2009 as %*
	1999	*2009*	*of 1999*	*1999*	*2009*	*of 1999*	*1999*	*2009*	*of 1999*
Republic of Kazakhstan	14981281	16009597	106,9	8455783	8662432	102,4	6525498	7347165	112,6
Akmola Oblast	827254	737495	89,1	380522	341915	89,9	446732	395580	88,5
Oktobe Oblast	682558	757768	111,0	377603	461050	122,1	304955	296718	97.3
Almaty Oblast	1557269	1807894	116,1	464953	416858	89,7	1092316	1391036	127,3
Atyrau Oblast	440286	510377	115,9	242673	238936	98,5	197613	271441	137,4
West Kazakhstan Oblast	616800	598880	97,1	251670	277751	110,4	365130	321129	87,9
Zhambyl Oblast	988840	1022129	103,4	452023	4044535	89,5	536817	617594	115,0
Karaganda Oblast	1410218	1341700	95,1	1158706	1040203	89,8	251512	301497	119,9
Kostanai Oblast	1017108	885570	87,1	554112	439554	79,3	462996	446016	96,3
Kyzylorda Oblast	624991	678794	108,6	389781	284248	72,9	235210	394546	167,7
Mangystan Oblast	314669	485392	154,3	246848	263182	106,6	67821	222210	327,6
South Kazakhstan Oblast	1978339	2469357	124,8	793241	972072	122,5	1185098	1497285	126,2
Pavlodar Oblast	806983	742475	92,0	511448	504579	98,7	295535	237896	80,5
North Kazakhstan Oblast	725980	596535	82,2	274744	237436	86,4	451236	359099	79,6
East Kazakhstan Oblast	1531024	1396593	91,2	898497	801475	89,2	632527	595118	94,1
Astama	328341	613006	186,7	328341	613006	186,7	0	0	0,0
Almaty	1130621	1365632	120,8	1130621	1365632	120,8	0	0	0,0

Sources: Results of the 2009 National Population Census of the Republic of Kazakhstan, Analytical Report, Astana 2011.

Regions of Kazakhstan

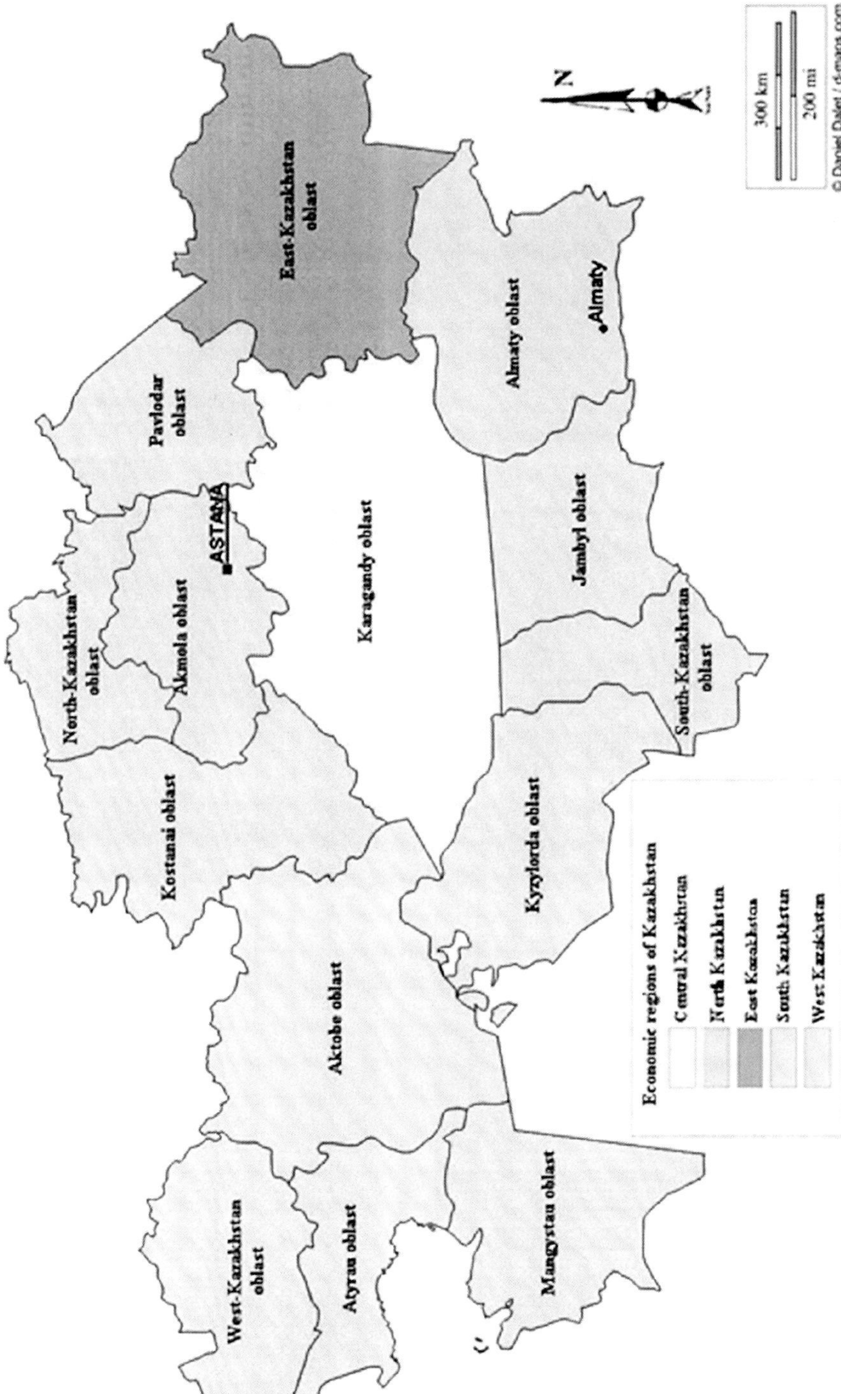

Source: Census and Yearbooks various issues.

Population of Kazakhstan, 1920-2010

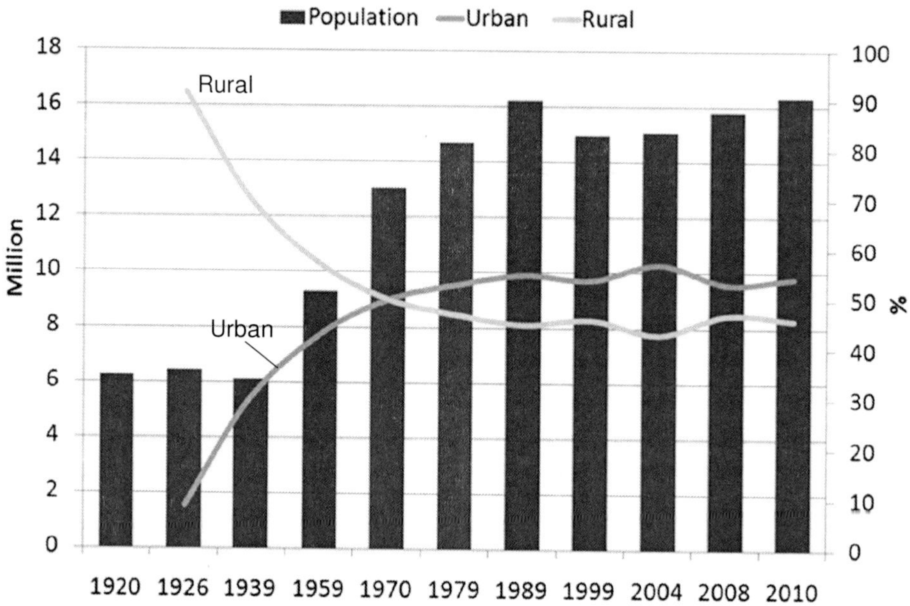

Source: Census and Yearbooks various issues.

Administrative-Territorial Breakdown

(as of January 1,2009)

Cities and Town Settlements

	Territory[17] thsd sq km	*Rayons[18]*	*Total[19]*	*Of which those of republican and oblast subordination*	*Village*	*Aul (rural)*
Republic of Kazakhstan	2724,9	175	86	41	35	7105
Akmolinskaya	146,2	17	10	2	5	660
Aktubinskaya	300,6	12	8	1	-	410
Almatinskaya	224,0	16	10	3	1	766
Atyrauskaya	188,6	7	2	1	2	175
Zapadno-Kazakhstanskaya	151,3	12	2	1	4	472
Zhambyiskaya	144,3	10	4	1	-	379
Karagandinskaya	428,0	11	11	9	11	438
Kostanaiskaya	196,0	16	5	4	3	669
Kyzylordinskaya	226,0	7	3	1	2	263
Mangistauskaya	165,6	5	3	2	-	57
Yuzhno-Kazakhstanskaya	117,3	14	8	4	-	873
Pavlodarskaya	124,8	10	3	3	4	408
Severo-Kazakhstanskaya	98,0	13	5	1	-	714
Vostochno-Kazakhstanskaya	283,2	15	10	6	3	821
Astana City	0,7	3	1	1	-	-
Almaty City	0,3	7	1	1	-	-

See: on Statistical Yearbook of Kazakhstan, p.n. 7-8,2009.

Administrative Structure

The country's administrative units consist of 14 *oblasts* (regions) and two cities of national significance (Almaty and Astana). The 14 *oblasts* are further divided into 160 *rayons* (districts), 39 *oblast* cities, 45 district towns, and 7,862 *auls* (villages). On December 10, 1997, Astana became the capital of the country.[20] Kazakhstan is politically divided into 14 *oblasts* and five economic regions. They are Aktyubinsk, Atyrau, Western Kazakhstan and Mangistau *oblasts* in Western Kazakhstan, Kostanai. Northern Kazakhstan *oblasts* in Northern Kazakhstan. Akmola. Karaganda *oblasts* in Central Kazakhstan, Almaty, Zhambyl, Kyzylorda and Southern Kazakhstan *oblasts* in Southern Kazakhstan and Pavlodar *oblasts* in Eastern Kazakhstan.[21]

There are 82 cities and towns in the Republic. The largest are: Almaty, Chimkent, Karaganda, Zhambyl, Semipalatinsk, Pavlodar, Ustkamenogorsk, Astana, Uralsk and Aktyubinsk.[22]

On January 1, 2011, the country's population was 16,442,000, having increased by 2.7 per cent from the 2009 PC, On November 1, 2011, the population was 16,638,000, having increased by 3.6 per cent from the 2009 PC.

Population by Age Groups

(*Thousand Persons*)

	2005	*2006*	*2007*	*2008*	*2009*
Total Population	15074,8	15219,3	15396,9	15571,5	15776,5
Of which at the age of years:					
Under 1 year	269,8	275,6	298,3	318,2	350,1
1-4	899,5	953,7	1013,3	1087,5	1160,2
5-9	1118,3	1088,2	1080,4	1088,9	1116,3
10-14	1413,0	1363,2	1299,7	1235,5	1183,5
15-19	1584,6	1578,6	1556,3	1512,7	1460,2
20-24	1362,4	1417,9	1481,1	1532,2	1568,8
25-29	1219,0	1232,6	1251,0	1281,8	1309,9
30-34	1131,2	1143,8	1156,1	1166,9	1180
35-39	1051,3	1057,7	1072,3	1087,7	1097,7
40-44	1125,7	1101,7	1078,3	1053,0	1036,8
45-49	995,4	1039,4	1073,2	1092,9	1098,0
50-54	797,5	813,8	837,2	866,3	908,4
55-59	542,8	618,8	663,8	688,3	712,5
60-64	401,0	340,4	328,1	353,7	412,0
65 and other	1163,3	1193,9	1207,8	1205,9	1176,1
Out of total population at the age:					
Under able-bodied age	4012,6	3982,1	3984,8	4011,6	4082,3
Of able-bodied age	9488,8	9652,5	9824,3	9967,2	10084,2
Over able-bodied age	1573,4	1584,7	1587,8	1592,7	1610,0

Sources: Statistical Yearbook of Kazakhstan, 2010.

Provinces

The provinces of Kazakhstan as well as all cities and settlements of more than 20,000 inhabitants

Name	*Abbr.*	*Status*	*Original*	*Capital*	*A(km)*	*E 01.01.2003*	*E 01.01.2009*
Almaty	AAO	Prov	Almaty	Almaty	224,000	1, 560,267	1,667,143
Almaty Qalasy	AAK	City	Almaty Qalasy	Almaty	300	1,149,641	1,365,105
Aqmola	AQM	Prov	Aqmola	Koksetan	124,200	748,167	741,897
Aqtobe	AQT	Prov	Aqtebe	Aqtobe	300,600	668,378	721,130
Astana Qalasy	AST	City	Astana Kalasai	Astana	700	501,998	639,311
Atyrau	ATY	Prov	Atairay	Atyran	118,600	451,928	501,623
Batys Qazakhstan Western Kazakhstan	BQA	Prov	Batais (Western Kazakhstan)	Oral	151,300	602,133	618,785
Mangystau	MAN	Prov	Mangystan	Aqtau	165, 600	338,612	425,684
Ontustik Qazakhstan (Southern Kazakhstan)	OQA	Prov	Ontustik (Southern Kazakhstan)	Symkent	117, 300	2,111,893	2,381,543
Pavlodar	PAV	Prov	Pavlodar	Pavlodar	124, 800	748,651	748,823
Qaragandy	QAR	Prov	Karagandy	Qaragandy	428, 000	1,333,656	1,346,373
Qostanaj	QOS	Prov	Kostanai	Qostanaj	196, 000	919,558	889,368
Qyzylorda	QYZ	Prov	Qyzylorda	Qyzylorda	226, 000	603,804	641,563
Soltustik Qazakhstan (Nothern Kazakhstan)	SQA	Prov	Soltustik	Petropavl	98, 000	682,148	648,236
Sygys Qazakhstan (Eastern Kazakhstan)	SHQ	Prov	Sygys	Oskemen	283, 200	1,465,931	1,417,764
Zambyl	ZHA	Prov	Zambail	Taraz	144, 300	980,072	1,031,144
Kazakhstan	KAZ	Prov		Astana	2, 724, 900	14,866,837	15,776,492

Sources: The Agency of Statistics cf the Republic of Kazakhstan (web).*According to the preliminary result of the census taken from 24 to 25 February 2009 the total population was 15,004,800. Taking this result into account, the estimated population at January 1st, 2010 was 16,196,800.*

HISTORICAL BACKGROUND

The process by which Kazakhs have become a nation involves a complicated and continuous historical ethno genesis. There are three historical phases in the history of Kazakhstan: the pre-Turkic (18th century B.C.-4th century A.D.), the Turkic (4th century A.D. to 13th century) and the Turk-Mongolian period (13th century till 15th century).[23]

The pre-Turkic period started in the Bronze Age and includes the period of Andronov tribes and the early nomads or "Saka period".[24] The territory of Central Asia was populated by tribes referred to by Persian sources as the Saka. The pre-Turkic tribes also included the Usun and Kaugli tribes. In the 3rd and 2nd centuries B.C. the Usun Tribal Confederation arose in Southeast Kazakhstan and tribes belonging to the Kaugli tribes union inhabited the Southwest.[25] These societies were essentially nomadic.

The Sakas were the first ever horsemen in the world to master arrow shooting at full tilt. In 6th-7th centuries BC, the Sakas set up their first state with its centre in the Zhetysu (Semireche) region. The king of the Sakas simultaneously performed the task of high priest. They had their own written language, mythology and art forms. In the Issyk burial mound that yieldedthe famous "Golden Man", the archeologists have unearthed a silver bowl having an inscription consisting of 26 characters on it.[26] This has not been deciphered as yet.

Being located in the center of Eurasia, Kazakhstan has long been at the intersection of ancient civilisations of world and at the crossroads of major transport arteries. Thus it has been a site for a negotiation of social and economic, cultural and ideological relations between East and West, North and South, between Europe and Asia. At different stages in history, Kazakhstan has been home to many nations with distinctive cultural histories which have, in turn, been absorbed into modern Kazakhstan.[27]

In the early part of the first millennium BC, the nomadic Scythian-Sakas prospered on the territory of the Central Asian steppes. Many of the cultural landmarks of this phase still exist on the steppe today. Especially impressive are articles of family life and decorations made of bronze and gold in the so-called "animist" style, excavated from mounds in different regions of Kazakhstan. The tomb of "The Gold Sakas Warrior Prince", discovered in the town of Issyk, close to the capital city of Almaty, is famous for its beauty and elegance.[28]

During the following centuries in the steppes of modern Kazakhstan, the powerful state of the Huns emerged. This exerted profound influence on the geopolitical map of contemporary world fabric. The Huns were succeeded in Central Asia by Turkic-speaking tribes. These groups founded several large state formations; know as *kaganats* (empires) which covered the region from the Yellow Sea in the east to the Black Sea in the west. These states were distinguished by a culture that was progressive for its time and based not only on a nomadic economy, but also on an urban oasis culture that had rich trade handicraft traditions. For instance, in the oases of Central Asia (the present day territory of southern Kazakhstan and Central Asia), cities and caravansaries were founded which helped to facilitate the famous trade route, known as the Great Silk Route which connected Byzantine and China. In addition, other important trade routes were eshttp://in.yahoo.com/tablished in the area, including a road running along the banks of the Syr Darya river leading to the Aral Sea and the South Ural, as well as the so-called "Sable Road" which connected Central Kazakhstan and the Altai with south-western regions of Siberia. A number of major cities and trade centers such as Otrar (Farab), Taraz, Rulan, Yassi (Turkistan), Sauran, Balasagun and others were founded on these routes.[29]

The Great Silk Road not only accelerated the development of trade, but also became a channel of processing progressive scientific and cultural ideas. For example, the life and creative activity of the great philosopher Al-Farabi (870-959) dates back to these times. Born in the district of Farab, Al-Farabi's fame was such that he was known in the East as the Second Teacher after Aristotle. He is best known for his detailed research into philosophy, astronomy, theory of music and mathematics. The well known 11th century scholar of Turkic philology, Mahmud Kashgari, also lived in the area. His three-volume *Dictionary of Turkic Dialects* even to this day serves as an important source of the history of Turkic folklore and literature. *KutadguBilig* (Blessed Knowledge), for example, which was written by the famous poet-philosopher Jusup Balasaguni, is recognised as having played an important role in the development of modern socio-political and ethnical thought. Likewise, the Sufi poet, Khoja Ahmet Yassawi lived in what is today southern Kazakhstan during the 12 century. His collection of poetic thoughts was called *Divan-i-Hikmet* (The Book of Wisdom). The rich cultural mosaic of the region influenced by centuries of trading contacts resulted in religious multiplicity and peaceful coexistence evident in the present day state of Kazakhstan.[30] There were Buddhists enclaves, Zoroastrian communities, a Nestorian Christian movement and Muslim mosques, as well as Sufi orders combining Islam with the traditional Turkic-Tengrian religion (a cult of the sky and other natural elements). This form of Islam influenced the world outlook of the Kazakh people for centuries to come.[31]

The greatest cultural legacy of this period is found in its architectural monuments which have been maintained and restored during the modern period. Architectural memorials, such as the mausoleums of Arystan Baba, the great Sufi Khoja Ahmet Yassawi (Turkistan) and Aisha Bibi (Taraz) are among the best preserved and most beautiful historic monuments in Kazakhstan today. Meanwhile, the ancient nomads of this region invented the *yurt,* an easily-dismantled and portable dome-shaped dwelling, made from wooden struts and felt, and suited the nomadic lifestyle and culture.

In 1221, Mongolian tribes, led by Chingiz Khan invaded and occupied Central Asia. The Mongolian invasion casted a considerable influence upon the history of the Kazakh people. One of the measures taken by Chingiz Khan regarding the Kazakhs was an attempt to replace the gender-tribal division with territorial administration and to unite nomads under the supreme power of Chingiz Khan himself, and his successors.[32] Most part of the modern Kazakhstan was included in the Golden Orda. Ulus (hereditary line) belonged to the successors of Dzhutchi, the eldest son of Chingiz Khan. Later, Kazakh Khans became his direct successors and enjoyed supreme power over the state. At the turn of the 15th century, the powerful empire of Tamarlane (1336-1405) http://in.yahoo.com/ was founded on the territory of Southern Kazakhstan and Central Asia.

TURKIC PERIOD

The Turkic period began in the middle of the first millennium A.D with a massive influx of Turks manifesting marked changes in the ethnic composition of the area. From that time, Turkic tribes became predominant starting from North Mongolia to the lower course of river Amu-Darya.[33] From 4th century to the beginning of 13th century, the territory of Kazakhstan was the seat of West-Turkic, Tyurgesh. Karluks. There were also states formed by the Oguzes, the Karakhanids, the Kimeks and the Kipchaks. These states successively replaced one another up to the very Mongol invasion.[34]

Seventh century AD was a memorable moment in the history of Central Asia as it saw the establishment of Turkic *kaghanate* in the middle of the sixth century with fragile existence-characteristic of nomadic empires.[35] The principal empires at this time were Tang China, Sasanian Iran and Byzantium. Besides, there were small principalities in Transoxiana (area beyond Oxus). Known in the history as the empire of Kok Turks, it lasted from 522 to 744 AD. The empire of Kok Turks expanded from Mongolia to Kyrgyzstan and to Kazakhstan. Among the two branches of the empire, the senior branch ruled northwestern Mongolia and was called Eastern Turks and the junior branch ruled in the West including the region of Semireche as its principal home and was known as Western Turks.[36] The Central Asian region during this time was under the sway of several suzerains and hence had multidimensionality. Several religions such as Zoroastrianism, Manichaeism, Buddhism, Christianity and Shamanistic cults coexisted in Central Asia at that time.[37] Following the formal founding of Islam in seventh century AD in Arabia, Central Asia was destined to come under Islamic influence. Persians made rare attempts to penetrate Transoxania. The Chinese Tang Empire, by 650 AD, made several attacks on the eastern wing of Kok Turkic empires finally reducing them to a position of a Chinese vassal.[38] Islamic armies under the Arabs invaded Central Asia after the conquest of Persia by 651 AD. However, unlike Persia in Transoxania the Arabs struggled for almost a full century to bring the province into the Islamic fold.[39] Qutaybaibn Muslim was the consolidator of

Arab and Islamic power in Tokharistan, Soghdi and Khwarezm. With Transoxania under in their control, the Arabs began to penetrate the territories beyond the river Syr Darya. This land was Semireche, under the control of western Kok Turks and by the middle of the 8th century the Arabs gained momentum in this area.[40]

The Arab victory in this area had far reaching impact in this region. The still Shamanistic Turks of Semireche encountered Islam and eventually were converted into the faith. The Arabs subsequently transmitted their religious zeal to the converts of the newly conquered Central Asian region which was explicitly led by a native Iranian dynasty of Transoxania, the Samanids. This laid the foundation of the rule of the 'native' whether Iranian or Turkic (later) to rein Islamic Central Asia.[41]

It was under the reign of the Samanids that Central Asia acquired major features of a mature Islamic civilisation.[42] One of these was its firm adherence to new religion. A new language, Persian came into being replacing the Sogdian and Khwarezmian idioms as the official language. The Samanid dynasty's power and glory peaked under the reign of three great Amirs—Ismail (892-907), Ahmad (907-13) and Nasr (913-43).[43] The Samanids are also remembered for the missionary propagation of Islam in Turkistan, Semireche and West Sinkiang. In this region, many Turkic chieftains chose to adopt the new religion and effected wholesale conversion of their tribes.

Modern historiography labeled these chieftains as Qarakhanids, a family dynasty whose origins are sought among the tribes of Qarluq of the Kazakh region.[44] Once they entered the community of Darul-Islam as believers, these Turks reversed the trend of actual conquest and conquered Transoxania. They begun the process of Turkicisation of Transoxania and the transformation of the entire region into Turkistan by 999-1005 AD by annihilating the last non – Turkic rule from the region.[45] The Turkicizingwave in Semireche (Kazakh region) and Turkmenistan was represented by Qarluq Turkic tribes. The turn of the millennium, thus, heralded political and military ascendancy of native Turks in the Central Asian region over the Iranian elements.

The Qarakhanids were Turks and their arrival signaled a definitive shift from Iranian to Turkic predominance in Central Asia. They ruled a confederation of tribes living in Semireche (South West Kazakhstan), Tianshan (present day Kyrgyzstan) and Western Sinkiang.[46] Whereas the Turks still adhered to the nomadic lifestyle of Inner Asia, Qarakhanids brought the entire population under Islam making broader social change in this region. One of the earliest *madrasas* was built in Samarkand and minarets were constructed in Bukhara. Contemporaneous with the political and linguistic Turkicisation of Central Asia under the Qarakhanids, a related process began simultaneously in the central lands of Islam under Seljuks (1055) and Ghaznavids.[47]

Seljuks and Ghaznavids also pursued large scale Turkicisation of the population. Both these dynasties originated in Central Asia and spoke Turkic. The Seljuks, who belonged to Oghuz Turkic tribes, moved westward into the steppe of Western Eurasia after the fall of Kok Turks and became dominant nomadic element there.[48] Before the great migration, they formed the majority of nomads in the steppe of modern day central and western Kazakhstan. It was also during this period of Oghuz migration and Islamisation that the 'ethnonym' Turkmen gained prominence.

Like Qarakhanids and Seljuks, the Ghaznavids were Turks with their roots among the nomads of Inner Asia and they were also recent converts to Islam.[49] Mahmud of Ghazna and his successors had relations with both the Qarakhanids and the Seljuks. However, the reign of Qarakhanids and the Seljuks witnessed an invasion by Qarakhitay, descendants of Khitan (who spoke a Mongolian language) in 1141 in Transoxania and made the Qarakhanid rulers their vassals.[50] They lived in Semireche with headquarter at Ordubaliq. Greater mobility together with superior maneuvering of cavalry and archers worked in favor of the Qarakhitay. Despite their Chinese veneer, the Qarakhitay remained essentially steppe nomads. However, by 1218 the Qarakhanids and their overlords—the Qarakhitay in Semireche were overthrown by Kuchlug.[51] Kuchlug killed the Qarluq ruler of Almaliq, whose son appealed to the Mongols for help. Kuchlug fled before the arrival of Mongol generals and later got killed while seeking refuge in the Pamir Mountains. His case is significant because it more drew Genghis Khan's attention to Inner Asia's western marches.[52] This event signaled the catastrophic turning point of Inner Asian *history*—the rise of Mongol empire.

TURKO-MONGOLOID PERIOD

The effects of Mongol invasion varied from cross-cultural exchange to horrifying massacres and devastation in the Central Asian region. By 1206 AD Temujin, emerged the leader of growing coalition of clans and tribes of Mongolia and later embraced the title of Genghiz Khan meaning "world-embracing."[53] He launched campaigns in lands beyond Mongolia and China, Central Asia and Russia to a large extent, thus creating the Mongol empire.

Mongols controlled all of Central Asia by 1223 AD. After Genghiz Khan's death the conquered territory was distributed among his four sons Juchi, Chaghatay, Ogedey and Toluy to administer, of which Chaghatay received the Central Asian region consisting of Transoxania, Semireche and Sinkiang.[54]

Chaghatay died in 1242 and was succeeded by his grandson QaraHulegu and thus began a new stage in Central Asia's history as Changhatayid dynasty came into front. Transoxania proper, Fergana, Semireche and western Sinkiang represented Chaghatayid territories, each of which gradually asserted its own individuality and distinctive evolution.[55] The Mongols plundered most of the cities of this area and decimated their population. In the Semireche region, not only cities but settled lives of the people were also attacked by the forced conversion of a territory with a thriving urban and agricultural civilisation into a nomad's steppe land. Babur, in his memoirs, wrote, "on the north (of Fergana), though in former times there must have been towns such as Almaliq, Almatu and Yangi which in books they write Taraz, at the present time all is desolate, no settled population, whatever remaining because of the Mongols."[56]

After a century of Mongol invasion, some Chaghatayid Khans began to get converted to Islam as they chose to live not in Semireche but in Transoxania, which was largely under the impact of Islamic civilisation.[57] In contrast, the Semireche and other adjoining territories had developed a special identity—that of a Mongol homeland (called as Moghulistan) reminding of the devastation and transformation carried out by Mongols in this region. It was this junction of civilisation which took a political form in 1370 AD when a Muslim Turk, Timur, seized power in Transoxania and gradually extended the same to some areas of Semireche i.e., Moghulistan and Sinkiang.[58] Timur's emergence in 1370 can be considered another turning point in the history of Central Asia which led to formal end of Mongol hegemony which was founded by the conquests of Genghis Khan a century and half earlier.

After the disturbing Mongol interlude, the Timurid period (1370-1507) can be viewed as a significant period in the history of Central Asia. Though Timur was occupied much of his life in military campaigns and destruction, he spared Central Asia. It is during this period that Islamic culture and art rose to a new stature in this area. Timur's military exploits were impressive and his reign extended from eastern Sinkiang to southern Russia including Transoxania to India, Syria and Anatolia. After Timur's death in 1405 AD, the territory of Transoxania and Khawarezm was succeeded by his son Sharukh and later by Sharukh's son Ulugh Beg.[59] During Ulugh's time, notable growth in mathematics and astronomy was witnessed in this region. He also built a *madrassa* in Samarkand for higher learning of Islamic theology.

During this time, Sufism had its influence in the Central Asian region. The most prominent one was *Naqshabanditariqa* founded by Khwaja Bahaa-ud-Din Naqshband and the other important was the *Yasaviyatariqa*.[60] Though Semireche and Moghulistan still remained with the Mongol Chaghatayid dynasty, by now they had converted to the natural trend of Islam. *Naqshbanditariqa* and Ahmad Yasavi's enduring example and continued to play their role as powerful anchors of Islam among the nomads of Kipchak steppe in Kazakhstan.[61] Although Kazakhstan was not directly ruled by Timur or Timurids, it was during this period that the region witnessed the revival of Islam and its wide propagation under Sufi *silislahs.* Owing to the weakness of the last Timurids some native nomadic group especially Uzbeks and Kalmyks started asserting their positions in Central Asia. Abulkhyar having Genghised ancestry was a Muslim and a Turk. Referred by the general name of the 'Uzbeks' (speaking Kipchak form of Turkic), the tribe under his leadership, swept down beyond the Syr Darya and captured Urgeneh and Samarkand.[62] The Uzbek Khan's move "made him the immediate neighbours of Timuridtransoxania and put him close to Chaghatayid Moghulistan. However, this situation was altered by the interruption of Kalmyks from east".[63]

Unlike the Genghis Khan clan, the Kalmyks Mongols used different dialects and were known as the "Western Mongols."[64] They momentarily rose to supremacy in Mongolia but great fortunes awaited them farther west in the Kipchak Steppe.[65] In 1456 AD, the Kalmyk khans entered into Moghulistan and the Kazakhstan steppe and defeated Chaghtayid Khans and later the Uzbek chieftains of Abulkhyar. These constant internecine wars resulted in the removal of many Uzbek tribesmen from Abulkhyar's authority, who now joined the followers of two other Genghisids Janibeg and Girey. These Genghisids had recently established the nucleus of a new Khanate in the territory of white Horde what is now central Kazakhstan.[66] Between 1465-66 AD, they had formed the Kazakh Khanate. By the end of the 15th century, the prolonged process of the formation of the Kazakh nation had been completed. These rebel Uzbeks came to be known as Kazakhs for the first time. Later, they were called as Kirghiz by the Russians to be finally reverted to Kazakh in 1925 by the *Soviets.*[67]

The Kalmyk Khans made no serious attempt to push south of Syr Darya i.e. Timurid Transoxania. However, the Timurid dynasty could not survive long. In the fifteenth century, the Shaybani Khans united the Uzbek clans into the Shaybani *Ulus* (gathering) and defeated the last Timurids and replaced them with the Shaybanids, thus restoring Genghisid rule in Central Asia.[68] By 1507, Muhammad Sliaybani crossed Syr Darya and seized Samarkand and Herat. The Shayabnids were Turks like the Timurids. Sufficiently exposed to Arabo-Persian Islamic culture, they spoke a different dialect called Kipchak.[69] This ensured a sort of continuity than change in this area.

From another perspective changes were taking place. During this time, the trans-continental Silk Road was losing importance against European maritime route.[70] Europe including Russia was undergoing a technological and economic revolution. The Shia Safavids started a new dynasty in Iran in 1501 and they developed hostile relations with Sunni Shaybanids. This impasse isolated Central Asia from orthodox Iran right up to its conquest by Russia in the 19th Century. The Shaybanid regime also witnessed a steady growth of *Naqshbandi* Sufism in Central Asia.

Apart from this, a segment of Shaybani *Ulus* later split away and sought refuge with the Chaghatai tribes on the Xinjiang-Kazakhstan border.[71] These tribes, who lived beyond the Shaybani control, came to be known by outsiders as "Kazakhs", possibly from the Arabic word Qazac which means 'outlaws'. They started forming a distinct Kazakh nationality which in actuality took shape during the sixteenth century.[72] Political structure in the Dasht-i-Kipchak of Kazakhs had become much looser than that was bequeathed by the Mongol empire. The most constant feature was the trend of alliances and conflicts. The Genghised ancestry of the Shaybanidline continued to play a role but it failed to produce personalities strong enough to create a realm and nation that could play a major role.

Although by sixteenth century Kazakhs had established their distinct identity, they were yet to establish any distinct political structure of a Khanate. Their first Chiefs Burunduk Khan (1488-1509) and Kasim Khan (1509-18) achieved their individual identity by fiercely resisting Uzbek advances and they could with legitimacy claim to speak for all Kazakhs.[73] For the first time, the Kazakh border with the Uzbeks was strung out along the Syr Darya river, with the Uzbeks to the south of the river and Kazakhs to the north. From the seventeenth century until the Russian conquest in the nineteenth century, these nomadic groups seldom and recognised the authority of a single Khan and that too for brief periods. Usually they formed three separate tribal confederations or "Hordes", called by the Russians as Orda in known as *zhuz* (Hundred) in Kazakh. The three groups occupied three separate regions, Lesser Horde in Western Kazakhstan, the Middle Horde in Central Kazakhstan and the Greater Horde in Southeastern Kazakhstan.[74] Each *Orda* was composed of tribal, clan and family, units ruled by a Khan. Together the Khans demarcated distinct areas in which to graze their flocks and organise their military forces. The Kazakh Khanates frequently engaged in wars against each other. This fragmentation could not but undermine their power to resist subsequent incursions by the Kalmyks and the eventual conquest of the land by the Russians.

In the early seventeenth century, the eastern Kazakhs were overrun by a Buddhist Mongolian confederacy called the Oirots.[75] Oirots were the native inhabitants of Mongolia. With the emergence of Ming dynasty in China, the last Yuan emperors of China fled to Mongolia and under Allan Khan they defeated Oirots. The Oirots retreated west after their defeat to join their kinsmen in the Eurasian Steppe and established Jungar Khanate in Sinkiang and Kalmyk Khanate in southern Russia.[76] It is during this period that the Oirols embraced Buddhism. After the defeat from Allan Khan, some of the tumultuous tribes collectively known as "Jungar" undertook second wave of raids in Kazakh territory. Kalmyk incursions into the Kazakh land led to the defeat of Tauke Khan of Middle Horde in 1698 AD and of his successor Pulat Khan in I723 AD.[77] The Oirots raided Kazakh territory all the way to the right bank of Syr Darya sacking the cities of Sayram, Tashkent and Turkistan. This raid displayed a resemblance to those of the 15th Century in which the Oirots (Kalmyks) had sacked the same area. The earlier raid shattered the prestige of the Uzbeks and the later one did the same to the Kazakhs. However, once the Oirots had pulled back, the Uzbeks and Kazakhs had regained their strength but during this time, they were defeated by the Russian empire, which having absorbed all of Siberia was beginning march towards Kazakhstan and Central Asia.[78] The *Oirots* raids caused misery, wide scale dislocation and migration among the Kazakh masses. The calamities caused by the Oirots came to an end when they were defeated by China's Manchu rulers in 1757 AD, but by then the Kazakhs had become too disorganised and weak to attempt any effective unified resistance to the incipient Russian expansion.

By 1730 AD, the Kazakhs had asserted themselves as a distinct group of nomadic tribes living in the eastern part of Dasht-i-Kipchak, speaking a distinctive Kipchak Turkic idiom but lacking overall political unity. The tribes had coalesced into three confederations, the aforementioned Greater, Middle and Lesser Hordes. Except for brief periods early in their history, the Kazakhs never managed to forge a united Khanate like their medieval Turkic and Mongol predecessors. One of the reasons for this may have been the proliferation of Sultans claiming Genghised descent—holding positions of prestige and authority but obstructing the rise of a truly charismatic leader able to repeat the exploits of their revered ancestor. On the other hand, the prestige enjoyed by the steppe aristocracy of Genghisid ancestry may have been a factor in the peculiar vertical division of Kazakh society into two layers, the so called "White Bone" and "Black Bone".[79] However, certain other credentials such as descent from eminent Muslim ancestors could also entitle some individuals to claim "White Bone" status.

TSARIST RUSSIAN CONQUEST OF KAZAKHSTAN

The rise of Russia began under Ivan IV (1547-84) and quickened by Peter the Great (1682-1725), who made Russia stronger than any of her Asian neighbors.[80] The Russians at first contended themselves with accepting offers of vassaldom from various Kazakh leaders, without actually acquiring military or administrative control over their territory. This complex process started in 1730 AD when Abulkhyar, Khan of Lesser Horde expressed his wish to accept Tsarist Russian suzerainty and the request was granted. Later Russia received similar assurances of loyalty from the other Kazakh leaders and by 1740 the Middle Horde and 1742 the Greater Horde signed treaties with Moscow.[81]

Totally dependent on forces of nature and located geopolitically between the two largest nations of Eurasia, China and Russia, the Kazakh nomads were often subject to invasion by their economically and politically stable and settled neighbors. During the 17th and 18th centuries, nomadic tribes of Jungars, led by Chinese Bogdy-Khans, began a large-scale war against the Kazakh state. Several factors were responsible behind the defeat of the Kazakhs among them—protracted battles throughout the steppe lands, and tribal and kin group divisions and regional affiliations played crucial role. The Kazakhs were defeated in 1723 AD. This defeat is remembered to this day as a tragedy and is known in Kazakh as *Ak Taban Shubyryndy* (The Great Calamity).[82]

During the reign of Catherine the Great (1762-96), colonisation process of the Central Asian lands was started by Russian peasants and military posts were set up deeper in Kazakh territory such as Akmolinsk and Turgai. They started using Tatar elites to propagate Russian commercial interests. The Russian idea was to entice the unruly nomads to a more sedate way of life so as to consolidate control over these areas. During the next fifty years, the deterioration of their nomadic life style caused by the devastation of the wars led to a series of revolts by Kazakh nomads against their own Khans, the most far reaching being the revolt of Batyr Srym in 1792. These revolts encouraged the Russians to abolish the Khanates and between 1822 and 1848 the entire Kazakh territory was incorporated into the Tsarist Empire.[83] The conquest of Central Asia, however, bore all the hallmarks of 19th century Europe's colonial expansion, the motivation ofacquiring abundant and cheap raw materials such as cotton for the Russian textile industry and inversely, of gaining a privileged position for Russia's commerce.[84]

However, *batyrs* (knights), the decisiveness of the Kazakh leader Ablai-khan, the diplomatic activities of the Kazakh *Biys* (sages) Tole bi, Kazdausty Kazybek bi, Ayteke bi, as well as the self-sacrifice of the people, the Kazakhs survived the onslaught. In order to obtain guarantees of independence and security, Kazakh khans started searching for the military assistance of the Russian Empire. While Russia's help saved the Kazakhs from annihilation, Russia also used this opportunity to build town-fortresses, move Russian population from internal regions of Russia into the steppe, transfer pastures to these Russian peasants and divide Kazakh steppe land according to Russia's administrative-territorial structure.[85] Finally, Kazakhstan lost its sovereignty. Despite the heroic resistance of Kenesary-Khan, leader of the peoples' volunteer corps, the insurrection of Batyr Syrym, the uprising of the eldest *zhuz* and other anti-colonial actions, Kazakhstan ceased to exist as an independent state in 1871 AD. The last stage of Russia's colonisation of Kazakhstan was the annexation of Southern Kazakhstan in the 1850s and 1860s, following a Russian military campaign against the Khanate of Kokand, Bukhara and Khiva, whose lands extended into what is today the territory of Southern Kazakhstan.

Russia devised a new administrative structure for the newly acquired Central Asian region. The, entire Central Asian region (except Kazakhstan) was divided into five regions (Syr Darya, Semireche, Fergana, Samarkand and Zukaspie) and two protectorates (Bukhara and Khiva) and was administered by Governor General of Turkistan residing in Tashkent.[86] However, owing to geographical and historical linkage with Russia proper and with Siberia, Kazakhstan was divided into three regions (*Oblasts*). The western most part-the area of Lesser Horde, now became *oblast* of Urals. Its administrative centre was the city of Uralsk and whose governor reported directly to the Ministry of Interior. The area of Middle Horde became the *oblast* of Turgai, whose Governor also reported to the Ministry *of* Interior.

The *oblasts* of Akmolinsk and Semipalatinsk had full fledged Governorate-General. The Semipalatinsk *Oblast* covered the territory of the Greater Horde.[87]

By the end of the 19th Century this process was complete, the Middle Horde was eliminated in 1822 AD, the Little Horde in 1824 AD and the Great Horde in 1848 AD. Although the political power of these Khanates was destroyed, the sense of belonging to a Horde remained a social identity that continues to this day. In 1854 the Russians set up a fortress at Verny, today's Almaty. Active involvement of Russia in the World War 1 triggered a severe economic crisis. The decree of the Russian emperor of June 25, 1916 that Central Asian Muslims be drafted for labour behind the battle lines during war time, primarily for digging trenches greatly hurt the Kazakhs sentiments.[88] In the Tsarist period up to 1917 AD, Kazakhstan remained overwhelmingly a rural and nomadic society. In 1900 AD, there were only four towns with a population exceeding 20,000 but changes were taking place. After the emancipation of serfs in Russia there was an influx of Russian and Ukranian peasants and then in the 1890's there began the process of industrialisation. In 1905, the Orenberg-Tashkent railway line was completed helping to open up Western Kazakhstan.

Subsequently, Kazakhstan's fate was closely linked to the European model of social progress in general and in particular to the fate of the Russian state and its people. During the first half of the 19th century an increasing number of Kazakh people turned to a settled way of life and abandoned pastoral nomadism in favor of agriculture. Gradually, the economy of Kazakhstan became increasingly integrated into the Russian economy. On the territory of Kazakhstan various industries, transport and trade were developed. As a result, a national working class and intelligentsia also began to develop. The Kazakh intelligentsia adapted them to European culture.

In the 19th century, there was a further development of national consciousness, a new appreciation of the Kazakh language, folklore, customs, music and an interest in the history with its "great" past and its heroic struggles. The two most prominent Kazakh figures in this process in establishing a national identity were both pro-Russian. Chokan Valikhanov (1835-65) was the grandson of the last Khan of the Middle Horde, an explorer, artist, liberal, Russian army intelligence officer. His notebooks reveal the value he placed on all aspects of Kazakh life. The second was Abay Kunanbayev (1845-1904) who was the founder of Kazakh as a literary language by translating Russian works into Kazakh. Like Valikhanov extolled the Kazakh culture. The Abay Museum in Semey was opened in 1995 on the 150th anniversary of his birth.

One of the Kazakh intellectuals who avidly supported such ideas was the scholar Chokan Walikhanov (1835-1865).[89] An outstanding scholar-orientalist, he is best remembered as the first scholar to have travelled from Kazakhstan to Xinjiang and thoroughly describe the region of Kashgharia. Another important

Kazakh intellectual from the Russian imperial period is the great poet-philosopher Abay Kunanbayev (1845-1904). Abai was one of the founders of Kazakh literary language and wrote many classics of Kazakh literature. He was not only a talented poet, but also a skillful translator of masterpieces from Eastern, Russian and European literature.

Russia brought peace and order in this area where internecine warfare had been endemic and surrendered the population's overall destiny to the discretion of a new and alien master. Under the new Russian system, Kazakhstan became a supplier of raw materials (especially cotton) for the Russian industry and a consumer of Russian products. The Russians encouraged the settlement of Cossacks in the Kazakh grazing and farming lands. Between 1783 and 1870 AD, there were at least eight major revolts by the Kazakh tribes against these Russian settlers but they were defeated by the Russian armies. By 1870 AD, The Kazakhs had lost an estimated one million people, a quarter of their population in wars, revolts and land grabbing by the settlers.[90] However, Central Asia's natives, having lost their political and economic independence retained their religion and remained Muslims in their religion, culture and way of life.

On the positive side, the population drew benefits from the *pax Russica* imposed on it by the colonizer. A minority of Central Asians did become exposed to modern education imparted by Russian schools. Besides, a movement known as *itsul-i-jadict* (new method) founded by a Crimean Tatar named Dismal Bey Gasprinskiy also helped introducing modern yet tradition based ideas. A number of *jaded* schools were opened to impart modern education in this area.

There were periodic revolts against Tsarist rule which were suppressed with harsh measures. At the time of the 1905 Revolution in Russia, a secret Nationalist Party, the *Alash Orda* was founded.[91] The major revolt was in 1916 in response to the efforts by a desperate Russian Tsarist government to mobilise men for military and labour service in the First World War. Many fled abroad. Months later the Tsar abdicated and in November 1917 the Bolsheviks took over.[92]

However, the new generation of Kazakh intellectuals formed a revolutionary party *Alash* in 1917-18, which aimed at liberating the Kazakh people from colonial oppression. Among the best known of these intellectuals were Alikhan Bukeikhanov, Ahmet Baitursynov and Mir Yakub Dulatov. They were engaged not only in political activity, but also in cultural and educational work, literary-public activity and scientific research. The distinguished poet-philosopher and historian Shakarim Khudaiberdiyev also played a special role in Kazakh development during these period, with his and philosophy advocating eternal and universal humanistic values. Almost all these intellectuals faced Stalinist repression and were executed during the years of Soviet domination.[93]

KAZAKHSTAN DURING THE SOVIET PERIOD

After the Bolshevik revolution of 1917 Soviet power was gradually established in Kazakhstan. The First World War and the Civil War adversely affected the economy of the area. Ahmad Baytursun wrote about the unpleasant choice facing the Kazakhs in 1918. "The Kazakhs received the First Revolution (February 1917) with joy and second with consternation and terror. The First Revolution had liberated them from the oppression of the Tsarist regime and the second was accompanied by violence, plunder and establishment of a dictatorial regime."[94]

Whilst the Bolsheviks could not afford to antagonize the Kazakh nationalists at a time when its power was not fully consolidated in Central Asia, *Alash* leaders were called to participate in a Communist Party Congress at Orenburg in March 1920. *Alash* had little choice but to join the victors of the civil war, if it was to survive. *Alash* leaders were also encouraged by Lenin's statement on autonomy stating that—"From now on your beliefs and customs, your national and cultural institutions are being declared free and inviolable. Arrange your national life freely and without hindrance". This statement from none other than Lenin generated hope of achieving their aim through the Bolsheviks.[95]

As a result of the Congress, *Alash*set up a government of the Eastern AlashOrda in Semipalatinsk and elected Ali Khan Bukeykhanov as President. They also formed western Alash Orda government in Zhambietu in Urals. For a time, *Alash* governments refused to join either Reds or Whites, resisting them both till January 1918, when Bosheviks captured Orenburg and disbanded Alash Orda government. Many *Alash* leaders began to negotiate with the White Armies. By the summer of 1918, the White armies under Admiral Kolchak had cut off Central Asia from Russia after defeating the Bolsheviks. After joining Admiral Kolchak, *Alash* leaders became quickly horrified at the cruelty of the White Armies, and Kolchak refused to allow any of the Kazakh demands of autonomy. By 1919, *Alash* had rejoined the Bolsheviks who by late 1920 defeated Kolchak, although sporadic fighting was continuing until 1923.[96]

On 10 July 1919, Lenin signed a decree creating a "Kazakh-Kirghiz Revolutionary Committee" and with the help of Red Army, liquidated all its nationalist opponents.On26 August 1920 the Kazakh Autonomous Soviet Socialist Republic was created and in October, the first constituent Congress of Soviets of the new Republic was held with the participation of many *Alash* leaders. Unlike Turkistan ASSR, the Kazakh ASSR was for the first time based on the ethno-linguistic factor of a native nationality, the Kazakhs. Later, the Republic became Kazakh ASSR in 1925 and on 5 December 1936, it became a full Soviet Socialist Republic within the USSR. However, all the expectations of seeking larger autonomy for Turkistan and Kazakhstan by the *Alash* leaders under the new Bolshevik regime were belied and all these nationalists were destined to die by 1934 as victims of Stalinist purges.[97]

In 1920, the Turkistan Commission was instructed to combat pan-Islamism and pan-Turkism. The Commission was also to organise the preparation of a map that would show the ethnic composition of Turkistan and to examine the question whether a fusion or delimitation was a preferable solution.[98] This process remained dormant until 1924 owing to complex situation in Central Asia and the Basmachi movement. In early 1924, shortly after the death of Lenin, Soviet leaders decided that the time had come for reshaping the borders within Central Asia along ethno-linguistic lines. In 31 January 1924, a decision was made to carry out national delimitation of Central Asia. This led to the transformation of Turkistan into a region of five national units, Kazakhstan, Kyrgyzstan, Uzbekistan, Tajikistan and Turkmenistan.[99] Each of the five Republics acquired the status of a Union Republic - Kazakhstan got it in 1936 and a new constitution was adopted by parliament of every Republic in 1937 (to be replaced by, the last Soviet constitution in 1977). Most striking privilege, explicitly stated in the 1936 constitution was their right to leave the Soviet Union altogether and become an independent country. Additional symbols of each Republic's sovereignty were its own flags, emblem and national anthem.

However, two clauses of Kazakhstan constitution, i.e. "Its government functions on its own territory in an independent manner except for those questions that pertain to the highest organs of USSR" and "the pivot of the republic's governmental and social organisms is the guiding and leading force of Soviet society, the Communist party of the Soviet Union and the Communist Party of Kazakhstan" showed Kazakhstan's close linkage with the Soviet Union.[100]

Since the national delimitation of 1924, Soviet officials worked hard to increase the distinctiveness of Central Asian nationalities.[101] The end result of this linguistic-cultural revolution was the creation of six new literary languages (Uzbek, Kazakh, Kyrgyz, Turkmen and Tajik) in a society that had previously used Chaghatay Turkic, or Persian. Education system was restructured, expanded and modernized along uniform Soviet lines. The Cyrillic alphabet was adopted in 1940. During Stalin's time, Kazakhstan was heavily industrialized and communications and infrastructure were improved. However, Kazakhstan was one of the worst affected regions during Stalin's campaigns in the early 1930s, to collectivize agriculture and settle nomadic population.[102] The introduction of a planned economy and the collectivisation of agriculture aggravated the dislocation of the traditional economy of Kazakhstan.[103] It increased the dominant role of cotton in the irrigated areas. One million people were estimated to have died as a result of starvation and the percentage of the Kazakhs in their own Republic fell to 29 per cent. Livestock losses were enormous as people killed their animals rather than had them over to collectives. The number of cattle shrank from 7.4 million heads in 1929 to 1.6 million in 1933 and of sheep from 21.9 million heads to 1.7 million.

Throughout Stalin's rule, the local communist parties were Russian dominated although the cadres in the countryside were drawn heavily from the indigenous population. The 1930s was the period of establishment of totalitarianism in Kazakhstan which entailed massive political repressions. All the leaders of *Alash* were executed during Stalin's purges of which Ahmed Baythrsun was first to be executed in 1925. The total power enjoyed by the communist elite created a new bureaucratic aristocracy in the supposedly classless society of the Kazakhs. The policy of cotton monoculture became pronounced in 1930s but from 1960s' it reached monstrous proportions. The Kazakhs ever since the civil war turned into minority in their own homeland. The official versions of the Republic's history portrayed the Russian conquest not as a conquest but as "voluntary unification" of Kazakhs.[104]

In the pre-World War-II period, mass deportation of many nationalities like Germans, Chechens, Bashkirs, and others had begun. In the World War II, Kazakhstan lost nearly 425,000 people. The war years were filled with millions of Soviet people in industries and agriculture. The Republic played host to hundreds of thousands of evacuated people. In the post-war period, under Khrushchev (1953-64), Kazakhstan entered the era of intensive economic development. Inauguration of the Academy of Sciences of the Kazakh SSR took place in 1946. Huge industrial complexes were built in north and east of Kazakhstan. Baikonur Space Centre was started at Leninsk.[105] The province of Semipalatinsk, in eastern Kazakhstan was chosen as the area for Soviet nuclear experiments.

In order to boost agricultural production in the Soviet Union, Khrushchev announced his Virgin Lands Scheme in February 1954. The Kazakh steppes were declared virgin territory.[106] The authorities allocated land to hundreds or thousands of volunteers from Russia and Ukraine for agricultural use. Some 62 million acres out of the 104 million acres ploughed between 1954 and 1960 were in Kazakhstan. But due to widespread storms and wind erosion between 1960 and 1964, four million hectares of farmland were ruined and 12 million hectares were damaged. However, this campaign resulted in the increase of the ethnic Russian population in the total population of Kazakhstan from 19.7 per cent in 1926 to 42.7 per cent in 1959.[107]

In the political arena, Khrushchev dismissed all Stalin era party leadership. However, the pattern established in the late Stalin years continued to predominate: first secretaries came from the indigenous nationality and second secretaries, generally charged with supervising personnel were Russians. The failure of Virgin Land campaign led Khrushchev to replace Ponomarcncko by Brezhnev in July 1955 as Secretary in Kazakhstan. He initiated a programme of transforming collective farms into state run enterprises, thus putting Kazakh farmers unfamiliar with modern agricultural and livestock breeding practices under the supervision of highly trained Slav cadres and improving output as well as economic integration of the new agricultural lands of Kazakhstan. Brezhnev was able to present Virgin Lands Scheme as a modern economic miracle.[108]

With the accession of Brezhnev as supreme leader (1964-82), the party elites of the local nationalists came to dominate the political life of Kazakhstan. The Brezhnev years were a period of remarkable political stability throughout Central Asia. The tenures of the Republican First Secretaries were marked by unprecedented longevity.[109] In 1964, Dinmuhamad Kunayev, a Kazakh and Brezhnev loyalist was party chief in Kazakhstan. He now controlled a Republic of about eleven million, which had during the past decade absorbed sizeable Slav work force. The arrival of hundreds of thousands of young politically conscious Russian and Ukrainian volunteers to participate in Grow More Food Campaign of 1954-63 led to a substantial increase in the membership of the CPK and strengthened the Slav hold over the party. Dinmuhamad Kunayev tried to redress the imbalance by reactivating the Kazakhs to join the party and play an active role. Gradually, Kunayev who stayed in Kazakhstan until December 1986 started building his own power base by putting members of his clan Great Orda into powerful bureaucratic positions. During his tenure, a new Kazakh political mafia developed, owing complete allegiance to Moscow but at the same lime consolidating Kazakh nationalism.[110]

During the final years of Brezhnev, the party hierarchy arrogated greater powers to itself and was losing touch with the Kazakh people. There was widespread pilferage, bribery and nepotism, giving impetus to a parallel economy. Under "scientific atheism" and communism, which was withering, Islam started revivalist tendency among Kazakhs because they felt a need to fill the moral-ethical vacuum left by the erosion of morality among the party cadres.

These developments occurred against the background of the diminishing power of Kunayev. The first sign came during the rule of Andropov. He wanted to diverge from the Brezhnevite line whereas Kunayev was for continuing the old policies. The brief tenure of Cherenenko, as the First Secretary of the CPSU failed to reverse the trend. This downslide was sought to be addressed by Mikhail Gorbachev, who after assuming the position of General Secretary in 1985 initiated his *perestroika* and *glasnost* to refurbish the entire politico-administrative system of the Soviet Union.

By mid-1980s, a practicality of radical changes in the Soviet policy became obvious and undeniable as ever before.[111] One problem was corruption among high officials. Soviet government was fully aware of the surge of native power in Kazakhstan but could not do anything to remedy the situation. The Kazakh leaders of the final Soviet era were Kazakh nationalists. Family, clan, tribe, Horde were determining factors by which power and positions of comfort were distributed and by the time Kunaev rose to be top leader, these considerations came to the fore. Though Moscow appeared satisfied with the state of affairs, doubts remained about the nepotism. The doubts burst into the open after Mikhail Gorbachev came to power in the Soviet Union. Gorbachev sought to rectify the situation by bringing openness in the system. This, however, brought about the collapse of thewhole system. After Gorbachev assumed the position of General Secretary in 1985, he made effort was made to clean up the Central Asian party and state organs. The corruption and inefficient management of the Central Asian Communist parties was discussed at length at the 27th Party Congress of the CPSU. The rampant corruption of the Kunayev regime and his mafia style politics led Gorbachev to dismiss him in December 1986. He was replaced by Gennadi Kolbin, an ethnic Russian outsider to clean up the Communist Party of Kazakhstan (CPKZ). His elevation to the highest party job in the second largest republic of USSR sent shock waves throughout Kazakhstan. The appointment of Zakash Kamalidenov—a Kazakh as Second Secretary failed to pacify the popular mood since it reversed the order of giving primacy to Kazakhs that had prevailed for the past 22 years. Replacing Kunayev with Kolbin only deepened the divide that had existed between the centre and the periphery, strengthening Kazakh nationalism even within the Kazakh ranks of the CPK. On 17 December 1986, a few days after Kolbin took over. Anti-Russian riots against Kolbin's appointment broke out in Alma Ata, the then capital of Kazakhstan.[112]

On 17 December 1986, some 10,000 people took to the streets in Almaty. A number of protesters mainly young people and students gathered on the main square of Almaty and staged demonstrations against Kolbin—what they viewed as an assault on their nationality. They carried placards saying, "We are for Kazakhstan", "Kazakhstan for Kazakhs." The Communist Party leadership organised a counter-demonstration by workers and they attacked the demonstrators. In the subsequent confrontation, which involved police opening fire, between two and twenty people lost their lives and between 763 and 1,137 received injuries; between 2,212 to 2,336 demonstrators were arrested.[113] Within two days, the riots spread to twelve other cities in the Republic. Chimkent and Zambyl were the other worst hit towns. The event was a watershed in the history of Kazakhstan, giving birth to a party called *Zeltoksan* (literally meaning December), the Decembrists. It was often portrayed as the first spontaneous democratic uprising of the Kazakhs.

Kolbin showed sensitivity towards the Kazakhs throughout his nearly five year tenure in the republic. He was responsible for legislation mandating Kazakh to become one of the two official languages of the Republic and he himself earned fluency in speaking Kazakh. However, Kolbin carried out purging of Communist Youth League Members. He also took action against those who were found participating in religious ceremonies. Said Aga Ziayev, the head of the party in Zambyl province was sacked for a public show of respect for religious rites. Both these cases were highly publicized, thus further inflaming Kazakh susceptibilities. In the spring of 1989, word went around in the cities of western Kazakhstan that the refugees from Armenia, which had suffered a devastating earthquake in December, were being offered scarce housing in Kazakhstan. This triggered riots which were quickly suppressed. The event which was symptomatic of rising resentment, especially among youth, provided Gorbachev with a rationale to return the top Republican Party job to a Kazakh.

In June 1989, when Nursultan Nazarbayev was elected as first Secretary of the CPK's Central Committee replacing Kolbin, he emerged as the most important leader. In September 1989, Kazakh Supreme Soviet passed a law making Kazakh the official language.[114] To meet the rising demand for autonomy, Kazakh Supreme Soviet declared the primacy of Kazakh legislation over Soviet laws.

In October 1991, Kazakhstan signed with seven other Republics, a treaty to establish an economic community with Presidents of Azerbaijan, Georgia, Moldova and Ukraine abstaining.[116] The new agreement was meant to provide a guideline for a similar set up in the political arena, the two together producing the Union of Sovereign States to replace USSR. In order to implement more effectively the forthcoming reforms in Kazakhstan, Nazarbayev decided to hold a popular ballot for the presidency. On 1st December 1991, Nazarbayev was elected President in the first direct Presidential election in Kazakhstan.

When the Presidents of three Slavic Republics of Russia, Ukraine and Belarus announced the creation of Commonwealth of Independent States by adopting the Belovezhskoye Agreement on December 8, 1991, they terminated Gorbachev's attempts to form a new confederation replacing USSR. Kazakhstan too agreed to join the new Commonwealth. On 16 December 1991, the Kazakh Supreme Soviet declared its Republic as an independent sovereign state. Finally, the agreement that was to break up the Soviet Union and change the map of the world was agreed by all the Republican leaders at Almaty on 21 December 1991. Thus, the Republic of Kazakhstan emerged on the political map of the world.[117]

NOTES

1. T.K Vineeth, *Kazakhstan: Commemorating 10 Years of Independence* (New Delhi, Embassy of Kazakhstan, 2001), p.12.
2. www.cia.gov/library/publications/the-world-factbook/geos/kz.html
3. B.K. Sultanov (ed), Kanat Saudabayev Secretary of State of the Republic of Kazakhstan-Ministry of Foreign Affairs of the Republic of Kazakhstan. Kazakhstan Today, Almaty 2010.
4. "Country Profile: Kazakhstan" (Federal Research Division; Library of Congress, September 2005)", p.3.
5. Vineeth, n.10, p.12
6. B.K. Sultanov (ed), Kanat Saudabayev Secretary of State of the Republic of Kazakhstan-Ministry of Foreign Affairs of the Republic of Kazakhstan. Kazakhstan Today, Almaty 2010, p.5.
7. T.K Vineeth, *Kazakhstan: Commemorating 10 Years of Independence* (New Delhi, Embassy of Kazakhstan, 2001), p.12.
8. Adel E. Abhishev, *Kazakhstan in focus: Ten Years of Independence* (Almaty, Centre for Foreign

Policy and Analysis, 2002), p.6.
9. Vineeth. n. 10, p.12.
10. Glenn E. Curtis, Kazakhstan*A Country Study* (Washington, Library of Congress 1996).
11. Country Profile: *Kazakhstan, Library of Congress* Federal Research Division, September 2005.
12. Nursultan Nazarbayev, Annual Address to the People of Kazakhstan, September 2001, at *http://www.akorda.kz/www/www_akorda_kz.nsf/section*
13. Statistical Agency of Kazakhstan, at http://www.stat.kz/RU/Pages/default.aspx (February 2, 2008)
14. Nazarbayev, Address to Third World Kazaklh Round-Table.
15. Nazarbayev, Address to the 12 Session of Assembly of the Nations of Kazakhstan.
16. M. Naribayev, "Economic Development Achievements in Kazakhstan as the Main Factor of Improving the Quality of Life for the Citizens," Kazakhstan Spectrum, No.3, 2007.
17. On the date of the Agency of Republic of Kazakhstan on Land Resources Management.
18. Including 15 rayons in cities and towns.
19. Including cities and towns of republican subordination.
20. Ministry of Education and Science of the Republic of Kazakhstan, *UNESCO Report* (Almaty, December 2004).
21. Vineeth, n. 10, p.12.
22. Ibid., p.12.
23. Bakhytnur, Otarbaeva, "Evolution of Ethnic Identity of Quazaq People", *Eurasian Studies*, no.13 (Ankara, Spring 1998), p. 34.
24. Abhishev, n.11, p.10.
25. Ibid.
26. Ibid.
27. *UNESCO Report*, n.6.
28. Ibid.
29. www.heritagenet.unesco.kz/kz/hn-english/history
30. Ibid.
31. Ibid.
32. http//www.state.gov/g/drl/rls/irf/2001, Human Rights and Labor: 2001 (online: web)URL
33. Otarbaeva, n.17, p.34.
34. Abhishev, n.11, p.10.
35. Svat Soucek, *A History of Inner Asia* (Cambridge University Press, London: 2000), p.46.
36. H.B Paksoy (ed), *Central Asia Reader The Rediscovery of History* (M.E. Sharpe, New York: 1994), p.33.
37. Soucek, pp.46-47.
38. Ibid.
39. Ibid.
40. Soucek, p.46.
41. Ibid., p.70.
42. Ibid., p.70
43. Ibid., p.71
44. Ibid., pp.71-72
45. Eric Hobswawn; Nation *and Nationalism since 1780* (Cambridge: 1992).pp.77-78.
46. Soucek, pp.83-84.
47. Ibid., p.93.
48. Ibid., pp.93-96.
49. Ibid., p.96.
50. Ibid., pp.99-100.
51. Ibid., p.100.

52. Soucek, pp.103-104.
53. C. Dawson (ed.), *The Mongol Mission.*(New York: 1955), pp.117-8.
54. Ibid., p.118.
55. Soucek, p.107.
56. Ibid., pp.114-115.
57. Ibid., p.117.
58. Soucek, p.123.
59. Ibid.
60. H. Algar, "The Naqshabandi Order: A Preliminary Survey of its History and Significance," *Studia Islamica*, 1976. p.54
61. Ibid., p.125.
62. Soucek, p.46, 144-47.
63. H. Algar, "The Naqshabandi Order: A Preliminary Survey of Its History and Significance," *Studia Islamica*, 1976, p.54.
64. Ibid. p.146, 54-55
65. Ibid., pp.146-147.
66. Otarbaeva, n.17 p.37.
67. H.B. Paksoy; (ed) *Central Asia Reader: The Rediscovery of History* (NewYork: M.E. Sharpe, 1994), pp.32-34.
68. Svat Soucek, *A History of Inner Asia* (Cambridge University Press, London: 2000), p.146
69. Ibid.
70. Ibid. p.150.
71. Ibid., pp.150-151
72. Ibid., pp.162-164
73. Ibid., p.164.
74. Soucek, pp.164-167.
75. Ibid.
76. Ibid.
77. Ibid., p.168.
78. Ibid.
79. Soucek, p.196.
80. Dilip Hiro; *Between Marx and Muhamad* (London: Harper Collis, 1994), p.107.
81. Rashid Ahamad, *The Resurgence of Central Asia: Islam or Nationalism* (Islamabad; Oxford University Press, 1994), p.111.
82. Dilip Hiro, *Between Marx and Muhamad* (London: Harper Collis, 1994). p.107.
83. Soucek, pp.200-201.
84. Jalalzai, Musa Khan, *Central Asia Political Situation and Economic Opportunities* (Lahore: The Frontier Post Publications, 1994), pp.166-67.
85. Abhishev, n.11, p.12.
86. Soucek, p.196.
87. Rashid Ahamad, *The Resurgence of Central Asia*: *Islam or Nationalism* (Islamabad; Oxford University Press, 1994), pp.111-112.
88. Soucek, p.213.
89. Soucek, pp. 200-201.
90. Soucek, p.111.
91. Rashid, Ahmad, n.20, p.112.
92. See, contents www.heritagenet.unesco.kz/kz/hn-english/history_en.htm
93. Rashid Ahmad, n.20, p.112.
94. Rashid, Ahmad, *The Resurgence of Central Asia*: *Islam or Nationalism* (Islamabad; Oxford University Press, 1994), pp.111-112.

95. Ibid. p.113
96. Ibid.
97. Rashid, Ahmad, *The Resurgence of Central Asia*: *Islam or Nationalism* (Islamabad; Oxford University Press, 1994) p.114.
98. Soucek, pp.255-27.
99. Ibid., p.226..
100. Ibid., p.227.
101. Martha Brill Olcott, "Central Asia: The Reformer's Challenge a Traditional Society" in Hajda Lubomyr and Beissinger Mark (ed.), *The Nationalities Factor in Soviet Politics and Society* (West View Press, USA: 1990), pp.225-256.
102. *Europa Year Book*, 1999, p. 2019.
103. Martha Brill Olcott, p.255.
104. Martha Brill Olcott, "Central Asia: The Reformer's Challenge a Traditional Society" in Hajda Lubomyr and Beissinger Mark (ed.), *The Nationalities Factor in Soviet Politics and Society* (West View Press, USA: 1990). p.255.
105. *Europa Year Book*, n.36, pp.2020-21.
106. Martha Brill, Olcott, P. "Central Asia: The Reformer's Challenge a Traditional Society" in Hajda Lubomyr and Beissinger Mark (ed.), *The Nationalities Factor in Soviet Politics and Society* (West View Press. USA: 1990), p. 256.
107. *Europa Year Book*, n.25, p.2022.
108. *Europa Year Book*, n.25, p.2022.
109. Martha Brill, Olcott, n.36, p.256.
110. Rashid Ahamad, *The Resurgence of Central Asia*: *Islam or Nationalism* (Islamabad; Oxford University Press, 1994) p.116.
111. Adel E. Abhishev, *Kazakhstan in focus: Ten Years of Independence* (Almaty, Centre for Foreign Policy and Analysis, 2002), p.14.
112. Soucek, pp.261-262.
113. Ibid.
114. *Europa Year Book*, p.2023.
115. Rashid Ahamad, *The Resurgence of Central Asia*: *Islam or Nationalism* (Islamabad; Oxford University Press, 1994), p.118.
116. *Europa Year Book*, n.25, p. 2020.
117. Rashid Ahmad, *The Resurgence of Central Asia: Islam orNationalism* (Islamabad; Oxford University Press, 1994), p.119.

2

Emergence of Independent Kazakhstan

The emergence of Kazakhstan, as an independent state in December 1991, was an event of importance not only for the Central Asian region, but it was also of equal significance to the world as well. For Kazakhstan, which is big in size, rich in oil, gas and mineral resources and vital due to its strategic location in Eurasia, independence came to the people of Kazakhstan as a momentous event. But the problems facing the new state were immense due to the troubles of transition, nation-building and economic development. The uncertainties were alarmingly visible in post-independent Kazakhstan. The sovereignty, territorial integrity and security of Kazakhstan had to be consolidated. Earlier, the economy had been planned and controlled by ministries in the Soviet Union and, it was almost completely integrated into the Soviet economy as a whole. That dependence was now ending and a free market economy had to be established.

With the collapse of old Communist political order, new political institutions, political reforms and modernisation were required. The industrial base and the communications infrastructure needed to be upgraded. The problems of pollution and environmental degradation, particularly in the areas of the Aral Sea and the nuclear testing site near Semipalatinsk, needed to be addressed. Given the rich resource base, realisation of its economic potential required a large volume of foreign investment. The task of nation building was complicated by the ethnic composition of the people living in its border areas, who are predominantly Kazakhs and Russians. The creation of a national identity, socio-political cohesion, and unity was not going to be easy. Besides, there were other problems like relations with Russia, China and relations with other newly independent states, and the instability and terrorism emanating from Afghanistan. Before analyzing the emergence of the independent Kazakh nation, it is imperative to go through the formation of the Kazakh nation with a brief historical background since the 15th Century.

FORMATION OF THE KAZAKH NATION

By the second half of the 15th century, a process of consolidation had begun among the nomadic peoples living on the territory of modern Kazakhstan. By the beginning of the 16th century, a united Kazakh nation had emerged.[1] After a long period of internecine power struggles, one of the Kazakh princes, Kasym-Khan, succeeded in uniting the main tribal groups in the early sixteenth century. From this time onwards it is possible to speak of a Kazakh nation, despite the fact that after Kasym's death the region was again torned by local wars.[2]

By the early seventeenth century three major groupings had emerged among the Kazakhs, each under the leadership of its own Khan (leader): the Great Horde (Ulu Zhuz), the territory of which lay to the south-east, between the Aral Sea and Lake Balkhash; the Middle Horde (Orta Zhuz), which controlled the central zone; and the Little Horde (Kishi Zhuz), with territory to the north of the Caspian Sea, between the Emba and the Ural rivers. These Hordes were further divided into tribes and clans. There was a extremely developed consciousness of genealogy, since it was lineage that determined both a man's place in society and his rights to pasture land. These features of Kazakh society, in one form or another, have survived up to the present.

During the first period of its existence, the Kazakh state was able to maintain a united state power and territorial integrity under the leadership of the wise Khans, Az-Djanibek and Tauke-khan. During this period, a legal system was established, reflecting the norms of the nomadic way of life and taking into account the relation between different groups within Kazakh society. The educational system and writing were built on the basis of the Arabic alphabet, the mores of Islam and the peoples' traditional nomadic upbringing. By this time, the verbal-poetic and musical traditions of the Kazakhs were already highly developed. To this day, these traditions remain a cultural trademark of the Kazakh nation. It could even be said that modern Kazakh spiritual culture is based on the reconstruction of the best examples of poetic improvisation and on the history of such well-known *Akyns* (poets) and *Biys* (sages) as Asan-kaygy, Kaztugan-zhyrau, Tole bi, Aiteke bi, Kazybek bi, Bukhar-zhyrau and others.[3] In spite of a large degree of ethnic and cultural unity, Kazakhstan this time essentially remained a "nomadic democracy" with a quite unstable political structure. The tribes of Southern and South-Eastern Kazakhstan grew into what was known as the Elder *zhuz*, the tribes of Central Kazakhstan into the Middle *zhuz* and the tribes of Western Kazakhstan into the Young *zhuz*. These tribes were, in turn, broken into kin groups and the leaders of each were known *Biys*. Some kin groups were led by "Sultan-Tores" (successors of Chingiz-Khan). At the head of the state was a Khan, elected from the "Sultan-Tores" by representatives of all tribes and kin groups of the Kazakh steppes.[4]

The Kazakh people traditionally travelled from place to place following warm weather. Each kin group had its own routes, which other kin groups were not permitted to follow. There was also a relatively strict system of land-utilisation and land-ownership, which was seasonally determined. Winter months were considered to be the most difficult. Livestock was fed on pasturage, and the starvation happening due to scarcity of grass in the harsh winter climate is known as '*Jut*' in Kazakhstan. Catastrophic *Juts* usually occurred once every 10-12 years and thoroughly devastated the nomadic economy of the Kazakhs. Some Kazakhs also engaged in agriculture, especially on the rich lands of Syr Darya, Talas, Chu river valley, on the edges of the Altai Mountains, in the Irtysh valley, and in the Zaisan depression. However, even in these areas, nomadic live-stock-breeding remained dominant.[5]

Kazakhstan is essentially a bi-cultural society with Russians being in majority in the northern region of the Republic. Kazakhstan, which has a history of the Khanates and mild Islamic culture, has no tradition of statehood or common culture other than that of the nomadic hordes.[6] The new Republic is devoid of having any consolidated national history and identity, which is now being consciously constructed. Nevertheless, it is possible to trace the contours of Kazakh philosophy on integration and nation-building.

Soon after their independence, there has been resurgence of the aspirations of native titular nationality—the Kazakhs. Despite all the propaganda about the multi-national Soviet state and the 'blossoming of nations', the Soviet Union, in many ways, looked like a Russian state.[7] In socio-cultural terms, the words 'Russian' and 'Soviet' overlapped and in many cases acted synonymous.[8] The Russian language and elements of Russian culture eventually turned out to be the normative all over the country. The socio-cultural integration in the former USSR was perceived by the Kazakh-national minorities as a camouflage of Russification and assimilation and evoked negative reaction among the indigenous elites.[9] The Soviet period witnessed Stalinist repression, deportations and even unprecedented famine, which are remembered by Kazakhs disapprovingly.

There are several other factors which present obstacles in adopting 'nation-state model' in Kazakhstan. The emergence of State has preceded the formation of ethno-nations as fairly homogenous socio-cultural and socio-political formations of modern type.[10] A low percentage of urban population, limited social and territorial mobility only reinforce traditional sub-ethnic divisions and identities among Kazakhs. The long history of the region, despite territorial reorganisation of 1924, was unable to familiarize the idea of ethno-nation-statehood as part of mass consciousness among the Kazakhs. The linguistic situation of having limited use of Kazakh language is also not conducive to the formation of 'nation-state'. In a way, post-Soviet Kazakhstan lacks any formidable national culture capable of performing normative functions for the new 'civil-society'.[11]

Another set of issues complicating the evolution of Kazakhstan as nation-state is presented by its ethno-demographic situation. The Russians mostly settled in north Kazakhstan and engaged almost exclusively in skilled jobs in modern economic sectors like industry, transport, engineering are economically strong section of the society. The historical memory of both native Kazakhs and the Russians contains a significant block of ideas, myths and images which adversely affect inter-ethnic relations in the region and the process of national integration.[12] The local history writing and mass media lay stress on the negative consequences of the incorporation and oppressive policies of the Russian empire in the region. There is a wide socio-cultural and psychological gap between the titular Kazakh nationalities and ethnic Russians. The Kazakh social scientists, A. Akhmedijanov and A. Sultangaliyeva comment about the differences: "While sharing a number of common features, the Kazakhs and Russians have different social and demographic structures, religion and political culture. These differences of their evolution, reinforced by the topological cleavage of the two ethno-systems are shaped originally by civilisational divergence."[13]

Thus culture, language, historical memory and social structure combine to draw a sharp line between the industrial, urbanised and Russian populated North and the predominantly rural Kazakh regions of the South. Unlike in other Central Asian Republics, the Russians are in a position to challenge the regime and its strategy of building a mono-ethnic nation state of Kazakhstan.[14] In a long term perspective, ethno-territorial conflicts or resurgence of separatist and irredentist movements, pose a grave threat in Northern Kazakhstan. Thus the post-Soviet Kazakh leadership is striving to ensure both the territorial integrity of Kazakhstan and the success of its strategies of building a nation state.[15]

INDEPENDENCE OF KAZAKHSTAN

In the new Commonwealth of Independent States (CIS), all the member states became truly independent and their membership in the CIS resulted from a decision made by the indigenous leaders of Central Asia, not the Russian authority in Moscow. Despite their newly acquired independence, Nazarbayev was well aware of 48 per cent of Central Asia's Slav population living in Kazakhstan. The late declaration of independence was attributed to Nazarbayev's concern to preserve the crucial inter-ethnic balance between Russians and Kazakhs and also to prevent further discussion on the cessation of Kazakhstan's northern territory to the Russian Federation. Nazarbayev retained many of the structures and members of the CPK (although renamed as *Socialist Party of Kazakhstan*), and he stressed that economic reform should take precedence over political change.[16] Decades of Moscow's hegemony, central economic planning and close transport/ communication linkages had only strengthened the bonds between Kazakhstan and Russia. Much of the political leadership and bureaucratic infrastructure of the Soviet regime remained the same in independent Kazakhstan. Thus, the totalitarian past of the Soviet period has been succeeded by the authoritarian regime of Nazarbayev. Nonetheless, Nazarbayev's popularity remained strong as testified by his re-election with 98.8 per cent of votes cast in his favour.[17]

The independence of Kazakhstan also witnessed the resurgence of Kazakh nationalist groups like *Adalat* and *Alash*, which were profoundly anti-Russian and wanted preferential treatment for native Kazakhs in their own Republic. The Russians were also opposed to discrimination against non-Kazakhs and sought equal status along with Kazakhs in the new Constitution. Nazarbayev in order to satisfy both these competing Kazakh and Slav interests, adopted a three pronged strategy since the creation of CIS—to preserve close links with Russia in order to pacify the local Russian population, to enhance Kazakhstan's historic and cultural identity in order to satisfy the aspirations of Kazakh nationalists and to strengthen links with other Central Asian states for whom he sought to be the leading spokesperson.[18]

In the early 1990s, the government of Kazakhstan brought about several changes in the socio-political system. On 24 April 1990, a law was passed declaring a Presidential form of the government in the Kazakh Soviet Socialist Republic (Kazakh SSR), with Nursultan Nazarbayev elected as its first President. On 25 October 1990, the Supreme Soviet of the Kazakh SSR approved the Declaration on State Sovereignty and the country's determination to be subject to international law, while the institution of citizenship as well as equality of forms of ownership were also introduced.[19]

On 10 December 1991, the country was officially renamed as the Republic of Kazakhstan. The events of August and December 1991 the unsuccessful coups and the Belovezhsk agreements—had caused the collapse of the USSR and subsequently, on 16 December 1991, the Parliament of the Republic declared the independence of the Republic of Kazakhstan.[20] During the period 1991-1995, the political system and Constitutional legislation of the Republic were formed.[21]

Nazarbayev, the first president of independent Kazakhstan views his country as a bridge between Russia and Central Asia. Both Russia and Kazakhstan signed an Economic and Military Cooperation Agreement on 26 May 1992.[22] At the same time, as a gesture to meet the nationalist demands, Nazarbayev signed a decree setting up Kazakhstan's own armed forces and creating a Defence Ministry. The new Constitution adopted in January 1993 established Kazakh as the State Language with Russian being the language of inter-ethnic communication. It was also specified that the President of the Republic should be a fluent speaker of Kazakh.[23]

By 1992, opposition to Nazarbayev's administration became more vocal and in June 1992, some 5,000 people demonstrated in Almaty against-continued communist predominance in the government and Supreme Kenges (i.e., legislature). In October 1992, three most prominent nationalist opposition parties (the *Azat,* the *Zheltoksan* and the *Republican Party)* united to form the Republication Party *Azat* to present a stronger opposition front.[24] On 7 March 1994, Kazakhstan's first multi-party elections were held with the participation of the 74 per cent of the electorate in which ethnic Kazakhs won majority of seats (59%).

In July 1994, the Supreme Kenges approved proposals to transfer capital to the northern city of Akmola (renamed as Astana) by the year 2000.[25] The proposal made by Nazarbayev emphasized Akmola's advantageous geographical location in contrast to Almaty's over crowded conditions. However, there was widespread speculation that the move was designed to strengthen government's control over the largely Russian populated northern regions. In November 1997, the new capital was officially inaugurated by Nazarbayev and a joint session of both the Chambers of Parliament was held for the first time in Akmola in December 1997.

Elections to the Senate and *Majalis* were held in December 1995.[26] Nazarbayev undertook several far reaching measures to restructure and nationalize state administration in March 1997. The existing 48 ministries and other government agencies were reduced to 25. Nazarbayev continued the reform process by reducing the number of administrative regions in Kazakhstan from 19 to 14. During 1997, Kazakhstan's opposition movement continued to denounce Nazarbayev's authoritarian regime and restrictions imposed on media. In March, the Republican coalition—a bloc of 10 opposition parties and movements including *Azamat* and the *CPK* organised a rally outside the Parliament building in Almaty to protest against the political persecution of opposition parties.[27]

In 1998, the Parliament voted overwhelmingly in favour of a parliamentary amendment in order to hold Presidential election before the expiry of Nazarbayev's extended mandate in 2000. Many opposition figures were disallowed to contest the presidency by the Central Election Commission. The applications of several opposition parties for registration were rejected by the Ministry of Justice. Despite appeals for postponement, voting for the Presidential election proceeded on 10 January 1999 and Nazarbayev was re-elected for a new term with 81.77 per cent of the total votes. Nazarbayev was sworn in for a new term of office on 20 January1999.[28]

In spite of President Nazarbayev's popularity, Kazakh nationalists insist that not enough is being done to cultivate a sense of Kazakh nationhood. Meanwhile, local Russians fear a Kazakh reaction. The fear that the majority Russian population in the north could decide to opt out by seceding from Kazakhstan and joining up with Russia remains a constant anxiety for Nazarbayev. In December 1992, some 15,000 Russians demonstrated in Ust-Kamenogrosk demanding that Russian be recognised along with Kazakh as state language and that dual citizenship with Russia be given to the Russians.[29]

After the collapse of the Soviet Union, Kazakhstan was considered to be one of themost potentially unstable post-Soviet States. Despite certain difficulties of initial years, the Kazakh authorities have managed to ensure economic and social development. There were only few incidents of inter-ethnic strife, and the country managed to preserve stability and unity among the people. Nazarbayev's acumen, authority and integrity and his temper for accommodation and harmony has brought a level of stability to Kazakhstan.[30]

For the first time since colonial conquest in the nineteenth century, Kazakhs are masters of their own destiny. Long treasured sense of Kazakh nationhood and "Kazakhstan for Kazakhs" has been realised. Russians may be welcome and even encouraged to continue living in the new Republic, but are no longer a privileged community. The vitality and stability of the post-Soviet Kazakhstan depends upon the sensibility and maturity of its leadership and citizens so that common interests, democratic principles are respected in governance and different ethnic groups are allowed to participate in building the political and economic future of the Republic in tune with the spirit of multi-ethnic and pluralistic society.

FOREIGN POLICY

Independent Republic of Kazakhstan has been working towards creating favorable conditions to integrate into the world community as a sovereign state and to find its appropriate place in it. The vast territory of Kazakhstan, the multi-ethnicity of population, the challenge of building communications and transport infrastructure, problem of accessibility to seas, typical in case of a land locked country, the dangerous proximity to Russia China and the Islamic world and the strategic location in the centre of Eurasia—are the determining factors in foreign policy of Kazakhstan. Its very geographical position being at the centre of Eurasia puts her into an advantageous position for becoming a link between the East and West of Eurasia.[31]

Therefore, to find its place in international community and to play the desired role in world affairs, Kazakhstan had to take into account the changing geopolitical environment in formulating its national security strategy, developing its foreign policy doctrine, selecting its allies in world politics in the field of military and defence, in the field of security matters as well as in the aspects of trade and economy.

The first foreign policy initiatives by sovereign Kazakhstan have been aimed at creating the atmosphere of mutual confidence, regional and international cooperation and development of relations with all the countries and international organisations on the basis of equality. Kazakhstan ventured for the creation of favourable external conditions for the drastic social, economic and political reforms in Kazakhstan, protection of the national and state interests, especially the country's territorial integrity and inviolability of the national borders.[32]

In his press conference held on December 2, 1991 after the Presidential election, Nursultan Nazarbayev outlined the main aspects of Kazakh foreign policy and emphasized that Kazakhstan should become a bridge between Europe and Asia due to its geographical location. When asked whether Kazakhstan was oriented towards Europe or Asia, Nazarbayev pointed out that Kazakhstan would like to establish multilateral economic and political contacts with all countries. The President maintained that these relations should not be limited to the Asian continent only.[33]

During the inauguration ceremony on December 10, 1991, President Nursultan Nazarbayev outlined his vision of Kazakhstan's foreign policy. According to Nazarbayev at the Presidential elections people voted for independence, sovereignty and democracy. During the meeting of the Central Asian leaders in Ashkabad on December 12, 1991, Kazakh President Nazarbayev, Kyrgyz President Akayev, Tajik President Nabiyev, Turkmen President Niyazov and Uzbek President Karimov unanimously stressed the importance and necessity of the coordination to strengthen the Commonwealth of Independent States (CIS). The following points were highlighted:

> The CIS should not be convoked on the basis of ethnic, religious or any other identity in violation of human rights.
>
> The CIS recognised the borders of the former Soviet republics as borders between the newly independent states as well as their territorial integrity and inviolability of the existing borders. It is put forward that the people of Central Asia are ready to become founders of the CIS on the equal basis with Russia, Ukraine and Byelorussia.[34]

The independence of the Republic of Kazakhstan was declared on December 16, 1991. The summit of eleven independent states (former Soviet Republics), was held in Almaty on December 21, 1991. These states signed the Almaty Declaration on the creation of Commonwealth of the Independent States. Once the CIS was created, the USSR ceased to exist.[35]

Independent Kazakhstan has been working to have its own foreign policy, its policy of national defence, a national security system and, to develop a strategy of foreign economic activity. Though Kazakhstan had never dealt with these issues until 1991, it prepared its foreign policy concepts and other principal documents. Keeping in mind its geographical environment, ethnic composition, economic situation and military structure, it was recognised that the principal tools to promote Kazakhstan's security were not military but on the contrary the political and economic ones.[36]

A quote from the speech of Kazakh president Nazarbayev will give a glimpse of the challenges and hopes for the tusk of the young nation.

> History made a provision for Kazakhstan to find itself in the very epicent world policy During the collapse of the bipolar world. The new states replaced

> one of the two ex-superpowers, and a special attention was paid to our country Twist of fate made the attention justified mainly by the fact that the USSR had placed a great portion of its nuclear potential on the territory of our country. Initially ignorance of our specifies has formed a negative image of Kazakhstan as an Islamic nation possessing nuclear weapons that threatened the entire world community. That Negative image became a disturbance not only for us, but for our future partners as well.[37]

Being conscious of these factors, priorities of Kazakhstan's foreign policy were identified as following:

- Maintenance of economic, cultural and humanitarian commonness within the CIS.
- Integration into the contemporary system of international relations and joining the UN, OSCE and other international organisations.
- Abandoning the nuclear status of Kazakhstan, which now looked for the traditional nuclear powers the United States, Russia, Great Britain, China, and France to extend security guarantees to Kazakhstan.
- Cooperation with the major international financial institutions—International Monetary Fund, World Bank, European Bank for Reconstruction and Development in order to attract funds for the economic reforms.
- Establishing the system of bilateral relations with other countries, especially with the neighbouring states of Russia, China, Uzbekistan, Kyrgyzstan, Turkmenistan and Tajikistan.

A cardinal feature of Kazakhstan's foreign policy was cooperation with the international security organisations, viz., the United Nations, Organisation on Security and Cooperation in Europe (OSCE) and North Atlantic Treaty Organisation (NATO). Kazakhstan joined the UN as a member state on March 5, 1992. At the 47th session of the UN General Assembly, the President of Kazakhstan advocated that the Conference on Interaction and Confidence-Building in Asia (CICA) should be conducted. In 1992 Kazakhstan obtained membership in the Organisation on Security and Cooperation in Europe (OSCE). So, somehow the nascent state of Kazakhstan earned admittance to the developed security and confidence infrastructure based on the common values that were laid down by OSCE and accepted by its 55 member countries. In 1992, Kazakhstan became a member of the Euro-Atlantic Cooperation Council (now the Euro-Atlantic Partnership Council), a special body that was created to establish cooperation with the East European and Federation of Soviet Union (FSU) states.[38]

Another priority of Kazakh foreign policy has been to on strengthen diplomatic relations with China which was formally established on January 3, 1992. A joint declaration on friendly relations was signed between Kazakhstan and China in Beijing on October 1993 and China also signed the Agreement on the Kazakh-Chinese state border in Almaty, in April 1994. Thus, Kazakhstan secured its borders with China and solved the problem that remained inflexible during the Soviet period. The first steps in its foreign policy showed that Kazakhstan consciously endeavoured beyond the region. So, from the very beginning the Kazakhstan government has been trying to develop friendly relations with all the countries, primarily with the USA, the EU, Japan, other nations of Asia Pacific, South Asia and Middle East.

The United States was among the first to recognise the independence of Kazakhstan. The United States prime concern to Kazakhstan was because of the nuclear weapons stored on the Kazakh territory whose prevention was considered to be the foremost objective of the US policy in the region. The diplomatic relations between Kazakhstan and the European Union was established in 1992 after Kazakhstan established the bilateral diplomatic relations with all the EU's members. The EU and Kazakhstan signed the Partnership and Cooperation Agreement in 1995. According to the Agreement, Kazakhstan and the EU develop a political dialogue and hold consultations on wide range of issues of mutual interest. Kazakhstan established the diplomatic relations with Bulgaria (March 1992), Hungary (March 1992), Poland (March 1992), Romania (July 1992), Slovakia (January 1993), Slovenia (Sep 1992), Croatia (October 1992), the Czech Republic (May 1992).[39]

Kazakhstan gave importance to its relations with the Islamic nations while the Kazakhstan government emphasized the fact that development of the relations with the Muslim countries will not be on ideological or religious basis but on the basis of the state interests and international law. In his address to the nation, Kazakhstan's President Nursultan Nazarbayev made it clear that his motto is not only to combat the problem terrorism, but also to prevent the kind of insurgent democratic movement that led to the downfall of Askar Akayev's regime in neighboring Kyrgyzstan.[40] Nazarbayev therefore wishes to accomplish a delicate geopolitical balance helping Kazakhstan to stand free from dependent relationships with Central Asia's main players—China, Russia and the United States. Nazarbayev appears to view neo-colonialism of the great-power as a threat tantamount to the dangerous of international terrorism and the so called "democracy-from-below" phenomenon.

Nazarbayev now advocates a certain distance from the United States. This attitude glaringly came out in the comments given by Kazakhstan's Ambassador to the United States, Kanat Saudabayev explaining Nazarbayev's state of the nation address. Building on the viewpoint of the president, the Kazakh ambassador to US indicated that the main spheres of US-Kazakh cooperation are trade and nuclear non-proliferation.[41] It is noteworthy that both Nazarbayev and Surabaya maintained a silence on the issues security and cooperation in fighting the menace of terrorism on a global scale. This silence is strange when one take into account its sending military personnel to Iraq.

The Kazakhstan is obviously uncomfortable with the Bush administration's efforts to globalize democratic values as the US weightage on democratisation is apparently viewed by the country's authority as misfit and destabilizing to Asian scenario. This apathy towards US policies manifested in Nazarbayev's drawing closer to Russia and China, the countries unlikely to cry about corruption and issues human rights violation in Kazakhstan.

Nazarbayev much proclaimed "multi-vectored" foreign policy shows signs of his drift toward Russia and China, intensifying after the Ukrainian revolution. Nazarbayev shared a similar strand in interpreting the Ukrainian revolution describing it as "stage-managed" from abroad by the United States devised to instigate a more pro-American leader in Kiev. It should be noted that a similar view was held by Russian foreign minister Igor Ivanov, when Eduard Shevarnadze's regime crumbled amid Georgia's Rose Revolution of November, 2003.

Given the prevailing opinion, it is widely perceived in the Kazakh diplomatic circle that the support for democracy is not a demand of inherent merit or a manifestation of the popular will, but a threat managed from outside. The functioning of the non-governmental organisations (NGOs) are often viewed suspiciously as US mechanisms to overthrow of Central Asia's existing political order and the installation of pro-Western or pro-American regimes.[42]

In his foreign policy statements, Nazarbayev emphasized Kazakhstan's continuing "activist, multifaceted, and balanced" foreign policy to defend the country's independence and national interests. Priority was accorded to relations with Russia, China, the United States and the European Union with reiteration of Kazakhstan's commitment to the Shanghai Cooperation Organisation (SCO) and the single Eurasian Economic Community (EEC), Russia's favorite project for integrating Central Asian economies under its patronage. During discussions with Russian President Vladimir Putin in Moscow on April 8 2003, Nazarbayev expressed his pleasure on the progress of Eurasian Economic Community (EEC).[43]

Moreover, Nazarbayev proposed in his address to establish a union of Central Asian states. Nazarbayev believes that closer cooperation among states in the region is the necessary precondition for facilitating stability and regional progress between Kazakhstan and its other Central Asian members and beneficial for economic-military-political independence for Kazakhstan. Nazarbayev is well aware of the threat facing Kazakhstan from outside to control the regional economy of the country. Though not categorically explicit it seems that the Kazakh president regards all the three countries of China, Russia and United States as posing equal dangers to Kazakhstan's economic and political sovereignty. To quote him, "Today, they are witnessing superpower rivalry for economic dominance in our region. We have to address correctly this global and geo-economics challenge. We have a choice between remaining the supplier of raw materials to the global markets and waiting patiently for the emergence of the next imperial master or to pursue genuine economic integration of the Central Asian region. I chose the latter."[44] Thus, Nazarbayev efforts to reduce Kazakhstan's economy from its dependence on the oil and gas sector and enhance the country's ability to remain an independent geopolitical player.

Several American and European experts consider that by historical standards, and in comparison to other states which came out of the grip of the Soviet Union in 1991, Kazakhstan has done remarkably well in establishing its independent foreign policy. In their opinion, Kazakh achievements are noteworthy. In fact, the formulation of conceptual basis and principles of Kazakh foreign policy was started soon after Kazakhstan became independent on December 16, 1991. It was based on the consideration that Kazakhstan is a large country not only located in Eurasia, i.e., Europe and Asia, but also its interest are multifaceted with no bias towards one continent or another. Moreover, its geographical location helped the country to define the key concerns of its foreign policy and influenced various directions of its diplomatic activities. President Nazarbayev clearly determined the main strategy of Kazakh diplomacy as well as creating and maintaining favourable conditions for the steady development of the country on the basis of political and economic reforms.[45]

The nature of political and economic reforms in Kazakhstan determined the main concerns or rather priorities of the country's foreign policy, apart from country's desire to involve itself in international and regional affairs. At that time, the Kazakh government had to take key decisions in military, political and economic affairs in order to give boost to democratic reforms and establish a new state governing system. These decisions were necessary to help integrate Kazakhstan smoothly into the world community. Today Kazakhstan's foreign policy is in harmony with the global political trend of leaning towards liberalisation.

Going through the main achievements in the independent development of Kazakhstan during the last two decades it is evident that one of the most important decisions made at that time was to achieve the status of a nuclear free state and to follow the policy of nuclear non-proliferation. Kazakhstan has indeed set an example of being a responsible state by demonstrating that it is not the nuclear arsenals, but a peaceful foreign policy, internal stability, sustainable economic and political development that guarantee the actual security of the state. To quote Winston Churchill who once said, "Generals always prepare for the last war". This is relevant in the case of Kazakhstan which was preparing for a new world, i.e., the nuclear weapon-free world and hence obviously became a vibrant example of mankind's increased responsibility in the face of the threat of total destruction.[46]

Over the years Kazakhstan has successfully developed cordial relations with United States, Russia, China, and several other European and Asian countries including the Central Asian countries. With Russia, Kazakhstan has longstanding historical ties and a physical link due to having a huge common border. In addition, a considerable proportion of Kazakh citizens (about 30 percent) are ethnic Slavs. Having a long border with China, Kazakhstan has well developed its relations in the post-independence period. On its part, China's desire for energy security and markets has led it to get intensely involved in Kazakh economy. This is in fact accelerating China's engagement with Kazakhstan as China's economy continues to grow including in its western regions adjoining Kazakhstan. On the other hand, in 2006, Kazakhstan established "strategic partnership" with the United States as well.[47]

As regards relations with its Central Asian neighbours, it is multidimensional due to the fact that globalisation is gaining momentum and so is the regional process of economic integration. Development of regional cooperation is now a world wide phenomenon. Numerous countries have realised that their national goals can be successfully achieved only through developing regional cooperation. Kazakhstan too has persistently been making efforts to promote regional economic integration. From the very beginning of its independence it took realistic measures on its cooperation within several regional organisations like the CIS, the Eurasian Economic Association, the Central Asian Economic Association as well as the Shanghai Cooperation Organisation (SCO). In early 2005, Kazakhstan pursued its neighbours to eventually establish the Central Asian Union based on commonality of historic, ethnic, cultural and economic backgrounds as well as on common future challenges and interests.

What has been achieved by strengthening friendly relations with its neighbours is that Kazakhstan has established a "security belt" across its borders. It resulted in the total absence of conflicts or confrontations between Kazakhstan and any other country. Besides, favourable external conditions have already been created so that sustainable development of political and economic interests of Kazakhstan can be achieved. Kazakhstan is also developing meaningful relations with other key Asian states such as India, Iran, Japan, South Korea, as well as Turkey and other European states.

Extending its influence beyond Central Asia Kazakhstan initiated the idea to create mechanisms of confidence building measures in Asia. In 2002, this idea was institutionalized into the Conference on Interaction and Confidence-Building Measures in Asia (CICA). A cooperative Endeavour of the CICA is involving 20 countries with a combined population of more than 3.5 billion that is designed as a setting for countering a multitude of threats, both traditional and new: wars among and within states, arms races, nuclear proliferation, terrorism, illegal migration, extremist ethnic and religious ideologies and movements, and environmental degradation. Besides identifying diverse threats and expanding the concept of "security" as traditionally conceived, the CICA proposal stresses the essentiality of collective action given that many of these threats are transnational in nature and immune to purely national solutions. CICA demonstrated that Kazakhstan is part of a larger Asian universe, just as its chairmanship of the

OSCE in 2010 establishes the length and validity of its ties to the European world.

Besides, Kazakhstan has built a strong and credible relationships with various organisations, foremost among them being 'the Collective Security Treaty Organisation' (CSTO), NATO's "Partnership for Peace" program (PFP), the European Union (EU), the Sanghai Cooperation Organisation (SCO), the Organisation for Security and Cooperation in Europe (OSCE), the Economic Cooperation Organisation (ECO), and finally the United Nations (UN). Since 1992, Kazakhstan continues creating a firm foundation for and expanding constructive cooperation with the NATO with a view to strengthening security in the Central Asian region and conduct joint efforts in anti-terror initiatives. NATO and Kazakhstan actively cooperate on democratic, institutional, and defense reforms, and have developed practical cooperation in many other areas. Kazakhstan joined NATO's Partnership for Peace program in 1995. This provided the country with an invaluable expertise and contacts with the military establishments of NATO members. Kazakh cooperation with the Alliance could be portrayed for internal domestic political purposes as promoting security in the region, and arguably by narrowing the focus of relations with NATO these elements have been more successful.

On June 24-25, 2009, Kazakhstan hosted the third Euro-Atlantic Partnership Council Security Forum for the first time in the history of NATO the Security Forum was held in the post-soviet space and Asian continent (last two meeting of the Council were hold in Sweden in 2005 and in Macedonia in 2007). The idea of holding the Forum in Astana was proposed by Kazakhstan's President Mr. Nursultan Nazarbayev and supported by the North-Atlantic Council. It was chaired by the NATO Secretary General, Jaap de Hoop Scheffer who said: "today, Kazakhstan is NATO's most active partner in the Central Asian region. The issues range security and other related topics that affect NATO Allies and Partner countries. Hence, each of them has a strong Partnership dimension with Kazakhstan". Kazakhstan-NATO effort in struggle against international terrorism, religious extremism, drug trafficking, and cooperation in science, education are priorities of Kazakh cooperation with the Alliance. According to the Kazakhstan-NATO treaty, the country allowed NATO aircrafts to cross its territory, as well as to land in case of emergency. More than 3,000 aircrafts have crossed country's air space.

Kazakhstan was accepted as a member of the United Nations in March 1992. Since then it has participated in many activities of the UN. In November 2006, Kazakhstan has been for the first time elected to the United Nations Economic and Social Council (ECOSOC). In the course of elections of 18 new ECOSOC members at the UN General Assembly, Kazakhstan was supported by 187 out of a total of 192 UN member states considerably exceeding the required minimum of two-thirds of the votes.

Through invitation from the Western countries, Kazakhstan joined the OSCE on January 30, 1992 and made a first step towards the formation of a new European security's architecture driven by equal rights and absence of dividing lines. By getting unanimously elected as OSCE Chairman in 2010 the Republic achieved a new level of international recognition. It is a paramount evidence of the country's growing importance in the international arena. The Madrid Statement by Foreign Minister Marat Tazhin of Kazakhstan at the OSCE Ministerial Meeting on November 29, 2007 chalked out the agenda for the forthcoming OSCE Chairmanship. Now it is clear that Kazakhstan's attention in 2010 will be focused on promoting tolerance, establishing Afghanistan within the OSCE mandate, strengthening all dimensions of the Organisation. On January 1, 2010 Kazakhstan took over Chairmanship of the OSCE. During its chairmanship, Kazakhstan was committed to a balanced development of OSCE activities in all three 'baskets', which included politico-military, economic and environmental, and human dimensions. Realising an initiative supported by the OSCE, Astana hosted OSCE High-level conference on tolerance and non-discrimination on June 29-30, 2010. Another important event held in 2010 was in Copenhagen, jointly organised by Kazakhstan and Denmark, which commemorated the 20th anniversary of the OSCE's Copenhagen Document on Human Dimension and review achievements in this area.

Yet another important initiative by Kazakhstan was to convene an OSCE Summit to gather all heads of the organisation's member states for the first time since meeting in Istanbul in 1999. The idea was to arrange a meeting of the OSCE leaders to discuss the contemporary challenges, including the impact on the region's political agenda of international terrorism since attacks of September 11, 2001, and of the latest global recession, and to state their common vision of the most pressing of common security concerns and of the agenda for international cooperation to promote the safer and better world.

Since obtaining independence Kazakhstan's foreign policy has based on a principle of multi-vector relations that was declared by Nazarbayev as soon as he was elected the country's first president on 1 December 1991. This position has largely been defined by the country's geopolitical position, its multiethnic and religiously diverse population and the level of economic development as a whole. Taking into account the current international realities the main emphasis in Kazakhstan's foreign policy strategy has been placed on ensuring an efficient security system in Central Asia which is aimed at preventing unconventional threats and challenges (international terrorism, religious extremism, drug trafficking and illegal migration) posed by Afghanistan and other countries bordering the region.

In order to solve this problem Kazakhstan found it expedient to focus on the following priority foreign policy aspects:

- Involvement in interstate associations—the Conference on Interaction and Confidence-Building Measures in Asia (CICA), the Shanghai Cooperation Organisation (SCO) and the Collective Security Treaty Organisation (CSTO).
- Strategic cooperation with Russia and China.
- Friendly relations with Kyrgyzstan, Tajikistan, Turkmenistan and Uzbekistan.
- Constructive cooperation with the USA, European Union countries and international organisations, such as the organisation for Security and Cooperation Organisation (the OSCE) and NATO.
- Cooperation with the countries of the Islamic World; and partner relations with Asia-Pacific countries.

Taking into account the situation developing in the world, we think that a quite promising international organisation is the CICA, whose main objective is to boost cooperation through multilateral approaches to ensuring peace, security and stability in Asia. From the very beginning the idea of convening the CICA was backed by a number of Asian countries that define the political climate on the continent and by leading international organisations.[48] The legislative basis for the Asian security system has already been laid out, with specific mechanisms to ensure stability in the region. As a result, the CICA is turning into a locomotive of mutual approaches in fighting challenges to security in Asia and making a significant contribution to ensuring peace and security in the entire world. The Eurasian Economic Community (EAEC) is also acquiring greater weight and reputation: it is aimed at economic integration that envisages the creation of a free trade zone and the formation of a customs union. At the summit of the heads of state of the EAEC member states in Dushanbe on 6 October 2007, the leaders of Belarus, Kazakhstan and Russia signed the documents to create the Customs Union. The creation of the legislative basis of the Customs Union is expected to be completed in 2010.

On 4 February 2009 the CSTO summit in Moscow decided to form the Collective Rapid Reaction Forces (CRRF). These forces should become an efficient and universal instrument to maintain security in the entire space of CSTO, including rebuffing military aggression, destroying terrorists, extremists, organised crime and drug trafficking gangs and the consequences of emergencies, if need be. The backbone of the CRRF will be one division and one brigade of air-borne forces (ABF) of Russia and one brigade of ABF of Kazakhstan. Cooperation within the SCO is also acquiring particular significance and it includes a wide range of mutual actions of an economic, military and political and humanitarian nature. At the same time, it is necessary to stress that the SCO is not a military political bloc and its activities are not aimed at other countries and regions. At the SCO summit in Dushanbe in August 2008 particular attention was placed on joint work on the Afghan issues. The SCO places a lot of attention increasing economic cooperation, including in the energy, transport, agricultural, trade and investment sectors, as well as the activities of an interbank association, the SCO Business Council and the creation of a transcontinental transport corridor between Europe and Asia.

Kazakhstan's cooperation with regional and international integration associations shows our government's openness and readiness to build and develop international relations both in bilateral and multilateral formats and on the basis of mutual respect, partnership and prospects.[49] Developing bilateral economic, political, cultural and humanitarian relations with close neighbours plays a key role in ensuring stability and security in Central Asia and creating conditions for mutually beneficial cooperation. Kazakhstan and Russia, as a result of various economic, political, ethnic, language, demographic, religious and geographical reasons (the world's longest land border, a significant share of Russian speakers in Kazakhstan and ethnic Kazakhs in Russia, interest in political and trade and economic cooperation and so on), are extremely intertwined countries.

Russian-Kazakh cooperation has been developed both in bilateral and multilateral formats within the CIS, the EAC, the CSTO, the SCO and the Central Asian Cooperation Organisation (CACO). It should also be noted that relations between Kazakhstan and Russia are a foundation for the creation of Eurasian financial, energy, transport and customs infrastructure. Kazakh President Nursultan Nazarbayev believes Kazakh-Russian relations enjoy a high level of trust and strategic partnership. He thinks that there are no political or economic problems between the two countries that cannot be solved "through a constructive dialogue and account of mutual interest."[50] This point of view is also shared by Russian President Medvedev who stressed at a meeting with President Nazarbayev on 4 February 2009 that Kazakhstan and Russia were developing a friendly and allied dialogue.

Cooperation with China remains a priority aspect of Kazakhstan's foreign policy and its long-term aim is to preserve the peaceful international situation, needed for the successful implementation of internal modernisation in the country. The Chinies leadership also showed readiness to start a large-scale dialogue with Kazakhstan on all aspects of bilateral relations. The former president of China, Jiang Zemin, said that China would always be a reliable friend and good neighbor despite any changes taking place in the world. China shows interest in, above all else, the energy sector. The West Kazakhstan-West China oil pipeline with a design capacity of 20 million tones of oil a year is expected to be completed by 2011. Two gas pipelines-one from Uzbekistan and the other from Turkmenistan-are being built through Kazakhstan to China.

Developing relations (bilateral and multilateral) with Central Asian countries-Kyrgyzstan, Tajikistan, Turkmenistan and Uzbekistan-is a strategic foreign policy priority for Kazakhstan. Astana proceeds from the fact that the regional countries are bound not only by economic interests but the common fates of the peoples, who are in a good sense doomed to live together in close friendship.

An important way of eliminating conventional and unconventional threats to Central Asian countries is regional integration. The Kazakh president's initiative to set up a Union of Central Asian States is still a topical issue. The initial stage of this project envisages the creation of a favorable business climate in the entire territory of the region. Kazakhstan favours expanding constructive interaction with the USA, taking into account this country's leading role in the world. Of particular significance in establishing constructive relations with the USA was the Kazakh leadership's decision to voluntarily give up the status of nuclear power. This fact largely predetermined the future nature of bilateral relations. The former US president, Bill Clinton said that the world had been saved from another threat of nuclear terrorism and nuclear proliferation and praised President Nursultan Nazarbayev for this. The USA is one of the largest investors in the Kazakh economy. Direct US investment totals about $15 bn. Kazakh-US trade stood at $2,046m in 2007 (2.5 per cent of Kazakhstan's total foreign trade). There are 374 Kazakh-US joint ventures and 91 representatives of US companies registered in Kazakhstan.

Maintaining relations with EU countries and expanding mutually beneficial political and economic contacts is another of the main foreign policy priorities of Kazakhstan. Kazakhstan, like Turkmenistan and Uzbekistan, is acquiring increasing importance for the EU (for example, in the energy security sphere). With regard to this, the European Union and Central Asia: *Strategy for a New Partnership*, adopted in 2007, stresses that new prospects are opening up for cooperation between the EU and Central Asia. Developing cooperation with EU countries is a very current priority for Kazakhstan. The main sphere of cooperation is energy. Kazakhstan is one of the EU's main suppliers of hydrocarbons, accounting for about 20% of its total oil and gas consumption.

Nazarbayev endorsed the Path to Europe Programme for 2009-2011 on 29 August 2008. This programme aimed at lifting Kazakhstan to the level of strategic partnership with leading European countries, with stress made on developing cooperation in the technological, energy, transport, trade and economic and humanitarian spheres. Taking into account the growing economic weight of Asia-Pacific countries, Kazakhstan has shown significant interest in expanding cooperation with Japan, India, South Korea, Pakistan, Malaysia, Singapore, Thailand and Indonesia. As a result, Kazakhstan, successfully pursuing its multi-vector foreign policy, has managed to occupy a well-deserved place in the system of international relations and claim a reputation as a reliable, pricipaled and predictable partner.

LANGUAGE, RELIGION AND CULTURE

Soon after independence, Kazakh language was conferred status of a state language in Kazakhstan. At the same time, Russian language has been playing a constructive role in stabilisation of inter-ethnic relations. The language policy of Kazakhstan has the following main characteristics: (a) Expansion and strengthening of the Kazakh language; (b) reservation of common cultural functions of Russian language for inter-ethnic dialogue; and (c) development of languages of other ethnic groups.[51]

Kazakh Language

In multiethnic Kazakhstan, the government adopted a go-slow, incremental approach to reviving the dominant role of the Kazakh language. The 1995 Constitution of Kazakhstan granted official status to the Russian language. Thus, the influence of Russian language, media, literature, theatre, and music has remained strong till date. Many Russian TV channels continue to broadcast, while most national and local newspapers appear in both Kazakh and Russian language. Ultimately, Kazakhstan has remained one of the most Russophone states in the CIS. In the educational sphere, while 60 percent of the secondary schools have switched to Kazakh as the principal language of instruction, 40 percent still teach in Russian. Secondary education in Kazakhstan is also available in 15 other languages. University instruction in both Kazakh and Russian continues while a few colleges teach in English, and students are able to select the language of instruction.

Language policy, nevertheless, remains a sensitive area for Kazakhstan. The state agencies have not yet completely transitioned into Kazakh, though the state launched a transition program in the late 1990s. Similarly, Kazakhstan has not completed the transition of the Kazakh language from Cyrillic to the Latin alphabet to this day. The Government has developed a policy of encouraging the non-Kazakh population to learn the state language without limiting the rights of the Russian-speaking community, as the state is trying to preserve the educated Russian population and prevent their migration to the more prosperous Russian Federation.[52]

The introduction of Kazakh as official language was planned in several stages: At the first level, translation of office-work in governmental bodies in the state language was planned. Governmental bodies arrange for conducting registration-statistical, financial and technical manuals in the state language by 2009. This process is expected to be completed in 2010. On the second stage, a huge amount of 600 million tenge has been allocated for language development and was made available. The Ministry of Culture and the Information intends to further increase this fund. Developing innovative and intensive techniques of teaching of Kazakh language including the use of audio-and video-materials and modern computer technologies are given serious thought. Thirdly, monitoring of broadcasting TV channels for observance of requirements of language legislation of the country is carried out. For maintenance of the Kazakh language proportion in the broadcasts funds have been allocated in the annual budget for development of qualitative television broadcast in the Kazakh language. Adding to this, necessary conditions for studying the state Kazakh language and preservation of languages of people of Kazakhstan are created. For example, "Republican center for accelerated teaching state language" is created for training civil servants. Teaching is conducted not only in Kazakh and Russian languages but also in 14 languages. The state promotes the system of Sabbath schools for teaching of vernacular language. Besides, over ten different newspapers and telecasts are issued in languages of other people in the Republic of Kazakhstan.[53]

Analysis of the political culture is especially important for the research of the states-in-transition like Kazakhstan. The indigenous traditions and values are an important component of the community's political culture. Before the Russian conquest, the Kazaks had a culture based on their nomadic pastoral economy. Traditional Kazak belief held that separate spirits inhabited and animated the earth, sky, water, and fire, as well as domestic animals. To this day, particularly honored guests in rural areas are treated to a feast of freshly killed lamb. Such guests are sometimes asked to bless the lamb and to ask its spirit for permission to partake of its flesh. Besides lamb, many other traditional foods retain symbolic value in Kazak culture.

Kazakh and Russian are official languages for commercial purposes. Kazakh, being spoken by 64.4 per cent of the population, is the official "state" language, and Russian, spoken by 95 per cent of the population, is designated as the "language of interethnic communication".[54] Because animal husbandry was central to the Kazakhs' traditional lifestyle, most of their nomadic practices and customs relate in some way to livestock. The traditional Kazak dwelling is the yurt, a tent consisting of a flexible framework of willow wood covered with varying thicknesses of felt. The open top permits smoke from the central hearth to escape; temperature and draft can be controlled by a flap that increases or decreases the size of the opening. A properly constructed *yurt* can be cooled in summer and warmed in winter, and it can be disassembled or set up in less than an hour. The interior of the *yurt* has ritual significance; the right side generally is reserved for men and the left for women.

The years following independence in 1991 have provided opportunities for greater cultural expression, but striking a balance between the Kazakh and Russian languages have become a constant political dilemma for Kazakhstan's policy makers. Kazakh first acquired the status of a state language in the late Soviet period, when few of the Republic's Russians thought of the possibility of compulsory learning of Kazakh to secure employment, to serve in the armed forces, or to have their children enroll in a Kazakh university. At that point, fewer than 5 per cent of Russians could speak Kazakh, although the majority of

Kazakhs could speak Russian. However, after the independence, Russian nationalist sentiment and objections to alleged discrimination in official language policies of Kazakhstan have increased, especially in the Russian dominated north, as they felt the threat of Kazakh becoming the sole legal state language. Meanwhile, Kazakhs have strongly defended the preeminence of their tongue, although mastery of the language is far from universal even among Kazakhs. According to some estimates, as much as 40 per cent of the Kazakh population is not fluent in Kazakh.[55] Even those who are fluent find Kazakh a difficult language to work with in science, business, and some administrative sectors. Thus, for most Kazakhs, Russian remains the primary "world language." Although president Nazarbayev defended making Kazakh the sole official language on the grounds that decades of *Russification* had endangered the survival of Kazakh as a language, the practical primacy of Russian is reflected in the school curriculums. In 1990 about twice as many schools taught in Russian as compared to Kazakh. Although institutions of higher learning now show a strong selection bias in favour of Kazakh students, Russian remains the medium of instruction in most disciplines.

The issue of languages is one of the most politicized and contentious issues in modern Kazakhstan. Demographic trends show that the next generation will have to learn Kazakh, a prospect that generates considerable discomfort in the non-Kazakh population. The 1995 constitution does not provide for dual citizenship, but it does ease Russian concerns by declaring Russian an official language. This status bestowed on the language suggests that Russian would continue as the primary language of communication for many ethnic Kazakhs, and it will remain acceptable for use in schools (a major concern of Russian citizens) and official documents.[56] Russian continues to be used regularly for general and business communication. At the same time, Kazakhstan is also promoting the use of English as the language keeping in minds the matter international affairs and business.[57]

By traditions, the Kazakhs are Sunni Muslims of the Hanafi School, and the Russians are followers of Russian Orthodox Church. In 1994, some 47 per cent of the population was Muslim, 44 per cent was Russian Orthodox christan, and 2 per cent was Protestant, mainly Baptist. Some Jews, Catholics, and Pentacostalists also live in Kazakhstan; a Roman Catholic diocese was established in 1991.[58] Although Islam was introduced to most of the Kazakhs in the seventeenth and eighteenth centuries, the religion was not fully assimilated until much later. As a result, it coexisted with earlier elements of Tengriism. Historically, the Kazakhs are the least Islamized of the Central Asian Republics. Nevertheless, Islam now holds a fascination for Kazakhs, not just for religious reasons but because it is a part of historical and national identity distinguishing them from the Russians. Kazakh nationalist groups like *Adalat, Alash* promote an amalgam of demands which include a call for a Greater Turkestan, closer ties with Turkey and elements of Islamic fundamentalism.[59] Since independence, over 4,000 mosques have been built.[60] The number of Muslims going to *Haj* pilgrimage is also growing up. Thus, the revival of Islam has added to the ethnic complexity in Kazakhstan.

Kazakh literary tradition is rich in oral histories. These histories were memorized and recited by the akyn, the elder responsible for remembering the legends and histories, and by jyrau, lyric poets who travelled with the high-placed Khans. Most of the legends concern the activities of a *batir* or hero-warrior. Among the tales that have survived are Koblandy-batir (fifteenth or sixteenth century), Er Sain (sixteenth century) and ErTargyn (sixteenth century), all of which concern the struggle against the Kalmyks; Kozy Korpeshand Bain sulu, both epic; and the love lyric Kyz-Zhibek. Usually these tales were recited in a song-like chant, frequently to the accompaniment of such traditional instruments as drums and thedombra, a mandolin-like string instrument. Kazakh writers and poets Akhmet Baitursynov, Bakhytzhan Kanapyanov, Mirjaqip Dulatuli, Bukhar-zhirau Kalmakanov, Abay Qunanbayuli, Makhambet Utemisov, Mukhtar Auezov, Gabit Musrepov, Abdilda Tazhibaev, Durnyam Mashurova and many others have enriched the Kazakh literature.[61]

For the most part, pre-independence cultural life in Kazakhstan was indistinguishable from that elsewhere in the Soviet Union. It featured the same plays, films, music, books, paintings, museums, and other cultural appurtenances in the former Soviet Union. This period produced many important figures of the early stages of Kazakh nationalist self-assertion, including novelist Anuar Alimzhanov, who became President of the last Soviet Congress of People's Deputies, and poets Mukhtar Shakhanov and Olzhas Suleymenov, who were co-Presidents of the political party Popular Congress of Kazakhstan. Shakhanov also chaired the commission that investigated the events surrounding the riots of December 1986 (Zheltoksan).

An even more powerful figure than Shakhanov, Suleymenov in 1975 became a pan-Central Asian hero by publishing a book, AziIa, examining the Layof Igor's Campaign. Later Suleymenov led the anti-nuclear Nevada-Semipalatinsk movement, which spurred the anti-nuclear movement leading to the end of nuclear testing in Kazakstan. He and Shakhanov originally organised their People's Congress Party as a pro-Nazarbayev movement, but Suleymenov eventually steered the party into an opposition role. In the short-lived parliament of 1994-95, Suleymenov was leader of the *Respublika* opposition coalition, and he was frequently mentioned as a possible Presidential candidate.

AGRICULTURE POLICY

Due to its geographical conditions, Kazakhstan is not capable to compete with the developed countries.[62] This is evidenced in the low rate of growth of production of agricultural commodities, low level of land productivity and animal farming, low labour productivity and ineffectiveness of different branches of agricultural production. The developed countries of Europe and Northern America employing advanced technologies in cultivation animal breeding, implementing complex mechanisation and by specialisation and concentration of production optimizing the organisational forms of the plants have transformed Agricultural Industrial Complexes into high-effective and immensely profitable sector of economy. Kazakhstan though succeeded in producing considerable amount of agricultural products with substantial labour force, land and other material resources, their volume and quality remains inadequate to solve the food problem of the country. After gaining independence, Kazakhstan like other post-soviet states, embark on a reorganisation of economy. It resulted in evolving the strategic directions of agrarian policy. Due to termination of inter-regional and inter-disciplinary economic links following the break up of USSR, there was decrease in agricultural production.[63]

The shock of privatisation of the property of agricultural sector with the loss of control on the part of the state caused difficulties, as it broke the stable activity of many state owned agricultural and refining plants. Many such units closed down. The agricultural sector in Kazakhstan has a huge potential. It has a considerable volume of land constituting 223 million hectares, including ploughed lands—21 million hectares (one inhabitant of the republic has almost 1. 5 hectares of ploughed lands). Besides, the animal rearing industry, especially sheep and horse breeding is practiced. The Republic is exporting grain, cotton, meat, wool and other agricultural commodity. About 45 per cent of the population lives in the countryside that represents a huge labour potential. However, according to statistics only 9.4 per cent of the people work in agriculture. The employment ratio of 12.8 per cent in the countryside will decrease, if agriculture sector is developed. Agricultural reforms henceforth include new emphasis on production of grains, which not only ensured the food security but also enabled Kazakhstan to export grains.[64]

Agriculture is the single largest employer, but between 1990 and 2004 its share in gross domestic product shrank from 35 per cent to 7.4 per cent. Few agricultural products have export value. The main agricultural products are grain, sugar beets, sunflower seed, fruits and vegetables, beef, and wool. Potatoes, fruits, and vegetables are other significant food crops. Kazakhstan has agricultural land of good quality, but its continental climate, exacerbated by soil-depleting agricultural practices cause hindrance in its proper exploitation. Land privatisation has been uneven and inefficient. In 2003, landholding law reforms failed to encourage trading in land, which would improve agricultural efficiency. In 1998, Kazakhstan had an estimated 30,135,000 ha (74,464,000 acres) of arable land, representing 11.3% of the total land area. Most cultivable land is found in the northern steppes, where the failed Virgin and Idle Land Project of the 1950s were implemented. Small-scale privatisation resulted in the formation of 31,055 private farms by 1995, up from 3,333 in 1991. The average peasant farm size in 1995 was 428 ha (1,058 acres). Between 1990 and 2000, annual agricultural output fall an average of 7.9%.[65]

Less than 2 per cent of agricultural land is used to cultivate commercial crops such as cotton, sugar beets, sunflowers, and flax. Kazakhstan is the only former Soviet Republic that exports grain. Wheat accounted for 29 per cent of all sown acreage in 1999. Wheat production declined from 18,285,000 tons in 1992 to 11,242,000 tons in 1999. Similarly, barley production fell from 8,511,000 tons to 2,265,000 tons during that time. Rice is produced in irrigated tracts along the Syr Darya near Qyzlorda and around Taldyqorghan in the east. Production amounted to 199,000 tons in 1999.[66]

ECONOMIC POLICY

The major industries of Kazakhstan are oil, coal, ore, lead, zinc, gold, silver, metals, construction materials, and small motors. Kazakhstan produces 40 per cent of the world's chrome ore, second only to South Africa besides the major fossil fuels and important minerals extractions. Kazakhstan trades oil, ferrous and non-ferrous metals, chemicals, grains, wool, meat, and coal on the international market mostly with Russia, the United Kingdom, Ukraine, Uzbekistan, the Netherlands, China, Italy and Germany.

The government maintains a virtual monopoly on energy industries. Despite its fossil fuel riches, Kazakhstan is a net importer of electricity, mainly from Russia. In 2004, Kazakhstan's 71 power plants produced 66.8 billion kilowatt-hours of electricity, 5 per cent more than in 2003. Demand was about 5 billion kilowatt-hours, which is higher than the actual production. Between 1996 and 2005, the share of thermo-electric generation declined steadily and the share of hydroelectric generation increased, reaching up 20 per cent in 2005. The main fuel for thermoelectric power generation is coal from the Ekibastuz mines in the northeast. A major cause of the energy imbalance is an extremely high ratio of energy consumption to gross domestic product output. Payment arrears to source countries lead to periodic power cuts. The state-owned oil and gas company, Kazmunaigaz, provides 20 per cent of output, with the remainder accounted for by three major foreign consortia: Tengizchevroil, the Karachaganak Integrated Operation, and the Agip Kazakhstan North Caspian Operating Company.

Throughout 2000-2005, oil and condensate production increased by 60 per cent. In 2005, Kazakhstan produced more than 51 million tones of oil. According to available data, the state-owned oil and gas company Kaz Munai Gaz produced 9,364,000 tones of oil and gas condensate in 2005, which are 445,000 tones more than its previous year's figures.[67] The company's share in total oil and gas condensate production amounted to 15 per cent. Oil production grew due to the application of new techniques to increase reservoir recovery. For 2006, oil and condensate production is forecasted to be 9,450,000 tones.[68]

Hydrocarbon Production in Kazakhstan (million tonnes)

	Oil	*Gas Condensate*
2000	30.65	4.67
2001	36.1	4.03
2002	42.1	5.2
2003	45.4	6.1
2004	50.7	8.8
2005	51.3	10.7

Source: Kazakhstan Paradise of Central Asia; 15 Years of Progress 1991-2006.

Because Kazakhstan's economy was closely linked to that of Russia in the centrally planned system of the Soviet Union, the breakup of USSR in 1991 caused an economic downslide in the immediate aftermath. In the 1990s, the contribution of industry to the gross domestic product (GDP) fell from 31 per cent to 21 per cent, and GDP fell by 36 per cent between 1990 and 1995. It was by 2002, new oil extraction operations restored the GDP share of industry to about 30 per cent, and overall economic indicators rose substantially. The government engaged in widespread privatisation, although many profitable enterprises went to members of the elite well connected with government.[69] However, the economy has remained poorly diversified. In the early 2000s, oil has accounted for more than half of Kazakhstan's industrial output, and many other industries are dependent on the oil industry. In the post-Soviet era, the labor-intensive agricultural sector became steadily less productive. The machine-building sector, producing construction equipment, agricultural machinery, and some defence items have grown.[70]

With a per capita GDP of $1,780, Kazakhstan is the wealthiest of the Central Asian Republics. It has made the most significant economic progress since independence, surpassing many other former Soviet countries in macro-economic reform. However, large income and social disparities continue to grow, with over 30% of the population living below the poverty line, according to official government statistics.[71] The shadow economy is estimated to account for 20 to 28% of GDP. The official unemployment rate is near 4%, but the real figure may be as high as 30%.[72] Kazakhs do rely on a local *bazaar*, where they buy clothes, electronics or other goods, mostly imported from Russia, Turkey, China, and South Korea. Urban Kazakhs rely much on grocery stores and now even big shopping malls in some cities for their goods and services.

For the last seven years, Kazakhstan's GDP has been growing by an average 10 per cent. Kazakhstan's banking system is among the best in the CIS countries. Since 1990s, Kazakhstan has attracted more than US$ 50 billion foreign capital. Now Kazakh has made foreign investments worth over US$ 17 billion, reflecting Kazakhstan's role in the growth of other economies of Central Asia.[73] In October 2000, the European Union raised Kazakhstan to the status of market economy.

In the past few years, Kazakhstan has been ranking the first in CIS in terms of foreign direct per capita investment. During the first half of 2006, FDI in Kazakhstan reached US$ 5.4 billion. Foreign investors are becoming increasingly interested in the Kazakh market considering that the total amount of FDI in Kazakhstan in 2005 leveled US$ 6.6 billion.[74] In January 2003, the Kazakh Law on Investment was passed based on the two previous laws. This law provides for equal investment incentives to foreign and local investors, protection of investors' rights, and procedure for setting investors' disputes.[75]

While addressing the joint session of the Parliament of Kazakhstan on March 1, 2006, President Nursultan Nazarbayev delivered his annual address to the nation, titled, "Strategy of Kazakhstan's Entry into the Ranks of the 50 Most Competitive Countries of the World".[76] He outlined the following main priorities for Kazakhstan to work on:

- Kazakhstan's successful integration into the world economy;
- Further modernisation and diversification of domestic economy;
- Modern social policy, protection of the most vulnerable walks of the population;
- Development of modern education, continuous improvement of human resources development, and the further prosperity of Kazakhstan's culture;
- Further democratisation and transformation of political system;
- National security strategy to meet modern threats and challenges;
- Balanced and responsible foreign policy course, given Kazakhstan's interests and dynamics of regional and world developments.[77]

Kazakhstan is now viewed as a model for other Central Asian Republics on account of its successful political, social and economic transformation, as well as for its social peace and stability. Kazakhstan has been pursuing a policy aimed at ensuring a staged democratisation of the fields of social and political life including the promotion of the citizens' rights and liberties, development of mass media, formation of the civil society's institutions.

The macro-economic stabilisation was complete by 1998 as was the implementation of the main economic and financial reforms. Liberal economy with advanced market-based infrastructure with stable national currency Tenge has been created. Kazakhstan has a favourable investment climate. It is experiencing the growth of domestic production and development of up-to-date information technologies.[78] An Assembly of Peoples of Kazakhstan—a unique body in the post-Soviet area representing the interests of all the ethnic groups living in Kazakhstan was established to deal with the inter-ethnic policy and relations.

As regards the military and defence field, Armed Forces, the reliable guarantor of the national security and territorial integrity of the state, have been formed after the independence of Kazakhstan. Meeting the aspirations of Kazakh people and contributing to global and regional security, President of Kazakhstan closed Semipalatinsk nuclear testing ground, obtained nuclear-free state status for Kazakhstan, as well as security guarantees from the nuclear states. Kazakhstan has gained international prestige, recognition and respect for its commitment to promote further internal economic and democratic development and contribute to global and regional stability and cooperation.[79] President Nazarbayev has pushed through the necessary measures, signed 400 treaties, and has promoted the sense of national consciousness and identity. The real impact of his numerous reforms began to bear fruits during 2000-01 given the huge investments in mining, industry and infrastructure.[80] Since then the country has been making an all-round progress in every sphere.

NOTES

1. See, Further Details, www.heritegenet.unesco.kz, Heritagenet Central Asia.
2. Adel E. Abbishev, Kazakhstan *in Focus: Ten Years of Independence* (Center for Foreign Policy and Analysis: Almaty,2002), p.129.
3. www.heritagenet.unesco.kz., Heritagenet Central Asia.
4. Ibid.
5. Ibid.
6. Lange, Keely, "Do Borders Make a Nation: A New Analysis of Identities with a Focus on Central Asia," Regional Studies (Islamabad: Autumn 1997), vol. xv, no.4, pp.87-91.
7. Prazauskas, Algis, "Ethnopolitical Issues and Emergence of Nation-State in Central Asia' in Zhang, Youngjin and Azizian Rouben (ed.), *Ethnic Challenges beyond Borders: Chinese and Russian Perspectives of the Central Asian Conundrum* (St. Anthony's College, Oxford:1998), pp.50-51.
8. Ibid., p.52.
9. Ibid., p.53.
10. Ibid., pp.54-55.
11. Ibid., p.55.
12. Prazauskas, Algis, "Ethnopolitical Issues and Emergence of Nation-State in Central Asia' in Zhang, Youngjin and Azizian Rouben (ed.), *Ethnic Challenges beyond Borders: Chinese and Russian Perspectives of the Central Asian Conundrum* (St. Anthony's College, Oxford:1998), pp.50-51.
13. Akhmedijanov, A and Sultangaliyeva A., *Eurasian Space: Potential for Integration and its Realization*, Almaty,1994, p.103.
14. Ibid., p.103.
15. Prazauskas, Algis, "Ethnopolitical Issues and Emergence of Nation-State in Central Asia' in Zhang, Youngjin and Azizian Rouben (ed.), *Ethnic Challenges beyond Borders: Chinese and Russian Perspectives of the Central Asian Conundrum* (St. Anthony's College, Oxford: 1998), pp.50-51.
16. Europa Year Book, 1999, p.2020.
17. Ibid., p.2020.
18. Rashid, Ahmad, *The Resurgence of Central Asia. Islam or Nationalism* (Islamabad: Oxford University Press, 1994), p.121.
19. Ibid.
20. Ibid.
21. Glenn E. Curtis, Kazakhstan A country Study: Federal Research Division Library of Congress, 1996.

22. Ibid.
23. Ibid.
24. Keesing's *Record of World Events.* 22 July 1994.
25. Europa Year Book.1999, p.2020.
26. Ibid, p.2021.
27. Ibid. p.2021.
28. Keesing's *Record of World Events.* 22 July 1994.
29. Rashid, Ahmad, p.131.
30. Vineeth. T.K., *Kazakhstan—Commemorating 10 Years of Independence* (New Delhi, Embassy of Kazakhstan: 2001).pp.36-37.
31. Adel E. Abbishev, Kazakhstan *in Focus: Ten Years of Independence* (Center for Foreign Policy and Analysis: Almaty,2002). P.129.
32. Ibid.
33. Adel E., Abishev, pp.129.130.
34. Ibid.,
35. Ibid.
36. Adel E., Abishev, p.131.
37. Ibid., p.133
38. Ibid., p.133.
39. Adel E., Abishev, pp.133-34.
40. Ibid.
41. Ibid.
42. Stephen Blank, "Kazakhstan's Foreign Policy in a Time of Turmoil", *A Eurasia Net Commentary.* 4/27/05.
43. Stephen Blank, n.15.
44. http://www.eurasianet.org/departments/insight/articles/eav042705.shtml
45. Kazakhstan Country Profile 2010; Committee for International Information Ministry of Foreign Affairs of Republic of Kazakhstan. www.osce.2010, p. 175.
46. Ibid., p. 176.
47. Ibid., p. 175.
48. B.K. Sultanov (ed), *Kazakhstan Today*, Almaty 2010, p. 128.
49. Ibid., p. 130.
50. Ibid., p. 131.
51. Ruslan Zhangazy, *About the Main Tendencies of Language Policy.* Institute for Strategic Studies under the President of the R?, July 12, 2006.
52. Ariel Cohen, *Kazakhstan: The Road to Independence Energy Policy and the Birth of a Nation*, Central Asia-Caucasus Institute Silk Road Studies Program, p. 23.
53. Ruslan Zhangazy, p.16.
54. Library of Congress-Federal Research Division, *Country Profile*: Kazakhstan, September 2005.
55. http://www.photius.com/countries/kazakhstan/society/kazakhstan_society_language.html
56. The information regarding Kazakhstan on this page is re-published from The Library of Congress Country Studies and the CIA World Factbook. No claims are made regarding the accuracy of Kazakhstan Language information contained here. All suggestions for corrections of any errors about Kazakhstan Language should be addressed to the Library of Congress and the CIA, Data as of March 1996.
57. *Kazakhstan Paradise of Central Asia; 15 years of Progress 1991-2006*, The Embassy of Kazakhstan, India.
58. http://www.photius.com/countries/kazakhstan/society/kazakhstan_society_religion.html. Sources: The Library of Congress Country Studies; CIA World Factbook.
59. Rashid. Ahmad, p.132.

60. Ibid., p.132.
61. Ibid, n.6, p.132.
62. G. Kurganbaeva, *The Analysis of the Development of the Agricultural Branch in Kazakhstan* (Kaz ISS October 10, 2002)
63. G. Kurganbaeva, p.64.
64. Ibid.
65. G. Kurganbaeva, n.64.
66. Ibid.
67. *Kazakhstan Paradise of Central Asia; 15 Years of Progress 1991-2006* (The Embassy of Kazakhstan, India).
68. *Kazakhstan Paradise of Central Asia*, n.22 p.22.
69. Country Profile: Kazakhstan, Library of Congress-Federal Research Division (Washington: September 2005).
70. Ibid.
71. See http://news.bbc.co.uk/1/hi/world/asia-pacific/country_profiles/1298071.stm
72. Ibid.
73. *Kazakhstan Paradise of Central Asia*.n.22 p.22.
74. Ibid.
75. Ibid., p.22.
76. Ibid., p.22.
77. Ibid., p.20.
78. Rashid, Ahmad, n.6. p.8.
79. Nation in Transit, 2004 unpan1.un.org/intradoc/groups/public/documents/nispacee/unpan016578.pdf.
80. Abhishev, n.2.

3

Constitutional Development in Kazakhstan

Constitution is described as a document or set of "documents, which lay down the framework of a political system."[1] Constitution also defines the very essence of the political system in some cases. In states, which are undergoing a process of a political change, Constitutions symbolize a transition from the old to the new, and set new goals and aspirations.[2]

FIRST CONSTITUTION

The first Constitution of the independent and sovereign Republic of Kazakhstan was adopted in January 1993. Amidst heated debate in the Supreme Soviet building and heckling by a crowd of protesters outside, the Kazakh Parliament ratified the country's first post-Soviet Constitution in January 1993. According to official statics, the referendum held on 30, 1993 attracted 91 per cent of eligible voters, of which 89 per cent supported the Constitution.[3] The Constitution of the Kazakhstan Republic, which established Presidential form of government, describes Kazakhstan as a "democratic, secular and unitary state", with emphasis on democratic principles.[4] Life, liberty, and the inalienable rights of the individual are held in high value. Citizens are guaranteed basic civil liberties including freedom of thought, expression and speech, freedom of media and right to receive information, freedom to demonstrate peacefully, and freedom to create public organisations.[5] The citizens of the Republic have the right to property, education and right to professor not to profess any religion. International human rights agreements signed by Kazakhstan have precedence over state law.[6]

The Constitution of the Republic, which lays emphasis upon establishing the government's fundamental objective of nation building strategy, also accommodates the aspirations of non-Kazakh population. While Kazakh is the state language, the 1993 Constitution accorded Russian a prominent position as the "language of inter ethnic communication" and prohibited any limitations on the rights of citizens who do not speak Kazakh. The Constitution granted automatic citizenship to all who desire it, with no language or residence requirements whatsoever. In line with the Constitution's declaration that Kazakhstan is a unitary state, regional governors (*Akims*) are appointed directly by the President. This ensures that local governments follow Nazarbayev's wishes and act as a check for ethno-national extremists from becoming powerful and disturbing socio-political stability. The Constitution of the Republic prohibits the establishment of any social organisation which seeks to forcibly change the Constitutional order and undermine the state security, violate territorial integrity, or promote 'social. Racial, national, religious, class or tribal discord'.[7] The new Constitution supplemented the legislation by an absolute ban on any propaganda or campaign directed towards the above aims. The creation of political parties based on religion is not allowed in the Republic. However the constitutional democracy is emphasized.[8]

The Supreme Soviet is the highest state representative body of the Republic exercising legislative powers and gets elected for five year term. The main functions of the supreme Soviet as determined by the Constitution of the Republic are to interpret the laws of the Republic, approve the Republican budget, give its consent to the President of the Republic appointing the Prime Minister, Deputy Prime Ministers, the Ministers of Foreign Affairs, Defence, Finance and Internal Affairs, the Chairman of National Security Committee, heads of the diplomatic representatives of the Republic of Kazakhstan, elect the judges of the Constitutional Court, Supreme Court and Higher Arbitration Court of the Republic and determine the procedure for the formation of lower courts, appoint Prosecutor General, Chairman of the National Bank, ratify and denounce international treaties and confirm the Presidential decrees on a state of emergency and resolve issues of war and peace.[9]

SECOND CONSTITUTION

In May 1995, President Nursultan Nazarbayev convened a council of experts to draw up a new constitution under his guidance. The prepared Constitution, which is, second since Kazakhstan became independent was adopted in August 1995 by a popular referendum. About 90 per cent participated in the vote as per official claims. The constitution guaranteed equal rights to all nationalities and prescribed both Kazakh and Russian as "official" state languages, suitable for use in government documents and education. The President and the legislature, the Supreme *Kenges* (Supreme Soviet), are to be elected by universal adult suffrage for five year terms. The President is the head of state. The second component of the executive branch is the Council of Ministers, key members of which are appointed by the President. The Prime Minister, as head of the Council of Ministers is the appointing authority of the other ministers.[10]

Constitutional Changes in Kazakhstan[11]

	1993	*1995*	*1998*	*2007*
President	Five-year term	Five-year term, abolition of the position of vice-president	Seven-year term, no maximum age limit, abolition of the 50% minimum voter turnout	Five-year term, no term limits (for Nazarbayev only)
Senate	Unicameral parliament; members reduced from 360 to 144	Four-year term, seven members are nominated by the president	Six-year term, 15 members are nominated by the president	—
Majilis	—	Four-year term, 67 members; total of 114 delegates in both houses of parliament	Five-year term, 77 members, abolition of the 50% minimum voter turnout, threshold increased from 5% to 7% of the votes	Five-year term, 107 members, abolition of majoritarian electoral system; the *Majilis* now only requires a simple majority to express a vote of no confidence in the government rather than the two-third majority previously required

THE NEW CONSTITUTION: A DEMOCRATIC START

The draft of the new Constitution of the Republic of Kazakhstan was originally planned to be submitted for the consideration of the re-elected Supreme Soviet of the 13th convocation, which at that time was already prepared to carry out constitutional reforms. In the meantime, on 6 March 1995, the Constitutional Court passed a ruling that the method of counting votes introduced by the Central Election Commission not only entailed a large-scale violation of the constitutional principle of 'one man, one vote', but might also distort election results and essentially change the electoral system established by the election code. In doing so, the Central Election Commission had violated Article 60 of the Constitution by exceeding its jurisdiction. Consequently the results of previous election and legitimacy of the authority of all the Supreme Soviet deputies came under the circle of doubt. Consequently, doubt was cast on the results of the previous election and legitimacy of the authority of all the Supreme Soviet deputies. In view of the complexity of the situation and in an attempt to avert the impending crisis, President Nazarbayev made a public statement on 8 March 1995 saying, "The Court's ruling has come as a total surprise to us all. Nothing like this has ever happened before in the history of the state. I was, and still am, an advocate of stable state authority."[12] He further stated that "a respectful attitude should be adopted to the Constitutional Court's rulings, regardless of whose interest they affect. Only then is it possible to speak of Kazakhstan's genuine move towards a rule-of-law state and of the triumph of the law."[13]

On the very same day, i.e., on 8 March 1995, Nazarbayev exercised his legal rights and raised an objection to the Constitutional Court's ruling. Next day, on 9 March 1995, an objection to it was also raised by Chairman of the Supreme Soviet Abish Kekilbayev. But in line with Article 131 of the Constitution,[14] the Constitutional Court overruled the objections raised and gave a ruling on 10 March 1995 stating that guided by Article 131 of the Constitution and also as per Articles 14, 25, 26 of the Law 'On constitutional judicial procedure in the Republic of Kazakhstan', the Constitutional Court decides to decline the objections of the President and Chairman of the Supreme Soviet of the Republic of Kazakhstan and reaffirms the ruling of the Constitutional Court of 6 March 1995. It was also made clear by the Constitutional Court that the decision was not a subject to appeal. However, despite this decision, on 11 March 1995, the Supreme Soviet passed the Constitutional Law on the implementation of amendments and addenda to the Constitution and resolution on suspending the activity of the Constitutional Court. However, from a legal viewpoint and pure common sense, these documents no longer had any bearing on the Constitutional Court's ruling. Considering the ruling, Nazarbayev made an inquiry to the court on the legal implications of this resolution. The inquiry reads as follows:

> In view of the passing into force of the resolution of the Constitutional Court of the Republic of Kazakhstan of the 6 March 1995, adopted in a accordance with the action brought by T.G. Kvyatkovskaya, I request an explanation of the following issues: does this ruling of the Constitutional Court signify the unconstitutionality of the election to the Supreme Soviet of the Republic of Kazakhstan that took place on 7 March 1994, and also the unconstitutionality of the authority of the deputies of the Supreme Soviet; if the authority of the deputies of the Supreme Soviet of the Republic of Kazakhstan is unconstitutional, who is entitled to make decisions of a legislative character; does the ruling of the Constitutional Court signify that the Law of the Republic of Kazakhstan "On the temporary delegation of additional powers to the President of the Republic of Kazakhstan and heads of the local administrations" adopted on 10 December 1993 continues in force?[15]

On the same day, i.e., on 11 March 1995, the Constitutional Court in its additional definition had already explained all the issues raised by the Kazakh President. Soon the Law of 10 December 1993 *On the temporary delegation of additional powers to the President of the Republic of Kazakhstan and heads of the local administrations,* granting the President the right to make decisions of a legislative character, came into force once again. This law continued in operation till the new Constitution was adopted. This intervening period marked the issuance of a total of roughly 140 Presidential decrees with respect to all the core directions of the state's vital functions which helped the country to speed up the reforms, particularly in the economic field and plan the course of future development.

The Presidential Decrees issued during this period directed towards liberalizing the economy, demonopolising the state, and giving freedom and support to enterprises. This also provided an opportunity to start work on a two-tiered banking system that was to develop into the best in the CIS, and enjoy considerable public confidence. The extensive systems of commercial banks that have opened across the country have, in turn, played a decisive role in the development of private enterprises. Kazakhstan has thus become an attractive location for the development of major international projects to exploit mineral resources, which has provided employment for thousands of Kazakh citizens and raised revenues for the state budget.

Following the Constitutional Court's ruling, Nazarbayev signed the Decree *On measures issuing from the ruling of the Constitutional Court of the Republic of Kazakhstan* of 6 March 1995. A state commission was set up in accordance with this decree to offer deputies assistance with finding employment, providing security for Supreme Soviet property, and resolving other issues relating to the cessation of the Supreme Soviet's term of office. On 11 March 1995, the government also offered its resignation, which was accepted by the President. The resignation of the Central Electoral Commission was also accepted at that time. Compliant with the Constitution and the *Law On the temporary delegation of additional plenary powers to the President of the Republic of Kazakhstan and heads of the local authorities*, Nazarbayev appointed Akejan Kazhegeldin as Prime Minister of the Republic of Kazakhstan and instructed him to implement the proposals on the new membership of the Government as a matter of urgency.[16]

Such events once again showed the aspiration of Kazakh leadership for stability and rigorous adherence to the legal principles of resolving conflicts. This was highlighted more than once by representatives of the international community. In the words of W. Courtney, the US Ambassador to the Republic of Kazakhstan:

> 'It's a triumph for democracy. There has been no crisis because all the branches of power have carried out their functions. The Constitutional Court has worked in a quite cautious and considered manner to reach the conclusion that the election was not legitimate...We respect the ruling of your Constitutional Court. The whole world understands today that democracy has been significantly strengthened in Kazakhstan. You have gone through all this calmly and very swiftly, and that's why there has been no crisis... This is a good model not just for the CIS states but also other countries who consider themselves democracies, including the US. Kazakhstan is no longer a student of democracy but a teacher. All Kazakhstanis may take pride in this, and the US had reason to be proud of Kazakhstan....The latest events...have consolidated the political rating of your leadership which has shown respect for the Constitution.'[17]

Work on the Draft Constitution

Following the recognition of the Supreme Soviet as illegitimate, it became clear that the new Constitution could be designed at its earliest. Now that the country had neither a Parliament nor a Government, it was important for the President to get support for his plans directly from the Kazakhstani people. The Assembly of the Peoples of Kazakhstan proposed holding an all-nation referendum on extending the President's plenary powers. The Decree *On the holding of a republican referendum on 29 April 1995*, No.2152, was published on 25 March 1995, which, in part, reads as follows:

> 'Given that the highest expression of the will of the people as the sole source of state power in the Republic of Kazakhstan is all-nation voting, with due regard for the appeal of the Assembly of the Peoples of Kazakhstan, and guided by Article 78 of the Constitution of the Republic of Kazakhstan, Article 3 of the Law of the Republic of Kazakhstan "On the temporary delegation of additional plenary powers to the President of the Republic of Kazakhstan and heads of the local authorities", Nazarbayev resolved to hold a republican referendum on 29 April 1995 and … to extend until 1 December 2000, the term of office of the President of the Republic of Kazakhstan.[18]

The referendum's results convincingly demonstrated Kazakhstanis' support for the reforms being carried out in the country. The Central Commission of the Referendum on the issue of extending the President's plenary powers summarized the results of the voting on 29 April 1995. The votes were cast by 8,309,637, or 91.21 percent of the republic's 9,110,156 citizens registered to take part in the referendum. A total of 7,932,834, or 95.46 percent of the total number of voters, were in favour of extending the plenary powers. After securing all-nation support, it was possible to focus on the design of the draft of the new Constitution. In the spring of 1995, President Nazarbaev invited B. Mukhamedzhanov and K. Kolpakov to work on the project under the supervision of Minister of Justice N. Shaikenov. Earlier, they both had worked actively on the 1993 draft Constitution, and so were familiar with all the Constitution's flaws and all the compromises the Kazakh leadership had been forced to make under pressure from the Supreme Soviet. The issue was now to design a more effective Constitution on the basis of which a modern and genuinely democratic state could be built.

Soon after the draft was ready, an Advisory Council of Experts was set up by a presidential resolution of 22 May 1995, to analyse it thoroughly. This Council consisted of twelve members. For the working group Shaikenov enlisted leading figures of the law Yuri Basin, Gairat Sapargaliev and Maidan Suleimenov.

The Adoption of the 1995 Constitution

Once the draft of the new Constitution was published in the media for a nationwide discussion, almost the whole country responded positively. Every day a summary was made of all the suggestions came from all over Kazakhstan. However, the discussion was undivided because everyone did not support the proposed draft Constitution. In addition, the idea of adopting a new constitution and its constructive aspect were not immediately appreciate even by specialists in jurisprudence. Just a few days after the draft Constitution's publication, six judges of the Constitutional Court functioning at the time issued a statement in the media which stressed that the proposed constitutional model did not provide grounds "for recognising the Republic as a fully-fledged democratic, rule-of-law and social state", while the distortion of the principle of apportioning power called into question "not only the presidential but the republican form of government as a whole". However, the other half of the Constitutional Court judges totally disagreed with their colleagues' viewpoint, and also issued a statement to that effect in the media. Such a confrontation inside the Constitutional Court points to the forceful discussions being conducted in the Kazakh society as a whole.[19]

The Kazakhstanis who took part in the discussions of the draft Constitution numbered over 3,345,000 who contributed 31,886 suggestions and comments which finally resulted in 1,100 amendments made to the draft, and 55 of the 98 articles under discussion changed, and also a new section and a number of new articles appeared in the Constitution.

In view of the suggestions a total of 18 versions of the Constitution's text were drawn up. When work on the draft Constitution was almost complete, President Nazarbayev signed the Decree *On the holding of an all-nation referendum on 30 August 1995* on 28 July 1995, No.2389. This Decree primarily resolved the following: [20]

1. To hold an all-nation referendum on 30 August 1995.
2. To submit to the all-nation referendum the draft of the new Constitution of the Republic of Kazakhstan with the question formulated as follows: "Do you accept the new Constitution of the Republic of Kazakhstan whose draft was published in the press on 1 August 1995?
3. To officially publish in the mass media on 1 August 1995 the draft Constitution, supplemented and amended to take into account the all-nation discussion of it.
4. To send the draft Constitution to the Central Election Commission of the Republic of Kazakhstan.

After the draft's publication it became clear that the new Constitution would definitely pave the way for Kazakhstan's stable development in a climate of international concord and civil peace, and for carrying out political and economic reforms in the years to come. Only after gaining the people's support it was possible to embark on constitutional reform. This was what lay behind the decision to step up work on the text of the new Constitution. President Nazarbayev was bombarded by a squall of criticism but he was given support by the Assembly of the Peoples of Kazakhstan who suggested choosing the option of a direct address to the people without waiting for the formation of a parliament.[21]

Finally, on 30 August 1995, an all-nation referendum was held on adopting the new Constitution of the Republic of Kazakhstan in accordance with the aforementioned Decree. The referendum was observed by around 1,000 representatives from 19 public associations. Also present were foreign observers from Hungary, Egypt, Canada, Poland, Rumania, Tajikistan, Ukraine and other countries beside. A total of 90.58 per cent of the voting public took part in the referendum, of which 89.14 per cent voted for the adoption of the new Constitution. The new Constitution of the Republic of Kazakhstan was adopted on the basis of the vote. It was a triumph. The high level of voting was an indication of Kazakhstani citizens' support for country's Basic Law. In the words of Nazarbayev:

> I felt an immense sense of gratitude. Every politician has his hour of glory when he gets his people's full support and gains tremendous satisfaction from the fact that he has done his duty. All those years of doubts and anxieties, and sometimes emptiness all around you, when the circle of like-minded colleagues seemed infinitesimally small compared to the huge mass of problems and endless pile of tasks, both great and small you were landed with – all of these now proved not to have been in vain.[22]

The 1995 Constitution truly became an expression of the entire people's will, and the Kazakhstani people themselves turned into the co-author of the Basic Law. To quote Nazarbayev:

> At the press conference on the referendum's results on 1 September 1995 I congratulated all Kazakhstanis on this historic event in the life of our young sovereign state. By voting for the draft of the country's new Constitution, our co-citizens had made a choice of great importance both for the country as a whole and for every individual citizen. It was arguably the first time in Kazakhstan's history that its future was in its people's hands and they were voting for it.[23]

The official presentation of the new Constitution took place at the residence of the Kazakhstan's President on 6 September 1995. On this ceremonial occasion the Chairman of the Central Electoral Committee Yuri Kim read out the resolution on the results of the all-nation vote on adopting the new Constitution and presented the original text of the country's new Basic Law to the President, who, in turn, signed the Decree *On the Constitution of the Republic of Kazakhstan.* At the same time, in his speech to the assembled Government members, public figures, heads of diplomatic representations and media officials, the President Nazarbayev said that it not only marked the start of a new phase of Kazakhstan's development, but also it offered a number of new issues to be solved. For example, in Nazarbayev's words:

1. How to integrate our economy into the global economic market? If we failed to, we were bound to end up as a peripheral country, and an inveterate outsider.
2. How to induce people used to meager but guaranteed state rations to grasp the nettle and show initiative? You see, unless a person realizes he is responsible for his own destiny and that of his family, he will never achieve real prosperity.
3. How to design a strong, modern state organisation as the main tool of radical social reforms?
4. How to preserve the original culture of every one of the peoples of Kazakhstan while avoiding isolationist extremes? We much understand that passivity, like intolerance, causes cultural stagnation.
5. How to cultivate in society the ideals of spirituality, inter-national concord and civic peace?
6. How, finally, to curb criminal activity and establish the supremacy of the law at all levels of authority in society, without resorting to repressive measures?

THE 1995 CONSTITUTION—THE 'FOUNDATION' OF NEW KAZAKHSTAN

> When the foundations of modern democracy were being laid some two hundred years ago, US President Thomas Jefferson, who was not a supporter of frequent changes to laws and constitutions, wrote that 'the laws and human institutions should go hand in hand with intellectual progress.' Two centuries later, this concept is just as relevant today. I can proudly say that the Constitution adopted in 1995 became a powerful driving force for carrying out reforms in Kazakhstan. It is in many respects thanks to its provisions that in a short period of time we have achieved tremendous positive results in the young state's economy and policy-making, and inter-national stability. With the adoption of the current Constitution we got the green light to carry through economic reforms in Kazakhstan. The Supreme Soviet that had governed, figuratively speaking, everything and nothing, was replaced by a professional bicameral Parliament whose laws over these past few years have changed the country's face.
>
> *Thomas Jefferson*

The 1995 Constitution gave a new impulse to the economic reforms, and provided for the setting up of an effective normative legislative base and legislative field for parliament and the Government to work within that met and continue to meet the modern demands of market relations. The Constitution provides for the equal protection of both state and private property.[24] It proclaims the genuinely state-guaranteed rights to freedom of labour and freedom of entrepreneurial activity; to receive free, extensive medical assistance established by legislation; to a free secondary education; to freedom of religion. In addition, it also guarantees the right to receive on a competitive basis a higher education; to social security in old age, and in the case of disease, disability or the loss of the breadwinner. Today these constitutional rights are consolidated in the specific norms of laws and part and parcel of people's everyday lives. The Constitution has strengthened basic individual rights and freedoms, providing for the equal rights of all our country's citizens, which enables fundamental democratic principles to be inculcated in society's political life.

In fact, basically the Constitution formulates both the essence and substance of citizen's constitutional rights, freedoms and obligations in keeping with the principles of a modern market economy, which in turn provides the opportunities for satisfying the multifaceted interests of the individual, subject to his specific contribution in the course of his work. A necessary basic level of free social services is also guaranteed by the state. The basic priorities of Kazakhstan's development include economic freedom, ideological and political diversity and every one's equality before the law.

The democratisation of the political regime has significantly broadened the range of social opportunities afforded the individual by the state. This has resulted in a substantial strengthening of the role of individual and civil rights and freedoms in the national legal system, their traditional legal guarantees receiving new input. After developing the conditions for fully executing the requirements of the UN international package on civil, political, economic, social and cultural rights, Kazakhstan has ratified these crucial documents. Besides, new legislation has been developed on the basis of the Constitution. Updated constitutional law has been introduced. Civil law regulating the relations of private ownership, civil society and free entrepreneurship has received further development. In keeping with the principles firmly established in the world community, substantial amendments have been made to the laws governing civil legal procedure, criminal legal procedure and criminal justice.

To quote President Nazarbayev, "A new hierarchy of social values to be protected was defined in criminal law and found expression in its principles. The Criminal Code was to be formed on the basis of them. Since it was a highly complex and responsible matter, I personally worked out nearly every article of the draft law along with working group leader I. Rogov and B. Mukhamedzhanov. It should be said that the Criminal Code won the international legal community's very high praise."[25]

Since a correctly defined criminal law policy is one of the means of guaranteeing the development of a rule-of-law state, in Kazakhstan it ensues from the Basic law which proclaims an individual, his life, rights and freedom as its highest values. Rejecting harshly repressive means of dealing with lawbreakers, the state is instead establishing judicious forms of accountability for them, thus making criminal policy more humane and the punitive justice system more liberal. However, in view of globalisation and the transformation of crime which is taking on ever more ominous aspects, the question of responsibility for all infringements of the law and, in particular, for the most dangerous types of crime is becoming increasingly topical.

So far Kazakhstan's main achievements include internal political and international stability, macroeconomic stabilisation, total control of inflation, the establishment of an effective financial and credit system, the normalisation of ownership relations, and the gradual introduction of privatisation. Industrial production has begun to grow steadily and agriculture is reviving. Nowadays we have reason to say that our Constitution and laws are not only people-oriented: they also activate a person's creative, constructive energy and stimulate his entrepreneurial initiative.[26]

Kazakhstan's economic success shows that economic liberalisation in a transitional period requires a sufficiently tough political structure, professional human resources and discipline in society. This makes it possible to carry out complex, frequently unpopular but absolutely essential economic reforms and guarantee political stability.[27] Setting out to establish a real presidential republic in 1995, the President's increased personal responsibility in the course of the reforms called for a parallel increase in a whole range of powers. From then on Parliament no longer became involved in the appointment of the heads of ministries and departments. Instead, they were appointed by the country's President. The Cabinet of Ministers was simplified as a collegial body. The Prime Minister appointed by Parliament on the President's recommendation was invested with the powers of "the country's chief crisis manager'. Later on, collegial councils such as the Economic Policy Council, the Board of the National Bank, the Board of the National Fund and the National Council were to acquire a legal form. They now have more specific orientation and are all under the direction of the Head of State and their membership is not restricted by the representatives of the executive branch of power.

The strengthening of the vertical of power in the center envisaged similar actions taking place in the provinces where *akims* continue to be appointed by the President while the institution of the President's representatives in the provinces was abolished. The role of provincial councils that had been reformed as provincial *maslikhats* was also reduced. On this count President Nazarbayev said:

> I realised that strengthening executive authority, particularly in the provinces, would have a whole series of systemic shortcomings. The main one was, and still is, corruption. When control over the representative bodies in authority is slackened, the appointees from the center often exceed their official plenary powers. Aware of how hard it is to keep an eye on everyone's activities, they often forget they are supposed to be serving the people. As a result, no sooner had the reform programme begun than the President's administration was inundated with complaints about provincial officials' arbitrary conduct... The people addressed their complaints to the 'Central Committee'.[28]

As corruption began penetrating other areas of state life, knocking economic policy and the country's development strategy out of track, the President made an appeal to the citizens of the Republic for their support in a decisive fight against it. At that time, lawyers were divided in their opinion regarding the need to pass a law aimed at eradicating the causes of corruption. However, on Nazarbayev's instructions, work began on the draft law *On fighting corruption* which was passed in June 1998. Incidentally, Kazakhstan was the first in the CIS to pass such a law. A programme for fighting corruption was worked out and accountability for corruption-related violations of the law was strengthened.

The people of Kazakhstan understand that each new phase of the political reforms must be closely coordinated with the level of development in the economy, and now that the main reforms in the economic sphere are complete, the country needed the economic successes to be accompanied by a similar liberalisation of the political system. President Nazarbayev once again stressed that "there is one crucial prerequisite for any political reforms to take place, and that is the formation of a middle class. Only a stable and flourishing society is capable of creating a stable political system." He continued that "...Before a society can successfully use such a (Western) democratic system, the people must achieve a high standard of education and economic development, create a substantial middle class, and people's life must cease to be struggle for survival…The middle class will not emerge without a sustainable economy which cannot exist without a sufficiently strong and wise leadership capable of getting the country out of freefall."[29]

In the period between 2005 and 2007, an urgent need was felt to introduce the system of appointing the *akims* of towns and other lower-ranking officials by election, and also officially rating their activities. Having completed these tasks, we shall be able to return to the and elevating Parliament's role. A number of problems at a constitutional level have been resolved for the political status of the country's Parliament to be strengthened. In recent years, all the conditions have been created for the development of the most crucial institute of democracy, i.e., parliamentary. The professional bicameral Parliament, providing for the representation of diverse interests, has successfully withstood the test of time, and Kazakhstan has been the first in Central Asia to decisively embark on this course of action.

Following the introduction of the 1995 Constitution, Kazakhstan did everything to maintain its reputation on the world map. The overwhelming majority of states in the modern world are multi-ethnic in composition, and one ethnic group makes up 90 per cent of the population in only 12 countries of the world. It is no coincidence that the Kazakhstan model of international relations has won the highest appraisal of the UN, OSCE (Organisation for Security and Cooperation in Europe) and a number of other authoritative international organisations. All the key development issues of the national groups have been advanced in a three-tiered regulatory system. The first level consists of the activity of the groups themselves. The country has supported the legitimate aspiration of all the national communities to further their culture. There are now several dozen national cultural centers in Kazakhstan. A unique instrument of inter-national relations was also created in the Assembly of the Peoples of Kazakhstan. No other country in the world today has a similar authoritative and representative national policy instrument.

There is also a state policy in the language sphere. The country has been able not only to confer on the Kazakh language the position of official state language, but also to resolve the issue of its full use in all areas of public life. Nowadays teaching in over 50 per cent of the country's educational establishments is conducted in Kazakh. One should not forget that Soviet national policy had the most destructive consequences for the state language in Kazakhstan. However, unlike many other countries, Kazakhstan went about this process in a dignified manner without any language discrimination. Besides, Political pluralism and a multi-party system are provided for in Kazakhstan. Major national parties operate in the country, including those in opposition, who all have an influence on the political process. There is also no doubt that such a crucial segment of a civil society as non-government organisations has grown noticeably stronger in our country. Whereas a decade ago there were about 400 of them, there are now over 5,000. What's more, the NGOs interact with the authorities as active, equal partners within the framework of the Citizens' Forum that has been set up on my initiative. And, revealingly, it is the NGOs that have now started taking the lead in these relations.

It is noteworthy that cardinal changes have taken place in the dissemination of information. Freedom to express one's opinion and criticize the authorities has genuinely been established in the Kazakhstan media, and citizens now have the right to alternative sources of information. The country now has over 2,000 publications of the most diverse political orientation, including some radically opposed to the government. And of all the mass media only 20 per cent are run by the state. Strict adherence to the Constitution is the basis for the state's successful development and civil concord in society. Learning to live by it—this is the greatest lesson in democracy: a lesson all of us are obliged to learn. The Constitution has laid the foundation for Kazaskhstani people's freedom and has consolidated all the various successes and acquisitions that brought their independence. Our Constitution has given us what matters most. The right to choose, to create one's own life, is the most precious gift of all.[30]

As already mentioned, the 1995 Constitution has given new impulse to economic development. Kazakhstan's economy is established as the driving force of progress—from the design of the new Constitution to the change in Kazakhstanis' way of life and, most importantly, mind-sets. And oil, the 'black gold' of Kazakh land, has at this stage become the life blood of overall country's economy. Oil and gas have become the main resource and acted as real start-up capital from the very first days of independence; and within the next 15-20 years Kazakhstan is expected to become a top supplier of hydrocarbons to the world market. Even President Nazarbayev stressed that "Our mineral resources have become an object not only of envy but also of claims that might well have cost us our independence.[31]

CONSTITUTIONAL AMENDMENTS

On 16 May 2007, President Nazarbayev and his government introduced several Constitutional amendments which enhanced the authority of the Parliament. This in turn would transform the republic from presidential to a parliamentary one. Nazarbayev stressed the need for strengthening the Parliament's role by increasing the number of deputies, introducing new procedures of forming the Government on the principles of parliamentary majority, introduction of proportional election system of deputies to the lower chamber of *Majilis,* cancellation of the party affiliation of the Senate deputies and many other political innovations.[32]

According to the new procedures of forming the Government, Prime Minister has to be appointed by the President after consultations with political parties and by the appropriation of a majority of the Parliament's deputies. The implementation of such an approach will first of all elevate the role of political parties in forming the Government. Secondly, the party having a parliamentary majority will be responsible for the formation of the Government and its consequent actions implementing the program of the winning party or coalition. The proposed election of *Majilis* deputies under proportional elective system would ensure representation and take into account the specific features of the country. The President also offered to develop practical mechanisms for partial support of the activities of political parties from the republican budget. The President porposed a reduction of the presidential term from seven down to five years and also that regional governors must be elected with the appropriation of corresponding *maslikhats* (regional elective entity).

In the area of judicial reform, not only legal confirmation of an arrest but also the abolition of the death penalty has been announced in Kazakhstan. It may be pointed out that the Constitution provides for death penalty to those who commit terrorist acts or violent crimes. President Nazarbayev underscored the need for the above stated amendments to the Constitution of Kazakhstan for ushering in a new stage in the democratisation of the nation.[33]

NEW REFERENDUM

Structure of Government in Kazakhstan

The post-independence government was structured by the 1993 constitution with a strong executive parliament and judiciary. In practice the administration of Nursultan Nazarbayev dominated the governance in the country after its independence.

The Executive

The constitution formalized the enhanced powers that President Nazarbayev assumed upon the dissolution of parliament in early 1995.It continued the previous constitutional definition of Kazakhstan as a unitary state with a Presidential form of government. The President is the highest state officer, responsible for forming the government, subject to parliamentary approval, and appointing all other republican officials. The 1995 constitution expanded the President's powers to introduce and veto legislation. The President has the powers to appoint the council of Ministers, headed by a Prime Minister, and several state committees. In October 1995, Nazarbayev himself assumed the *portfolio* of the Ministry of National Security. In early 1996, after Nazarbayev had reshuffled the government in October 1995, the Council of Ministers included the heads of twenty-one ministries and nine state committees, the Prime Minister being Akezhan Kazhegeldin.[34]

The new constitution does not provide for the position of Vice President. However, it permitted the incumbent Vice President, Yerik Asanbayev to remain in office till 1996. The President has the power to declare state of emergency during which the constitution can be suspended. The President is the sponsor of legislation and the guarantor of the constitution and of the proper functioning of government, with the power to override the decisions and actions of local authorities and councils. The only grounds on which a President can be removed are infirmity and treason, either of which must be confirmed by a majority of the joint Upper and Lower House of the new parliament. In the event of such a removal from power, the Prime Minister would become the temporary President.[35]

The Legislative

The 1993 constitution created a unicameral parliament, which was to replace the 350 seat Supreme Soviet when the mandates of its deputies expired in 1995. The 1990 parliament, which was composed of the former communists, was dissolved early under the pressure of President Nazarbayev in December 1993 in order to pave way for a smaller and presumably more flexible parliament. Under the 1995 constitution, the parliament consisted of two houses, the Senate and the *Majilis*, both operating in continuous sessions. All the provinces of Kazakhstan and the city of Almaty, which had provincial status, had two senators, chosen for four-year terms by the joint sessions of the provincial legislative bodies. Additional seven senators were appointed directly by the President. In addition, ex-Presidents automatically receive the status of senators-for-life. The *Majilis* had 67 representatives, including one from each of 55 districts having roughly equal population, and the *Senate* has forty seats. Direct elections for half of the seats are held every two years. In the first election under the new parliamentary structure, all the seats in both houses of parliament were contested in December 1995; renoff elections filled twenty-three seats in the *Majilis* for which the initial vote was inconclusive. The new parliament, which assembled in January 1996, included sixty-eight Kazakh and thirty-one Russian deputies, among whom only ten were women. The initiative for most legislative actions originated with the President. If a law passed by the parliament faces the President's veto, a two-third vote of both houses is mandatory to override the veto. A similar margin is needed to express no confidence in a Prime Minister, an action that requires the President to name a new Prim Minister and Council of Ministers.[36]

Judiciary

The judiciary system is the least developed of Kazakhstan's three branches of government. The constitution retains the provision of Presidential appointment of all judges in the republic. Whereas, the 1993 constitution specified the terms of service for judges, the 1995 document made no mention of length of service, suggesting that judges would serve at the discretion of the President.[37] Under the constitution of 1993, lines of judicial authority were poorly defined, in part because the republic had three "highest courts", the Supreme Court, the State Arbitrate Court, and the Constitutional Court employing a total of sixty six senior judges. Many of these senior judges, as well as numerous judges in lower courts, had been retained from the Soviet era, when the judicial branch was entirely under the control of the central government. The 1995 constitution makes no provision for the State Arbitrate Court Provisions, for the new judiciary clearly subordinates all other courts to the Supreme Court, which has a consultative role in appointing senior judges.[38]

Local Government

Kazakhstan is divided into fourteen provinces, and the city of Almaty has administrative status equal to that of a province. In turn, the provinces are divided into regions that consist of a number of settlements. Each province or region and most settlements have their own elected councils, entrusted with making a budget and supervising local tax collections. Cities have their own local councils as well, and large cities are divided into regions, each having its own council.[39]

The local legislature lack the authority to choose the local executives, who are directly appointed by the President. The duty of a local executive is to ensure the enforcement of the decisions of the national government and a proper observance of the constitution. Provincial and regional "heads of administration", known by the Russian term *Glav* or the kazakh term *Akim*, are Presidential appointees. The *Akim*, in turm, appoints the members of his staff, who function as departmental heads. The *Hakim* also can reverse budgetary decisions of the local council.[40]

There has been considerable pressure, especially in the predominantly Russian north, to alter the nature of the post of *Akim* making it elective rather than through appointment by the Presidential. The 1995 constitution provides that only the local councils have the capacity to express no confidence in their *Akim* by a two-thirds majority. The President has the power to override or revoke the decisions taken by local councils.

Kazakhstan is divided in the following tiers of local government:

1. First (rural) tier, which includes the local administrations, that is, executive bodies in towns, villages (auls) and rural countries
2. Second (raion) tier, which includes the local state administrations, that is, the executive and representative bodies in 160 raions and seventy-nine cities of raion status
3. Third (oblast) tier, which includes the local state administrations, that is, the executive and representative bodies in fourtieen oblasts and two cities, Almaty and Astana.[41]

POLITICAL STRUCTURE IN KAZAKHSTAN

Reformation period of Kazakhstan's political system began immediately after its independence. Transition to democracy commenced under dificult conditions: The country was then experiencing socio-economic crisis due to decline in industrial and agricultural production, hyperinflation (up to 3,000 per cent), and drastic decline in living standards. After the collapse of the USSR, former Soviet states experienced a crisis situation. Kazakhstan too experienced the same and tried to overcome the problems related to democratisation of political institutions, so as to strengthen the political system in Kazakhstan.

In accordance with the 1995 Kazakh constitution, the government exercises the executive power. The government is composed of the Prime Minister, the deputy ministers, heads of the government departments, ministers and Chairpersons of state committees. According to Act 166 of the Kazakh Constitution (1995), the government works out the basic socio-economic directions of the state policy, its defense preparedness and security, ensures social order and organises their implementation. The government presents state budget to the parliament. Among other factions performed by the government mention may be made of tabling laws in the *Majilis* (Parliament) and administration of state properties, working out measures for conducting foreign policy; guiding the activities of the ministers, state committees, other central and local executive organs, keeping vigilance on the actions of the ministers and state committees as well as on other central and local executive organs of the republic, appointment and removal of the heads of the central executive organs not forming part of the government. In short, the government is liable to discharge functions entrusted to it by the constitution, laws and acts of the President.[42]

The new constitution of 1995 preserved the extensive executive powers of the President and also abolished the post of Vice-President. The Supreme *Kenges* was replaced by a bicameral Parliament, comprising a 47 member Senate (the Upper Chamber with 40 members elected by Kazakhstan's regional administrative bodies and seven appointed by the President) and 67 directly elected members of *Majilis* (Assembly).[43] The Constitutional Court was replaced by a Constitutional Council, whose decisions are subject to a Presidential right of veto. The Constitution retained Kazakh as the state language but guaranteed the development of all other languages, making Russian the language of inter-ethnic communication.

Notwithstanding the sufficient authority regarding the implementation of the executive powers, the government is extremely dependent on the President. A number of mechanisms are incorporated in the constitution through which the President is in a position not only to form the government in the manner he considers fit but also to influence its day to day functions. According to the constitution, the President of Kazakhstan being the head of the state, remains the key figure to which all executive powers are subordinated. The President, with the consent of the parliament, appoints the Prime Minister; removes him from his post determines the structure of Government on the recommendation of the Prime Minister, appoint6s and terminates from the post all its members all implying to a high degree of personal influence of President on the composition of the government. In general, the level of participation of the President in the government formation in Kazakhstan is compared with the prerogatives of the President of the Russian Federation in regard to the government formation.

Questions related to the resignation of the government are regulated by the constitution in such a fashion that the government or its individual members can relinquish office only when it is sanctioned by the president. President's power in deciding over the resignation of the government is not limited by any provision whatsoever. The strong of the dependence of the government on the president follows from the fact that the decisions and acts of the government can be altered or stopped by the President in full or in part if he views them as being contradictory to the constitution, legislative acts or Presidential decrees and others. The subordinate character of the government before the President is manifested in the fact that the government's powers are terminated before the new President is elected. This provides ample opportunity to the next President to appoint a new government.[44]

The correlation in the system of state power is defined in the Constitution of the Republic of Kazakhstan in such a way that the executive power is independent of legislative power and the latter is comparatively weaker. Article 53 of the constitution, which provides for the consent of the President to the appointment of the head of the government, curtails the jurisdiction on of the Parliament. The Parliament can reject the candidate proposed by the President but if this happens twice the President holds the power to appoint a person of his choice as head of the government. The parliament faces the risk of dissolution and fresh elections in case it tries to obstruct the President for the third time.[45] Secondly, the Parliament can express its lack of confidence in the government through a No-Confidence Motion in two cases: When a draft law introduced by the government gets rejected, the Prime Minister has the right to raise the question of confidence in his government by proposing it for the second time. The second instance of the no confidence motion occurs in the case when the parliament expresses its rejection twice to a government's proposal by a two thirds majority in the house. The fact remains that parliament's role in deciding the question of confidence in the government is *de jure* while the President acts as the *de facto* arbitrator. If the Parliament express its lack of confidence in the government, it hands over its own fate to the President by doing so. The Parliament decides the question of its agreement or disagreement with the President over the issue of the appointment of the Prime Minister.[46]

The Parliament, in reality, has limited powers on framing the budget.

According to Article 61 of the constitution, all draft legislations concerning reduction of state revenues or increase in government expenditure should be introduced in the Parliament by the government alone. In October 1998, several alterations and additions were made in the constitution of the Republic of Kazakhstan. Firstly, the powers of the Parliament in relation to the government were enhanced. In case members of the Parliament were to demand that a member of the government be relieved of his post, the President has to either take a definite decision over it or if the President turns down the demand of the members of the Parliament for removal of a member of the government, they can repeat the same demand after a period of six months. Such a demand is constitutionally valid if it is supported by two-third members of the Parliament. In such a case, the President is bound to relieve the member of his post.[47]

The history of building national statehood of sovereign Kazakhstan is the history of establishing and strengthening the Presidential powers. As a result Kazakhstan's President is endowed with extraordinary powers. In October 1998,both Houses of Kazakhstan's Parliament amended the law to further enhance President's powers. Such amendments have extended President's tenure up to seven years (as opposed to five years under the earlier constitutional provisions); they have extended the qualifying age for the Presidential candidates (earlier upper age limit was 65 years). The President has the right to establish rules and procedures for appointment or "election" of *Hakims* (heads of *oblast*, district, city and local administration).[48]

In 2007, the Parliament of Kazakhstan underwent its most radical transformation over a decade when seats were added to both senate and *Majilis*, with the latter body elected exclusively through a system of proportional representation, with nine members elected from within the 400 member Assembly of Peoples.[49] But it is noteworthy that the concentration of power in the hands of an experienced statesman and administrator like Nazarbayev during the critical years of transition has proved fruitful for Kazakhstan which has withstood the difficulties in its economic and socio-political transition. Following are some features of the domestic reforms:

- Kazakhstan passed to a new form of governance with many powers of the President being transferred to the Parliament, thus effectively constituting a presidential-parliamentary Republic.
- The Government is to be formed on the basis of the Parliament majority;
- The size of the Parliament is expanded with the Lower House being formed on a proportional basis;
- Term of the President has been cut form 7 years to 5 years starting form 2012.
- Kazakhstan de-facto abolished the death penalty, which is allowed only in case of terrorism with heavy human casualties and mass killing at the time of war.

As an outcome of the amendments, the key powers are transferred from the President to the Parliament. The new changes are thus aimed at increasing Parliament's authority in forming the Government.

The Prime Minister, who will represent the party holding majority in the Parliament, will be appointed by the President after consultations with political parties and with the consent of the majority of the Parliament. Some factions of political parties may be established only in *Majilis*, lower house, its role will increase many fold. Thus, the Government will be accountable not only before the Head of State, but also the Parliament. In its turn the Parliament will be responsible for the government policy and accountable for its outcome.

No Confidence Motion of the *Majilis*, lower house of the Parliament, has been greatly simplified. Now a simple majority of *Majilis* may express no confidence in the Government, while as earlier, the Constitution required two thirds majority for the same. The Parliament will also have a greater say in forming, such important bodies as the Constitutional Council, Central Election Commission and Accounts Committee.

The Senate, the upper house, will be given additional powers to pass laws during the temporary absence of *Majilis*. This will ensure continuous functioning of political processes in the country in case the *Majilis* is dissolved before its term ends.

In addition, the Senate will approve the nomination of the Chairman of the National Bank of Kazakhstan, which will ensure autonomy of the National Bank from the executive branch in running monetary and credit policy as well as institute its accountability before the Parliament.

Under the reforms, the number of seats in the two chambers Parliament has been increased from 116 to 154, with 9 seats in the Lower House allocated for the members of Assembly of the Ethnic Groups of Kazakhstan. With a view to ensure inter-ethnic and religious accord and also ensure representation of interests of 130 ethnic groups.

In the 154 seat Parliament, 98 seats in *Majilis* are to be filled by voting for political parties on a proportional basis rather than individual candidates. Earlier only 10 seats were given to political parties.

The same procedure of checks and balances at the Centre level is applicable in the local governance. *Aakims* (head of local governments, major cities and the capital) are to be appointed with the consent of *Maslikhats*, local Legislative Assemblies. The *Maslikhats* can also express no-confidence in *Hakims* through a simple majority of votes.

The Council of Ministers exercises the executive powers and is responsible to the President of the Republic. Local state administration is exercised by local representative and executive bodies, which are responsible for the state of affairs on their own territory. The local representative bodies, the councils (*Maslikhats*) express the will of the people of the corresponding administrative areas. Councils are elected for a period of five years by a secret ballot on the basis of equal and direct suffrage. The local executive bodies are part of the unified system of executive body and are headed by the *Hakims* of the corresponding administrative/territorial unit, who act as the representatives of the President of the Republic of Kazakhstan.[50] The judicial authority in the state is independent and subject only to the Constitution and laws of the Republic of Kazakhstan.

On 20 October 2002, experimental local district *Hakim* elections were held, representing the first move away from the Presidential appointment of local district *Hakims*. In each of the 14 oblasts, elections were held to fill 2 local *Hakim* positions. The positions to be elected were chosen by the oblast administration. The local *Hakims* were elected through secret ballot by a group of "elector" who were chosen by local residents through a public "show of hands" vote. Although minority ethnic groups are represented in the Government, ethnic Kazakhs hold majority of the high positions. Nearly half of the population is non-Kazakh according to the national census completed in 1999. Non-Kazakhs hold one out of three positions of Vice Premier and two out of 14 heads of government ministries and the national bank. Non-Kazakhs are under–represented in the *Majilis* and the Senate. In Parliament, seven senators were non-Kazakhs, and 19 members of the *Majilis* were non-Kazakhs.

The task of economic reconstruction undertaken immediately after independence was extremely complex. The Soviet styled planned management of economy was dismantled; government finance and the banking system were reformed and the new currency, the *Tenge* (KZT) was introduced. Small and middle size businesses and housing were privatized. Foreign investment flowed into the country to develop the rich natural resources. Though immediately after independence there was hardship and a decline in the economy and by the end of 1990's economic restructuring bore fruit. In 1999, the economy began to grow and the take off phase started. GDP in the first half of 2001 was 13 percent higher than in the year 2000 and the rate of inflation declined to 7 percent. In the year 2000, the government introduced its Strategy 2030 outlining the economic priorities and objectives over a thirty years. In an important speech made in September 2001, the President outlined the aims for the tears up to 2010 in political and economic matters. This included the doubling of GDP by that date and increase in investment.

Role of Religion

Though Kazakhstan professes to be a secular state, Islam, in its orthodox Sunni form, has been accorded special status *Akim* to that of state religion. While the Government unsuccessfully sought to amend the National Religion Law to give the Muslim Spiritual Association a quasi-official role, both the Government and the Association denied any official connection. Other religions that have long been established on the territory of Kazakhstan including the Russian Orthodox Church and Judaism are also treated with respect and do not suffer any discernible harassment.[51] Recently the complex of Hare Krishna Movement near Almaty was demolished. There is also particular concern about the activities of some of the Protestant sects. Several of these missions (mostly form the US and South Korea) are extremely well funded and these seek converts. Many Kazakhs regard this as a dangerous phenomenon, on the grounds that it "steals" vulnerable young people away from the faith of their ancestors. This is regarded as a threat to national unity. There are also concerns about the nature of the teachings of some of these faiths.[52] President Nazarbayev emphasizes the importance of equality, stating that "it is necessary to stress our commitment to the principle of equality of all citizens of the Republic regardless of their nationality, race, or religion."

The Constitution provides for freedom of religion. The Government invited the leaders of the two largest religions, Islam and Russian Orthodoxy, to participate jointly in some state events. The leaders of the Catholic and Jewish religions, which were represented by small proportions of the population, also participated in some official events. Religious organisations need to be registered to receive legal status in order to act as a legal entity to buy or rent property, hire employees, or engage in other legal transactions.

The administrative law allows national and local authorities to suspended activities or fine the leaders of unregistered religious organisations. Local officials, particularly in remote areas, often insisted that religious organisations should register at the local level, despite the fact that registration at the national or at the national or at the oblast level was sufficient to obtain the right that registration offers. Members of the Council of Churches of Evangelical Christians and Baptists reported that they were harassed by law enforcement for not being registered. Although the Council of Churches was reported to act as a legal entity, it has a policy of not seeking or accepting registration in former Soviet Republics. The Government dropped criminal cases and did not fulfill court orders that would have compelled congregations affiliated with the Council of Churches of Evangelical Christians and Baptists to register. In Nikolayevka, Almaty Oblast, Aleksandr Kalmakov was fined for his group's failure to register.[53]

As per the Law on National Security, a permanent exit visa is required for emigrants and obtaining this visa requires criminal checks, credit checks, and letters from any dependents concurring to the exit visa. Foreigners are required to have exit visa, which they receive routinely with entry visa. Foreign visitors intending to stay in Kazakhstan for three months are required to register, either with the airport immigration officials or local migration police.

The Government accords special treatment to those ethnic Kazakhs and their families who left the country in Stalin's era and wished to return. These returnees are now entitled to citizenship and many other privileges. Other ethnic Kazakhs living abroad were also encouraged and promised assistance when returned. The Chair of the Agency for Migration and Demography reported that between 1991 and 1 April 2002, approximately 322,500 ethnic Kazakhs immigrated to the country, mostly from other former Soviet Republics, Iran, Afghanistan, Mongolia, Turkey, China, and Saudi Arabia. The Government maintained a quota for such immigrant families that kept on increasing annually; during the year 2000 it was 10,000.[54] The Government provided such families with facilities like housing, stipends, and other benefits.

To conclude, the first Constitution of sovereign Kazakhstan adopted in January 1993 was to some extent a compromise between the old and new political systems. It has been an attempt to introduce a Western democratic model in the post-Soviet context. As a result of the referendum held on 30 August 1995, a second Constitution of the Republic of Kazakhstan was adopted, removing the shortcomings of the preceding Constitution. So far as the political opposition in Kazakhstan is concerned, currently it is weak. To quote Anthony Cliv Bowyer, "the state of multi-party system can be seen as going through a crisis phase at present, with no party strong enough in terms of its popularity, influence, outreach, financial wherewithal, or stature to be considered an effective counterweight to official power in the country".[55]

NOTES

1. J. Denis Derbyshire and Ian Derbyshire, *Political System of the World*, London: Helocon Publication, 1996, p.11.
2. John Anderson, "Constitutional Development in Central Asia", *Central Asian Survey*, vol.16, no.3, 1997, pp.301-320.
3. Ian Bremmer and Cory Welt, "The Trouble with Democracy in Kazakhstan", *Central Asian Survey*, vol.15, 2002, p.183.
4. Constitution of Republic of Kazakhstan (References regarding Articles of the Constitution are based on the text published in the FBIS: Central Eurasia, 1993), pp. 67-78.
5. Constitution of the Republic of Kazakhstan, Article 10.
6. Ibid., Article 3.
7. Ibid., Article 55.
8. Ibid., Article 58 (Paragraph 2).
9. Ibid., Article 64 (1-21).
10. E. Curtis Glenjn, Kazakhstan: A Country Study, Federal Research Division Library of Congress, Washington, 1996.
11. Andreas Heinrich, "The Formal Political System in Azerbaijan and Kazakhstan, A background Study". Forschungsstelle Osteuropa an der Universitat Bremen Klagenfurter Strabe, Germany.
12. Nursultan Nazarbayev, Foreword by Margaret Thatcher O.M., *The Kazakhstan Way*, London, p.55.
13. Ibid., p.56.
14. Article 131 of the Constitution states that 'if the Constitutional Court by a majority of no

less than two thirds of the votes of the total number of judges shall approve a previously adopted ruling, it will pass into effect from the moment of its adoption,'

15. Nursultan Nazarbayev, The Kazakhstan Way, Forewarded by Margaret Thatcher O.M Source: Archive of the President of the Republic of Kazakhstan, p.57.
16. Ibid.
17. From an interview with W. Courtney, US Ambassador to the Republic of Kazakhstan. Archive of the President.
18. Nursultan Nazarbayev, The Kazakhstan Way, Forewarded by Margaret Thatcher O.M, from From the Archive of the President of the Republic of Kazakhstan, p.60.
19. Nursultan Nazarbayev, foreworded by Margrate Thatcher O.M, "The Kazakhstan Way", Stacey International, London 2008, p.73.
20. Nursultan Nazarbayev, Foreword by Margrate Thatcher O.M, "The Kazakhstan Way", from Archive of the President of the Republic of Kazakhstan, p.74.
21. Nursultan Nazarbayev, Foreword by Margrate Thatcher O.M, "The Kazakhstan Way", from Archive of the President of the Republic of Kazakhstan, p.75.
22. Ibid.
23. Nursultan Nazarbayev, Foreword by Margrate Thatcher O.M, "The Kazakhstan Way", Archive of the President of the Republic of Kazakhstan, p.76.
24. Nursultan Nazarbayev, Foreword by Margrate Thatcher O.M, "The Kazakhstan Way", Stacey International, London 2008, p.78-79.
25. Ibid.
26. Ibid.
27. Nursultan Nazarbayev, Foreword by Margrate Thatcher O.M., "The Kazakhstan Way", Stacey International, London, 2008, p.81.
28. Ibid.
29. Lee Kwan Yew, *Singaporean History*: From the '*Third World*' into the '*First*' (1965-2000).
30. Ibid.
31. Ibid.
32. Marat Yermukanov, CACI Analyst, 30 May 2007.
33. www.akorda.kz, 16 May 2007.
34. E. Curtis Glenn, *op. cit.*
35. Ibid.
36. http:www.president.kz
37. E. Curtis Glenn, *op. cit.*
38. Ibid
39. Kazakhstan and CIS Countries 1 (2000), p.41.
40. Ibid.
41. http://lgi.osi.hu/publications/2001/84/Ch8-Kazakstan.pdf.
42. D. Galyamova, "Division of Powers in Kazakhstan: Constitutional Experience of Independent Development", *Contemporary Central Asia*, vol.11, no.3, December 1998.
43. Ibid
44. D. Galyamova, "Division of Powers in Kazakhstan: Constitutional Experience of Independent Development", *Contemporary Central Asia*, vol.11, no.3, December 1998.
45. Osnovnoi Zakon, Konstitutisia Respubliki Kazakhsta, 28 January 1993.
46. Ibid
47. Ibid.
48. United Nations Development Report, Almaty.1999, p 42.
49. Anthony Clive Bowyer, "Parliament and Political Parties in Kazakhstan" *Silk Road Paper*, Washington DC: John Hopkins University—SAIS, 2008, p. 7.
50. The Constitution of the Republic of Kazakhstan, Article 92.

51. The Constitution of the Republic of Kazakhstan, Article 92.
52. Adel E. Abishev, Kazakhstan in Focus: Ten Years of Independence, Almaty, 2002, p.147.
53. Ibid.
54. Ibid.
55. Anthony Clive Bowyer, op.cit, p.12.

4

Democratisation Process in Kazakhstan

The Central Asian elite belonged to the most conservative and hardline element of the Soviet political establishment which strongly resisted Mikhail Gorbachev's policy of *Glasnost* (openness) and democratisation. Even during the *Perestroika* period, the Central Asian leaders perceived the emergence of various opposition parties and groups in their Republics as a direct challenge to their position and power. They were preoccupied with the idea of preventing "unproductive and damaging reforms" and of consolidating their power without democratisation and radical changes in political and state institutions.[1] This, however, did not stop the discussion of possible "models of development" for the Central Asian Republics (CARs), which dominated the intellectual discourse in the region throughout the 1990s. It was especially intensive in Kazakhstan, Kyrgyzstan and Uzbekistan on the eve of the dissolution of the Soviet Union and during the very first stage of independence. A number of developmental models were floated around—the Turkish secular political model versus the Iranian theocratic model, the Chinese model of gradual economic reform versus Russia's shock therapy model etc., to mention a few.

In each of the five countries of Central Asia—Kazakhstan, Kyrgyzstan, Tajikistan, Turkmenistan and Uzbekistan, political institutions of democratic government and market-oriented economies were adopted soon after these nations attained independence in 1991. As these countries entered into the first stages of transition, the leaders of each of the Central Asian countries spoke in favor of the establishment of democratic institutions and secular government. Following independence, each of them adopted a constitutionally limited, representative form of government and a legal and regulatory framework in accordance with international standards.[2] Today Kazakhstan and Kyrgyzstan seem to be making steady progress towards the development of democratic or quasi-democratic polities.[3] Evidently, the current Constitution of the Republic of Kazakhstan approved through a national referendum in August 1995 and ratified in September 1995 replaced the previous constitution of 1993. The Constitution provides for a democratic, secular state and a Presidential system of government. State governance is divided among the executive, legislative and judicial branches. The

President is considered the supreme authority of the state. In October 1998, the Constitution was amended to provide for a 7-year Presidential term instead of 5 years. However, in 2007 the term of the President has reverted back to 5 years from the existing 7 years starting from 2012. The first election under the amended constitution was held in January 1999 which resulted in the re-election of President Nazarbayev.[4] Such developments in the democratisation of Kazakhstan politics have given the country a new identity in the post-Soviet world.

It is against this background that this paper seeks to examine the process of democratisation in Kazakhstan since it got independence, with particular focus on the reforms in the country's political structure, apart from highlighting the challenges lie ahead in the democratic developments of the country.

Beginning of Kazakh Democratisation Process

Kazakhstan can take pride of certain achievements, having avoided the bloody chaos of a civil war like Tajikistan's and the dictatorial backsliding as in Turkmenistan and, to a lesser degree, in Uzbekistan. Possessing abundant hydrocarbon resources and buoyed by high oil prices, Kazakhstan's economy has outperformed its regional competitors.[5] Zohvtis, who talks about the process of democratisation in Kazakhstan, divides this process into three stages. He opines that Kazakhstan was 'freer' or more democratic in the first stage, between 1991 and 1994, when "there were significant developments in freedom of speech and in media in Kazakhstan."[6] However, the second stage which began in 1994 and early 1995 witnessed the Constitutional court making a decision to dissolve the Supreme Soviet (the Parliament) of Kazakhstan. According to Zohvits, "this decision of the highest Judicial body broke the evolutionary development of the political system in Kazakhstan and left the state and the people of the republic without legislative and representative power." Even in the third stage, beginning in 1997 and 1998, one can witness a glaring contrast to the first stage, when "the government is alleged to have begun direct repression aimed at the participants of protest marches and unsanctioned meetings, as well as representatives of the political opposition."[7] Zohvtis points out that even though the rights and freedoms are guaranteed in the state's constitution, these may be whittled away in "second and third levels of enabling legislation."[8]

When we talk about the process of Kazakh democratisation, there are two positive factors which can be highlighted. The first has been the introduction of Ombudsman under the President of Kazakhstan in autumn of 2002 and the second is a Permanently Acting Deliberation (PAD) created in December 2002 in Almaty. PAD is a body working on democratisation and the development of civil society, initiated by the Government of Kazakhstan. All political parties, movements, public organisations and trade unions were invited to have dialogue with the government. Only the *Communist Party*, *Republican People's Party of Kazakhstan* and *Democratic Choice* ignored PAD and expressed their irreconcilability with the organs of power. *Majilis* Deputy, Erasyl Abylqasymov has warned that PAD can toe the line of the government if the ideas of only one organisation or party are lobbied for. The third meeting of PAD held in Astana, failed because of disagreement among the participants on issues of the laws on elections, mass media, and political parties. Serik Abdrahmanov, another *Majilis* Deputy, demanded the isolation of *akims* (provincial and municipal heads) from the election process because of their tendency to abuse of power. PAD is expected to improve its effectiveness with the growing interest in public organisations for democratisation and establishment of civil society.[9] Legal reforms constitute another important aspect in post-independence Kazakhstan. The Western countries have helped Kazakhstan enormously in political and legal reforms, through assistance in the establishment and funding of Non-Governmental Organisations. NGOs are oriented to the programme of educational improvement in Kazakhstan aiming at promoting consciousness for the need of political, legal, social and economic reforms in Kazakhstan. The object behind this is to make people aware of the process of transition from totalitarianism of the past to democracy.[10]

Kazakhstan's transition to democracy forms the subject of several scholarly analyses. Martha Brill Olcott's seminal work, *Kazakhstan: Unfulfilled Promise* (2002), chronicles the recent political history of the country since independence and identifies several challenges to the state-building process. She also notes the need for more attention to such factors as civil society when examining democracy in Kazakhstan. Olcott cites the political obstacles instituted by the Nazarbayev regime as a factor impeding democratisation.[11] In an article "Democratic Transition in Central Asia: An Assessment" (1998), Juliana Geran Pilon asserts that the people of Central Asia would like to participate more actively in political life and that they support democratic rights. However, she observes that local cultural factors would determine the depth of civic associational activities that make civil society an effective vehicle for democratic change.[12]

President Nazarbayev identifies seven fundamental elements of democratisation and political liberalisation which are necessary for political reform in Kazakhstan:[13]

a) The electoral process must be honest, representative and encourage the fullest participation of candidates and voters. Free and fair elections are at the heart of any democracy and Kazakhstan should be no exception. Quoting a popular proverb Nazarbayev argues that "The people seldom speak but when they speak they never make mistakes." Elections are the manifestations of people's verdict. Our goal should be clear: to make the upcoming national elections a model for free and fair elections. According to Nazarbayev Kazakhstan should develop "a comprehensive step-by-step programme of election of leaders at all levels."[14]
b) The second major element underlined by the President in political democratisation package is the strengthening of the role of parties in

the country's political system. Political parties are the basic building blocks of democracy, and, the need of the hour is to help them grow and develop. The President also encourages international groups, and Non-governmental Organisations, to come to Kazakhstan to educate and train the political parties. Calling upon all parties, regardless their political orientation, he urges them to respect and preserve political and inter-ethnic stability in the country as the future of the State system and democracy depends on this.[15]

c) For stability and succession of power in Kazakhstan strengthening and providing autonomy for *Majilis* and Senate seemed appropriate to the President. The President believes in the greater responsibility of the Parliament to build up a responsive government in the coming years. Representation by political parties according to proportional representation will make the *Majilis* better reflect the full spectrum of political views in Kazakhstan. The President proposes that to ensure representation of a broader range of ethnic and religious minorities of the country in Parliament, some of the Presidential appointees to the Senate shall be from candidates recommended by the People's Assembly.

d) A key element of democratisation is recognised as strengthening the role of Non-Governmental Organisations in building a civil society. A democratic structure does not in itself guarantee a democratic society. Democracy depends on private voluntary institutions which allow citizens to be politically involved, aware enough to volunteer their services, and express their grievances to advocate their interests.[16] To ensure that civic groups can operate freely, the Ministry of Justice is asked to simplify registration and supervision procedures for domestic and international Non-Governmental Organisations who wish to work in Kazakhstan, and encouraging and accelerating operation.

e) The President acknowledged an independent judiciary as the pillar of a democratic society. An autonomous judicial system is absolutely necessary that decides issues on their merits and is free from corruption. Training process of judges should be improved. Vigorous enforcement of the recently enacted Anti-Corruption Law was stressed. It is also pointed out that the Higher Judiciary Council should not be headed by the President.[17]

f) Nazarbayev emphasized the building of free, uncensored and independent press. According to him the Government should consider the free access of journalists to information not as a favor of the Government but as its commitment to public opinion. The work to remove any remaining impediments to a free press from the nation is accorded importance. Privatisation process of many state publishing houses and the availability and increase in the number of independent mass media means the growth of openness in society.

g) The progress of the society can be measured by its attitude to women. The President therefore intends to increase the role of the Council on Problems of Family, Women and Demographic Policy or reorganise it into a Special Commission on women issues. It must become a Chief Advisor both to the President and the Government in solving important problems pertaining to this sphere. It is necessary to increase women's representation in all branches of authority. This is a question of social equality.

President Nazarbayev insists that his observations are based on survey of the situation in his country and the world scenario. He is of opinion that some forces including those who are skillfully hiding behind the mask of pseudo-democrats in public become more authoritarian. He expressed his belief that "Only a free democratic society will be a guarantor of our stable and happy life in the near future. My nation deserves freedom in this terrible and bloody century."[18]

Reforms in Political Structure

The post-independence government was structured by the 1993 constitution with a strong executive parliament and judiciary. In practice the administration of Nursultan Nazarbayev dominated the governance in the country after its independence.[19]

The Executive

The constitution formalized the enhanced powers that President Nazarbayev assumed upon the dissolution of parliament in early 1995. It continued the previous constitutional definition of Kazakhstan as a unitary state with a Presidential form of government. The President is the highest state officer, responsible for forming the government, subject to parliamentary approval, and appointing all other republican officials. The 1995 constitution expanded the President's powers to introduce and veto legislation. The President has the powers to appoint the council of Ministers, headed by a Prime Minister, and several state committees. In October 1995, Nazarbayev himself assumed the portfolio of the Ministry of National Security. In early 1996, after Nazarbayev had reshuffled the government in October 1995, the Council of Ministers included the heads of twenty-one ministries and nine state committees, the Prime Minister being Akezhan Kazhegeldin.[20]

The new constitution does not provide for the position of Vice President. However, it permitted the incumbent Vice President, Yerik Asanbayev to remain in office till 1996. The President has the power to declare state of emergency during which the constitution can be suspended. The President is the sponsor of legislation and the guarantor of the constitution and of the proper functioning of government, with the power to override the decisions and actions of local authorities and councils. The only grounds on which a President can be removed are infirmity and treason, either of which must be confirmed by a majority of the joint Upper and Lower *House* of the new parliament. In the event of such a removal from power, the Prime Minister would become the temporary President.[21]

The Legislative

The 1993 constitution created a unicameral parliament, which was to replace the 350 seat Supreme Soviet when the mandates of its deputies expired in 1995. The 1990 parliament, which was composed of the former communists, was dissolved early under the pressure of President Nazarbayev in December 1993 in order to pave way for a smaller and presumably more flexible parliament. Under the 1995 constitution, the parliament consisted of two houses, the Senate and the *Majilis*, both operating in continuous sessions. All the provinces of Kazakhstan and the city of Almaty, which had provincial status, had two senators, chosen for four-year terms by the joint sessions of the provincial legislative bodies. Additional seven senators were appointed directly by the President. In addition, ex-Presidents automatically receive the status of senators-for-life. The *Majilis* had 67 representatives, including one from each of 55 districts having roughly equal population, and the *Senate* has forty seats. Direct elections for half of the seats are held every two years. In the first election under the new parliamentary structure, all the seats in both houses of parliament were contested in December 1995; runoff elections filled twenty-three seats in the *Majilis* for which the initial vote was inconclusive. The new parliament, which assembled in January 1996, included sixty-eight Kazakh and thirty-one Russian deputies, among whom only ten were women. The initiative for most legislative actions originated with the President. If a law passed by the parliament faces the President's veto, a two-third vote of both houses is mandatory to override the veto. A similar margin is needed to express no confidence in a Prime Minister, an action that requires the President to name a new Prime Minister and Council of Ministers.[22]

Judiciary

The judiciary system is the least developed of Kazakhstan's three branches of government. The constitution retains the provision of Presidential appointment of all judges in the republic. Whereas, the 1993 constitution specified the terms of service for judges, the 1995 document made no mention of length of service, suggesting that judges would serve at the discretion of the President.[23] Under the constitution of 1993, lines of judicial authority were poorly defined, in part because the republic had three "highest courts", the Supreme Court, the State Arbitrate Court, and the Constitutional Court employing a total of sixty six senior judges. Many of these senior judges, as well as numerous judges in lower courts, had been retained from the Soviet era, when the judicial branch was entirely under the control of the central government. The 1995 constitution makes no provision for the State Arbitrate Court Provisions, for the new judiciary clearly subordinates all other courts to the Supreme Court, which has a consultative role in appointing senior judges.[24]

Local Government

Kazakhstan is divided into fourteen provinces, and the city of Almaty has administrative status equal to that of a province. In turn, the provinces are divided into regions that consist of a number of settlements. Each province or region and most settlements have their own elected councils, entrusted with making a budget and supervising local tax collections. Cities have their own local councils as well, and large cities are divided into regions, each having its own council.[25]

The local legislature lacks the authority to choose the local executives, who are directly appointed by the President. The duty of a local executive is to ensure the enforcement of the decisions of the national government and a proper observance of the constitution. Provincial and regional "heads of administration", known by the Russian term *Glav* or the Kazakh term *Akim*, are Presidential appointees. The *Akim*, in term, appoints the members of his staff, who function as departmental heads. The *Akim* also can reveres budgetary decisions of the local council.[26] There has been considerable pressure, especially in the predominantly Russian north, to alter the nature of the post of *Akim* making it elective rather than through appointment by the President. The 1995 constitution provides that only the local councils have the capacity to express no confidence in their *Akim* by a two-thirds majority. The President has the power to override or revoke the decisions taken by local councils. So far as influence of the *Akims* on the electoral process is concerned, *Akims* determine electoral precincts in order to hold elections and calculate votes in coordination with the district electoral commissions. These precincts are created with consideration of conditions that include: (a) no constituency should have more than three thousand voters; (b) the boundaries of administrative-territorial units should be observed; and (c) boundaries of electoral districts should not overlap boundaries of electoral precincts.[27]

It is to be noted that the reformation period of Kazakhstan's political system began immediately after its independence. Transition to democracy commenced under difficult conditions: The country was then experiencing socio-economic crisis due to decline in industrial and agricultural production, hyperinflation (up to 3,000 per cent), and drastic decline in living standards. After the collapse of the USSR, former Soviet states experienced a crisis situation. Kazakhstan too experienced the same and tried to overcome the problems related to democratisation of political institutions, so as to strengthen the political system in Kazakhstan. In accordance with the 1995 Kazakh constitution, the government exercises the executive power. The government is composed of the Prime Minister, the deputy ministers, heads of the government departments, ministers and Chairpersons of state committees. According to Act 166 of the Kazakh

Constitution (1995), the government works out the basic socio-economic directions of the state policy, its defense preparedness and security, ensures social order and organises their implementation. The government presents state budget to the parliament. Among other factions performed by the government mention may be made of tabling laws in the *Majilis* (Parliament) and administration of state properties, working out measures for conducting foreign policy; guiding the activities of the ministers, state committees, other central and local executive organs, keeping vigilance on the actions of the ministers and state committees as well as on other central and local executive organs of the republic, appointment and removal of the heads of the central executive organs not forming part of the government. In short, the government is liable to discharge functions entrusted to it by the constitution, laws and acts of the President.[28]

The new constitution of 1995 preserved the extensive executive powers of the President and also abolished the post of Vice-President. The Supreme *Kenges* was replaced by a bicameral Parliament, comprising a 47 member Senate (the Upper Chamber with 40 members elected by Kazakhstan's regional administrative bodies and seven appointed by the President) and 67 directly elected members of *Majilis* (Assembly).[29] The Constitutional Court was replaced by a Constitutional Council, whose decisions are subject to a Presidential right of veto. The Constitution retained Kazakh as the state language but guaranteed the development of all other languages, making Russian the language of inter-ethnic communication.

Notwithstanding the sufficient authority regarding the implementation of the executive powers, the government is extremely dependent on the President. A number of mechanisms are incorporated in the constitution through which the President is in a position not only to form the government in the manner he considers fit but also to influence its day to day functions. According to the constitution, the President of Kazakhstan being the head of the state, remains the key figure to which all executive powers are subordinated. The President, with the consent of the parliament, appoints the Prime Minister; removes him from his post, determines the structure of Government on the recommendation of the Prime Minister, appoints and terminates from the post all its members all implying to a high degree of personal influence of President on the composition of the government. In general, the level of participation of the President in the government formation in Kazakhstan is compared with the prerogatives of the President of the Russian Federation in regard to the government formation.

In 2007, the Parliament of Kazakhstan underwent its most radical transformation over a decade when seats were added to both senate and *Majilis*, with the latter body elected exclusively through a system of proportional representation, with nine members elected from within the 400 member Assembly of Peoples.[30] But it is noteworthy that the concentration of power in the hands of an experienced statesman and administrator like Nazarbayev during the critical years of transition has proved fruitful for Kazakhstan which has withstood the difficulties in its economic and socio-political transition. Following are some features of the domestic reforms:

1. Kazakhstan passed to a new form of governance with many powers of the President being transferred to the Parliament, thus effectively constituting a presidential-parliamentary Republic.
2. The Government is to be formed on the basis of the Parliament majority;
3. The size of the Parliament is expanded with the Lower House being formed on a proportional basis;
4. Term of the President has been cut from 7 years to 5 years starting from 2012.
5. Kazakhstan de-facto abolished the death penalty, which is allowed only in case of terrorism with heavy human casualties and mass killing at the time of war.

As an outcome of the 2007 amendments, the key powers are transferred from the President to the Parliament. The new changes are thus aimed at increasing Parliament's authority in forming the Government, thus reducing the powers of President.

The task of economic reconstruction undertaken immediately after independence was extremely complex. The Soviet styled planned management of economy was dismantled; government finance and the banking system were reformed and the new currency, the *Tenge* (KZT) was introduced. Small and middle size businesses and housing were privatized. Foreign investment flowed into the country to develop the rich natural resources. Though immediately after independence there was hardship and a decline in the economy and by the end of 1990's economic restructuring bore fruit. In 1999, the economy began to grow and the take off phase started. GDP in the first half of 2001 was 13 percent higher than in the year 2000 and the rate of inflation declined to 7 percent. In the year 2000, the government introduced its Strategy 2030 outlining the economic priorities and objectives over a thirty years. In an important speech made in September 2001, the President outlined the aims for the tears up to 2010 in political and economic matters. This included the doubling of GDP by that date and increase in investment.

Restructuring of Political Parties

Law on political parties has achieved the intended objective of disbursing and legalizing power through pro-regime parties, thereby pushing out both existing and potential opposition. The number of registered parties fell from 19 in late 2002 to 8 in November 2003. These include the prominent pro-regime *Otan*, the *Civil Party* and *Ak Zhol*, as well as 4 smaller parties enjoying varying degrees of official patronage—the *Agrarian Party*, the *Party of Patriots*, *Aul*, and *Rukhaniyat*.

The *Communist Party* is the only independent party to maintain its registration. It has been in opposition since 1999 but is considered less threatening than other opposition parties. The *Democratic Choice of Kazakhstan*, better known by its Russian name DVK (*Demokraticheskii Vybor Kazakhstana*), was denied registration. The DVK was founded in 2001 by Ghalymzhan Zhakiyanov, the former administrative head of Pavlodar, and the powerful former Minister Mukhtar Ablyazov, who was jailed in March 2002 for alleged misuse of office and subsequently given a Presidential pardon in April 2003. Retaining its Russian acronym, the DVK renamed itself *Democratic Power of Kazakhstan* (*Demokraticheskaya vlast Kazakhstana*) to obtain registration as a new entity but could not succeeded. A number of opposition parties, which include the *People's Congress*, the *Socialist Party*, the *Justice Party*, the *Republican People's Party*, and *Azamat*, refused to seek re-registration. Almost all the parties in Kazakhstan, whether pro-regime or opposition, lack well-developed organisational structures or significant national membership. Though it no longer has legal status, the DVK enjoys the support of independent deputies Tolen Toktasynov and Zauresh Battalova as well as numerous activists in Almaty, Astana and Zhakiyanov's native land Pavlodar.

The notable pro-regime parties are *Otan*, the *Civil Party*, and the newly formed *Ak Zhol*. *Otan*, which was launched in January 1999 following the Presidential elections, secured 24 seats, the largest share, in the 1999 parliamentary elections. It has formed a large membership base, presumed to be at least 300,000, that includes numerous state employees.[31]

The *Civil Party*, formed a few months before the 1999 parliamentary elections, is the political platform of the Eurasia corporate group. This party includes Aleksandr Mashkevich and Azar Peruashev among its leaders and controls six major metallurgical enterprises in Kazakhstan, the most important being located in Pavlodar. All employees of these enterprises and their families are included in the membership register of the party. *Ak Zhol* was founded in late 2001 by Alikhan Baimenov, Uraz Zhandosov and Bulat Abilov—known as the Young Turks, as an opposition party. However, it was soon co-opted as a pro-regime force. It claims to represent young entrepreneurs and technocrats who advocate greater economic and political reform.

An overall lack of leadership and scarcity of resources and the regime's relentless drive to either co-opt or remove any opposition have made it difficult for any opposition to get organised. The Kazhegeldin-sponsored *Republican Party* suffered a major blow in 2003 with the sentencing of its leader, Amirzhan Kosanov, to one year's probation and a fine of about US $225,000 for tax evasion. The alliance between former premier Kazhegeldin and the DVK appear to have ended, as most members of the *Republican Party* have defected to the DVK or other opposition parties.[32]

A new development with important implications occurred during the 2004 parliamentary elections with the launch of the party named Asar by Dariga Nazarbayeva (daughter of the Kazakhstan's President) in October 2003. *Asar* is expected to dominate the electoral scene and weaken the deep-rooted bureaucratic interests that support *Otan*. The new party is likely to draft individuals and interests currently associated with other pro-Presidential parties. *Ak Zhol* may suffer a setback from *Asar's* rise, since both parties aim to rally the support of young professionals, entrepreneurs, and rally the support of big businesses by advancing an economic reform agenda. *Ak Zhol* has advocated greater economic freedom, local elections, and party law reforms. By contrast, *Asar* has pledged loyalty to the President and emphasized social reforms and poverty reduction without reference to any party politics. Presidential spokesperson Ermukhan Ertysbaev has frequently referred to *Ak Zhol* as a "constructive" and "legal" opposition.[33]

In the new ethnic hierarchy prevalent since 1991, Kazakhs enjoy the status of "first among equals," whereas Russians and other non-Kazakh groups no longer enjoy their previous privileged position. Kazakhs form 53.4 per cent of the population, according to the 1999 census, up from 39.7 per cent in 1989, and their share continues to rise. The Russians' share has continued to decline, down to 29.9 per cent from 37.7 per cent in 1989, though their portion among the elderly and pensioner population is much higher. Among other ethnic groups, Uzbeks form 2.5 per cent, Ukrainians 3.6 per cent, Tatars 1.7 per cent, and Germans 2.4 per cent. Kazakh is the sole state language, though Russian is granted the status of language of communication.

The Constitution authorizes ethnic groups to form 'National Cultural Centers' committed to protecting their cultural heritage. However, it prohibits the formation of public associations or political parties based on ethnic, religious, or nationalist agendas. The national centers are encouraged and expected to seek support from their "kin" states for the cultural and material advancement of their respective groups. The German and Korean centers have received material support from their kin states as well as from individual ethnic sponsors. However, most other ethnic centers remain dependent on modest state support. A law requiring such centers to be registered with the Ministry of Justice serves as an important screening mechanism. Groups championing the rights of ethnic Uighurs, for example, have faced obstacles due to the widespread perception among officials that many Uighurs are involved in separatists or terrorist activities.

Nazarbayev has used his personal patronage to create symbolic institutions of ethnic representation, such as the Assembly of Peoples of Kazakhstan, established in 1995. Its members are nominated by the officially recognised national cultural centers and by the President, who also serves as the Assembly's Chairman. Lacking juridical power or a representative base, the Assembly serves as an instrument for co-opting leading ethnic figures into the existing political system. Its members are encouraged to engage in cultural activities and steer clear of politics.[34] However, it is to be noted that Kazakhstan's political party landscape is currently dominated by the ruling Nur-Otan party, which dominates parliament and the public debate, despite the existence of numerous other political parties.[35] Outside of Nur-Otan, the present-day political parties in Kazakhstan can be grouped into three categories: Pro-presidential, Soft Opposition, and Hard Opposition. Numbering among the current Pro-presidential political parties are Rukhaniyat and the Party of Patriots. Those falling into the category of Soft Opposition are the recently reconstituted party Adilet, Ak-Zhol, Auyl, the Communist Party, and the Communist People's Party. Those in the category of Hard Opposition, i.e., those most opposed to the current leadership, include the All-National Social Democratic Party, Azat (formerly Naghyz Ak-Zhol) and the unregistered political movement Alga.

Following the August 2007 elections to the *Majilis*, the political opposition in Kazakhstan has been exceptionally weak. The state of multipartyism was seen as going through a crisis phase, with no party strong enough in terms of its popularity, influence, outreach, financial wherewithal, or stature to be considered an effective counterweight to official power in the country. This is largely, as Anthony Clive Bowyer opines, "due to a combination of factors, some directly attributable to the parties' own conduct, and much due to the political environment in which they currently find themselves, and in which they have been mired for nearly last fifteen years."[36] In fact, Kazakhstan's law on political parties prohibits parties based on ethnic origin, religion, or gender. A law came into force in 2002 raised the number of members that a party must have in its ranks from 3,000 to 50,000 in order to register with the Ministry of Justice, divided up proportionally by oblast with no fewer than 700 members in each of the fourteen oblasts and two major cities. In order to gain seats in the parliament, a party must attain no less than 7 per cent of all votes cast, a high percentage retained from the previous mixed system parliamentary election. In an all party-list election this percentage is inordinately high. Given the weakness of the opposition and the extremely short turnaround time from the adoption of a new constitution to the dismissal of parliament and holding of elections (a matter of three months), any but the most organised and well-financed political parties would face serious challenges in competing. Nur-Otan's sweep of all 98 party list seats can be understood in light of the party's presidential status, its expansive platform, virtually limitless resources, and the opposition's own reliance on personality-driven politics, all within the limited preparation and campaign time. In order to understand the present status of party politics, a review of the origins of organised political movements in Kazakhstan is required which has been dealt with in the following paragraphs.

The first political movement that led to the formation of a party, with broad organisational structure and popular support, was the Alash Orda movement, borne out of the chaos of the civil war in the Russian Empire in 1917 and officially constituted in November of that year. The Party was formed by the intellectual elite and essentially became a Kazakh nationalist movement, the precursor of similar movements that developed in the late 1980s and early 1990s as a result of the decline of the Soviet Union and reinvigoration of Kazakh nationalism. Prior to the Alash Orda movement, governance in the ethnic Kazakh territories of the steppe was divided among the middle, small and great hordes of the Kazakh Khanates, each in turn being ruled by local clans and alliances. The events in the Russian Empire of 1917 enabled the Kazakh elite to pursue the possibility of creating a territorially-defined state for the first time with an ethnic Kazakh "home rule" majority. The Alash Orda Central Executive Body consisted of eight ethnic Kazakh members representing each of the seven regions plus the chairman[37] as well as fifteen deputies of non-Kazakh origin. It is interesting to note the participation of deputies of non-Kazakh origin, which included members of Tatar-Turkic tribes, as recognition of the multi-ethnic nature of the steppe and the desire to include representatives of such groups to help legitimize the government. This legitimacy was necessary particularly to support a tottering regime in the face of serous external and internal pressures, when not all of the Kazakh people could be comfortably labeled as enthusiasts of the Alash Orda regime. The main issue seemed to stem over tribal differences and an East-West cleavage in Kazakh society at that time, which was essentially related to ownership of land. Public opinion seemed to be divided between pro-Alash Orda or indifferent.[38] The nature of political parties up to 1995 was somewhat confined, with parties clearly based upon personal appeal or narrow platform interests. The Communist Party was not allowed to field candidates in the 1994 elections, thus removing from the ballot the one party that enjoyed any kind of name recognition. Fourteen years later, parties are still largely known for their leaders or leadership conflicts than for ideas. Some would argue that this condition applies to Nur-Otan as well which is being led by President Nazarbayev.

CURRENT POLITICAL PARTY LANDSCAPE

Kazakhstan's political party landscape is currently dominated by the ruling Nur-Otan party, which dominates parliament and the public debate. However, numerous other political parties exist. Outside of Nur-Otan, the Present-day political parties in Kazakhstan can be grouped into three categories: Pro-presidential, "Soft" Opposition, and "Hard" Opposition. Numbering among the current Pro-presidential political parties are Rukhaniyat and the Party of Patriots. Those falling into the category of Soft Opposition are the recently reconstituted party Adilet, Ak-Zhol, Auyl, the Communist Party, and the Communist People's Party. Those in the category of Hard Opposition, those most opposed to the current leadership, include the All-National Social Democratic Party, Azat (formerly *Naghyz Ak-Zhol*) and the unregistered political movement Alga. As will be discussed, the present political opposition in Kazakhstan is exceptionally weak and on its heels following the August 2007 elections to the *Majilis*. The state of multipartyism can be seen as going through a crisis phase at present, with no party strong enough in terms of its popularity, influence, outreach, financial wherewithal, or stature to be considered as an effective counterweight to official power in the country. This is of course due to a combination of factors, some directly attributable to the parties' own conduct, and much due to the political environment in which they currently find themselves, and in which they have been mired for nearly the last fifteen years.[39]

Nur-Otan

Nur-Otan's party headquarters in Astana sits at a stone's throw from the gleaming new buildings that are home to the Senate and *Majilis* of the parliament. One could argue that the *Majilis* building itself serves as a de facto second headquarters for the party, which occupies all of the 98 party list seats in the 107 member *Majilis*. The 47-member Senate, comprised of 32 deputies elected by Oblast Maslikhats as well as another 15 appointed by the President[40] (half are elected every three years with each Senator serving six-year terms) can also be considered unanimous supporters of the President. Upon entering the *Majilis* building, one is struck not only by the numerous display cases housing the many awards presented by foreign parliamentary delegations and dignitaries, but also by the larger-than-life Nur-Otan poster that greets visitors to the building. In fact, one can hardly consider Nur-Otan without the parliament, and likewise cannot consider the parliament without a discussion of Nur-Otan. Such is the present state of political affairs in Kazakhstan, where the distinction between the parliament and the presidential super-party are blurred. By far the largest political party in the country, Nur-Otan has 740,000 members nationwide, with 3400 deputies serving in oblast maslikhats and lower levels of government.

Nur-Otan formally came into being in 2006 as a result of the merging of two other pro-presidential parties which had competed separately during the 2004 parliamentary elections, the Civic Party (*grazhdanskaya partiya*) and Asar (led by President Nazarbayev's daughter, Dariga Nazarbayeva) with the Otan party, which had won 4 party list seats (and 24 overall) in the 1999 elections to the *Majilis*. While harboring few ideological differences, the parties were united in their support for the president and the chance to compete as a "super party" in subsequent elections, with the promise of a centralized structure and the allure of being on the "winning team." At the same time, the move signaled the decreasing independent political authority of Dariga Nazarbayeva, which had been eroding since the President failed to make his customary appearance at the Dariga-organised annual international media conference conducted in 2005. In addition, with President Nazarbayev indicating he would run again for the presidency, it eliminated the immediate need to elevate presidential daughter Dariga to prominent role in party politics, and as a result Asar's mandate and popularity began to wane. With the power of the Otan organisational structure, unlimited financial resources, and of course the backing of the president, the union of these three parties created the first Central Asian "super Party" which would go on to dominate the August 2007 parliamentary elections. The high 7 per cent party threshold added another barrier and created a nearly insurmountable hurdle for an already weakened and fractured opposition, none of whom could muster enough votes to win a single seat. The relatively modest state of financial wherewithal of the opposition, and restrictions on its ability to campaign, were two additional confining conditions for the opposition parties to deal with during the hastily-scheduled elections.

One of the more noteworthy conditions hampering parties' effectiveness is the fact that parties still tend to revolve around one or more magnanimous personalities, and less on ideas and issue-based platforms. Even the fractured Communist Party faces this, having split into two different parties, one led by the "godfather" of post-Soviet communism in Kazakhstan, Serikbolsyn Abdilding, and the other by his former associate, the head of the People's Communist Party of Kazakhstan, Vladislav Kosarev. The Ak-Zhol party faced a similar circumstance, with Bulat Abilov, Altynbek Sarsenbaev, Oraz Zhandosov, and Tulegen Zhukeyev breaking away from co-leader Alikzhan Baimenov to form the "True Ak-Zhol" (*Naghyz Ak Zhol*) party in 2006. They announced a merger in June before the parliamentary elections, though efforts to form an electoral bloc were rebuffed by a new law that prohibited the forming of electoral coalitions. The party did not compete independently, with their former colleagues in Ak-Zhol, now nominally pro-presidential, receiving but 3.09 per cent of the party list vote and falling short of the minimum required to win seats. Cynics in the parties affected suggest that the fracturing of their parties was in fact orchestrated by the government or Nur-Otan. The truth may lie as much in personality clashes and egos, however, as in the nefarious actions of the government or Nur-Otan.

Nur-Otan claims to have 740,000 members nationwide, with 3400 deputies elected to oblast or local Maslikhats. Nur-Otan claims to be the only party in Kazakhstan to have representation in every electoral district in the country. In fact it certainly is the only one to have the resources to operate in every electoral district. It reaches out to constituents through its party newspaper, via its website in Kazakh, Russian and English language, and through the quarterly meetings that the 98 Nur-Otan members of the *Majilis* conduct in their "home" districts. The party's youth wing, Zhas-Otan, has over 200,000 persons younger than 30 as members. Three have become deputies of the *Majilis*, and 220 (age 36 or younger) have been elected as deputies to Maslikhats at different levels.[41] In keeping with its emphasis on youth, the party states that every third member is younger than 30 years of age. The party is already discussing strategy for the next elections in 2012, and continues to forge alliances and work cooperatively with NGOs, private businesses, and trade unions. Indeed, one is struck at the fact that the party is omnipresent handling affairs of the state and intends, by all appearances, to be accountable to the voters. As one deputy put it, "we won the elections. Now we have to fulfill our promises."[42] As further evidence of its benevolence, the party has undertaken a number of local community improvement projects as well as instituted a grievances department, through which people can appeal to *Majilis* or Maslikhat deputies and file complaints. For example, in 2007 the party reported that 1727 grievances were received by the Astana branch out of a total of 66,230 nationwide. It is not clear how many were resolved successfully, but it does seem, on the surface, to challenge the notion that citizens are entirely apathetic or unenthusiastic about addressing their problems to their local Nur-Otan or local government official.

Among Nur-Otan's most signaled achievements is the formation of local anti-corruption councils, charged with investigating reported instances of official abuse and taking corrective action. While the typical forms of official abuse are most often associated with shakedowns by traffic police, increasingly cases have been brought to light of corruption among local government officials. With Nur-Otan dominating government at all levels, this effort amounts to essentially an internal housecleaning. Nonetheless, acknowledgement of the problem and a mandate for addressing corruption now exists at the level of government and not only on the agendas of special interest groups. Nur-Otan underscores its strong "everyday" contacts with people and the party's philosophy of "maximizing the intellectual potential" of every person in the country, using the "best mix of European and Asian experiences."[43] When asked about the merits of a party list system over elections of individual deputies via single mandate, this author suggested that the exclusive party list method removes the degree of personal responsibility and accountability of each deputy to his or her region of origin, along with personal contact with constituents, creating an ambiguous collection of deputies for whom no citizen directly voted. This is typically one of the arguments levied against proportional representation systems, that direct accountability of members elected via party list is absent and they are somehow less legitimate in their position than those elected through single mandate constituency voting. However, this is often balanced by mixed systems in which a proportion of deputies are elected by either method, such as the system Kazakhstan had up until the 2007 elections. In response, the Nur-Otan senior leadership countered that the party list system is actually more legitimate than previous elections to the *Majilis* in that for the first time the election centered around ideas and not around personalities. In other words, the element of individuals winning seats due to their charismatic personalities was a dangerous thing of the past, to be avoided. Indeed, those who re-engineered the constitution believed the Kazakhstani electorate's maturation allowed it to focus exclusively on judging parties' ideas for addressing the most pressing needs of the country. In this sense, Nur-Otan claims, the electorate dismissed the opposition parties precisely for their deficit of clear ideas as well as personality-driven "politics as usual."

It can be argued that political parties in Kazakhstan and elsewhere in Central Asia have always tended to revolve around one or more charismatic leaders. In fact a public opinion survey conducted in Kazakhstan by the International Republican Institute in 2004 suggested that more voters still believe that a party's leader was the most important factor in deciding whether or not to vote for them (38%), with the party and its ideas second (26%) and another 22 per cent who believe both factors are equally as important.[44] Looking back eight years, when asked whether people were more likely to vote for a candidate affiliated with a political party or one who was not, 54 per cent of respondents would have chosen an independent candidate over a party-backed one, with 26 per cent stating that they would more likely select a party-backed one.[45] It is exactly the reliance of personalities and deficit of ideas that, in the minds of Nur-Otan leaders, doomed the opposition political parties. One could reasonably add to the argument that a lack of funding and political space played as much a role in this, as did the fracturing of two of the more well known opposition parties, Ak-Zhol and the Communist Party, prior to the 2007 elections as well as the prohibition of party coalitions. The irony in suggesting that personalities have been driven out of politics or discredited as a factor in parliamentary elections, is of course, the ever-present image of President Nazarbayev as leader of Nur-Otan. Nazarbayev's popularity and image as "Papa" to the masses certainly has had a positive impact on the party he governs, which is visible on the billboards and literature maintained and distributed by the party across the country.

When asked whether the party list system of voting and the 4th session of the *Majilis* represents the "evolutionary goal" of Kazakhstani political reformation, few were in agreement that the current system is perfect, though, it was stated, it does appear to best suit the realities in Kazakhstan, and moreover, why shouldn't one party claim all the seats. Results also suggest that the country is still recovering from a post-election "trauma", with a low level of political activity. Respondents were also diagnosed with a "very low level" of recognition for political parties, with an equally low level of interest in politics and the work of political parties.[46] Dr. Bakytzhamal Bekturganova, Head of the Association, suggests that Nur-Otan and the government is "seriously out of touch with the rest of the country", that they are operating in a vacuum and are unable to see the "real situation" beyond their own immediate interests, while the opposition, stinging from electoral defeat and the massive changes in the political landscape, is at present "weak and passive."[47] One metaphor used more than once to describe the current state of Nur-Otan (by members themselves) and the state of the parliament was that a "crystallisation" of the system had taken place after the August 2007 elections. Whether this crystallisation was natural or artificial remains to be seen, as does the verdict on whether the process has led to a desirable result.

Nur-Otan in the Parliament

Though dominant in the *Majilis* for at least the next five years, Nur-Otan does not appear to take for granted its role as custodian of a multi-party political system. Though vocal of other parties' failure to successfully oppose them, they do make an attempt to reach out to citizens, businesses and other political parties through a forum known as the Citizens Alliance of Kazakhstan, with which Nur-Otan shares a Memorandum of Understanding. This forum is set up as an all inclusive "open microphone" type of discussion opportunity in which ideas can be freely shared and criticisms expressed. Opposition parties interviewed confirmed that Nur-Otan has led such outreach sessions, though dismissed them as ideologically biased. Actual levels of public participation were difficult to ascertain, though it is true that Nur-Otan members of parliament are required on a quarterly basis to visit their constituencies for no less than ten days, which reflects the irony that a party-list elected parliament in essence functions as if its members were individually elected. The answer is, of course, that by winning all of the 98 seats in the *Majilis* Nur-Otan has the ability to meet with constituents in all Oblasts and major regions of the country without exception, having members in parliament from most major cities in each oblast of the country. In addition, television coverage on state-run channels is frequent, and showcases the party's latest initiatives.

Nur-Otan keeps abreast of the mood of the electorate through quarterly surveys conducted through its Centrer for Social Research, via which it measures the problems and issues most pressing to voters. The surveys provide data based on which the party makes any necessary "course corrections". Bakytzhamal Bekturganova confirmed that Nur-Otan contacts her Association regularly to obtain comparative polling data, though often does not agree with the results.If debate cannot be reasonably had within a one-party parliament on ideological grounds, then on what basis can we compare this parliament with those in other fully-fledged or emerging democracies? How do we assess the state of parliamentary democracy in Kazakhstan in 2008, less than two years removed from Kazakhstan's ascension to the Chairmanship of the OSCE? The casual observer might invoke the dreaded "rubber stamp" moniker or suggest Nur-Otan's status as a Super-Party. The latter of these statements invariably elicits a negative response from Nur-Otan members, who consider the Super-Party term more in line comparatively with the Communist Party of the Soviet Union, not a progressive party in post-Soviet independent Kazakhstan. As for the rubber stamp notion, it is dismissed as well though acknowledged that disagreements with the president on substantive issues are few and far between. "it cannot happen," remarked one deputy, "we are all from the same party."[48]

Still, members of parliament have the right to voice their opinions during parliamentary sessions and object to particular course of action proposed. For example, deputies cannot approve of ministers appointed by the Nazarbayev, but they do vote on his choice for Prime Minister. If members of parliament don't vote to confirm the nominated candidate for prime ministers post, the president must nominate a different one. They can discuss the merits of individual cabinet ministers but they don't have any power to vote against them, as outlined in the constitution. This was one of the constitutional amendments approved in 2007, as previously it was the President who appointed the Cabinet of Ministers. Party fractions in the parliament have "serious discussions" on major issues including: the state budget, development of Kazakhstan's territory, social protection, cultural issues, tariffs and tax law. Taking exception to the notion of the fourth convocation of the parliament being entirely submissive to the president, deputies in both the Senate and *Majilis* insist that the government "has no carte blanche over this parliament!"[49] If there are any internal disagreements among Nur-Otan members, it exists on a regional basis. Deputies do hold spirited discussions on issues such as resource allocation and infrastructure development, arguing in favor of their "home" regions, a condition unique to Kazakhstan's party list system and resulting one-party parliament. This now allows deputies to function as individuals within the party structure. Competition along regional lines within Nur-Otan is likely to continue. The party dismisses any notion of disunity and points out that they have the only political party capable of addressing all regional needs systematically. It can be argued that not all parties are capable of mounting national programs to the degree that Nur-Otan is, although as will be seen many claim a high level of activism in all oblasts (among these the "soft opposition People's Communist and Auyl parties).

The lack of a serious political opposition from among the ranks of political parties or individual leaders does not necessarily signal that there is no opposition whatsoever to speak of; rather, it may lay in "islands of power"[50] related to business leaders or oligarchs within Kazakhstan that affect the course of discussion to a greater degree than other forces outside of the president or parliament. Though not a topic of the present paper, the business elite do have serious influence when contemplating the centers of power beyond the President and his Nur-Otan party.

PRO-PRESIDENTIAL PARTIES

Rukhaniyat

The Rukhaniyat ('Rebirth') Party is a small party that was registered in 2003. Led by Altynshash Zhaganova, it tends to support the ruling government's position. Zhaganova is a well-known writer and worker in state television dating back to Kazakhstan's days as a Soviet republic. The party pledges to expand the economy, address social issues and develop the spirituality of society. Rukhaniyat registered a proportional list consisting of nine candidates for the 2007 elections, receiving 1.51 per cent of the party list vote in 2007, a slight improvement over the 0.44 per cent received in 2004. It maintains a party website, www.rukhaniyat.kz, and claims a nationwide base of constituents.

Party of Patriots

The Party of Patriots of Kazakhstan (PPK) was established in 2000 and had eleven candidates on its party list for the 2007 elections. A small party, like Rukhaniyat, the PPK is sometimes critical of certain government policies, but in general supports most presidential initiatives. Led by Gani Kasimov, who once ran opposite Nursultan Nazarbayev as a candidate for the presidency, the party aims to establish a governmental system based on the rule of law and democratic principles, and promote a civil society with a market economy where living standards are raised. In addition to its party newspaper, it maintains a website www.ppk.gl.kz. Having won 0.6 per cent and 0.75 per cent in the 2004 and 2007 elections, respectively, it appears to lack broad appeal. The party claims to have over 130,000 members and attracts the support of military officers and the official endorsement of the Union of Officers.

"SOFT" OPPOSITION

Adilet ("Justice")

The recently re-constituted Adilet Party, which merged with Ak-Zhol for the 2007 elections, has assumed the status of a pro-presidential party. It maintains an extensive website of information,[51] and fights for justice and against corruption. It developed out of the foundation of the Democratic Party and the "For a Just Kazakhstan" movement in 2004. It is led by Maksut Naribayev, and is active in its critique of government, recently criticizing a state project on economic development of the regions of the country.

Ak-Zhol ("Bright Path")

Ak-Zhol is led by Alikhan Baimenov, who ran as the party's candidate for president in the 2005 election Just before that election, Ak-Zhol split, with the more vocally critical wing of the party re-registering under the name Naghyz (True) Ak Zhol. The only opposition party to win a seat in the 2004 elections, Ak-Zhol characterizes itself as 'constructive opposition,' with Mr. Baimenov later becoming a key player in the President's Commission for Further Democratisation of Kazakhstan. In 2006 the party signed an agreement of cooperation with the Adilet party and the two parties ran a joint list consisting of 98 candidates for the 2007 elections. Ak-Zhol advocates an independent, democratic and free Kazakhstan, and supports the fundamental values of democracy, independence, freedom and fairness. Ak-Zhol claims over 150,000 members nationally, though acknowledges that their ranks have likely thinned somewhat since the August 2007 elections. They acknowledge that the reality of their situation, and for that matter of all parties, is that they need to maintain good relations with Nur-Otan in order to advance their own interests. But when looking back at the 2007 elections, Ak-Zhol leader Baimenov acknowledged that financing and public exposure were among the biggest downfalls the party faced in order to be able to compete on a level playing field.[52] While the party does publish a newspaper (dormant since the elections, however) and maintains a website, *www.akzhol.kz*, a more important, and expensive, medium is television. Baimenov outlined an interesting problem: most citizens of Kazakhstan have access to Russian Federation television, which portrays political change in other republics, the so-called "color revolutions", in a very negative light. This affects public opinion on opposition parties inside Kazakhstan, he claims, as citizens are fearful of what their true objectives are, and see them not as potential agents of change but agents of disorder.

Baimenov believes a 50-50 split between proportional representation and single-mandate elections would be optimal, arguing that single-mandate elections are better for voters on a regional level, but the party list votes are better to "diffuse tribalism" in Kazakhstan. He admits that one of the problems is that political parties are still largely personality-driven. As with other parties, Ak-Zhol found it pointless to press their electoral grievances far in the court system, though it did try, albeit unsuccessfully. Ak-Zhol claims to be best in tune with the public interest, a public that they claim has become more religiously devout. Religion in society is seen as a positive element that Ak-Zhol has developed plans to address. Its other plans focus on literacy and empowerment of young persons. Although they cooperate with trade unions, their access to finances have been significantly reduced since the elections, a problem which Baimenov suggests is endemic among all opposition parties, Ak-Zhol does not participate in the Nur-Otan led "discussion groups," instead preferring to wait to dialogue with the dominant party in the forum of parliament (should it win seats in the future). It does hold its own inclusive discussion groups in Almaty and Astana, though it was unclear whether Nur-Otan or other parties participated in those sessions.

It appears that being an outspoken member of Ak-Zhol in the regions of the country elicits a negative response these days, as those many members of the party who function in local Maslikhats and Akims must conceal their party allegiance.[53] Of the split with his former colleagues, who went on to form True Ak-Zhol and newly renamed Azat Party, Baimenov is reflective in suggesting that all the likes of his former colleagues wanted were "money and power", and left while acknowledging that they could not win an internal struggle for the hearts and minds of the party faithful. Baimenov added proudly that 80 per cent of Ak-Zhol party members stuck with the party during the split. Ak Zhol gained 12.4 per cent of the vote in 2004 but fell to just over 3 per cent in the 2007 elections.

The Kazakh Social Democratic Party Auyl ("Village")

Auyl was established in 2002 and promotes itself as a party for the defense of rural districts and social justice. As such it focuses on the development of agriculture and the protection of the interests of agricultural workers. Auyl furthermore supports economic and political reforms aimed at the further democratisation of society, and increasing the living standards of citizens. It works cooperatively with the president and Nur-Otan (though likening it to a "communist party"),[54] generally supporting the president's policies. Auyl is headed by Gani Kaliyev and succeeded in registering 33 candidates on its proportional list, though did not have any members elected to the *Majilis* in the 2007 (or preceding) elections, as it earned but 1.51% of the vote. In the 2004 elections it had received 1.73 per cent of the vote. It maintains representation in all 14 oblasts, 160 regions and in the cities of Almaty and Astana, claiming it is the only party to have such widespread support in the country. It has earned seven seats in oblast Maslikhats and another 30 in local Maslikhats around the country.

Auyl members found the election results from August 2007 to have been "problematic", as they feel they should have won "at least 20 per cent of the seats." They found it pointless to appeal the results, however, citing their experience from past elections. It goes without saying that they are against the current party list system, and feel that the system will change before the next elections. They do acknowledge having financial issues, though cited some private financing and sponsors. When asked whether they have heard of the discussion groups led by Nur-Otan, they acknowledged they had (and mentioned their own discussion clubs), but said they refused to participate in them. The party tries to meet with representatives of other parties, and participated in the *For Fair Elections* coalition. Auyl publishes a monthly newspaper for supporters, conducts regular meetings at the oblast level, holds four party meetings per year, and maintains a party website, www.ksdp-auyl.kz.

Communist Party of Kazakhstan (CPK)

The Communist Party of Kazakhstan, the original successor to the Communist Party of the Kazakhstan SSR, was reformed in October 1991 and registered in February 1994. The party has been led by Serikbolsyn Abdildin since its re-inception, and functioned as the only registered communist political movement in the country until 2004. In that year, Abdildin and prominent party member Vladislav Kosyrev split when the latter accused Abdildin of questionable fundraising practices. The resulting schism led to the forming of the Communist People's Party, which ran as a separate party in both the 2004 and 2007 elections (failing to win seats on either occasion). Abdildin's Communist Party boycotted the 2007 elections and has arguably suffered a drop off in prominence vis-à-vis the Communist People's party led by Kosyrev, which tends to support the policies of the President.

The Communist Party in its post-1991 history has frequently cooperated with other movements, having participated in the opposition coalition entities Azamat and Pokolenie ("Generation") as well as initiating the unregistered "National-Patriotic Movement-Republic" in 1996. In 1998 it joined the "People's Front of Kazakhstan" movement, an opposition bloc, and during the December

2005 presidential elections the Communist Party, Democratic Choice of Kazakhstan and Naghyz Ak Zhol Party formed a coalition movement, "For a Just Kazakhstan", and supported Zhamarkan Tuyakbai as its presidential candidate, who was soundly defeated by President Nazarbayev.

The party's electoral history in the 1990s was consistent (if unspectacular, considering its relative popularity among all political parties during the period) after its organisational reformation, winning two seats in both the 1995 and 1999 elections. The party was not permitted to field candidates in the 1994 elections. In the 2000s once again the Communist Party sought alliances and in 2004 it joined with the Democratic Choice of Kazakhstan and won 3.4 per cent short of the 5 per cent threshold and resulting in no seats gained in the parliament. In addition to its electoral boycott of 2007, the party remains in a low intensity conflict with the Communist People's Party for the hearts and minds of its constituents, many of whom are older-generation voters.

Communist People's Party

The Communist People's Party of Kazakhstan (CPPK) was registered prior to the 2004 parliamentary elections, competing with the opposition Communist Party of Kazakhstan, though not winning any seats in parliament. The CPPK, headed by Vladislav Kosarev, registered a proportional list numbering 20 candidates for the 2007 elections. Largely pro-presidential, the party promotes Marxist-Leninist ideology, but adapted to the new realities of social development. They "expected" to have won at least seven seats during the 2007 elections, and claim that they were unfairly denied these seats but did not take the matter to court. While recognising that cooperation with Nur-Otan is a necessity, they do not embrace this alliance, referring to their Nur-Otan colleagues instead as "fanatics." The party claims that 30 per cent of its 70,000 members are younger than age 30, addressing the charge that the party only appeals to nostalgic, older-generation citizens. They maintain contacts with other communist parties throughout the world, including those from Kyrgyzstan, China, Cuba and the Czech. When describing the split with Serikbolsyn Abdildin and the other communists, Kosarev claimed that those who split away from the CPPK were interested only in power, not in serving the people based on true Marxist ideology.[55]

The party does not appear to have representatives in local government, though it holds that the actual process of the election is more important that the outcome, an oblique reference to electoral struggles at the lower levels. While unabashedly anti-western, the party leadership does agree with the OSCE on at least one thing, that the threshold, or barrier, for parties to have members elected via party list should be lowered, in the CPPK's opinion to 3 per cent, and that each registered party should have at least some members serving in parliament. The party acknowledges having participated once in the Nur-Otan led all-party discussion groups, but refused further invitations to participate due to the "heavy-handed" nature of Nur-Otan's leadership of those sessions.[56] The party publishes newsletters regularly and maintains a party website at www.knpk.kz.

"HARD" OPPOSITION

Azad (former Naghyz Ak-Zhol, "True Bright Path")

The newly-renamed Azat party claims to be the most structured and popular democratic opposition party in the country. Its founders, which split with Alikzhan Baimenov's Ak-Zhol party in 2005, include famous businessman Bulat Abilov, ex-governor of the National Bank Oraz Jandosov, and the late Altynbek Sarsenbayev, ex-minister of information, murdered in February 2006. They claim their former Ak-Zhol colleagues to be "puppets of the administration," while they alone are true standard-bearers of opposition to the ruling elite. In February 2008 the party called a congress and formally changed its name to "Azat" [Freedom] party. The name selection was the result of a context, in which party leaders selected two names to put to a vote out of some 300 suggestions received: Azat and Azamat (the name of a political movement from the late 1990s), meaning "citizen." Azat won overwhelmingly with 88 votes to Azamat's 58. Other popular suggestions included Akikat (truth), Adal (honesty), and even the names of some political movements, which already exist, such as Adilet (justice) and Atameken (fatherland).[57] The re-branding of the party included not only a new name, but a leadership shake-up as well (Abilov was elected party chairman). Party leaders hope that the makeover will infuse new energy and momentum into attempts to open up Kazakhstan's political system.

The party, which still needs to register with the Ministry of Justice (rarely an easy or straightforward process), abandoned its policy of having three co-chairs. Another former co-leader, Tolegen Zhukeyev, was elected secretary-general, with overall responsibility for party strategy. The third former co-chairman, Oraz Zhandosov, is likely to become a deputy leader and will remain the party's chief economic strategist. The existence of two similarly named parties had been a source of confusion to voters, and Azat's leaders are hoping they can finally put the split behind them and create a new brand that will have public recognition by the next parliamentary election, due in 2012. The new name has positive connotations for many Kazakhstanis: a movement called Azat was formed in 1990 and lobbied for independence from the Soviet Union.[58] Leaders of that movement, which still exists but is not active, condemned the decision to adopt the name. "We are surprised and perturbed that they have taken the name Azat, as if there weren't any other words in Kazakh," the movement's former chairman, Toleubek Seytkaly-Uly, said during a March 4 news conference, as reported by the Interfax-Kazakhstan news agency. The party claimed that the parliamentary vote was marred by widespread fraud, as have been previous elections, according to Zhukeyev. Votes are regularly stolen from the opposition, Zhukeyev said, who added that if conducted fairly, the party would have gained 30 to 40 percent of the vote.[59]

As Kazakhstan continues to be hurt by the effects of the global credit crunch, and as public dissatisfaction rises along with the country's inflation rate, Abilov's demand that the party of power must take responsibility is not lost on many Kazakhstanis. Therein lies political opportunity, Abilov believes. Azat's leaders insist they don't need seats in parliament to influence the legislative and policy process, and are able to put pressure on the regime from the outside. Azat, which will now have to seek re-registration under its new name, plans to draw up as three-year political strategy and a longer-term program, "Azat-2012", to prepare for the next parliamentary elections. It will be pushing for laws to improve the lives of ordinary people, Abilov said, singling out several priorities: making public information about foreign companies' role in energy exploration, resource export issues, labor migration restrictions, setting up a public-service TV channel; bringing laws on elections, the media, and freedom of assembly into line with OSCE commitments; introducing elections for all mayors and governors; and lobbying for Kazakhstan to join the Council of Europe.[60]

All-National Social Democratic Party (NDSP)

Following his unsuccessful presidential bid in 2005, Zharmakhan Tuyakbai established the NSDP in January 2007. In June 2007, before the elections were called, it announced its intention to unite with True Ak Zhol jointly run candidates. In the end it won 4.62% of the vote, which was good enough for second place but not enough to gain any representation in parliament. NSDP positions itself as a radical opposition. The party platform emphasizes the establishment of democracy, rule of law, and a socially-oriented state, an innovative economy and a new 'humanist' system of politics, as well as the principles of the social-democratic movement. The weakness of the All-National Social-Democratic Party is that, like many parties, it does not enjoy broad, genuine popular support. Tuyakbai appears to have lost a measure of his political prestige after his defeat in the last elections; he has done relatively little to maintain his hard-won image of a political leader.[61]

The party appears somewhat distant and alienated from the ethnic values of Kazakhs. Such popular demands as the promotion of the Kazakh language in public offices, or social and financial aid to repatriated Kazakhs, have never been on the priority list of the Social Democratic party. Ironically, party Tuyakbai comes from South Kazakhstan, the most densely Kazakh-populated region, with a host of lingering social problems. When Tuyakbai toured South Kazakhstan during the presidential election as part of his election campaign, residents of the cities of Shymkent and Turkistan posed many questions on how he was going to address the long overdue problems of improving of education and medical service standards, the rising costs of public utilities, and unemployment. Zharmakhan Tuyakbai walked away with "another heap of promises."[62] Nevertheless Tuyakbai remains a well-known figure through his ability to mount a serious opposition. Although more successful in this regard that other individuals, his popularity and drawing power over the long term, are, at best, questionable.

Alga ("Forward") People's Party (unregistered)

The Alga Party, still unregistered and not a participant in the 2007 elections, faced a leadership void in 2007. In spite of the apparent disarray, the party's headquarters office in Almaty is relatively opulent by the standards of most opposition parties in Kazakhstan, maintains two newspapers, conducts its own public opinion surveys, and monitors the work of parliamentary deputies. They appear not to share the same challenges of funding as their opposition cohorts, yet appear part of a reactive political opposition instead of a proactive one. Alga emerged from the banned, former Democratic Choice of Kazakhstan (DCK) after that movement weakened in early 2005. The DCK had been among the country's strongest opposition groupings before its demise. Alga has had continual issues with registration, being denied registration four times since its inception. The decision to apply for registration was adopted at the founding conference of the newly born movement, which took place on September 10, 2006. Since then, the Ministry of Justice has repeatedly declined to register the party under various pretexts. Opposition leaders capitalized on the delayed registration of Alga to win back public sympathy, albeit with little success. Similar protest actions in support of Alga were simultaneously organised by opposition activists in some regions, but failed to gain popular support.[63]

POLITICAL MOVEMENTS

Republican People's Party (RNPK)

In October 1998, after a reported falling out with President Nazarbayev, former Prime Minister Akezhan Kazhegeldin announced the formation of the Republican People's Party (RNPK) and his decision to run in the 1999 presidential elections. Soon thereafter, the government declared his candidacy void due to an administrative conviction for participating in an unsanctioned public gathering. In October 1999, member of the opposition founded the Forum of the Democratic Forces of Kazakhstan to strengthen their efforts against the increasing power of President Nazarbayev. Kazhegeldin was named chairman of the Forum, though obstacles erected by the government as well as internal organisational issues stunted its development. For two years it remained nearly dormant and in the end Kazhegeldin himself had to flee the country and seek exile abroad.

Azamat

In 1996 the *Azamat* political movement was founded by former prominent government officials Peter Svoik, Murat Auezov, and Galym Abilseitov. Azamat attempted to play the role of "constructive opposition," and formally registered in 1999 to participate in parliamentary elections of that year. It did not reregister in 2003, a prerequisite for participation in the 2004 parliamentary elections. In 2003, Auezov accepted a government-funded position as the head of the National Library. In late 2001, Sovik joined forces with the Republican People's Party and the People's Congress to form the United Democratic Party, whose slogan was "Kazakhstan without Nazarbayev". Neither Party, however, participated in the 2004 elections. Because both Azamat and the United Democratic Party were plagued by a lack of funding, neither became a viable force capable of opposing Nazarbayev. In fact, neither the first nor second generation of political opposition could effectively overcome the general problem of disorganisation and lack of resources.

A key commonality that these opposition movements shared is that, during their emergence, Kazakhstan's elite base had not yet undergone the process of division and conflict that later arose as a result of diversifying economic interests. In addition to their lack of independent economic resources, opposition leaders including Suleimenov and Auezov were unable to overcome social and political cleavages that they shared with others from their generation of intellectuals. Until economic interests caused a split, elites of this generation were more or less homogenous. Their political movements thus did not represent intra-elite competition, which is important to party leadership development.[64] Azamat is no longer an influential movement, having suffered from financial woes and intimidation that weakened the movement's leadership and support base.

Democratic Choice of Kazakhstan (DCK)

The Democratic Choice of Kazakhstan movement represented a new stage in the evolution of opposition movements in Kazakhstan, if not all of post Soviet Central Asia, brought on by the emergence of a new economic cleavage within the country's previously homogenous elite. In November 2001, ten years removed from Kazakhstan's declaration of independence, the growing authoritarian rule of President Nazarbayev experienced perhaps its most significant political challenge to date. The DCK movement was created by elements of Kazakhstan's business and political elite to challenge the leadership of the country, and called for decentralisation of political authority (via the direct election of regional governors), a strong legislature and independent judiciary to balance presidential power.

The DCK's driving force to create a competitive political system represented its desire to ensure that fair, transparent, and impartial laws would apply to everyone, including the presidents family and associates-irrespective of position in the patrimonial hierarchy. The government's response to the new political movement was quick and decisive. In an early speech, then-Prime Minister Kasymzhomart Tokaev condemned the DCK and demanded the resignation of "all those who disagree with the government's policy and wish to be involved in political movements," calling the movement's founders "nonprofessionals" and "schemers". Within weeks, DCK members holding government posts were replaced through presidential decree, and criminal charges alleging tax evasion and misuse of office were filed against the movement's two most outspoken leaders, Galymzhan Zhakiyano and Mukhtar Ablyazov. Unknown "hooligans" shot up a television station sympathetic to the new movement, and firebombs were detonated in the offices of a newspaper run by one of DCK's founders.

As a result of this pressure, some of the DCK's original members renounced their support for the movement, while others outright withdrew their participation. Some joined to create the new, moderate Ak-Zhol political party. Zhakiyanov and Ablyazov were jailed on criminal chares. Foreign observers, including the OSCE, characterized their trials as suspicious and politically-motivated. In the case of the DCK, the opposition's key interest and political agenda is more fully understood in the context of, and in opposition to, "the existing clientelistic or patrimonial system rather than the expression of competition between clans or other traditional forms of social cleavage."[65] Although many of their founders had managed to amass large personal fortunes, they were "not permitted to compete with those in the inner circle made up of Nazarbayev's family and close associates."[66]

As Barbara Junisbai writes in *Demokratizatsiya*:

> As many Central Asian political observers have noted, Kazakhstan's political opposition is the most developed in the region in terms of its organisational abilities and resources. Armed with their own financial assets, direct experience with and knowledge of the government's decision-making processes, as well as public relations savvy, they have yet to translate these organisational advantages into the creation of a wide base of popular support. Sergei Duvanov, a well-known Kazakhstani journalist, has criticized the opposition's inability to rouse public sentiment in its favor, noting that not only is Kazakhstan far from Ukraine in terms of its chances for mass support for widespread political change, but also that Kyrgyzstan's opposition has been more successful at garnering public support than have their counterparts in Kazakhstan. At the same time, Duvanov argues...that as the initial elite split that the DCK signaled continues, and as more of the elite flock to the opposition and take their government experience with them, the opposition will grow more credible and stronger, and there will be greater chance for real political reform.[67]

In the years since DCL's primacy among alternative political movements, the opposition has stagnated and largely failed to generate public excitement or work under a unified banner, and was later officially banned.

For a Just Kazakhstan

Perhaps the most significant event that occurred in 2004 was the resignation of Otan party leader and parliamentary speaker Zharmakhan Tuyakbai in the aftermath of the parliamentary elections. Publicly condemning local election officials for deliberately rigging the election results and stating that he could no longer represent a party that had won due to fraud, Tuyakbai joined the opposition and was elected the chair of the opposition coalition 'For A Just Kazakhstan'. The 'For A Just Kazakhstan' (also known as For a Fair Kazakhstan) political movement was founded by a coalition including the Communist Party of Kazakhstan, the Ak Zhol Party and Democratic Choice of Kazakhstan as an opposition coalition to nominate a single candidate in the 2005 presidential elections. Gearing up for the 2006 presidential elections, this "radical opposition" united with the express purpose of presenting a unified political platform and nominating a viable single candidate for president. 'For a Just Kazakhstan' advocated democratisation of the political system, election of the regional governors, investigation of corruption cases involving the family of the president Nazarbayev and the fair redistribution of national wealth.[68]

Tuyakbai was officially declared the united opposition's presidential candidate in March 2005. Many political anaysts in Kazakhstan have concluded that Tuyakbai's defection to the opposition signaled the continuation of internal conflict and division within the country's political elite. Taken together, these developments suggest that Kazakhstan's current political evolution is a "direct result of an ongoing intra-elite competition, which was brought on by the twin processes of economic liberalisation and interest diversification among the country's elite."[69]

The 'For Just Kazakhstan' opposition alliance suffered numerous attacks and incidents of harassment against its members throughout the year preceding the presidential elections in 2005. In May, a group of men stormed a 'For a Just Kazakhstan meeting' and threatened to kill Tuyakbai, who escaped unharmed. Several people suffered minor injuries while police on the scene reportedly did not intervene to stop the violence. In November 1995, For a Just Kazakhstan member Zamanbek Nurkadilov was found shot dead in his home, and two nephews of Naghyz Ak Zhol leader Altynbek Saresenbayev were beaten by off-duty police officers.[70] As with other inspired political movements of this decade, For a Just Kazakhstan's leadership suffered under pressure and intimidation. It eventually would form the All-National Social Democratic Party and run for seats in the 2007 elections.

What is noteworthy here is that the present state of multi-partyism in Kazakhstan would seem to suggest a period of pause and reflection for the opposition, which has been fragmented due to internal dissention and external pressures. While some parties such as Adilet and Azat have plans to play the role of overseers of the parliament and government, their overall popularity remains a question among a very skeptical, depressed electorate. Nur-Otan has successfully fended off all challengers though a mix of bullying and immense, almost bottomless, financial and political resources. The current period will undoubtedly give way at some point to a more pluralistic system, though the prospects of outside voices being heard and listened to remains questionable in the short term, even with the seemingly well-intentioned efforts of Nur-Otan to reach out to other political parties and movements. At the same time, opposition political parties in Kazakhstan have truly moved from needing basic organisational assistance or help in campaigning or strategizing to becoming a more sophisticated "loyal opposition" that doesn't blindly accept its fate as outsiders to the political process but which does not continue to keep itself perpetually at odds with the authorities. This is not to say that opposition parties need to "fall into line" or begin attending the Nur-Otan sponsored discussion clubs, but rather focus on positive elements and connecting with voters on a grassroots level that they have previously not seen.

PRESIDENTIAL ELECTION OF 2005

Kazakhstan's Presidential election of 2005 became an important milestone in Kazakhstan's history with implications for the future and the wider region. In September 2005, Kazakhstan's President Nursultan Nazarbayev had declared his commitment to ensure the forthcoming election to be "free, fair and transparent."[71] US Secretary of State Condoleezza Rice, on a visit to Astana earlier in October 2005, said "with the Presidential election in December 2005, Kazakhstan has an unprecedented opportunity to lead Central Asia toward a future of democracy and to elevate US-Kazakhstani relations to a new level."[72] The election campaign started on October 25, 2005. Kazakhstan's Central Election Commission registered five candidates who met all the requirements:

1. Yerassyl Abylkassymov, a leader of the Communist People's Party of Kazakhstan and a deputy of the *Majilis*.
2. Alikhan Baimenov, Chairman of the *Ak Zhol* political party.
3. Mels Eleusizov, leader of the *Tabigat* (Nature) environmental protection Nongovernmental organisation.
4. Nursultan Nazarbayev, the President of Kazakhstan and the leader of the *Otan* political party, and
5. Zharmakhan Tuyakbai, Chairman of *For a Fair Kazakhstan Movement*.

Nursultan Nazarbayev was re-elected for a new term in the Presidential election held on 4 December 2005 receiving the support of more than 90 per cent of those who voted. More than three-fourth of registered voters exercised their right to vote and cast ballots on Election Day which went in a mostly calm and amicable atmosphere. Onalsyn Zhumabekov, Chairman of Kazakhstan's Central Election Commission, declared the election valid and said that Nazarbayev had received 6,100,694 votes cast, or 91.01 per cent; Zharmakhan Tuyakbai of *For a Fair Kazakhstan Movement* came second with 445,047 votes, or 6.64 per cent, while Alikhan Baimenov of the *Ak Zhol Democratic Party* was third with 1.65 per cent. Yerassyl Abylkassymov finished fourth with 0.38 per cent, while Mels Yeleusizov of the *Tabigat* (Nature) *Environmental Movement* was fifth with 0.32 per cent.[73]

More than three-fourths of registered voters in Kazakhstan had turned out at polling stations on December 4 to cast their ballots. Out of a total of 8,874,968 voters in voter lists, 6,850,000, or more than 77 per cent, voted. Slightly less than 400,000 people, or 13.80 per cent of those who voted, chose to do it through the Sailau Electronic Voting System, out of about 3,000,000, or 35 per cent, had such an option. The election was observed by 11,086 trustees of candidates for President, more than 1,000 observers from foreign countries, international organisations and foreign reporters, 16,458 observers from political parties, 5,652 observers from public associations, and 500 Kazakh reporters.[74] The Organisation for Security and Cooperation in Europe (OSCE) set up an office in Astana with a staff of 43 long term observers. Four hundred more observers from the OSCE came to Kazakhstan later.[75] OSCE maintained that Kazakhstan had fallen far short of international norms.[76]

Foreign Minister of Kazakhstan Tokaev voiced on December 3, 2005 that the presence of OSCE in Almaty would help promote the development of a civic society in Kazakhstan, but he stressed that building democracy in Central Asia is a slow process: "One should duly appreciate the willingness of the new democracies to advance gradually." Tokaev also emphasized that stability in Kazakhstan was a "significant contribution to global and regional security."[77]

Four days before the elections of Kazakhstan President, the American human rights monitors expressed their doubt as to its fairness. According to Human Rights Watch, "Coercion, threats and repression in relation to oppositionists are typical features of the election campaign in Kazakhstan".[78] Human Right Watch was critical of Nazarbayev for his decision to call early elections, leaving no time for the opposition to organise any serious confrontation. A group of human rights activists also declared that some candidates, including chief oppositionist and former Prime Minister Akezhan Kazhegeldin, were forced out of the Presidential races on the pretext of some administrative irregularities.

It is believed that Nazarbayev drew lessons from the Presidential elections in other transitional countries in Central Asia. In other elections in democratic and semi-democratic regimes in the CIS, incumbent Presidents lost office. This happened to Kravchuk of the Ukraine and Shushkevitch of Belorussia in 1994 in spite of their emphasis on 'patriotism' and anti-Russian sentiments.[79] And it was not possible to use same jargon in multi-ethnic and multicultural Kazakhstan. Second, the Kazakhstani elite widely perceived the Russian Presidential elections as deceitful elections accompanied by a high level of corruption and a very expensive election campaign. Although Boris Yeltsin won the elections in Russia, he and his regime lost both moral and political grounds. Third, the experience of neighbouring Kyrgyzstan showed that the best way to assure victory is to follow some democratic procedures (like conducting relatively free elections), but to set some limits and new 'rules of the game' (like banning potentially strong opponents from registration on technical grounds and through harsh electoral rules). As such the Kazakhstani ruling elite followed the Kyrgyzstan model during the December 1995 Presidential elections by banning strong potential and undesirable candidates from the registration process.

PRESIDENTIAL ELECTION OF 2011

President Nazarbayev once again saw a resounding victory in the presidential election held on 3 April 2011. Soon after his reelection he declared that he now had "carte blanche" to continue national reform.[80] According to the Kazakhstan's Central Election Commission, the incumbent President, Nursultan Nazarbayev, won over 95 percent of the vote in the presidential election defeating three rival candidates environmentalist Mels Yeleusizov of the Green Party, Gani Kasymov of the Party of Patriots, and Zhambyl Akhmetbekov of the Communist People's Party. The Association of Sociologists and Political Scientists (ASIP) in its exit poll gave Nazarbayev 94.82 percent, followed by Patriots Party Senator Gani Kasimov 2.17 percent, Communist People's Party of Kazakhstan candidate Zhambyl Ahmetbekov 1.57 percent, and Tabigat environmental group leader Mels Eleusizov 1.44 percent. About 110,000 people were surveyed, or around 1.2 percent of voters. A second poll, of 50,000 people at 333 polling stations by the Democracy Institute, gave Nazarbayev 95.1 percent of the vote.

Election observers reported no major violations on polling day, although it was noted that Nazarbayev's campaign was far more prominent than any of his rivals. "We visited several sites in and near Astana, and I did not see any gross violations there," said Alexander Brod, a member of Russia's Public Chamber who monitored the election. "In the pre-election period we found a predominance of campaign material from the incumbent president," the Russian human rights activist added. Three opposition parties boycotted the election, saying holding the vote with two months' warning did not give them time to mount a serious challenge to the incumbent, who has been in power in Kazakhstan since before the breakup of the Soviet Union in 1991. Despite the call for a boycott, the Central Election Commission reported turnout of 89.8 percent. Nazarbayev called the early poll after rejecting parliament's vote for a referendum to extend his term until 2020, bypassing presidential elections scheduled for 2012 and 2017.[81]

After winning the election Nazarbayev told his supporters that he would "continue the course of economic, political and social reforms". David Witherspoon of the *Daily Telegraph* reported that most Kazakhs who were interviewed before and after the election said the country had made rapid progress under Nazarbayev, and they wanted it to continue. They added that the president had provided Kazakhstan with the stability it needed to move ahead.[82] In his report he informed that more than 1,000 international observers came to Kazakhstan to ensure the fairness of the election. According to him, the Organisation for Security and Cooperation in Europe (OSCE), which brought hundreds of observers, noted some irregularities while also saying that Kazakhstan had made progress toward achieving fairness since the last presidential election in 2005. At a press conference in Astana on April 4, when asked whether this election could be considered a step forward towards greater democracy, Tonino Picula, who led the short-term OSCE observer mission and headed the delegation of the OSCE Parliamentary Assembly, said: "We believe so... We already said that earlier in our conclusions... We believe this election has been an honest attempt to improve the election process."[83]

The Parliamentary Assembly of the Council of Europe said in a statement that "despite certain imperfections that invariably mar all elections in any country, the outcome of this vote truly reflects the will of Kazakhstan's electorate." The Independent International Observer Mission said that it assessed the election as successful on three levels: (1) it clearly reflects the political choice of Kazakhstan's voters; (2) it marks a definite advance in the transparency of the electoral process, compared with previous elections; and (3) it opens the prospect for the formation of a more pluralist (multiparty) Parliament in the next legislative elections.[84] The Mission's members included experts from the United States, England and Germany from institutions such as Washington-based Institute for New Democracies, Center for Strategic and International Studies, Georgetown University, Jamestown Foundation, and the Hudson Institute, as well as the International Tax and Investment Centre.

Similarly Professor Dr. Anton Caragea, President of European Council on International Relations presented the Final Report of EU Monitoring Mission on 12 April 2011. It concluded that "The Election Process was on all his duration and in all his faze in conformity with international standards, international accepted norms and Copenhagen Criteria and is recognising the April 3 Presidential Elections in Kazakhstan as free, fair, open and in complying with democratic values and criteria's." Today democratic and prosperous Kazakhstan is building a new euro-asian relation. Once Kazakhstan had obtained the democratic credentials European Union is having a stable and open partner in Central Asia. The involvement of European Council on International Relations in supporting democratic process in Kazakhstan is a new bridge that is uniting the two countries.

Campaigning for this poll was low-key. The most organised and visible being by the main pro-presidential party Nur Otan. Nazarbayev had no real competition and no previous elections in Kazakhstan had ever been judged free and fair by independent monitors. Human Rights leader Zauresh Battalova who was a former Senate member stated that "we have not had fair elections in 20 years". On the other hand, Nazarbayev argued that economic prosperity should come before democracy: "without such strength, as we have seen repeatedly around the world, stability is put at risk and democratic reform can founder".[85]

ASSUMPTION OF OSCE LEADERSHIP

Less than one year now remains until Kazakhstan takes over the rotating function of OSCE leadership. But before that something significant will need to take place particularly in the area of legislative change so as to enable Kazakhstan to meet the requirements for incoming Chair in 2010. During its campaign for the Chairmanship of the OSCE, several Participating States raised questions regarding Kazakhstan's suitability for the position by doubting its efforts on democratisation.[86] Reacting to these concerns, at the Madrid OSCE Ministerial Council on 29-30 November 2007, Kazakhstan's Foreign Minister committed his country to amend its laws on elections, political parties, local governance and the media by the end of 2008 to bring them into compliance with international norms. He promised that "the Kazakhstani government would take steps to strengthen cooperation with civil society in order to promote greater transparency in the policy-making process." He also stressed that Kazakhstan, once it becomes Chairman-in-Office, would support the work of the OSCE's Office of Democratic Institutions and Human Rights (ODIHR) under the terms of its current mandate.[87]

What is to be noted here is that the legitimacy of the new Kazakh Parliament following August 2007 general elections appears to have been widely accepted, both in Kazakhstan and abroad, as demonstrated by the consensus among OSCE members to elect Kazakhstan as its chair for 2010. However, it is worth to be highlighted here that while it is inevitable that some form of single-mandate voting will return to the Kazakhstani electoral system, as the requirements of an OSCE-member state insist that at least one House of Parliament has its deputies elected directly. But such is not the case now and parties need to plan accordingly. Besides, the democratic reforms have increased the role of the Assembly of Peoples of Kazakhstan (APK), a nationwide ethnic minority representation body, as a unique instrument to preserve the religious and ethnic peace and promote mutual tolerance within the multi-ethnic and multi-confessional society of Kazakhstan. However, arguments have also been made that the body lacks democratic legitimacy, with its top members being presidential appointees.[88]

As election analysts from the Organisation for Security and Cooperation in Europe, Office for Democratic Institutions and Human Rights (OSCE/ODIHR) have pointed out, "a general electoral vote does not determine the full membership of either house of Kazakhstan's Parliament." This is more so because the election of nine of the *Majilis* members by the APK falls short of meeting the OSCE's provision, which says that the popular vote should determine all seats in at least one chamber of the national legislature.[89] In response to these criticism, officials from Kazakhstan's CEC have referred to the OSCE's provisions permitting members states to implement special measures to guarantee full equality to persons belonging to ethnic minorities, which is what the APK quota aspires to achieve.

In addition, Kazakhstan has worked to balance both Russian and Chinese interest with its many suitors in the west. Kazakhstan's pending chairmanship of the OSCE next year places it in an exceptionally unique position to be a bridge between East and West, all the more reason to engage it on a full and equal level. Notwithstanding the period leading up to Kazakhstan's assumption of the OSCE Chairmanship provides a window of opportunity for progress on democratisation process.

To conclude, the technocratic model and the programme of reforms make Nazarbayev's regime quite different from the regimes of Turkmenistan and Uzbekistan, and from that of Russia. Nazarbayev did not ignore democratic procedure. However, he limits this 'procedure' within certain framework and his 'rules of the game'. Nazarbayev and some other Central Asian Presidents have been emphasizing on 'Asian values' and peculiarities of Central Asian democracy. Besides, the policy of manoeuvres and compromises with different social, ethnic, tribal and political groups, and the moderate technocratic programme of reforms, allows Nazarbayev to broaden the social and political base of the President of Kazakhstan.[90] His flexibility has attracted wide social support in Kazakhstan and even the Russian ethnic community voted for Nazarbayev. At the same time it may be emphasized here that there are no middle class, no strong democratic institutions, or no democratic traditions in Kazakhstan. So, Kazakhstan is definitely not a democracy from the Western standards, but can be termed as "delegative democracy" if we use the terminology of G. O'Donnell.[91] Even the OSCE officials commenting about the election said that "they [Kazakhstan authorities] made a good effort in terms of voter education, and we are looking rather optimistically at the future, in that we have had some commitments to cooperate in the future."[92] Though Kazakhstan government does crack down on some opposition groups and newspapers, the country is still much freer than neighbouring Turkmenistan, Uzbekistan and China and the country has a strong basis on which it could move foreword to democratisation.

NOTES

1. For an excellent discussion of Central Asia's quest of an appropriate model of development see Rafis Abazov, "Central Asian Republics: Search For a Model of Development", *Central Asia in Transition,* Slavic Research Center, Hokkaido, 1998.
2. S. Frederic Starr, For a discussion of Central Asia's democratic accomplishments "Democratisation in Central Asia: the public's view," *Central Asia Institute Briefing Paper*, The Paul H. Nitze School of Advanced International Studies, 1997.
3. Human Rights Watch, Memorandum: U.S. Policy in Central Asia, May 2001.
4. Republic of Kazakhstan Country Profile www.mfa.kz/eng/index.php?base=3&article_id=31 - 335k.
5. Martha Brill Olcott, "Democratisation and the Growth of Political Participation in Kazakhstan," in Karen Dawisha & Bruce Parrot, eds., *Conflict, Cleavage, and Change in Central Asia and the Caucasus* (Cambridge, 1997), p.211.
6. M.Holt Ruffin and Daniel Waugh (Edited), *Civil Society in Central Asia,* Center for Civil

Society International (Washington, 1999), pp.58-60.
7. Ibid.
8. Ibid.
9. Thomas, Carother, "Democracy without Illusions", *Foreign Affairs*, January-February, 1997, p.17.
10. Ibid., p.18.
11. Martha Brill Olcott, *Kazakhstan: Unfulfilled Promise,* Washington DC: Carnegie Endowment for International Peace, 2002.
12. Juliana Geran Pilon, *Democratic Transition in Central Asia: An Assessment*, SAIS Review(1998). pp.89-103.
13. *Nazarbayev Speeches, On the Situation in the Country and major Directions of Domestic and Foreign Policy: Democratisation, Economic and Political Reform for the New Century: September 30, 1998.*
14. Ibid.
15. Ibid.
16. For a discussion of Central Asia's flawed democratic process see Gregory Gleason, "Asian Values and the Democratic Transition in Central Asia," (*Harvard Asia Quarterly*, May 2001).
17. *Nazarbayev Speeches, On the Situation in the Country and major Directions of Domestic and Foreign Policy: Democratisation, Economic and Political Reform for the New Century,* September 30, 1998.
18. Ibid.
19. For more details on the Constitutional Development in Kazakhstan, see Mukesh Kumar Mishra, "Constitutional Development in Independent Kazakhstan: A Review", *Himalayan and Central Asian Studies*, vol.12, nos. 3-4, July-December 2008, pp.115-129.
20. E. Curtis Glenn, *Kazakhstan: A Country Study* (Washington, Library of Congress 1996).
21. Ibid.
22. See Presidential Speech at http:www.president.kz
23. E. Curtis Glenn, *Kazakhstan: A Country Study* (Washington, Library of Congress 1996).
24. Ibid.
25. Kazakhstan and CIS Countries 1 (2000), p. 41.
26. Ibid.
27. Meruert Makhmutova, *Local Government in Kazakhstan*, at http://lgi.osi.hu/publications/2001/84/Ch8-Kazakstan.pdf.
28. D. Galyamova, "Division of Powers in Kazakhstan: Constitutional Experience of Independent Development", *Contemporary Central Asia*, vol.11, no.3, December 1998.
29. Ibid.
30. Anthony Clive Bowyer, "Parliament and Political Parties in Kazakhstan" *Silk Road Paper*, Washington DC: John Hopkins University – SAIS, 2008, p. 7.
31. Adel E. Abbishev, *Kazakhstan in Focus: Ten Years of Independence*. Almaty: Center for Foreign Policy and Analysis, 2002, p. 77.
32. Ibid., p.79.
33. Ibid., p.77.
34. Ibid.
35. Anthony Clive Bowyer, *Parliament and Political Parties in Kazakhstan*, Silk Road paper, May 2008.
36. Ibid.
37. Martha Brill Olcott, *The Kazakhs,* Hoover Institutions Press, 1995, p.143.
38. Olcott, *The Kazakhs*, p.140.
39. Anthony Clive Bowyer, Parliament and Political Parties in Kazakhstan, Central Asia-Caucasus Institute Silk Road Studies Programme, Silk Road Paper, May 2008, p. 12.

40. Eight additional deputies to be appointed by the President was added to the Constitution as part of the May 2007 constitutional amendments.
41. From Nur-Otan website, www.ndp-nurotan.kz
42. Interview with members of the Senate and Majilis, March 19, 2008.
43. Interview with Nur-Otan members, March 19, 2008.
44. IRI Public Opinion Survey, 2004.
45. IFES Public Opinion Survey in Kazakhstan, 1996.
46. Public Opinion Survey, Association of Sociologist and Politologists of Kazakhstan, December 2007, www.asip.kz
47. Interview with Dr. Bakytzymal Bekturganova, March 21, 2008.
48. Interview with members of the Senate and Majilis, March 19, 2008.
49. Interview with members of Nur-Otan, March 19, 2008.
50. Public Opinion Survey, Association of Sociologist and Politologists of Kazakhstan, December 2007, www.asip.kz.
51. www.dp-adilet.kz
52. Interview with Alikhan Baimenov, March 20, 2008.
53. Ibid.
54. Interview with Auyl party representatives, March 20, 2008.
55. Interview with Vladislav Kosarev, March 21, 2008.
56. Ibid.
57. Joanna Lillis, "Kazakhstan: Opposition Party Tries to Make a Fresh Start," Eurasia Insight, 4 March 2008.
58. Ibid.
59. Ibid.
60. Ibid.
61. Tuyakbai finished second in the 2005 presidential election with 6.61% of the vote.
62. Marat Yermukanov, "Election Authorities in Kazakhstan Warn of Balck PR Syndrome," *Central Asia-Caucasus Analyst*, 25 July 2007.
63. Marat Yermukanov, "Kazakh Opposition Forces Press Government For Genuine Democracy," *Central Asia-Caucasus Analyst*, 2 May 2007.
64. Barbara Junishbai, "Democratic Choice of Kazakhstan: A Case Study in Economic Liberalization, Intra-elite Cleavage, and the Political Opposition," Demokratizatsiya Heldref Publications, Summer 2005, p.6.
65. Barbara Junisbai, "Democratic Choice of Kazakhstan: A Case Study in Economic Liberalization, Intra-elite Cleavage, and the Political Opposition," Demokratizatsiya, Heldref Publications, Summer 2005, p.12.
66. Ibid, p.12.
67. Ibid, p.17.
68. Pannier, Bruce. "Kazakhstan: Can Opposition Compete In Presidential Elections?" RFE/RL Daily Report, August 22, 2005.
69. Barbara Junisbai, "Democratic Choice of Kazakhstan: A Case Study in Economic Liberalization, Intra-elite Cleavage, and the Political Opposition," Demokratizatsiya Heldref Publications, Summer 2005, p.15.
70. Freedom House, *Freedom in the World Report*, 2006.
71. OSCE/ODIHR, Report on the Presidential Elections in the Republic of Kazakhstan on December 4, 2005.
72. Ibid.
73. Ibid.
74. Ibid.
75. www.homestead.com/prosites-kazakhembus/Election-2005.html

76. Report OSCE, Office for Democratic Institutions and Human Rights, 2 August 2004.
77. Kassymzhomart K. Tokaev cited from OSCE Report, 2005.
78. See, International Helsinki Federation for Human Rights, Annual Report, 1999.
79. See Wolczuk, K., "Presidentialism in Ukraine: A Mid-Term Review of the Second Presidency", *Democratisation*, Vol. 4, No.3, 1997, pp.152-171.
80. "Kazakhstan President Nazarbayev wins re-election", 4 April 2011, http://www.bbc.co.uk/news/world-asia-pacific-12949853
81. RIA Novosti, Almaty, 3 April 2011.
82. David Witherspoon, "Nazarbayev Election Victory spells Economic stability, More Growth", http://www.kazakhstanlive.com/Documents/KazakhstanSpotlight.pdf
83. Ibid.
84. Ibid.
85. http://www.bbc.co.uk/news/world-asia-pacific-12949853
86. "Kazakhstan's Record on Human Rights, Democratisation and Fulfilling Its OSCE Chairmanship Commitments Executive Summary", June 10, 2008, at www.freedomhouse.org
87. Ibid.
88. Joanna Lillis, "Kiazakhstan Set to Have One-party Parliament Following Disputed Elections," Eurasianet, August 20, 2007, at http://www.eurasianet.org/departments/insight/articles/eavo82007.shtml (March 31, 2008).
89. Turgankulov, "Parliamentary Election in Kazakhstan and OSCE: Assessment, Reality and Outlook," Kazakhstanskaya Pravda, No.175, November 9, 2007 (Russian), at www.kazpravda.kz (December 18, 2008).
90. Rafis Abazov, "The Presidential Elections in Kazakhstan", *Contemporary Central Asia*, Vol. 3, No.2, 1999.
91. G.O. Donnell, "Delegative Democracy", *Journal of Democracy*, Vol.5, No.1, January1994, pp.55-56. Delegative Democracy is a form of democratic control whereby voting power is vested in delegates, rather than representatives. A general model of delegative democracy contains such principles as Choice of Role; Low Barrier to Participation; Delegated Authority; Privacy of the Individual; Accountability of the delegates; and Specialization by Re-Delegation. For more on these principles, see Bryan Ford, "Delegative Democracy", 15 May 2002 at http://www.brynosaurus.com/deleg/deleg.pdf
92. "Kazakhstan: OSCE Critical of Presidential Election", Report RFE/RL, 12 January 1999.

5

Powers of President

The creation of the new system of government in the Republic of Kazakhstan following independence in 1991 took place in three stages. Firstly, the Soviet era political system was disbanded within two years. Communist Party's dominance, the system of Soviets (representative bodies from the federal to the local level), and the Congress of People's Deputies were phased out. A second stage involved the implementation of a new constitution and a new system of government,[1] which also took two years. A revised constitution was adopted in August 1995 and there were elections to the new Parliament in December 1995. In a referendum in April 1995 the President's term of office was extended to 2000. Subsequently, in 1999, he was re-elected for a term that was to run until 2006. The constitutional changes made in 1995 strengthened Presidential powers. The third stage has been the period since August 1995 during which the new constitution has been in force. The 1995 Constitution is a long document with 98 articles. Section III of the constitution deals with the Presidency or the Institution of President.

Evolution of Institution of President

One of the most significant events of the 20th century was the disintegration of the Soviet political system. But transition to democracy in the Central Asian States including Kazakhstan had demonstrated systemic change and also continuity of this very process at the initial stage. Yet there are several experts who have opined that this process was not a sort of continuity, rather it was a combination of several phases with its own specificities.

After declaring its independence on 16 December 1991, Kazakhstan entered the first phase of transition in which fundamental changes in the former political and economic processes were expected. This was the phase of creation of a new political system wherein the first and then the second Constitution were adopted, presidential and parliamentary elections were held and democratic political institutions started to function. Consequently, Kazakh society was experiencing unique changes that were connected with several difficult transitions. Objective analysis of unprecedented social reforms in the post-Soviet states, including Kazakhstan, shows that the transition to democracy has not been a linear process rather it came along the possibilities of serious threats to the socio-political development of the country.

A distinctive feature of the constitutional development of independent Kazakhstan is that the reform in the whole political system being carried out by the state itself. It is noteworthy that Kazakhstan was able to avoid political crises which might have led to destabilisation of the Kazakh society. Clean and positive results have been achieved in Kazakhstan's evolutionary reformation of the political system with a Presidential system of rule.

The institution of President in Kazakhstan has been formed in an environment with a combination of political and economic systems.[2] Since then it has undergone evolution in many respects. The institution of President was introduced in the Constitution of 1993. It is true that the provisions of the first Constitution of independent Kazakhstan were so restrictive that it hardly had a Presidential form of rule in the classical sense.

On 30 August 1995, a national referendum was conducted which approved the new Constitution. The Constitution came into force on 5 September 1995, the day when the results of the referendum were published.[3] Kazakh scholars have rightly pointed out that as per the new Constitution the main feature of the system of rule in Kazakhstan is a strong Presidential system.[4] Commenting on the adoption of the new Constitution, the President of Kazakhstan, N.A. Nazarbayev himself declared:

> The Constitution of Kazakhstan, through its statutes, has laid the foundation of a strong Presidential Republic and division of authority between various branches of power. Institutions of civil society have been formed, human rights are being observed, mass media is working in a free atmosphere. The revived statehood of Kazakhstan forms the basis for building up democracy and a marked economy.[5]

Like other post-Soviet countries Kazakhstan also witnessed the formation of a national sovereign state along with their inclusion in the globalisation process. Radical transformation of social and economic systems was initiated even though there was lack of experience and absence of democratic traditions in society. Looking at the developments taking place in today's world, it must be admitted that globalisation has become an objective reality which is connected with the functioning of a world market economy as a system by itself. Globalisation is influencing not only the existing world order but rather it is also directly influencing the internal political scene and the role of the state in this entire process. It is desirable that any State should be capable of suitably reacting to new challenges and threats. Under conditions of globalisation, the State has to expand its role in socio-economic, political and other areas. It is only the State that can formulate and implement a long-term strategy for the development of the country and make it capable of facing challenges of the twenty-first century.

HOW TO BUILD A STRONG STATE?

One of the pertinent questions informing the process of nation building would be, "What are the conditions necessary for the transitional countries for building up a 'strong state' of such a kind? And secondly, how are they to be created?"

The process of building a strong state should start with strengthening of political institutions with Head of State as its centre with the wide powers. The Presidential system of rule by itself has several variations and flexibilities in well-tested democracies of the world. The Kazakh model of Presidential system of rule has acquired its present shape on the basis of the Constitution of 1995.

Presently, the President of Kazakhstan by his position does not have executive functions. His main prerogative is to decide the strategic directions of internal and foreign policies of the country. The Head of State has the right to interfere in the work of representative organ on matters of special importance by taking over legislative functions. That is, the constitutional set up of the Republic of Kazakhstan is such that the President is equidistant from the executive as well the legislature. In this sense, the Presidential system of Kazakhstan is an institution for ensuring harmonious functioning of all the branches of power and ensuring their responsibility to the people. In short, the President of Kazakhstan is an arbiter who maintains balance between various organs of powers.[6] While implementing the Presidential system of rule, certain adjustments have been made in division of power, keeping local conditions in mind.

Establishment of the Presidential system of rule in Kazakhstan has been borrowed as a foreign political and state institution. This system is functional in more than 63 countries of the world. In general, Presidential system in Kazakhstan has been successful during the period of important reforms, proved its worth and established stability. During the period of transition, a strong Presidential system was in a position to control contradictions that might have posed a threat to national harmony and political stability in Kazakhstan.[7]

Experience shows that a strong Presidential system is not an obstacle in the path of democracy. On the other hand, in France, as well in US, long democratic traditions do not permit anyone, including the President, to trample democracy. That is why many countries of the world are showing interest in the Presidential system. This political institution means that it is the President who ensures the integrity of the country, optimum and balanced functioning of the legislative, executive and judicial organs as well as being the arbiter in disputes. The greatest advantage of the Presidential system is that it facilitates a unified and stable executive power.

Further, Kazakhstan has used the 1958 model of the French Constitution. A comparative study of the constitutions of Kazakhstan and France shows that Kazakhstan can be called a mixed semi-Presidential Republic. It is important to recall that in France, the authors of the Constitution of 1958 initially wanted to give more powers to the President. But, later, they included in the Constitution several provisions which restricted the powers of the President. In this connection, French scholars introduced a new concept of "Presidentialisation" to explain the specific character of the state system in France. By "Presidentialisation" they mean more powers to the President while, simultaneously, strengthening democratic institutions of the society. The other feature of "Presidentialisation" is insulation of the post of President from individual temperament, political beliefs and other intentions of the person occupying this post.

The 1995 Constitution of the Republic of Kazakhstan, based on the French model, has given a different kind of status to the President of Kazakhstan. He is Head of State, holds the highest post, and is a symbol and guarantor as well as protector of the unity of peoples, of the Constitution, human rights and freedoms.[8] This high status of the President flows from the constitutional character of the country which has accepted the Presidential form of rule.

Further, the doctrine and practice of the Kazakh model of Presidential system is based on the principles of state power, namely, (a) political and lawful recognition of the universal norm of division of power, (b) adapting the constitutional experience of other countries according to the conditions of Kazakh society, (c) maintenance of political stability by means of legislative regulation of relations between different organs of state power and d)an independent legal authority.

Though the institution of President in Kazakhstan has a lot of potential for further growth, there is it still a need to rectify some of the provisions. In order to avoid a situation that may lead to misuse Presidential powers, candidature for the post of future President should be left to political parties. Secondly, it is necessary to develop stable democratic traditions among the citizens. The 1995 Constitution of Kazakhstan helped the country to make the transition to a real sovereign state, a modern, democratic economic order. It has become clear that this process is not a sort of continuity but a combination of different transition phases. Amendments and additions to the Constitution were initiated by the President himself. In May 2007, the Parliament of Kazakhstan passed these amendments and additions.[9]

A special feature of the amendments was that they were oriented towards the growth of Kazakhstan into an economically and democratically strong country. Implementation of these amendments in the Constitution will give further impetus to the economic progress achievements of Kazakhstan along with political stability.

The constitutional reforms have four directions, namely:

- giving more powers to the Parliament;

- more increased role of political parties in the life of the country;
- improving the judicial system and strengthening protection of human rights; and
- Strengthening of local self-government and Maslikhats in performing their functions.

The continuing process of democratic reforms calls for increased effectiveness in governance in the sense that organs of state should be able to respond adequately to the changes taking place within the country as well as outside its borders. Ensuring political stability essentially implies building up of a democratic political system which is legitimate and effective in governance.[10] Besides, the problem of comprehending socio-political processes to minimize risks to internal political stability and sustainable development of the Kazakh society and state itself is very complex. "Internal security would be long-lasting if it is consolidated by democratic changes in the political system."[11]

The President of Kazakhstan since independence has been Nursultan Nazarbayev. He demonstrated his statesmanship, determination and vision during this period, which witnessed the evolution of a Presidential democracy in Kazakhstan. Nazarbayev has been instrumental to provide political stability, social harmony and economic development. The President has expressed his commitment to develop free political institutions. Nazarbayev has a well set task before him to secure the territorial integrity, inviolability of the borders, and the sovereignty of the new state.[12] This has been done with a proactive and peaceful foreign policy by establishing good relations with all neighbors. The government of Nursultan Nazarbayev has signed 350 treaties in the ten years since independence in 1991. Treaties have been signed with all neighboring states as well as with other states and also the European Union. Important agreements were signed with China in 1994 and 1996 delineating common order and regulating cross-border trade etc. Kazakhstan signed the Nuclear Test Ban Treaty in 1994 and closed its semi-nuclear base. There has been a very strong commitment to global and regional security.

CONSTITUTIONAL PROVISIONS REGARDING PRESIDENT

Section III of the Constitution of Kazakhstan elaborates the powers of the President. As per constitution, the President of the Republic shall be elected by universal, equal and direct suffrage under a secret ballot for a seven-year term. The President heads the executive branch of government. Nazarbayev was originally elected as President in 1991 for a seven-year term, and had his term extended to 2000, but in 1999 presidential elections, he was re-elected for a seven year period to 2006 with 82 per cent of the total votes cast.[13] In December 2005 presidential elections, he was again elected. A citizen of the Republic is eligible for the office of the President of the Republic of Kazakhstan, if he is by birth not younger than forty and has a perfect command of the state language —Kazakh, and has lived in Kazakhstan for not less than fifteen years.[14] Regular elections of the President of the Republic are to be held on the first Sunday of the month of December and should not coincide with the election of a new Parliament of the Republic. The candidate who receives more than 50 per cent of the votes of the constituents that took part in the election shall be deemed elected. If none of the candidates receives the above number of votes, a second round of elections would be held between the two candidates who obtained the largest number of votes. The candidate who receives the larger number of votes of the people who take part in the second round of elections, is deemed to have been elected.[15]

According to Section III of the Constitution of Kazakhstan, the President of the Republic of Kazakhstan is the head of state, its highest official determining the main directions of the domestic and foreign policy of the state and representing Kazakhstan within the country and abroad. The President of the Republic is described as the symbol and guarantor of the unity of the people and the state power, inviolability of the Constitution, rights and freedoms of an individual and citizen. The President of the Republic is required to ensure by his arbitration concerted functioning of all branches of state power and responsibility of the institutions of power before the people.[16]

The President has two important tasks:

i) To create new political institutions within the framework of the written constitution, adopted in 1993, then endorsed by referendum in 1995. The Cabinet is appointed by him and is responsible to him. His continuity in office has been essential to the continuity of policy and the political stability of the country. The system of government is Presidential and Republican in a secular state. The strong executive has been the basis for social and political cohesion and one of the principal factors in Kazakhstan's socio-economic and political stability.

ii) To create a new national identity and to produce social harmony and peace. Having over a hundred ethnic groups, there is a strong potential of social and political discord in Kazakhstan. The President has placed the highest priority on ethnic peace and reconciliation as he did in 1995, "at every opportunity I try to persuade every Kazakhstani that our main treasure during the recent past is social stability and the absence of inter-ethnic discord and bloodshed".[17] He quotes the Kazakh proverb "Unity of power means to be on the eve of happiness."[18]

The President of the Republic of Kazakhstan takes office after swearing to the people the oath: "I solemnly swear that I will faithfully serve the people of Kazakhstan, strictly observe the Constitution and the laws of the Republic of Kazakhstan, guarantee the rights and freedoms of the citizens, honestly perform the high duties of the President of the Republic of Kazakhstan entrusted to me."[19] The oath is taken on the second Wednesday of the month of January in a ceremony in the presence of the deputies of Parliament, the members of the Constitutional Council, the judges of the Supreme Court as well as all former Presidents of the Republic. As stipulated by Article 48 of the Constitution, the oath is to be taken within one month since taking the powers of the President of the Republic.[20] The powers of the former President of the Republic terminate from the moment the newly elected President of the Republic takes office as well as in the case of premature release from office, resignation or death. All former Presidents of the Republic except those who were discharged from office would have the title of ex-President of the Republic of Kazakhstan.[21] The President of the Republic of Kazakhstan shall not have the right to be a deputy of a representative body, hold other paid offices and engage in entrepreneurial-activity.

TERMINATION OF PRESIDENT

The President of the Republic of Kazakhstan may be prematurely ousted from office in the case of his/her continued incapacity to perform duties due to illness. In this case, the Parliament shall form a Commission consisting of equal numbers of deputies from each Chamber and specialists of the respective areas. The decision of premature ouster based on the conclusion of the Commission and that of the Constitutional Council confirming observance of the established constitutional procedures is to be adopted at a joint sitting of the Parliament by the majority of no less than three-fourths from the total number of deputies of each Chamber.[22]

The President of the Republic is responsible for the actions performed while exercising his duties and only in the case of high treason may be discharged from office by Parliament. The decision to bring an accusation and conduct its investigation may be adopted by the majority of the deputies of the *Majilis* at the initiative of no less than one-third of the total number of its deputies. Investigation of the accusation shall be organised by the Senate and by the majority of votes of the total number of the deputies of the Senate. Its result is communicated are transferred for consideration at a joint session of the Parliament. The issue is finally decided at a joint session of the Parliament by the majority of no less than three-fourth of the total number of the deputies of each Chamber, provided the Supreme Court concludes the validity of the accusation and conclusion by the Constitutional Council that the established constitutional procedures were observed. The failure to arrive at a final decision within two months from the moment of the accusation would mean that the accusation against the President of the Republic is rejected. Rejection of the accusation of the President of the Republic in perpetration of high treason at any stage shall result in premature termination of the powers of the deputies of the *Majilis* who initiated the consideration of this issue. The issue of discharge of the President of the Republic from office may not be initiated in the period when the President is considering premature termination of the powers of the Parliament of the Republic.[23]

According to Article 48, in case of premature release or discharge of the President of the Republic of Kazakhstan from office as well as in case of his death, the powers of the President of the Republic shall be transmitted to the Chairperson of the Senate of the Parliament for the rest of the tenure; if the Chairperson of the Senate is unable to assume the powers of the President they shall be transmitted to the Chairperson of the *Majilis* of the Parliament; if the Chairperson of the *Majilis* is unable to assume the powers of the President they shall be transmitted to the Prime Minister of the Republic.[24] A person who has taken the powers of the President of the Republic shall correspondingly withdraw his powers of the Chairperson of the Senate, the *Majilis*, the Prime Minister. In this case filling of those state positions shall be carried out in the order, stipulated by the Constitution. A person who has taken the powers of the President of the Republic of Kazakhstan, as per Paragraph 1 of the article 53, has no right to initiate amendments and additions to the Constitution of the Republic of Kazakhstan.[25]

POWERS OF PRESIDENT

- The President of the Republic of Kazakhstan makes an annual address to the people of Kazakhstan explaining the state of affairs in the country and main directions of the domestic and foreign policy of the Republic of Kazakhstan;
- The President has the powers to announce regular and extraordinary elections to the Parliament of the Republic, convene the first session of Parliament and accept the oath of its members to the people of Kazakhstan, call extraordinary joint sessions of the Chambers of Parliament, sign laws submitted by the Senate of Parliament within fifteen working days, promulgate the law or return the law or its separate articles for a second discussion and vote. Parliament is bicameral with a lower house, the *Majilis*, of 77 deputies, 67 of whom are elected by constituencies, and ten are drawn under proportional representation from party lists. Deputies have a five-year term. The Upper House is having 47 members. Forty members are elected on the basis of two from each oblast and big city. And there are seven members appointed by the President. Senate members have a six year term with half the membership retiring every three years.[26] There is a built-in system of checks and balances. Parliament has the power of approval over the government programme, the budget, many appointments recommended by the President, and issues of war and peace. It can override the Presidential veto on legislation with a two-thirds majority; it can call for a referendum. A two thirds majority against the government programme counts as a vote of no confidence in the government;

- The President appoints a Prime Minister of the Republic with the Parliament's consent. He has the powers to remove him from office; determine the structure of the Government of the Republic as proposed by the Prime Minister, appoint to and release from office its members, as well as form, abolish and reorganise central executive bodies of the Republic which are not included into the Government; accept the oath of the members of the Government; preside at the meetings of the Government on important issues; charge the Government with bringing a bill into the *Majilis* of Parliament; annul or suspend completely or partially the effect of the Government's acts and those of the *Akims* of the oblasts, major cities and the capital;[27]
- The President appoints the Chairperson of the National Bank of the Republic of Kazakhstan with the Parliament's consent; removes him from office;
- The President appoints the Prosecutor General and Chairperson of the (Committee of National Security of the Republic with the consent of the Senate of Parliament; removes them from office;
- The President appoints and recalls the heads of diplomatic representative offices of the Republic;
- The President appoints the Chairperson and two members of the Estimation Committee for control over implementation of the Republican Budget for a five-year term;
- The President approves state programmes of the Republic;
- The President approves a unified system of financing and labor payment for all bodies financed by the state budget of the Republic at the proposal of the Prime Minister of the Republic;
- The President adopts measures on conducting the all-nation referendum.
- The President conducts negotiations and signs international treaties of the Republic; sign ratification instruments; receives letters of credentials and recall from diplomatic and other representatives of foreign states accredited to him.
- The President acts as the Commander-in-Chief of the Armed Forces of the Republic, appoints and replaces the highest command of the Armed Forces.[28]
- The President gives away awards and state decorations of the Republic and confers honorary, highest military and other ranks, ranked positions, diplomatic ranks and qualification degrees;
- The President resolves issues of citizenship of the Republic, and political asylum;
- The President grants pardon to citizens;
- In the event of a serious and immediate threat to the democratic institutions of the Republic, its independence and territorial integrity, political stability of the Republic, security of its citizens and the disruption of normal functioning of the Constitutional bodies of the state caused by a state of emergency on the entire territory or in particular areas of Kazakhstan, the President in consultation with the Prime Minister and Chairpersons of the

Parliamentary Chambers of the Republic takes measures, and immediately inform the Parliament of the use of the Armed Forces of the Republic;

- In the case of aggression against the Republic or immediate external threat to its security, the President shall impose martial law on the entire territory of the Republic or in particular areas declare a partial or total mobilisation and immediately inform the Parliament of the Republic to the effect;
- The President forms the Republican Guard as well as the Presidential Guard;
- The President appoints to and removes from office the State Secretary of the Republic of Kazakhstan, define his status and powers;
- The President forms the Security Council, the Higher Judicial Council and other consultative and advisory bodies;
- The President exercises other powers in accordance with the Constitution and the laws of the Republic.[29]

The President of the Republic of Kazakhstan, on the basis of and with the exercise of the Constitution and the laws, issues decrees and resolutions, which are binding on the entire territory of the Republic. As provided in the sub-paragraph IV of Article 53 of the Constitution, the President of the Republic issues laws, and in accordance with the provisions of the sub-paragraph II of Article 61 of the Constitution, the President or the Republic issues decrees having the force of laws in the Republic. The acts of Parliament signed by the President of the Republic as well as the acts of the President issued on the initiative of the Government are to be signed respectively by the Chairperson of each Parliament or the Prime Minister who is responsible for the legality of these acts. The President of the Republic of Kazakhstan, his honour and dignity shall be inviolable. Provisions, services, and guard of the President of the Republic and his family are borne by the state. This provision extends to ex-Presidents of the Republic as well.[30]

The constitution increased the powers of President Nazarbayev after the dissolution of Parliament in early 1995. It continues with the previous constitutional definition of Kazakhstan as a unitary state with a Presidential form of government. The President is the highest state officer, responsible for naming the government-subject to Parliamentary approval-and all other Republican officials. The 1995 constitution expanded the President's power to introduce and veto legislation. The government appointed by the President comprises the Council of Ministers, headed by a Prime Minister, and several state committees. Nazarbayev reshuffled the government in October 1995, and in early 1996, the Council of Ministers included the heads of twenty-one ministries and nine state committees with the Prime Minister as its head namely Akezhan Kazhegeldin. In a reshuffle in October 1995, Nazarbayev himself assumed the portfolio of the Minister of National Security.[31]

The new constitution does not provide for the position of Vice President, although it allowed the incumbent Vice President to be in his office. The President has the power to declare states of emergency during which the constitution can be suspended. The President is the sponsor of legislation and the guarantor of the constitution and of the proper functioning of government, with the power to override the decisions and actions of local authorities and councils.

Expansion of Presidential Powers by Parliament

A significant development related to the institution of President is that Kazakhstan's parliament made legislative changes through constitutional amendment on 13 May 2010 that bestowed new powers on President Nursultan Nazarbayev. In addition to granting Nazarbayev the title of "leader of the nation," he now gained the right to intervene in politics after he officially retires from the presidency and would enjoy enhanced immunity from prosecution.[32] Parliamentary deputies promoting the amendments, argues that Nazarbayev occupies a special role in Kazakhstan's national psyche. They defended him for his role in shaping Kazakh statehood since independence in 1991, and commended him for successfully steering the country out of the ruins of Communist central planning and transforming it into an energy-rich regional economic powerhouse. For example: As quoted by the state controlled *Kazakhstanskaya Pravda* newspaper Svetlana Ferkho, the Member of Parliament told the *Mazhilis* (lower house) on May 5, 2013 that "I believe the achievements of our president give us the right to acknowledge him as leader of the nation, and that status needs to be legislatively enshrined,". She went on to compare Nazarbayev to historical figures who are viewed as the fathers of their respective countries: "Nursultan Nazarbayev ranks with such great personalities as George Washington, Mustafa Kemal Ataturk, and Mahatma Gandhi, who in the interests of their states did truly historic deeds and remained in the memories of their people for eternity". Further, Deputy Amzebek Zholshibekov said that the legislation would grant Nazarbayev a political role even after he retires. In effect, he would retain de facto veto authority over state policy. "The draft law stipulates the need to agree with the first president and leader of the nation [on] initiatives that are being elaborated in the main directions of the state's foreign and domestic policy," Zholshibekov said in his remarks quoted by the Kazakhstan Today news agency.

Nazarbayev, who has been at the helm of Kazakhstan since becoming first secretary of the Soviet republic's Communist Party in 1989, was already exempted from term limits following a controversial constitutional amendment introduced in May 2007. Today he enjoys a genuine measure of public popularity as his administration has been successful in keeping public dissatisfaction in check. However, critics say that the legislative amendments contradict the principle that everyone should be equal before the law. Many who lobbied in favor of Kazakhstan's OSCE chairmanship in 2010 argued that granting it to Astana would encourage political liberalisation. Skeptics, however, said that the chairmanship has instead given Astana a green light to cement a fairly constricted political status quo in place. The administration's actions "prove the correctness of those who predicted that awarding Nazarbayev the OSCE chairmanship while commitments were not fulfilled would be assessed as carte blanche for anything to be permitted," wrote columnist Sergey Duvanov, a fierce Nazarabayev critic, in a commentary posted on the Respublika news website on May 6, 2013.[33]

Legislature

The 1993 constitution created a unicameral Parliament, which was to replace the 350-member Supreme Soviet when their term expired in 1995. Composed mainly of career communists, the 1990 Parliament was a difficult partner in the task of economic and political reform. Nazarbayev pressured this Parliament into a "voluntary" early dissolution in December 1993 in order to allow the elections of a smaller and presumably more pliant "professional Parliament".[34] Under the 1995 constitution, the Parliament consists of two houses, the Senate and the *Majilis*, both operating in continuous sessions. Each of Kazakhstan's fourteen provinces and the city of Almaty, which has province status, has two Senators, who are chosen for four-year terms by joint sessions of the provincial legislative bodies. An additional seven senators are appointed directly by the President. In addition, ex-Presidents automatically receive the status of senators-for-life. The *Majilis* has 67 representatives, including one from each of fifty-five districts drawn to have roughly equal populations, and the Senate has forty seats. Direct elections for half the seats are held every two years. In the first election under the new Parliamentary structure, all seats in both the houses of Parliament were contested in December 1995; runoff elections filled twenty-three seats in the *Majilis* for which the initial vote was inconclusive.[35] The new Parliament, which was seated in January 1996, included sixty-eight Kazak and thirty-one Russian deputies; only ten deputies were women. The initiative for most legislative actions originates with the President. If Parliament passes a law that the President vetoes, a two-thirds vote of both houses is required to override the veto. A similar margin is needed to express no confidence in a Prime Minister, an action that requires the President to name a new Prime Minister and Council of Ministers.[36]

Judiciary

The judicial system is the least developed of three branches of the Kazakh government. Although Minister of Justice, Nagashibay Shaykenov objected strenuously, the constitution retains the practice of Presidential appointment of all judges in the republic. The 1993 constitution specified terms of service for judges, but the 1995 document makes no mention of length of service, suggesting that judges will serve at the President's pleasure.

Under the 1993 constitution, lines of judicial authority were poorly defined, because the Republic had three "highest courts" such as the Supreme Court, the

State Arbitrage Court, and the Constitutional Court which among them employed a total of sixty six senior judges. Many of these senior judges as well as numerous judges in lower courts, had been retained from the Soviet era, when the judicial branch was entirely under the control of the Central government. The 1995 constitution makes no provision for the State Arbitrage Court. Provisions for the new judiciary clearly subordinate all other courts to the Supreme Court, which has a consultative role in appointing senior judges.[37] Ministers are not allowed to sit in Parliament as is the case in the US system of government. They are responsible to the Prime Minister. If they do not agree with government policy they are bound to resign under Article 68 of the Constitution.[38]

According to the Constitution, the President proposes to the Upper House of Parliament (the Senate) nominees for the Supreme Court. Specifically nominees are recommended by the Supreme Judicial Council, which includes the Chairperson of the Constitutional Council, the Chairperson of the Supreme Court, the Prosecutor General, the Minister of Justice, Senators, judges, and other persons appointed by the President. The President appoints *oblast* judges (nominated by the Supreme Judicial Council) and local level judges from a list presented by the Ministry of Justice. The list is based on recommendations from the Qualification Collegium of Justice, an institution made up of deputies from the Lower House of Parliament (the *Majilis*), judges, public prosecutors, legal experts, and Ministry of Justice officials.

The President appoints the Collegium's Chairman. Under the law, judges are appointed for life, although in practice this means until the mandatory retirement age of 65 years. Under a 1995 Presidential decree, the President may remove judges, except members of the Supreme Court or chairmen of judicial collegia, on the recommendation of the Minister of Justice. The Minister's recommendations must be based on findings by either the Supreme Judicial Council or the Qualification Collegium of Justice that the judge failed to, or was no longer capable of, performing his duties. The President can request, based upon recommendations from the Supreme Judicial Council, that the Senate remove members of the Supreme Court or chairpersons of Judicial Collegium, which are judicial councils that judges serve on at the local, city, *oblast* and Supreme Court levels.

The Constitution abolished the Constitutional Court and established Constitutional Council in 1995. The Council makes rules on election and referendum challenges, interprets the Constitution, and determines the constitutionality of laws adopted by Parliament.[39] The President directly appoints three of its seven members, including the Chairman, and has the right to veto the Council decisions. The Council may overturn a Presidential veto if at least two-thirds (five) of its members vote to do so. Therefore, at least one Presidential appointee must vote to overturn the President's veto in order for the Council to overrule the President. Citizens do not have the right to appeal to the Council regarding the constitutionality of government actions, although they were allowed to make such appeals to the former Constitutional Court. Under the Constitution, only the President, Chairperson of the Senate, Chairperson of the *Majilis*, Prime Minister, one-fifth of the members of Parliament, or a Court of Law may appeal to the Constitutional Council.[40] The Constitution states that a court shall appeal to the Council if it "finds that a law or other regulatory legal act subject to application undermined the rights and liberties of an individual and a citizen."[41] The Constitution and the law establish the necessary procedures for a fair trial. Trials are public with the exception of instances in which an open hearing could result in state secrets being divulged, or when the private life or personal family concerns of a citizen must be protected. If a defendant cannot afford an Attorney, the Constitution rules that the Government must provide one free of charge.[42]

According to the Constitution, defendants have the right to be present, the right to counsel, and the right to be heard in court and call witnesses for the defence. Defendants enjoy a presumption of innocence, are protected from self-incrimination, and have the right to appeal against a decision to a higher court. Legal proceedings are conducted in the state language, Kazakh, although Russian may also be used officially in the courts. Proceedings also may be held in the language of the majority of the population in a particular area.[43]

The concentration of powers in the presidency, the presence in the Parliament of powerful, regime-connected financial interests, and the prevalence of personal patronage over formal rules have contributed to the continuing subordination of the judiciary to political interests. Kazakhstan's judicial system has deficit of its credibility by acting in full compliance with the regime's interests rather than stepping in to protect civil liberties. The local courts have been accused of many procedural and politically motivated charges. Though Kazakhstan has revoked the death penalty, it has not passed an amended Law on Life Sentences. The Supreme Court has refused to review the case against a prominent opposition leader Ghalymzhan Zhakiyanov, who remains in jail since April 2003 on politically motivated charges of corruption despite serious allegations of torture.

Recent "Colour Revolutions" in the former Soviet republics of Georgia, Ukraine, and Kyrgyzstan have revitalized the opposition and civil society. There has been speculation of discord within the regime between Nazarbayev and the *Asar* party of his daughter Dariga Nazarbayeva and her husband, Rakhat Aliev, between *Otan* and the *Civil Party*, and between the two sons-in-law of Nazarbayev. These growing signs of competition and discord among pro-regime groups as well as within the Presidential family, possible defections of some regime associates to the opposition and the uprising in Kyrgyzstan have the potential to unite the opposition for putting up a common front against President Nazarbayev and his regime.

ROLE OF NURSULTAN NAZARBAYEV AS PRESIDENT

In December 1991, Nursultan Nazarbayev became the first elected President of Kazakhstan, for a five-year term of office, enjoying extensive personal powers which included the authority to appoint and dismiss officials at the all levels and to issue decrees counteracting laws passed by the Parliament. It was during the Soviet period that Nazarbayev had been appointed to the post of Chairman of the Council of Ministers (head of Government) of Kazakhstan in 1984, and subsequently to that of First Secretary of the Communist Party of Kazakhstan in 1989.[44] He introduced political and administrative reforms in September 1989, including the introduction of extra-executive duties for the Chairman of the Supreme Soviet of Kazakhstan.[45] He was duly elected to this post in February 1990, thus becoming, the *de facto* head of state. He was elected to the newly created post of President by the Supreme Soviet in April 1990.

On 1 December 1991, he was the sole candidate in a general election to the Presidency, in which he secured the support of 98.8 per cent of the total votes cast.[46] In November 1993, President Nazarbayev announced plans for a reform of the Supreme *Kenges*, the legislative body that had been inherited from the Soviet period. He proposed that the number of seats should be halved from the current total of 360, and also that the new deputies should receive a salary and devote themselves full-time to Parliamentary work. The Supreme *Kenges* thereupon agreed to dissolve itself in December 1993, in preparation for elections to the new Parliament, and on 7 March 1994 elections to the new Parliament were held.[47] Of the 177 seats in the new Parliament, 42 had to be chosen from a specially selected list of Presidential nominees. Deputies who were critical of government policies won only 23 seats. The ethnic mix of the new legislative body was tilted in favour of the Kazakh population, with some two thirds of the new deputies being drawn from the titular people, although within the population as a whole the Kazakhs represented less than half the total.[48] When the new Parliament was convened in April 1994, President Nazarbayev promised that more constitutional safeguards would be introduced. He indicated that there would be a clearer definition of the conditions under which the President could be impeached, or Parliament be dissolved. However, government strengthened its control on the state television and radio. A new decree was passed that gave the President the right to appoint the head of the organisation for radio and television.[49]

Centralisation under the President is certainly a characteristic of the Kazakh system of government. The party system is developing slowly. The largest party is the *Otan* or *Fatherland Party* and then there are a number of smaller parties in a multi-party system. Control over the regions is provided by government appointed *Akims* or regional governors. Each of the 14 regions has an elected council. The emphasis has been on dynamic Presidential leadership necessitated by prolonged crisis management and on the need to push ahead rapidly with reform and restructuring. The President has constantly emphasized the need for unity,[50] which is necessary for protecting the vital interests of Kazakhstan in its period of transition. With two powerful neighbours, Russia with a population of 150 million and China with a population of over 1.2 billion, and with powerful multinational corporations deeply involved in the economy of the country, Kazakhstan with its population of under 16 million inhabitants scattered across a vast area, requires strong leadership in keeping the country united and stable.

In March 1994, Kazakhstan held Parliamentary elections that created the first post-independence national Parliament (until that election, the republican Supreme Soviet deputies elected in 1989, despite its disbanding, remained in office). Seventy-two of the new 177-member lower house were directly linked to the President, whose *Union of Popular Unity* (SNEK) won 30 seats, while candidates from a Presidential list filled forty-two of the seats.[51] The Constitutional Court ruled in March 1995 that the 1994 general elections that had created the Parliament were unconstitutional. In response, Parliament voted to suspend the Constitutional Court. Within days, President Nazarbayev dissolved the Parliament, and ruled for the rest of 1995 by a Presidential decree. In March 1995, the President decreed several amendments purportedly "to strengthen the fight against organised crime," but actually to create additional legal safeguards to prevent organised opposition to the disbanding of Parliament. Among the amendments was one "outlawing any participation in an as yet unregistered public association (Article, 188) or an association that has been suspended or closed."[52] Penalties included up to fifteen days, or fine of from five to ten times the minimum monthly wage. In another referendum in August 1995, 89 per cent of the total voters supported a draft constitution vastly expanding Presidential powers.[53]

A legislation passed in June 2000 allowed the President to maintain certain policy prerogatives and a seat on the National Security Council after he leaves office. The Constitution limits Parliament's powers by precluding it from appropriating state money or lowering taxes without the approval of the executive. However, Members of Parliament (MPs) have the right to introduce legislation, and some bills introduced by MPs have become laws. Parliamentary elections held in October 1999 were an improvement on the Presidential election.[54] The Committee for National Security (KNB) is responsible for national security, intelligence, and counterintelligence. The KNB also plays a law enforcement role in border security, internal security, and anti-terrorism efforts, and oversees the external intelligence service, Barlau. The chairman of the KNB reports directly to the President. The Ministry of Interior (MVD) supervises the criminal police, who are poorly paid and are widely believed to be corrupt. The KNB continued efforts to improve its public image by focusing on fighting corruption, religious extremism, terrorism, illegal arms exports, and organised crime.[55] The Constitution also provides for the protection of the dignity of the President, and the law prohibits insulting the President and other officials. Media outlets generally practice self-censorship regarding information on the President and his family in order to avoid possible legal action.

However, media outlets freely published detailed reports in 2000 on allegations against Rakhat Aliyev, the President's son-in-law, and first Deputy Chairman of the KNB. The Aliyev affair provided an opportunity for the public criticism of the President's immediate family. Aliyev filed libel lawsuits against *Internews*, The *Globe*, *Novaya Gazyeta*, *Yevrasia Website*, and *Aziopa Website*. A libel provision of the new Media Law, which was enacted on April 16, 2000,[56] held owners, editors, distributors, and journalists responsible for content and promotes self-censorship at each level.

There is no doubt that Independence and sovereignty of Kazakhstan is directly related with the name of the First President of Kazakhstan Nursultan Nazarbayev. For over twenty years the political leadership of the republic have been pursuing a multi-vector foreign policy on the background of successful and dynamic development, national and cultural revival of the Kazakh people, political reforms and formation of a modern social and economic model. The foreign policy strategy of the President enabled the republic to posture itself in the international arena. Kazakhstan plays a significant role in the world politics and economy due to its membership in a great number of international organisations and friendly and constructive partnership relations with all countries within international community. The dissent role of Kazakhstan is reorganised internationally and its Chairmanship in the Commonwealth of Independent States (CIS), Shanghai Cooperation Organisation (SCO), Eurasian Economic Community (EurAsEC), Organisation for Security and Cooperation in Europe (OSCE), and the forthcoming Chairmanship on the 38th session of the Council of foreign Minister of the Organisation of Islamic Cooperation (CFM OIC) in June 2011 prove that. Moreover, a number of global initiatives made by President Nazarbayev have been acknowledged by the world community.

Earlier, Kazakhstan's admission as a member of the United Nations Organisation (UNO) on March 2, 1992 was one of the important stages in formation of the Kazakhstan foreign policy. The 47th session of the United Nations General Assembly (UNGA) became the first international forum where Kazakhstan participated as an independent state headed by President Nazarbayev. This event had a great historical importance for Kazakhstan as Nazarbayev delivered a speech on October 5, 1992 in UNGA touching upon the issues of systematic changes in the world community. He made a number of initiatives, namely he proposed the 'one plus one' formula as the basis for the UN peacemaking efforts. The initiative to establish the Conference on Interaction and Confidence-building Measures in Asia (CICA) in particular is worth mentioning.

The Kazakhstan OSCE Chairmanship in 2010 became a triumph for Kazakhstan's diplomacy. The President of Kazakhstan proposed to hold the OSCE Summit in Astana. Personal authority of the Kazakhstan leader was one of the reason that the summit in Astana was held at the highest international level. The final document approved by the Summit covered the major directions of the world development towards maintenance of international peace and stability in the Euro-Atlantic and Eurasian regions. The Astana Commemorative Declaration 'Towards a Security Community' confirmed once again the principle of indivisible nature of security. The CICA initiative of Nazarbayev is increasingly acknowledged in the world community for being significant for formation of the international security system on regional and global levels. The idea was lately transformed into providing a suitable "platform" for international consultations on Asian security issues and became an integral part of the new global world order. In April 2010, the Kazakh President suggested that the world community would take the actions aimed at practical implementation of the measures to enhance global nuclear security system, in the course of the Global Nuclear Security Summit in Washington. In particular, Nazarbayev proposed to elaborate an effective mechanism to monitor the distribution and usage of radioactive materials conducted by the United Nations special institutions in order to increase the responsibility of all the parties of international relations having an access to nuclear technologies and power engineering.

At present, people of over 130 ethnic backgrounds and more than 46 confessions live in peace and consent in Kazakhstan. The uniqueness and effectiveness of the Kazakhstan model of harmonious multi-ethnic society is internationally recognised. In addition, the Congress of World Religions initiated by Nazarbayev is regularly held in Astana being a unique in the history of development of the world culture and religion. This is a positive example of cultural and equitable dialogue on inter-confessional understanding in the changing world. The main characteristic and key values of the policy pursued by the President are peace, consent, tolerance and stability. Following this policy the inter-ethnic and inter-confessional peace became the key elements of development of Kazakhstan over the years of its independence. As the world experience shows, the national interests are best met via collective adherence of sovereignty in the contemporary global environment of increasing interdependence. Therefore, Nazarbayev considers the regional integration as one of the most effective ways to address the threats and challenges of economic globalisation and to retain a strong position in the world. He is paying due regard to the development of foreign relations of Kazakhstan and Islamic world on the basis of the national interests and generally recognised norms of international law. Great opportunities and new prospects especially in economic sphere are opened in mutual relations with the countries of the Asia-Pacific region and Latin America.

Thus, the role of Nazarbayev as the President of Kazakhstan is multifaceted as he greatly contributed to the development of mutually beneficial cooperation and constructive relations with the international organisations, regional associations and other countries. It is significant to note here that for more than twenty years in Kazakhstan's independent development there has been no change in its foreign policy priorities, and the credit goes to the charismatic personality of Nazarbaev.[57]

NOTES

1. Country Reports on Human Rights Practice, 1999, p.27.
2. Zakon Kazakhskoi SSR, "Ob uchrezhdeniiposta Prezidenta Kazakhskoi SSR ivneseniiizmeneniiidopolnenii v Konstitutsiyu Kazakhskoi SSR".
3. Konstitutsiya Respubliki Kazakhstan 1995 goda, Almaty,1995.
4. See Nurpeisov E.K., Kotov A.K. Gosudarstvo Kazakhstan: otkhanskoivlasti-k prezidentskoirespublike. Almaty, 1995, p. 67.
5. Nazarbayev N.A. Na porog xx1 veka. Almaty: Oner,1998, p.165.
6. Konstitutsiya Respubliki Kazakhstan, 1995 goda, Almaty, 1995.
7. Akimbekov S. Syroezhkin K. Respublika Kazakhstan: poiskputeiustoichivovorazvitiya // Tsentralnaya Aziyai Kavkaz, 1999, No.2, p.121.
8. Konstitutsiya Respubliki Kazakhstan 1995 goda, Almaty, 1995, Article 48.
9. Zakon Respubliki Kazakhstan. O vneseniiizmeneniiidopolnenii v Konstitutsiya Respubliki Kazakhstan// Kazakhstanskaya Pravda. 22 May 2007.
10. Bizhanov A.KH. Stabilnost v Kazakhstane: sostoyanieiproblemy// Kazakhstan-spektr, 2005, No.1, p.19.
11. Poslanie Prezidenta RK Nursultan Nazarbayevanarodu Kazakhstana "Strategiyavkhozhdeniya Kazakhstana v chislopyatidesyatinaiboleekokurentosposobnykhstanmira" //Mysl. 2006, No. 3, pp.2-18.
12. Martha Brill Olcott; "Kazakhstan," *Collier Encyclopedia* (New York: Macmillan, Vol. 14, 1993), p.7.
13. "Kazakhstan's Presidential Campaign Found Grossly Unfair," press release, Human Rights Watch/Europe and Central Asia Division, 5 January 1999.
14. www.missions.itu.int, Permanent Mission of the Republic of Kazakhstan.
15. Ibid.
16. The Constitution of the Republic of Kazakhstan, Article 40, p. 9.
17. Ibid.
18. Interview of Prof. Kozhakhmetov Kenes Kozhakhmetovich, Department of History (Al-Farabi Kazakh National University, Almaty, 2006).
19. Interview of Prof. Kozhakhmetov Kenes Kozhakhmetovich, n. p.3.
20. Ibid.
21. The Constitution of the Republic of Kazakhstan, Article 42, p.12.
22. Ibid.
23. Ibid., pp.13-14.
24. Ibid., Article 48, pp.15-16.
25. Ibid.
26. The Constitution of the Republic of Kazakhstan, n.5, pp.15-16.
27. Ibid., p.16.
28. The Constitution of the Republic of Kazakhstan, Articles 44, pp.13-14.
29. Ibid., pp.12-13.

30. The Constitution of the Republic of Kazakhstan 1995, Articles 44, p.14.
31. Glenn E. Curtis, *Kazakhstan A Country Study*, Federal Research Division Library of Congress, Washington, p.56.
32. Jay Carmella, "Kazakhstan approves constitutional amendment to increase presidential powers", Jurist, 13 May 2013, http://jurist.org/paperchase/2010/05/kazakhstan-approves-constitutional-amendments-to-increase-presidential-powers.php
33. Joanna Lillis is a freelance writer who specializes in Central Asia, May 10, 2010 eurasianet.org
34. The Constitution of the Republic of Kazakhstan, 1993, Article 62, p. 11.
35. Ibid.
36. Ibid., pp.11-12
37. Ibid.
38. The Constitution of the Republic of Kazakhstan, 1993, Article 68, p.13.
39. Frederic Starr, "Democratisation in Central Asia: the public's view," (*Central Asia Institute Briefing Paper*), The Paul H. Nitze School of Advanced International Studies, 1997.
40. Ragov, Igor, Ivanovich (Formation and development of the Constitutional control in the Republic of Kazakhstan*)*, www.const council.kz/eng/
41. The Constitution of the Republic of Kazakhstan, 1993, Article 43, p.8.
42. Ibid.
43. Ibid.
44. Shirin Akiner, Kazakhstan An Overview. UNHCR Emergency & Security Service (Council of the European Union: Brussels, 18 June 2002), p.7.
45. Ibid., p.7.
46. Ibid., n.14, p.7
47. Ibid.
48. Ibid.
49. Ibid.
50. D. Galyamova, "Division of Powers in Kazakhstan: Constitutional Experience of Independent Development" (Contemporary Central Asia), Vol.2, No.3.
51. Ibid., p.3.
52. Shirin Akiner, n.14, p.8.
53. Organization for Security and Co-operation in Europe (OSCE) Report, Almaty: 1998.
54. Ibid.
55. According to UNDP Report, Almaty: 1999.
56. United Nation Development Report, Almaty: 2000.
57. For more details, see Bulat Auelbayev, "President of the Republic of Kazakhstan N. Nazarbayev and Foreign Policy of Kazakhstan", Central Asia's Affairs, No. 3, 2011, pp.15 17.

6

Civil Society in Kazakhstan

In a democracy, the civil society works as a cushion against authoritarianism and a propellant for liberalism. The idea of state support for civil society gained momentum after President Nursultan Nazarbayev announced his ideas for cooperation between the government and civil society at the Civic Forum that took place in October 2003 in Astana. Now the authorities acknowledged that civil society is beneficial for the government, and that cooperation between the two sectors should include state support of social activities of Civil Society Organisations (CSOs).[1]

THEORETICAL CONSTRUCT ON CIVIL SOCIETY

Modern political thought from Hobbes to Hegel is marked by a constant tendency to consider "the state or political society, in relation to the state of nature (or natural society), as the supreme and definitive stage in the common and collective life of humanity perceived as a rational entity, as the most perfect or least imperfect result of that process of rationalisation of the instincts or passions or interests via which the rule of uncoordinated force is transformed into one of coordinated liberty."[2]

The state is conceived as a product of reason, or as a rational society, the only one in which human beings can lead a life which conforms to reason, that is, which conforms to their nature. This conception merges and fuses both the realist theories.[3] Theories of natural law (from Hobbes to Rousseau and Kant) propose ideal models of the state, defining how a state should be in order to realize its true purpose.[4] The process of rationalisation of the state (the state as rational society), which is characteristic of theories of natural law, merges with the process of 'statisation' of reasons, which is characteristic of theories of the reason of state.[5] In Hegel, who represents the decisive break with this tradition of political thought as well as its culmination, the two processes are synthesized, so that in the Philosophy of Right, the rationalisation of the state achieves its ultimate expression for an ideal model, but as the key to understanding the real movement of history.[6] Rationality of state is no longer just a necessity but a reality, not just an ideal but a historical event.[7] Karl Marx showed a deep insight into this feature of Hegel's philosophy of right when he wrote in an early comment: "Hegel is not to be blamed for depicting the nature of the modern state as it is, but for presenting that which exists as the essence of the state".[8] The rationalisation of the state came about through the constant use of a dichotomic model, where the state is conceived as a positive moment in contrast to a pre-state or anti-state society, which is relegated to a negative moment. One can distinguish, even if in a rather schematic way, three principle variants of this model: the political state as a radical negation which, therefore, eliminates and overthrows the state of nature that is as a renewal, compared to the phase of human development which precedes the state (Hobbes-Rousseau).[9]

With Hegel, the process of rationalisation of the state reaches the highest point of the parabola. In those same years, with the works of Saint Simon, which took account of the profound transformation of society resulting not from political revolution but from the Industrial Revolution and predicted the coming of a new order which would be regulated by scientists and industrialists as opposed to the traditional order upheld by metaphysicians and the military, the parabola had begun its decline and the theory, or simply the belief (the myth), of the inevitable withering away of the state began to be formulated. This belief was to become a characteristic feature of the political ideologies prevalent in the nineteenth century.[10] Marx and Engels would use it as one of the central ideas of their thesis: the state is no longer the reality of the ethical idea, the rational per se, but according to the famous definition in *Das Capital* it is the 'concentrated and organised violence of society. The antithesis to the tradition of the philosophy of natural law which culminated in Hegel could not be more complete. In contrast to the first model, the state is no longer conceived as an elimination of the state of nature but rather as its conservation, prolongation and stabilisation. In the state, the reign of force has not been suppressed but perpetuated, with the only difference that the war of all against all has now been replaced by a way of one side against the other (class struggle, of which the state is the expression and instrument). In contrast with the second model, the society in which the state is the supreme ruler is not a natural society, which conforms to the eternal nature of humanity, but a historically determined society characterized by certain forms of production and certain social relations. Therefore, the state, as an institution of the dominant class, instead of being the expression of a universal and rational need is both the repetition and reinforcement of particularistic interests. Finally, in contrast to the third model, the state is no longer presented as the transcendence of civil society but merely as its reflection: as civil society is, so is the state. The state incorporates civil society not in order to transform into something else but to keep it as it is; civil society, which is historically determined, does not disappear into the state but reappears in the state in all its concrete manifestations. From this three-fold antithesis, one can derive the three basic elements of Marx and Engels' Doctrine of the State:

- The state as a coercive apparatus or as the 'concentrated and organised violence of society': an instrumental conception of the state, which is the opposite of the ethical or finalistic one.
- The state as an instrument of class domination, where 'the executive of the modern State is but a committee for managing the common affairs of the whole bourgeoisie': a particularistic conception of the state as opposed to the universalistic conception characteristic of all the theories of natural law including Hegel's.
- The state as a secondary or subordinate phenomenon in relation to civil society where 'it is not the State which conditions and regulates civil society, but it is civil society which conditions and regulates the State': a negative conception of the state which is in complete opposition to the positive conception found in rationalistic thought.

GRAMSCI'S CONCEPT OF CIVIL SOCIETY

Gramsci's theory introduces a profound innovation with respect to the whole Marxist tradition. Civil Society, according to Gramsci, does not belong to the structure, but to the super-structure. In spite of the many analyses that have been made in the last few years of Gramsci's concept of civil society, it seems that this fundamental point, upon which his conceptual system hinges, has not been sufficiently stressed. Gramsci cites a major historical example: civil society in the Middle Age is the Church understood as 'the hegemonic apparatus of the ruling group, which did not have its own apparatus, i.e. cultural and intellectual organisation, but regarded the universal, ecclesiastical organisation as being that.[11] For Gramsci, civil society comprises not 'all material relationships', but all ideological-cultural relations; not 'the whole of commercial and industrial life', but the whole of spiritual and intellectual life. According to Marx and Gramsci, civil society, and not the state as in Hegel, represents the active and positive stage of historical development. However, in Marx this active and positive stage is structure, while in Gramsci, it is superstructure.

Gramsci derives his thesis concerning civil society from Hegel and sees it as belonging to the super structural sphere and not to the structural. On the other hand, Marx also involves Hegel's civil society when he identifies civil society with all economic relations, that is, with the structural sphere.[12]

Hegel stresses on the institutions which regulate them, the corporations, which as Hegel says, along with the family, constitute 'the ethical root of the state, the one planted in civil society',[13] which he calls elsewhere 'the firm foundation of the State', the pillars of public freedom'. In short, the civil society which Gramsci has in mind when he refers to Hegel is the final stage, when the organisation and regulation of the various interests (the corporations) provide the basis for the transition towards the state.[14]

RELATIONS BETWEEN STATE AND CIVIL SOCIETY

A paper prepared by John Beauclerk (Programme Manager, Eastern Europe) and Simon Heap (Senior Researcher) examines global trends in civil society-state engagements and presents the simplistic model of State-Civil Society relations and a more complex dynamic model looking at both the oppositional and complimentary tendencies of the relationship.[15] Major global economic and political trends show that the Civil Society-State nexus is a fundamental driver for social development, democracy-building and economic delivery. Some argue that civil society is a bulwark against government; others see it as an indispensable support for government. In terms of the role of a strong civil society in relation to the state and formal power and authority, there are two contrasting schools of thought. One views the relationship as essentially oppositional, antagonistic and conflicting. This notion is found inWestern liberal thought in which the Civil Society is seen as the means by which individuals are protected from incursion of the state and by which state power is limited. This view puts forth the argument that the civil society must be strengthened in order to serve as a buttress against the state and to redress the massive imbalance between state and citizen power.[16]

A second view sees Civil Society and the State as mutually interdependent and complementary rather than as antagonistic. This view regards Civil Society and the State as neither fully autonomous nor fully self-sufficient. According to this view, Civil Society[17] strengthening cannot be done independently of the State and certainly not at the expense of the State (Clayton 1996).[18] This thesis, originally developed by de Tocqueville and, updated for the contemporary world by Robert Putnam (1993), postulates that democratic government is strengthened, not weakened, when it faces a vigorous civil society. In countries, where the State is relatively weak and fragile, the second view may be more appropriate in order to promote long-term democratic governance.[19]

A weak State will not be able to provide political stability and legislative framework in which a civil society can develop. The Static Model offers a broad analysis of state-civil society relationships. It, however, does not provide the concepts of multiple levels of relationship with the state according to particular circumstances, nor says anything about the modalities of joint work, nor allows civil society actors to assess their particular situations and plan their moves accordingly. One need not emphasise that civil society actors work in a range of circumstances, adapting their strategies to need and to the space available to them. Fowler analyses the characteristics and functions of civil society in terms of the ability of actors to choose a purpose or role in society (varying between service and reform) and their ability to retain and exert control over decisions (on a scale of degree of autonomy ranging between the contained and the independent).

In transition countries, civil society actors can chose to move either towards a contracting role in service provision or aim for reform through advocacy. Some believe that the state fully arbitrates in questions of civil society. Yet in Latin America, CSOs and NGOs developed and grew during military dictatorships. Serbia is also an example from Europe where civil society flourished despite its opposition to Milosevic. According to Alan Fowler, several key factors are placing pressure on, and creating more scope for closer cooperation between the state and civil society: "The emergence of civil society in the international development agenda provides the political complement to the economies of adjustment; these two pillars being bridged by the concern for good governance".[20]

Civil society interacts with governments on many levels due to several factors: (i) reform in the role of the state, (ii) specifically privatisation of public services and state control of the economy; (iii) the continuing decentralisation of public administration; and (iv) The devolution of responsibility for authority over public services to local or regional institutions; and democratisation, with its implicit goal of opening space for and stimulating wider inclusion, equality before the law, civic mobilisation and citizen engagement in public affairs and policy making. Decentralisation is an explanation of increased State-Civil Society connections. Most NGOs act at the local level; generally isolated from, and in competition with, local government, but often dependent on them for facilities, funds and political access.[21] Civil society actors who are close to community needs, familiar with setting local agendas, and locally accountable stand to benefit from decentralisation.

The concept of civil society and its relationship to the democracy literature is a relatively recent development. According to the proponents of civil society, democracy occurs when subordinated social groups achieve sufficient access to the state so as to change the patterns of representation contained within it[22] (Rueschemeyer, Stephans and Stephans, 1992). A truly democratic society must embrace all members within the society, including subordinated social groups and a society is not democratic when it serves simply as an instrument to protect the dominant class. The strength of civil society is almost a test of the strength of democracy itself (Grugel, 1992).[23] Civil society groups occupy the political space between the state and the individual and encompass subordinated social groups as well as other groups across the social strata. The mobilisation and activism of civil society groups can enact change and aid in democratic transition (Bernard, 1993).[24]

Figure 6.1: Civil Society Index Diamond for Kazakhstan

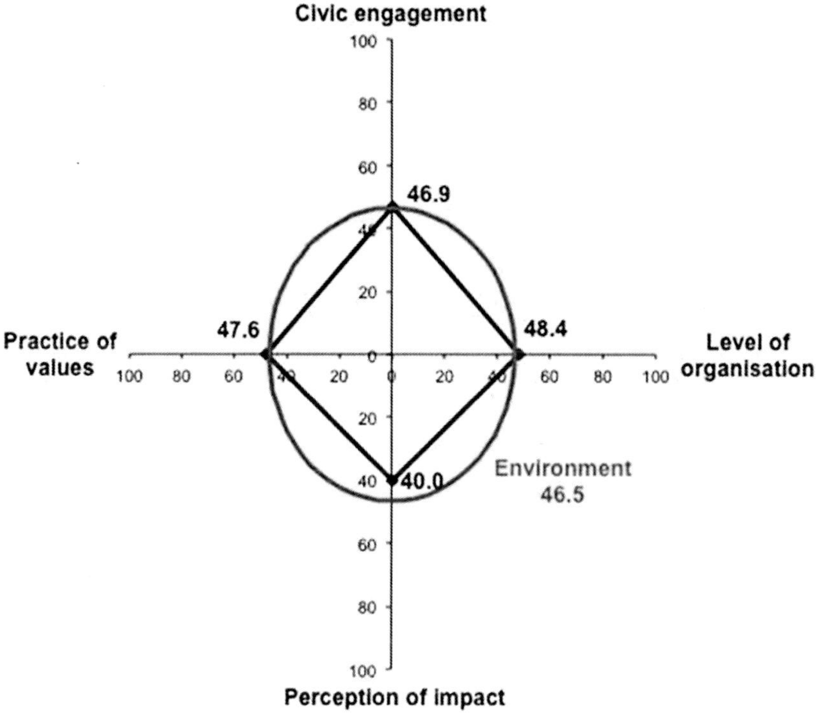

CIVIL SOCIETY IN KAZAKHSTAN

CSI Implementation

There are several key CSI programme implementation activities as well as several structure sinvolved, as summarized by Figure 6.1.[25]

The concept and development of civil society in Central Asia is a recent one which came to fore only after the emergence of independent Central Asian Republics. The issue was the theme of a two-day conference held in 1998, organised by the Centre for Civil Society International, based in Seattle, Washington, and the Central Asia-Caucasus Institute of the Paul J. Nitze School of Advanced International Studies, Johns Hopkins University, Washington DC, which resulted in a book titled *Civil Society in Central Asia*. The book has articles dealing with all the five countries in Central Asia—Kazakhstan, Turkmenistan, Uzbekistan, Kyrgyzstan, and Tajikistan—besides covering specific issues like the status and applicability of 'civil society' in Central Asia, the role of Islam, and NGOs.[26] The book is a modest attempt to examine the state of development in Central Asia regarding civil society.[27]

In his introduction to this book, Ruffin acknowledges that it would not be realistic to expect the development of civil society on the Western model in the countries where societies and traditions are so different. He adds, "Even if one were to grant the desirability of fostering the emergence of 'civil society' along the Western models, is it reasonable to expect that such a transformation can occur in a matter of years, when the institutions in question took generations to evolve in other societies?".[28] Starr's article, "Civil Society in Central Asia," gives a quick overview of the development of the idea of civil society in the West, its development in Eastern Europe, and its potential in Central Asia.[29] The state of civil society in Central Asia is not in a developed stage. Polat points out, "the basis for creating civil society does not yet exist in Uzbekistan".[30] It is important to understand the religious and social context in Kazakhstan in order to understand the social, civic, and democratic possibilities there. Islam is a powerful religious tradition, but the details of Islam's "social, civic and democratic possibilities" have not been thoroughly explored.[31]

The impact of NGOs in Central Asia varies by country and even within a country. In Tajikistan for instance, "amid the economic, political, and social chaos caused by a civil war, NGOs, surprisingly, have been able to gain a solid and relatively influential foothold in society". However, the impact of NGOs in the region has been limited. Some important NGOs have been founded by women who are former researchers, educators, attorneys and other professionals. Many NGOs were created by small groups of women, who united after losing their jobs.[32] However, the problem of sustainability and potential and actual problems are associated with particular types of projects in Kazakhstan.[33]

The ideas of a vibrant civil society, a law-abiding state and a free market oriented economy were taken as the main foundation of Kazakhstan's development. Basic principles of a civil society in Kazakhstan are the recognition of ideological and political pluralism and separation of state and public institutions. Citizen's rights to establish political, public and professional organisation are legally protected. The development of non-governmental organisations (NGOs) is one of the most significant achievements. They carry out a role of intermediaries between the State and citizens; perform many functions of social transformation in the society, and work in the fields of human rights, democracy, election, ecology, equal rights of women in the society, consumer rights, youth rights, lonely mothers and families with many children, orphans, invalids, victims of illegal reprisals, etc.

More than 4,500 non-governmental organisations are functioning in Kazakhstan today, resolving social problems and promoting more active involvement of citizens in the society's democratisation processes. About 35,000 individuals are permanently employed, and 50,000are temporarily employed by NGOs as experts and more than 100,000 individuals act as volunteers.[34] At the first stage of the development, Non-Governmental Organisations existed basically on foreign grants and over 500 Non-Governmental Organisations were established in this process basically working for civil rights protection. The 1998 programme of democratisation of the country increased the role of non-governmental organisations as key element of democratisation of Kazakhstan society. The quality of organisational and practical support by the state to non-governmental organisations acquires has improved since then.

In 2001, the adoption of Law of the Republic of Kazakhstan regarding "NPOs" became a real step towards the recognition of the role and place of non-governmental organisations.[35] Registration of the non-governmental organisations was radically simplified. The code of the Republic of Kazakhstan "taxes and other obligatory payments in the budget" No 209-II, 12 June 2001 stipulates significant tax advantages for the non-governmental organisations.[36] The policy of the "State support of the non-governmental organisations" was adopted in January 2002.It determines the purposes and priorities of the state support of the non-governmental organisations. Recognised leaders of non-governmental sector, as well as representatives of international organisations (UNDP, TASIS and Counterpart Consortium) took part in the development of the concept'.[37]

The resolution, "the Programme of the state support of non-governmental organisations of Republic of Kazakhstan for 2003-05 years", outlining the government's policy towards civil society organisations, was adopted in 2003.[38] The purpose of the Programme is the creation of conditions for sustainable development of non-governmental organisations as an indispensable part of the civil society and strengthening of their role in resolving significant social problems of the society on the basis of interaction with the Government.

Development of the new Laws "non-governmental organisations in the Republic of Kazakhstan and the State social order" are aimed at the formation of the new model of relations in realisation of the social policy in the Republic of Kazakhstan, creation of steady and effective system of relations between the state and public sector, maintenance of the legal basis of activity of non-governmental organisations and carrying out the State social order by them on a competitive basis. Kazakhstan has maintained a unitary and centralized administration, resisting domestic and international pressures to introduce direct elections of regional and local *Akims* (heads). The President appoints the *Akims* of the 14 *oblasts* and major cities such as Astana and Almaty, and they in turn appoint local district administrators. *Oblast Akims* are accountable solely to the President. Following the September 2003 local elections, several leaders of *Ak Zhol* called for reforms in the Law on Elections and urged a rapid introduction of elections for the positions of *Akims* at all levels. Notwithstanding the tight control wielded by the central government, the power and authority of *Akims* has continued to rise, contributing to a de facto decentralisation in various regions. *Akims* in the regions that have attracted the most foreign investment, such as west Kazakhstan, have exercised considerable control over budgetary matters and have even extracted significant contributions from foreign investors to various "social and welfare projects."

Kazakhstan held elections to the *Maslihats* in September and October 2003. Although the *Maslihats* have virtually no political power and are used to rubber-stamp laws introduced by the local heads, each *oblast Maslihat* nominates two members to the Senate. Out of the 2,852 candidates elected, 1,696 were party affiliated and the remaining were elected as independents. According to the available results, *Otan* was at the top with 1,477 candidates, followed by the *Agrarian Party* (109), *Azamat* (87), *Aul* (18) and *AkZhol* (5). Out of 250 *AkZhol* members, who ran as independents to minimize the interference by local officials, 140 won. There was an average of seven candidates for each council seat. Only 56.4 percent of the population voted in the local elections.

Kazakhstan has taken some steps toward introducing a career civil service system also. The Civil Service Agency, created to implement the 1999 Law on Civil Service,[39] plays a leading role in administrative reform and the downsizing of ministries, which have traditionally controlled recruitment, promotion, and dismissal procedures. USAID and TACIS, the technical assistance programme sponsored by the European Union (EU), have offered assistance in developing training programmes, job descriptions, and classifications for civil servants. Kazakhstan has established major institutions in Almaty and Astana to train civil servants and management cadres, with financial assistance from TACIS under the European Commission office in Kazakhstan. These institutions include the Academy of Civil Service, the International Business School at the Kazakhstan Academy of Management, and the Almaty School of Management at the International Academy of Business, the Institute for Development of Kazakhstan, and the Eurasian Civil Service Training Centre.

Thus, while there is a general lack of literature on the history of civil society in Kazakhstan, reviews of the current state of civil society are more readily available.[40]

Overview of the Concept of Civil Society

The CSI methodology defines civil society as "the arena, outside of the family, the state, and the market, which is created by individual and collective actions, organisations and institutions to advance shared interests." In envisaging civil society as an arena, the CSI recognises the importance of civil society's role in creating public spaces where diverse societal values and interests interact. The usage of the term arena is implies a particular realm or space in a society where people come together to debate, discuss, associate, and seek to influence broader society. As per CSI's pragmatic interest in strengthening civil society, the civil society is conceptualized as primarily a political term (rather than in economic terms as a synonym for the 'non-profit sector'). This helps to explore collective public action in greater depth in the broader context of governance and development and not primarily in the economic role of non-profit organisations. This political perspective of civil society leads the CSI to focus on issues of power, both within the civil society arena and between civil society actors and the institutions of the state and the private sector. Members of the Advisory Committee for the Kazakhstan CSI project discussed civil society's broad definition during their first meeting, and decided to adopt the CSI definition above without modification.

The preamble of the current Constitution, adopted in 1995, envisages Kazakhstan having a peaceful "civil society following ideals of freedom, equality and harmony." The prominence of the term "civil society," along with the term "Non-Governmental Organisation" (NGO) came with the influx of donor support in the 1990s. National legislation uses the term "noncommercial organisation" to include organisations with various legal forms, such as institutions, public associations, non-commercial joint stock companies, consumer cooperatives, foundations, religious associations, and associations of legal entities. The Law on Non-Commercial Organisations (2001) defines non-commercial organisations as legal entities that do not make profit and whose incomes are not distributed among their participants.

Further, the civil society as a concept has been recognised in other official legal documents in Kazakhstan. A presidential decree in June 2006 entitled "The Concept of Civil Society Development for 2006-11" offers a formal definition. According to the decree, "civil society is a society where the individual, with all his or her needs, interests and values, is at the centre of all processes and relations." Civil society means all social relations—political, economic, cultural, national, religious, family and other—that are independent from the state and reflect a variety of private interests. The task of civil society, then, is defined here as mediating between individuals and state. Its main aims are to protect the interests of every member of society and represent them against authorities and society, to conduct public oversight of the authorities' activities and to formulate internal and external policy. According to the decree, CSOs are political parties, local communities, religious organisations, professional and scientific unions and associations, mass media and NGOs. As per the decree an NGO is formally defined as a non-commercial organisation (excluding political parties, trade unions, professional unions and religious organisations) established by the initiative of individuals and/or non-state legal entities on a voluntary basis for the achievement of common goals.

When we look at the background of the developmental trajectory of civil society in Kazakhstan, we find that during the Soviet period it can roughly be divided into two stages: (1) Pre-1985 period; and (2) The *perestroika* era (1985-1991). In fact, it was the communist party that controlled all forms of public life within the Soviet framework. Nevertheless, there were a limited number of civil society organisations connected to the party such as *Komsomol* (the youth wing of the party), *Pioneer* organisations, trade unions and other public associations (mostly formed in the 1930s), voluntary organisations supporting the armed forces, and party-linked sport unions. It were these organisations that later became the basis for the development of CSOs during the transition period.

In the mid-1980s, when *perestroika* allowed for more civic participation, environmental and democratic issues became hot topics. However, the communist regime continued to limit basic human rights such as freedom of public assembly and freedom of speech. For example, in 1986, in Alma-Ata, when a civil movement of students and workers mobilised against Moscow's appointment of the First Secretary of the Central Committee of the Kazakhstan Communist Party, the movement was crudely crushed by the army. With most of the movement's participants imprisoned, the authorities failed to formally recognise the final number of victims.

Nevertheless, public movements played an important part in the democratic transition. Environmental movements such as Nevada-Semey, which sought the closure of nuclear test sites in Kazakhstan, diversified into democratic movements, opening up the political scene and serving as the basis for the first political parties in the newly independent Kazakhstan. After independence, organised civil society in Kazakhstan became more diverse, visible and robust (ADB, 2007). Since then, it has undergone three periods of development (UNDP, 2002). During the first period, the early 1990s, more than 400 non-governmental organisations (NGOs) were established, mostly involved in rights protection. The second period (1994-2001) was characterised by growth in the diversity and quality of NGO activity. NGOs were financially, technically and ideologically supported by a number of international organisations. The international support provided a critical foundation for the emergence and institutionalisation of NGOs. In the third period (2001 to the present) the environment for a healthy civil society seems to have blossomed. Greater recognition from state bodies, formal arrangements for civil society-government cooperation, the establishment of public financing mechanisms for CSOs, and further growth in the number of registered NGOs all form the groundwork for the continued growth and entrenchment of civil society in Kazakhstan.

Mapping Civil Society

This section provides a brief overview of the civil society landscape in Kazakhstan. Key social actors were identified and ranked by members of the CSI project's Advisory Committee as part of a Social Forces Analysis. The largest circle in the first figure showing Social Forces Analysis represents the actor with the greatest social impact, while the smallest represents the actor with the least impact. The president, presidential family, the Nur-Otan ruling party, state executive authorities and financial-industrial groups are society's most important and influential actors. The amended election law of 2007 resulted in the president's Nur-Otan party capturing all seats in that year's lower house (*Mazhilis*) election (Freedom House 2010).

Figure 6.2: Social Forces Analysis

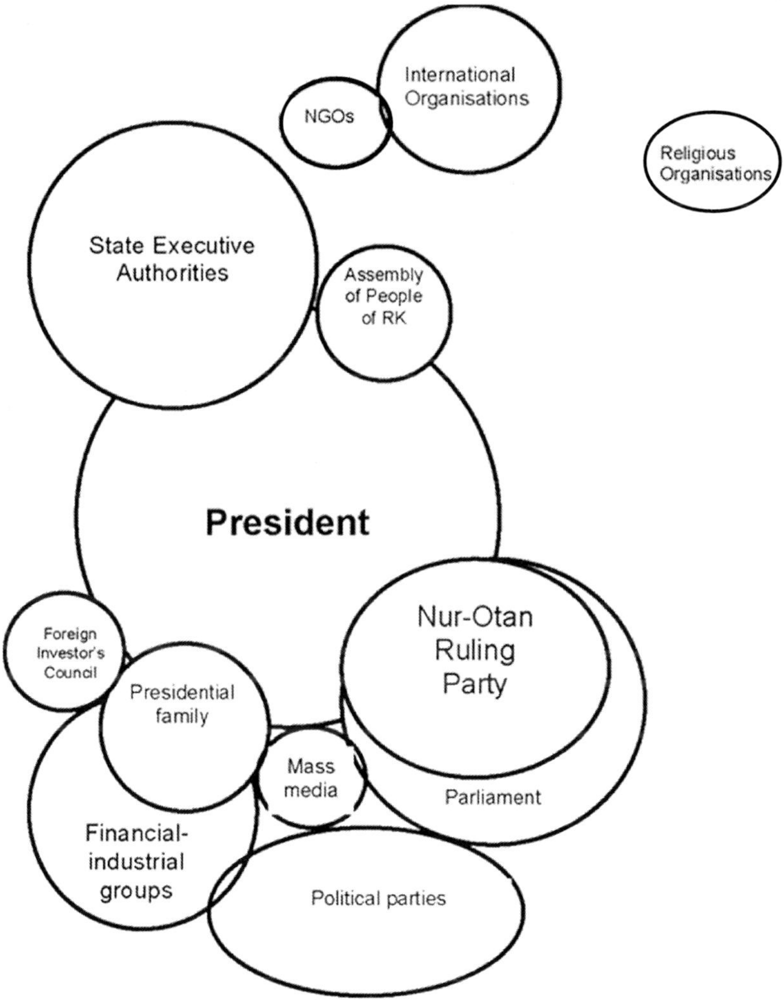

Key actors in the civil society include the Foreign Investor's Council, media organisations, the Assembly of the People of Kazakhstan, international organisations, political parties, CSOs such as NGOs, and religious organisations.

The second figure showing mapping of Kazakhstan's Civil Society presents the key civil society actors within the country's civil society and also includes local and international actors.

Kazakhstan has a large number of professional and business associations and NGOs active in the areas of human rights, women's issues, ecology, youth and others. However, the activities of CSOs depend on various factors. According to Freedom House reports,[41] the government uses its enormous power of patronage to target nascent NGOs and public associations for co-option, aiming to promote

Figure 6.3: Kazakhstan's Civil Society Mapping

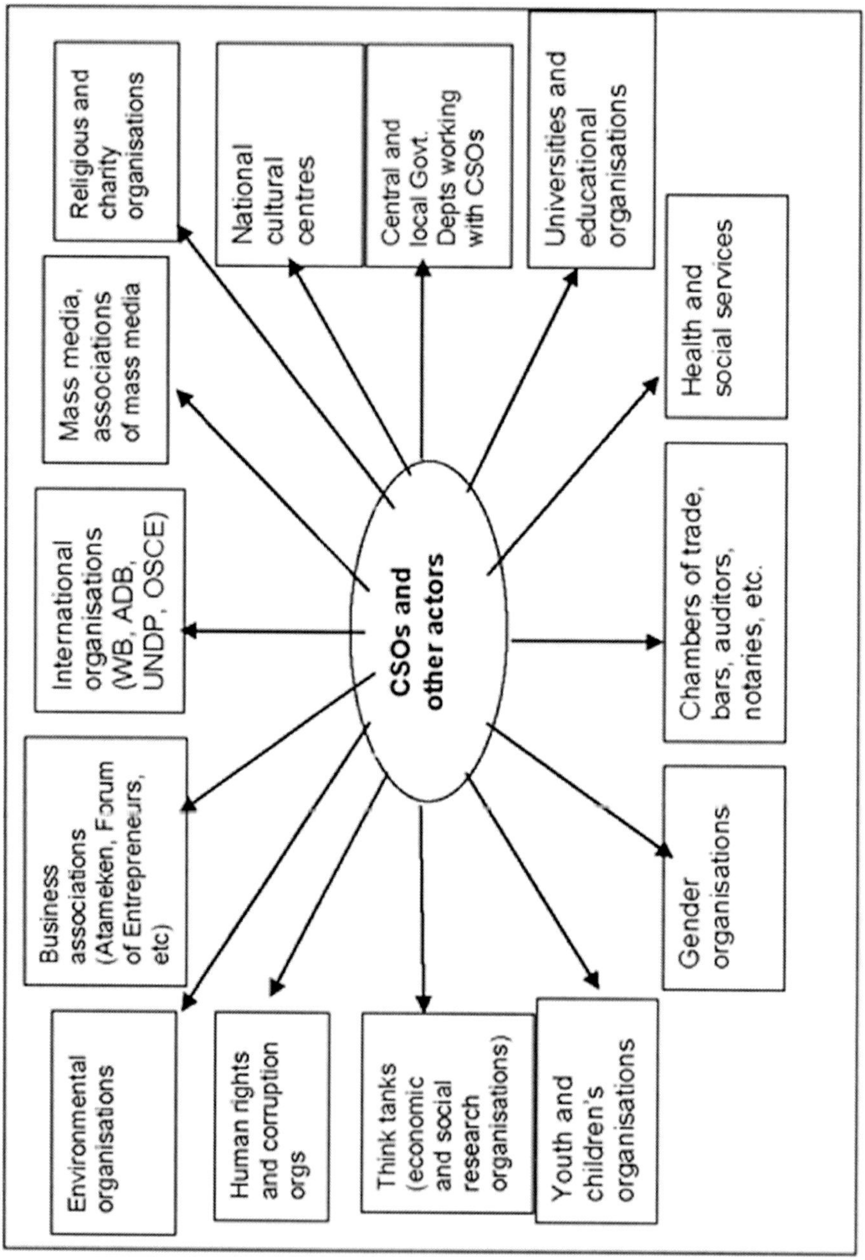

its own agenda of social and infrastructural development rather than allowing the nongovernmental sector to develop independently. While pro-government NGOs are offered funds, publicity, and recognition for engaging in 'constructive cooperation' with the government, independent NGOs that resist such pressures tend to be portrayed as either irresponsible, serving outside interests, or opposed to reform and prosperity.

Vitalino (2005)[42] notes that the state, the ruling party and oligarchic economic interests associated with the Nazarbaev family have been active in recent years in shaping quasi-official NGOs. Some even registered on the eve of the 2004 parliamentary election, and exist on paper only as government showcases of democracy. According to the Minister of Foreign Affairs, of over 25,000 CSOs in Kazakhstan, almost 13,000 are NGOs and more than half a million people are employed in the sector.[43] However, these figures vary from source to source; the Ministry of Justice data on 'non-commercial organisations' (NCOs) in Table 6.1 below is different.

Table 6.1: CSOs Registered in Kazakhstan by Type

	Form	*Dec 2003*	*Apr 2006*	*Nov 2008*	*May 2010*
1.	State institutions	15,502	20,840	21,280	21,334
2.	Private institutions	7,351	6,097	5,688	*(5,500)
3.	Public associations	4,763	5,820	7,204	8,034
4.	Foundations	2,690	3,340	4,204	4,751
5.	Religious associations	1,265	1,360	1,399	1,388
6.	Associations (unions) of legal entities	949	1,072	1,210	1,324
7.	Consumer cooperatives	4,791	4,846	5,319	5,553
8.	Rural consumer cooperatives	450	833	1,517	1,769
9.	Housing and building cooperatives	273	215	290	339
10.	Non-commercial joint-stock companies	22	*	3	63
11.	Housing owners' cooperatives	2,040	2,186	2,363	2,417
12.	Notary chambers	18	16	16	18
13.	Bar colleges (associations)	14	14	15	16
14.	Auditors' chambers	16	16	13	*(13)
15.	Chambers of trade and industry	29	16	16	*(16)
16.	Agricultural partnerships	430	29	35	29
	Subtotal (private NCOs)	25,101	25,860	29,292	(31,201)c
	Total (including state NCOs)	40,603	47,600	50,572	(52,564)c

[a] Legal entities issuing shares with the aim or raising funds for the implementation of activities, the profit of which will be used only for their own development.

[b]Organisations created to manage a condominium of a multi-apartment residential building or a group of nearly located homes.

[c]Total numbers, as well as their analyses, are estimates due to absence of information on three types.

* No official data available.

Source: ICNL, 2010. Figures are based on official information from the Ministry of Justice of Republic of Kazakhstan; the number of organisations according to ICNL's assessment is given in parentheses.

The government has increased its involvement in civil society by establishing state NCOs. The *number of state institutions is only about one-third less than the number of private NCOs*. By contrast, in the United States, there are one-tenth as many governmental institutions as there are non-governmental entities (ICNL, 2010).

There is a steady growth in the number of registered non-commercial organisations. The most popular forms of NCOs are public associations and foundations. The number of public associations grew by 69 per cent from December 2003 to May 2010; the number of foundations grew by 77 per cent in the same period. It is necessary to take into account that several organisations can be established by the same people. There is a new abbreviation present in Kazakhstan, 'GONGO,' referring to Government Operated Non-Governmental Organisation. Ziegler has argued that only a small fraction of registered NGOs are active, while the rest exist only on paper. Many are 'dormant' or are quasi-NGOs created by government agencies (Ziegler, 2008). Most active NGOs tend to be concentrated in cities, while they are mostly absent from the rural areas.

Civil Society in Kazakhstan: CSI Project Findings

The CSI project includes an analysis of individual indicators, sub-dimensions and dimensions in various levels of detail, with the intention of identifying the key findings. For this purpose the whole findings can be divided into five dimensions of the CSI diamond: Civic Engagement, Level of Organisation, Practice of Values, Perception of Impact and External Environment. However, the Civic Engagement dimension is of primary importance to understand the civil society in Kazakhstan.

Figure 6.4: Civic Engagement Sub-Dimensions

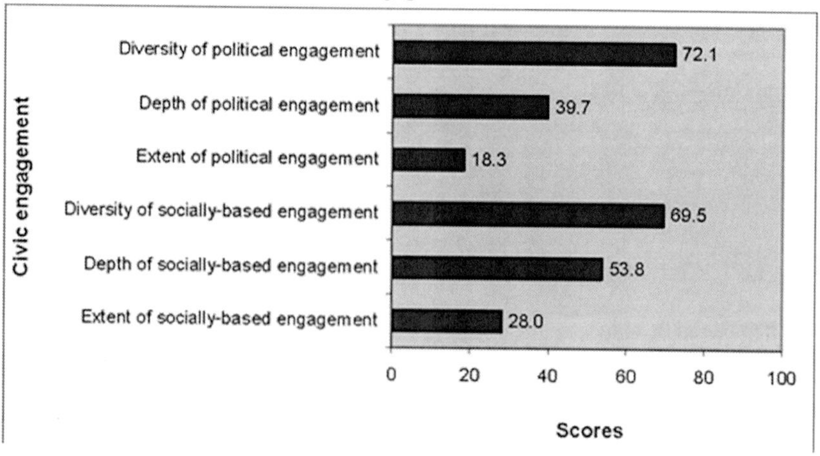

Civic Engagement

The overall size, strength and vibrancy of civic engagement in Kazakhstan can be gauged on the basis of scores from the population survey. The score for this dimension is 46.9 per cent. Figure 6.4 provides the scores for the six sub-dimensions: the extent, depth and diversity of socially-based engagement and the extent, depth and diversity of political engagement.

Extent of Socially-based Engagement

This sub-dimension concerns the proportion of citizens engaging socially in Kazakhstan, and scored 28.0 per cent. Of the population survey respondents, 36.5 per cent are active members of a social organisation such as a mosque, church, religious organisation, sporting, recreational, arts, music or educational, humanitarian or charitable organisations. Also, 19.7 per cent of respondents said that they do voluntary work for at least one social organisation, while 27.9 per cent of respondents engage in social activities in sports, voluntary or service-based organisations several times a year.

BUILDING CIVIL SOCIETY IN KAZAKHSTAN

On providing support to civil society development in Central Asia, Anne Garbutt (INTRAC Regional Manager for the Former Soviet Union) and Brenda Lipson (Training and Capacity Building Director) look at those initiatives set out to develop the capacities of civil society organisations, either as a means to a further end or as an end in itself.[44]

The Republic of Kazakhstan has introduced several social-economic, political and ethical-cultural reforms and established democratic institutions of civil society and a state laws. In the process of civil society formation, special attention has been paid to the social and cultural values and spiritual heritage of the past. Nazarbayev understood well that fundamental reforms of Kazakh society should be implemented not as a thoughtless copying of the Western experience of modernisation and transformation, but should be based on the historic development of Kazakhstan in terms of globalisation. He stated that in order to set up a civil society, it is crucial to utilize the positive potential of our past, both Soviet and traditional. Based on these values it is possible to reach a consensus and to establish and develop the institutions of civil society. In creating conditions for interest in private-ownership, for the development of individualism, and for the education of a sense of ownership—all these issues are complicated by the fact that such conditions are not found in the framework of traditional society. Strengthening the values of the Kazakh nation is necessary for the revival of the institutions of civil society institutes.[45]

The development of multi-structural economics is crucial for the establishment of civil society. Equitable and diversified forms of property, adjusted by market mechanism, contribute to freedom of choice in economic activity, and lead to economic freedom. It is necessary to restore the genuine feeling of community for which the development of communal forms of property (co-operative, joint stock, rent) should provide an objective basis. Freedom is the major value of the civil society being formed in Kazakhstan. Nomads have always been famous for a freedom-loving spirit.[46]

Elaborating on Kazakhstan's experience of civil society, Nazarbayev stated, "A civil society comprises various cultural, national, labour, territorial and other units, which carry out their activity based upon genuine self-government. History tells us that a Kazakh village (*aul*) had a peculiar institution of self-government which co-existed with the traditional power. It was formed as result of elections by members of the community or *aksakal*, who solved the various issues of fellow-tribesmen. Contemporary researchers see a rational nucleus in this form of self-government and possibilities for applying it in modern society. The formation of civil society institutions is impossible without the development of a patriotism shared by the entire Kazakhstan, and with deep roots in the culture, psychology, and historical past of the Kazakhs. In a traditional Kazakh society such values as love of the Motherland (*atameken*), its veneration and care have also been strong. The values of inter-ethnic and intra-ethnic consent and stability have a special place among the unifying values received from the past. They provide a valuable foundation for poly-ethnic Kazakh society with which it is possible to strengthen the democratic values in Kazakhstan. Civil society should be formed on their basis. Religious tolerance, absence of fanaticism and religious aggression are historic traditions of the Kazakh nation. Respect of elders and of the spiritual freedom of other nations is principal values. It is important to develop a productive dialogue between confessions and to acknowledge religion as an element of civil society. Thus, revival of the culture and spirituality of the Kazakh nation which was lost in the period of totalitarianism and the development of Kazakh philosophy in line with traditional culture must play important roles in ensuring the spiritual freedom and independence of Kazakhstan in the context of world development. This is important for the growth of national self-consciousness and the consolidation of the nation."[47] Cooperation between the state and civil society can be carried out through various means as discussed below.

Public Participation

Public participation in Kazakhstan is evident in the form of civil society representatives' participation in drafting various normative acts at different levels (national, regional, and local). Representatives of NGOs are increasingly involved in working groups drafting normative acts. The most recent example is the revocation by the President of his directive to enact the Law on NGOs, a repressive and anti-NGO draft that was broadly criticized and opposed by NGOs throughout the country. For the past three years, NGOs have participated in,

Cooperation Councils that operate in five *Oblasts* (Provinces) of Kazakhstan. These boards advise the government on strategies of cooperation with civil society. In addition, at the national level, three NGOs (Confederation of NGOs of Kazakhstan, Diabetic Association of the Republic of Kazakhstan, and Consumers Rights' Protection League) were included in the National Council, the Advisory Board of the President of Kazakhstan. These Cooperation Councils represent a first step in creating a structure for long-term engagement of the state with civil society organisations.[48]

State Sponsorship of the CSOs

The financial support provided by the government to Civil Society Organisations (CSOs) can be labeled as direct or indirect, ranging from the direct funding of activities to mere tax preferences. Subsidies (Grants), including "Natural Subsidies" Kazakhstan legislation provides for the granting of subsidies to youth and children's organisations, but does not specify any criteria for identifying such organisations. Several municipal laws, including those of Almaty, Kazakhstan's biggest city, provide for a considerable discount in rental payments for public organisations leasing premises on municipal property. This amounts to about tenth of the average market value for similar premises. Such a discount is called a "natural subsidy." However, local legislation does not specify what organisations are eligible. Thus, this leasing discount is left to the unlimited discretion of local officials administering municipal property.

Grants Given under State Procurement Contracts

During the summer of 2003, the Ministry of Culture, Information and Public Accord (now split into the Ministry of Culture and the Ministry of Information) distributed grants among NGOs using state procurement procedures and state procurement contracts. Such tenders had a closed nature and only NGOs were eligible to participate. However, only selected invited NGOs could participate in this process.[49]

State Procurement Legislation

State procurement legislation in Kazakhstan does not preclude NGOs from participation in state procurement contracts. Several problems have crept in while applying such legislation to NGOs over the last five years. State Procurement Law formally provides for equal treatment of all potential vendors under state procurement contracts. In reality, NGOs have less opportunity to compete with commercial vendors because of the limited and restricted assets they possess. This prevents them from being able to place a compulsory security deposit along with a tender application—three percent of the contract price. Moreover, state procurement legislation does not stipulate special procedures for procurement of social services. Also, there are no special criteria to evaluate tenders for services—the law only stipulates that the "lowest price" be sought. This ignores the quality of services, qualifications, reputation, and other non-price factors. As a result, both NGO participation in state procurement of social services and procurement of social services by the state are discouraged due to inadequate regulations.

Pending Law on State Social Contracting

After prolonged lobbying by certain NGO activists, the government finally agreed to draft and submit to parliament a Law on State Social Contracting, which would stimulate and develop state procurement of social services from NGOs.[50] During the last few years, many tax benefits for Non-Commercial Organisations (NCOs) and Social Sphere Organisations (SSOs) have been incorporated into Kazakhstan's tax legislation. However, practical difficulties remain while these benefits. Individuals are still unable to claim any deductions from taxable income for their charitable donations to NCOs and SSOs. There is still no opportunity for legal entities to deduct from their income tax charitable donations transferred to SSOs (including, but not limited to schools, universities, institutions for the disabled, theaters, and museums).[51]

The legislative framework is critical to NGO-government cooperation and economic support for NGOs. The Kazakh government's interest in civil society and civil society's interest in working with the government presents an opportunity to transform the current and past sporadic *ad hoc* experiments in state support of civil society into a regulated system that is open and transparent. Though there are indications of growing state-civil society relationship, additional steps need to be taken to ensure the delivery of efficient and effective social services in Kazakhstan.

According to Vsevolod Ovcharenko, who is Legal Consultant for Kazakhstan at the Central Asia office of the International Centre for Not-for-Profit Law (ICNL) in Almaty, "one can expect that the state-civil society relationship will escape the negative public image most often associated with practices that look to be mere political patronage. The state can use the upcoming legislative agenda to remedy any current inefficiency within the state-civil society relationship."[52]

While developing of institutions of civil society in Kazakhstan, development of the guarantees of the rights and freedoms of the citizens of Kazakhstan—freedom of speech, freedom of assembly, and the right to express political will—is important. In accordance with the Presidential decree, on the "Future Development of the System of Constitutional Laws and Freedoms of Persons and Citizen", the resources of Ombudsmen for protecting human rights have been broadened. Freedom of speech is one of the fundamental conditions for the continued democratic development of Kazakhstan.[53] However, there is need for a clear legislative shield against the abuse of freedom of speech.

Combating Corruption and Crime

Kazakhstan has been one of the first Post-Soviet states to pass anti-corruption legislation. Quite a few officials have been punished. However, legislation requires thorough analysis and revision of all the regulations that willfully or unwittingly create conditions conducive to corrupt actions by officials, separating business from civil services, transparency in stock companies, their owners and related parties, the banking system, the multitude of licensing bodies, etc. To achieve these goals, the country needs to follow these points:

- Create comprehensive "one-stop" public service Centres, where in one location it is possible to apply for a passport, receive a tax ID number, a driver's license, etc. This can be done on a pilot basis in Astana and Almaty.
- Sharply reduce the number of licenses and permits.
- Pass appropriate amendments in the law, "On Stock Companies in the Republic of Kazakhstan".[54]
- A civil servant should make public his past and current assets, business etc.
- It is essential to develop an Ethics Code for civil servants to prohibit them from engaging in private business, or lobbying in the interests of companies.
- Disciplinary councils should finally be given over to the Agency on Civil Service Affairs, and transferred to the central budget; the councils should be strengthened with legal personnel. The Council should be charged with assuring that civil servants act ethically, and in compliance with the Ethics Code.
- Punishment should be handed out not only to those taking bribes, but also to those giving them.
- The salary of civil servants should be raised to a level comparable to the salary earned in business. The Agency on Fighting Economic Crimes and Corruption must be independent. It is appropriate to bring it under the direct control of the President.

In Kazakhstan, bountiful natural resources (particularly oil reserves) and a lack of democratic oversight have together created an ideal environment for corruption. Those individuals who stand to gain the most from this advantage are found in public office or are closely tied to key public officials. Corruption exists at all levels of the government, bureaucracy, and legal system, and in education as well in varying degrees. In 2003, Kazakhstan and Uzbekistan ranked 100th (out of 133 countries) on the Berlin-based Transparency International's Corruption Perceptions Index. Kyrgyzstan and Tajikistan had lower score; Turkmenistan was not included. Kazakhstan's ranking has continued to deteriorate. It ranked 65th (out of 91) in 2000, 71st (out of 91) in 2001, and 88th (out of 102) in 2002.

The United States Justice Department continued in 2003 its investigation into the scandal known as Kazakhgate, involving the suspected funneling of millions of dollars from U.S. oil companies to top Kazakh officials via the U.S. businessman James Giffen. Giffen was indicted in a New York Federal Court for offering bribes, though he is currently out on US $10 million bail as investigations continue. Independent parliamentary deputies who support the *DVK* have appealed to the U.S. government to provide information, since the Kazakh Parliament has refused to discuss the case. Transparency Kazakhstan Foundation, a member of Transparency International, conducted a poll among 55 experts (including members of Parliament, NGOs, journalists, civil servants, businessmen, and independent specialists) to evaluate the transparency of the Kazakh budgetary system. Only 16.7 percent of the respondents described the process for drawing up the budget as fully transparent, whereas 9.3 percent said that the process of passing the budget was fully transparent; 68.5 percent noted that some of the budget funds were misused, as reported in 2003 by *Interfax*-Kazakhstan.[55]

The Office of the Prosecutor-General formally handles inquiries on corruption among government officials in conjunction with the Ministries of Justice and of Internal Affairs. The Prosecutor-General, however, is appointed by the President and is not accountable to the government. Though the government has punished some low-level political figures to demonstrate its commitment to check corruption, the top regime associates and supporters are beyond the reach of inquiry. Marat Koishibaev, a member of the Senate and an affiliate of *Otan*, was found guilty in 2003 of large-scale embezzlement and abuse of office. He received a relatively light 5½-year suspended sentence and a 2-year ban on holding public office. The pattern set by the trials and sentencing of influential political figures such as Kazhegeldin, Ablyazov, and Zhakiyanov illustrates that individuals challenging or competing with the financial or political interests of the Nazarbayev family will invariably be accused of some financial misdemeanor.[56]

In the new millennium, Nazarbayev endorsed a number of amendments to laws as part of a state programme to fight corruption designed for 2001–2005. These amendments include a specific definition of corruption that covers gifts or property received indirectly. Also included is an extensive list of actions that are defined as corruption and a prohibition on government employment for eight years after a person has served a sentence for corruption. Georgiy Kim, head of the State Commission under the President for Observance of Public Official Ethics and the Fight against Corruption, reported that complaints about law enforcement agencies and justice bodies accounted for 29.7 per cent in 1997 and 42.4 per cent in 2002 of the total complaints received.[57] Most of the complaints came from Almaty, south Kazakhstan, Karaganda and east Kazakhstan. Kim blamed regional governors and the mayors of Astana and Almaty for insufficiently implementing the state anti-corruption programme for 2001-05.[58] Kazakhstan still lacks a professional stratum of civil servants with a strong public ethics. As shown by the increase in corruption-related offences by civil servants, the penalties for such lawbreakers are not commensurate with the seriousness of the crimes committed. Yevgenii Zhovtis, head of Kazakhstan's International Bureau for Human Rights and the Observance of Legality, claims that pervasive corruption and an extremely low level of trust in laws and the judiciary are the main factors limiting investment in Kazakhstan.[59] This has driven away small and medium-scale investors. In contrast, investors in large companies tend to seek business protection from the political elite rather than the judiciary.

MASS MEDIA AND PROTECTION OF JOURNALISTS' RIGHTS

By 1990, only 10 national newspapers and magazines were published and 21 TV and radio stations existed. By 1 July 2004, 2,041 mass media bodies exist, including 1,211 newspapers, 477 magazines, 124 TV and radio stations, 15 news agencies and 159 electronic media outlets. Eighty five per cent of media outlets in Kazakhstan are non-governmental ones. Public associations own 159 media outlets, 11 publications belong to political parties and movements, and 10 are owned by religious associations. The media market is characterised by considerable diversity such as political newspapers and magazines as well as information, advertising, entertainment, religious, women, youth, children, technical and many other special publications. The newspapers and magazines are published and TV and radio stations broadcast in 11 languages. Besides the main Kazakh and Russian, there are Ukrainian, Polish, English, German, Korean, Uyghur, Turkish, Dungan etc. These ethnic minorities' mass media outlets receive government financial support.[60]

Internet, air-cable and cable TV are rapidly developing. Up-to-date technologies are widely used in the information market—national TV and radio stations broadcast via national satellite TV system, Kazakhstan TV and radio broadcasters widely use digital technology. The international Caspio Net Satellite Channel (the operator is Eutelsat) was opened in 2002. Programmes of the BBC, CNN, Deutsche Welle, Freedom Radio Station, Polish TV Polonia, Russian and other TV channels are widely telecast. Over 80 representatives of foreign mass media from 20 countries including the largest news agencies such as the *BBC, Associated Press, Interfax, Agence France Press, Xinhua, Reuters, ITAR-TASS, Bridge news,* etc. are accredited in Kazakhstan.[61] This diversity of companies and languages promote rapid development of the Kazakhstan mass media.

Key mechanisms of the government information policy are:[62]

- Legal guaranties and practical insurance of the principles of freedom of speech, free receiving and spreading of information, censorship prohibition;
- Continuing improvement of legal framework of mass media activity;
- Annual placing of budget financed government order for implementation

of the government information policy. A right to get this order is assigned through a contest among mass media bodies irrespective of their ownership. It helped in creating equal conditions for receiving government financial support by both government and non-government press consequently encouraging their creative activity and business initiative;

- Transparent process of receiving frequencies for TV and radio broadcasting. The Commission on providing rights for radio frequency use comprises representatives of the Parliament, international and Kazakhstan public associations. Activity of the Commission is widely covered by the mass media;
- Creation of economic conditions for mass media growth. All publications and TV stations are exempted from VAT. Charges for use of radio frequency decrease almost every year;
- Continuing and constructive cooperation with public associations, international organisations, media research institutes in the area of mass media development. Journalists rights associations such as the Journalists Congress of Kazakhstan, Journalists Union of Kazakhstan, Tele-Radio Broadcasters Association of Kazakhstan, offices of international organisations (the OSCE, Human Rights Watch, Internews network, Adil Soz etc.) fruitfully work in Kazakhstan;
- Close attention to journalists development. To this end every year the government provides grants and loans for education in this field and a TV Journalism School has been established.

A Public Council on Mass Media (information policy) has also been created. It comprises MPs, the Chairman of the Board of the Journalists Union of Kazakhstan, President of the Tele-radiobroadcasters Association of Kazakhstan, Editors-in-Chief and journalists of leading mass media bodies. A new Law on Mass Media that is aimed at further improvement of journalist's rights protection and parity of information law of Kazakhstan with international standards and practice is being developed.[63]

Restrictions on Freedom of the Press

However, several violations of right to freely disseminate and receive information through the media in several ways exist in Kazakhstan. Direct and indirect censorship have intensified as elections have neared. In early 1997, the government of Kazakhstan stripped the independent, privately owned broadcast media of their broadcasting rights, as the government directed re-sale of frequencies held by these firms. The owners of the frequencies were not informed of the conditions or rules of sale and they were able to retain their channels. Kazakhstan courts repeatedly refused to consider the substance of the appeals they had lodged against the government decision. The new owners of these frequencies, several of whom are related to or have close ties to President Nazarbayev, considerably changed the content of the programmes aired, replacing news and information with music and entertainment.[64]

In September, 1998, the government of Kazakhstan began to exert pressure against an array of privately-owned newspapers with ties to former Prime Minister Akezhan Kazhegeldin. The editorial office of the paper *XXI Vek* was extensively damaged by a firebomb on 26 September 1998. First, printing presses broke contracts and unilaterally refused to continue printing several papers. Secondly, the state tax police began investigations against several papers, seizing their property and bank accounts. Thirdly, Kazakh Customs Officers began to seize print runs of several papers, which were printed outside Kazakhstan. President Nazarbayev asserted that the former Prime Minister staged the 26 September firebombing of an opposition newspaper and 13 October 1998 incident in which Kazhegeldin had come under gunfire.[65]

MAJOR CHALLENGES BEFORE KAZAKH CIVIL SOCIETY

US donor interest to strengthen civil society in Kazakhstan has its prime objective of giving boost to democratisation. Therefore, US aid support to civil society is biased towards those groups, which similarly promote this goal. In fact, civil society assistance is not only limited to fostering democratisation but also promotes the neo-liberal economic policies. Donor efforts to strengthen civil society include the establishment of specific programmes that often revolve around democracy and governance; specific projects to build the institutional capacity of civil society organisations; setting up partnerships between civil society organisations, business and government; promoting the financial sustainability of civil society organisations through support to local foundations and philanthropic institutions. These attempts to operationalise the concept of civil society are innovative and imaginative, promising to open up new avenues of participation for otherwise marginalized voices. They suggest cooperative rather than antagonistic forms of engagement between the civil society and state. They also recognise the multi-dimensionality of individuals, the plurality of their identities, the coexistence of contradictory motives and interests. However, the donors face three challenges: politics of plurality and choice, politics of universality, and politics of autonomy and dependence.[66]

Donors start out with two implicit assumptions, namely, that democracy contributes positively towards development and that civil society is an important democratic check upon the state. In particular, the US approach views the task of 'civil society' as system maintenance—or the creation or strengthening of democratic institutions which protect the rule of law and legitimate peaceful opposition, and the expression of dissent in acceptable ways—facilitating economic progress and prosperity.[67] However, this is, in many respects, a deeply conservative vision where political stability is as important as political freedom, and protection form the state more important. An alternative approach to democracy and its relationship with civil society is the radical continental European tradition with particular influence among grass-roots organisations and development NGOs. Civil society is an arena to debate and challenge the prevailing ideas of progress and development through active participation in non-formal and non-institutionalised spaces.

The Constitution provides for freedom of association; however, the Government and the law impose significant restrictions on this right. Organisations that conduct public activities, hold public meetings, participate in conferences, or have bank accounts must be registered with the Government. "Membership organisations," such as churches, religious groups, or political parties, must register in each of the 14 provinces where they have active members, whereas "non-membership organisations", such as NGOs, must register only at the national level. Registration at the local level requires a minimum of 10 members and on the national level, a minimum of 10 members in at least 7 of the 14 *oblasts*. In addition, a registration fee of $135 (19,845 Tenge) is required. Most organisations must hire lawyers or other consultants to expedite their registrations through the bureaucracy, which increases the registration cost by approximately $200 (29,400 Tenge). Some groups consider these costs to be a deterrent to registration. According to government regulations, registration is supposed to be granted within 15 days; however, according to local NGO's, registration often takes 1 month to a year because the Government may return applications for additional information or require investigations into certain portions of the application. There have been numerous cases of the activities of religious groups being suspended for pending registration.

The Constitution prohibits political parties established on a religious basis. The Government also has refused to register ethnically based political parties on the grounds that their activities could spark ethnic violence; however, the small Kazakh ethnic nationalist *Alash Party* was registered for the 1999 Parliamentary elections. In February 1999, the Government refused registration to a newly established ethnic-Russian party; the pro-Presidential *Civic Party* stated that the creation of an ethnic-Russian party would have "an adverse effect on inter-ethnic stability." The Constitution bans "public associations"—including political parties—whose "goals or actions are directed at a violent change of the Constitutional system, violation of the integrity of the republic, undermining of the security of the state (and), fanning of social, racial, national, religious, class, and tribal enmity."[68] All of the major religious and ethnic groups have independently functioning cultural Centres. To participate in elections, a political party must register with the Government. Under the law, a party must submit a list of at least 3,000 members from a minimum of nine *oblasts* (the cities of Almaty and Astana count as *oblast*-equivalents in addition to the 14 *oblasts* for this purpose). The list must provide personal information about members, including date and place of birth, address, and place of employment. For many citizens, the requirement to submit such personal data to the Government inhibits them from joining political parties. Membership in political parties or trade unions is forbidden to members of the armed forces, employees of national security and law enforcement organisations, and judges.[69] The Constitution also prohibits foreign political parties and foreign trade unions from operating in the territory of Kazakhstan. In addition, the Constitution prohibits the financing of political parties and trade unions by foreign legal entities and citizens, foreign states, and international organisations.

Overall, the picture of civil society in Kazakhstan seems to be optimistic. But the road ahead will require real focus and commitment from the government, civil society and the donor community if the considerable challenges the civil society in Kazakhstan are to be overcome.

NOTES

1. See, UNDP Report, Almaty, 1998.
2. Neera, Chandhoke, *State and Civil Society: Exploration in Political Theory* (New Delhi: Sage Publication, 1995). pp.80-81.
3. Ibid.
4. Ibid.
5. Neera, Chandhoke, *State and Civil Society: Exploration in Political Theory* (New Delhi: Sage Publication, 1995), pp. 80-81.
6. Ibid., p.81.
7. Ibid., p.83.
8. Andre Beteille, "Civil Society and Good Society", *Sociological Bulletin* (Journal of the Indian Sociological Society), Vol. 50, p.288.
9. Ibid., p.289.
10. Andre Beteille, n.2, p.288.
11. Neera, Chandhoke, *State and Civil Society: Exploration in Political Theory* (New Delhi: Sage Publication, 1995), pp.80-81.
12. Andre Beteille, "Civil Society and Good Society", *Sociological Bulletin* (Journal of the Indian Sociological Society), Vol. 50, p.288.
13. Andre Beteille, n.2, pp.288-289.
14. Ibid., p.290.
15. Ibid.
16. Ibid.
17. Kadir Z. Alimov, *Prospects For Development of Institutions* (Washington, Central Asia Institute, School of Advanced International Studies Johns Hopkins University) 1995.
18. Andre Beteille, n.2, pp.288-289.
19. Ibid.
20. Ibid.
21. Ibid.
22. Ibid., pp.290-291.
23. Kadir Z. Alimov, *Prospects For Development of Institutions* (Washington DC, Central Asia Institute, School of Advanced International Studies Johns Hopkins University), 1995.

24. Ibid.
25. For a detailed discussion on each of these steps in the process, please see Matiet al.2008.
26. J. Beauclerk, and S. Heap, "Civil Society-State Relationships: Models and Actualities', Background Paper for INTRAC's 10th Anniversary Conference, *Changing Expectations? The Concept and Practice of Civil Society in International Development* (Balliol College, Oxford, 13-15 Dec, 2001).
27. For further details see, *Civil Society in Central Asia, B.C. Asian Review 12* (Spring 2000), pp. 128-132.
28. Ibid.
29. J, Beauclerk, and S, Heap, "Civil Society-State Relationships: Models and Actualities', Background Paper for INTRAC's 10th Anniversary Conference, *Changing Expectations? The Concept and Practice of Civil Society in International Development* (Balliol College, Oxford, 13-15 Dec, 2001).
30. R. James (ed.), *Power and Partnership? Experiences of NGO Capacity-Building* (Oxford: INTRAC), 2001.
31. See, UNDP Report, Almaty 1999.
32. Ibid.
33. M. Hott Ruffin and Daniel Waugh (eds), *Civil Society in Central Asia* (Seattle: Centre for Civil Society International and the Central Asia-Caucasus Institute, John Hopkins University in association with University of Washington Press, 1999, pp.129-130.
34. Ibid.
35. Ibid.
36. R. James (ed) *Power and Partnership? Experiences of NGO Capacity-Building* (Oxford: INTRAC), 2001.
37. See, UNDP Report, Almaty, 1998.
38. Ibid.
39. UNDP Report, Almaty, 1999.
40. Meruert Makhmutova and Aitzhan Akhmetova, Civics Civil Society Index 2008-2010, Analytical Report, Public Policy Research Center, Almat 2011.
41. Freedom House (2010), Nations in Transit 2010.Kazakhstan Country Report.
42. Canas Vitalino (2005), NATO and Kazakhstan, 165 CDS 05.
43. Ibid.
44. Anne Garbutt and Simon Heap (eds) *Growing Civil Society in Central Asia* (*INTRAC*'s First Central Asia Regional Conference, Almaty, Kazakhstan, 13-14 June), 2002.
45. Nation in Transition 2004 unpan1.un.org/intradoc/groups/ public/documents/nispacee/ unpan016578.pdf
46. Ibid.
47. See, UNDP Report, Almaty, 2001.
48. See B.C. Review 12 (Spring 200), pp.128-132.
49. UNDP Report, Almaty, 2001.
50. UNDP Report, Almaty, 1998.
51. Vsevolod Ovcharenko, "The State-Civil Society Relationship in Kazakhstan: Mechanisms of Cooperation and Support." in *The International Journal of Not-for-Profit Law,* Vol. 6, No. 3, June 2004.
52. See; www.icnl.org/JOURNAL/vol6iss3/ar_ovcharenko.htm
53. R. James (ed.), *Power and Partnership? Experiences of NGO Capacity-Building* (Oxford: INTRAC), 2001.
54. Vsevolod Ovcharenko, n.17, p.310.
55. R. James (ed) *Power and Partnership? Experiences of NGO Capacity-Building* (Oxford: INTRAC), 2001.

56. Interview of Republican Network of Independent Monitors, Almaty, 2005.
57. Ibid.
58. Ibid.
59. Vsevolod Ovcharenko, n.17, p.310.
60. Ibid.
61. Interview of Republican Network of Independent Monitors, Almaty, 2005.
62. Ibid.
63. Republic of Kazakhstan Country Profilewww.mfa.kz/eng/index.php?base=3&article_id=31 - 335k
64. Ibid.
65. OSCE, Office for Democratic Institutions and Human Rights, 2 August 2004.
66. Anne Garbutt and Simon Heap (eds) "Growing Civil Society in Central Asia", *INTRAC's* First Central Asia Regional Conference, Almaty, Kazakhstan, 13-14 June 2002.
67. Republic of Kazakhstan Country Profilewww.mfa.kz/eng/index.php?base=3&article_id=31 - 335k
68. Ibid.
69. Ibid.

APPENDICES

Appendix-1

The Constitution of the Republic of Kazakhstan (1993)

We, the people of Kazakhstan, united by a common historic fate, creating a state on the indigenous Kazakh land, considering ourselves a peace loving and civil society, dedicated to the ideals of freedom, equality and concord, wishing to take a worthy place in the world community, realising our high responsibility before the present and future generations, proceeding from our sovereign right, accept this Constitution.

SECTION I
GENERAL PROVISIONS

Article 1

1. The Republic of Kazakhstan proclaims itself a democratic, secular, legal and social state whose highest values are an individual, his life, rights and freedoms.
2. The fundamental principles of the activity of the Republic are public concord and political stability; economic development for the benefit of all the nation; Kazakhstan patriotism and resolution of the most important issues of the affairs of state by democratic methods including voting at an all-nation referendum or in the Parliament.

Article 2

The Republic of Kazakhstan is a unitary state with a Presidential form of government.

The sovereignty of the Republic extends to its entire territory. The state ensures the integrity, inviolability and inalienability of its territory.

The administrative-territorial division of the Republic of Kazakhstan, location and status of its capital are determined by law.

The names "Republic of Kazakhstan" and "Kazakhstan" have the same meaning.

Article 3

1. The people shall be the only source of state power.
2. The people shall exercise power directly through an all-nation referendum and free elections as well as delegate the execution of their power to state institutions.

3. Nobody shall have the right to appropriate power in the Republic of Kazakhstan. Appropriation of power shall be persecuted by law. The right to act on behalf of the people and the state shall belong to the President as well as to Parliament of the Republic within the limits of the constitutional powers. The government and other state bodies shall act on behalf of the state only within the limits of their delegated authorities.
4. The state power in the Republic of Kazakhstan is unified and executed on the basis of the Constitution and laws in accordance with the principle of its division into the legislative, executive and judicial branches and a system of checks and balances that governs their interaction.

Article 4

The provisions of the Constitution, the laws corresponding to it, other regulatory legal acts, international treaty and other commitments of the Republic as well as regulatory resolutions of Constitutional Council and the Supreme Court of the Republic shall be the functioning law in the Republic of Kazakhstan.

The Constitution shall have the highest juridical force and direct effect on the entire territory of the Republic.

International treaties ratified by the Republic shall have priority over its laws and be directly implemented except in cases when the application of an international treaty shall require the promulgation of a law.

All laws, international treaties of which the Republic is a party shall be published.

Official publication of regulatory legal acts dealing with the rights, freedoms and responsibilities of citizens shall be a necessary condition for their application.

Article 5

1. The Republic of Kazakhstan shall recognise ideological and political diversity. The merging of public and state institutions and the formation of political party organisations in state bodies shall not be permitted.
2. Public associations shall be equal before the law. Illegal interference of the state in the affairs of public associations and of public associations in the affairs of the state, imposing the functions of state institutions on public associations, and financing of public associations by the state shall not be permitted.
3. Formation and functioning of public associations pursuing the goals or actions directed toward a violent change of the constitutional system, violation of the integrity of the Republic, undermining the security of the state, inciting social, racial, national, religious, class and tribal enmity, as well as formation of unauthorized paramilitary units shall be prohibited.
4. Activities of political parties and trade unions of other states, religious parties as well as financing political parties and trade unions by foreign legal entities

and citizens, foreign states and international organisations shall not be permitted in the Republic.

5. Activities of foreign religious associations on the territory of the Republic as well as appointment of heads of religious associations in the Republic by foreign religious centers shall be carried out in coordination with the respective state institutions of the Republic.

Article 6

The Republic of Kazakhstan shall recognise and by the same token protect state and private property.

Property shall impose obligations, and its use must simultaneously benefit the society. Subjects and objects of ownership, the scope and limits of the rights of proprietors, and guarantees of their protection shall be determined by law.

The land and underground resources, waters, flora and fauna, other natural resources shall be owned by the state. The land may also be privately owned on terms, conditions and within the limits established by legislation.

Article 7

1. The state language of the Republic of Kazakhstan shall be the Kazak language.
2. In state institutions and local self-administrative bodies the Russian language shall be officially used on equal grounds along with the Kazak language.
3. The state shall promote conditions for the study and development of the languages of the people of Kazakhstan.

Article 8

The Republic of Kazakhstan shall respect principles and norms of international law, pursue the policy of cooperation and good-neighborly relations between states, their equality and non-interference in each other's domestic affairs, peaceful settlement of international disputes and renounce the first use of the military force.

Article 9

The Republic of Kazakhstan shall have its state symbols—the flag, emblem and anthem. Their description and order of official use shall be established by the constitutional law.

SECTION II
THE INDIVIDUAL AND CITIZEN

Article 10

Citizenship of the Republic of Kazakhstan shall be acquired and terminated as prescribed by law, shall be indivisible and equal regardless of the grounds of its acquisition.

A citizen of the Republic of Kazakhstan under no circumstances may be deprived of citizenship of the right to change his citizenship, and may not be exiled from the territory of Kazakhstan.

Foreign citizenship of a citizen of the Republic shall not be recognised.

Article 11

1. A citizen of the Republic of Kazakhstan may not be extradited to a foreign state unless otherwise stipulated by international treaties of the Republic.
2. The Republic shall guarantee its citizens protection and patronage outside its boundaries.

Article 12

Human rights and freedoms in the Republic of Kazakhstan shall be recognised and guaranteed in accordance with this Constitution.

Human rights and freedoms shall belong to everyone by virtue of birth, be recognised as absolute and inalienable, and define the contents and implementation of laws and other regulatory legal acts.

Every citizen of the Republic shall have rights and bear responsibilities owing to his citizenship.

Foreigners and stateless persons in the Republic shall enjoy rights and freedoms as well as bear responsibilities established for the citizens unless otherwise stipulated by the Constitution, laws and international treaties.

Exercise of a citizen's human rights and freedoms must not violate rights and freedoms of other persons, infringe on the constitutional system and public morals.

Article 13

1. Everyone shall have the right to be recognised as subject of the law and protect his rights and freedoms with all means not contradicting the law including self-defense.
2. Everyone shall have the right to judicial defense of his rights and freedoms.
3. Everyone shall have the right to qualified legal assistance. In cases stipulated by law, legal assistance shall be provided free of charge.

Article 14

Everyone shall be equal before the law and court.

No one shall be subject to any discrimination for reasons of origin, social, property status, occupation, sex, race, nationality, language, attitude towards religion, convictions, place of residence or any other circumstances.

Article 15

1. Everyone shall have the right to life.
2. No one shall have the right to arbitrarily deprive a person of life. The law shall establish the death penalty as an extraordinary measure of punishment

for especially grave crimes and grant the sentenced person the right to appeal for pardon.

Article 16

Everyone shall have the right to personal freedom.

Arrest and detention shall be allowed only in cases stipulated by law and only with the sanction of a court or prosecutor of law. The detained person shall be provided with the right to appeal. Without the sanction of a procurator, a person may be detained for a period no more than seventy-two hours.

Every person detained, arrested and accused of committing a crime shall have the right to the assistance of a defense lawyer (defender) from the moment of detention, arrest or accusation.

Article 17

1. A person's dignity shall be inviolable.
2. No one must be subject to torture, violence or other treatment and punishment that is cruel or humiliating to human dignity.

Article 18

Everyone shall have the right to inviolability of private life, personal or family secrets, protection of honor and dignity.

Everyone shall have the right to confidentiality of personal deposits and savings, correspondence, telephone conversations, postal, telegraph and other messages. Limitation of this right shall be permitted only in the cases and according to the procedure directly established by law.

State bodies, public associations, officials, and the mass media must provide every citizen with the possibility to obtain access to documents, decisions and other sources of information concerning his rights and interests.

Article 19

1. Everyone shall have the right to determine and indicate or not to indicate his national, party and religious affiliation.
2. Everyone shall have the right to use his native language and culture, to freely choose the language of communication, education, instruction and creative activities.

Article 20

The freedom of speech and creative activities shall be guaranteed. Censorship shall be prohibited.

Everyone shall have the right to freely receive and disseminate information by any means not prohibited by law. The list of items constituting state secrets of the Republic of Kazakhstan shall be determined by law.

Propaganda of or agitation for the forcible change of the constitutional system, violation of the integrity of the Republic, undermining of state security, and advocating war, social, racial, national, religious, class and clannish superiority as well as the cult of cruelty and violence shall not be allowed.

Article 21

1. Everyone who has a legal right to stay on the territory of the Republic of Kazakhstan shall have the right to freely move about its territory and freely choose a place of residence except in cases stipulated by law.
2. Everyone shall have the right to leave the territory of the Republic. Citizens of the Republic shall have the right to freely return to the Republic.

Article 22

Everyone shall have the right to freedom of conscience.

The right to freedom of conscience must not specify or limit universal human and civil rights and responsibilities before the state.

Article 23

1. Citizens of the Republic of Kazakhstan shall have the right to freedom of forming associations. The activities of public associations shall be regulated by law.
2. The military, employees of national security, law-enforcement bodies and judges must abstain from membership in political parties, trade unions, and actions in support of any political party.

Article 24

Everyone shall have the right to freedom of labor, and the free choice of occupation and profession. Involuntary labor shall be permitted only on a sentence of court or in the conditions of a state of emergency or martial law.

Everyone shall have the right to safe and hygienic working conditions, to just remuneration for labor without discrimination, as well as to social protection against unemployment.

The right to individual and collective labor disputes with the use of methods for resolving them, stipulated by law including the right to strike, shall be recognised.

Everyone shall have the right to rest. Working labor agreements stipulating the length of working time, days-off and holidays, and paid annual leave shall be guaranteed by law.

Article 25

1. Housing shall be inviolable. Deprivation of housing shall not be permitted unless otherwise stipulated by a court decision. Penetration into housing, its inspection and search shall be permitted only in cases and according to the procedure stipulated by law.
2. Conditions shall be created in the Republic of Kazakhstan to provide citizens with housing. Citizens in need of housing shall be categorized in a manner

to be prescribed by law and provided with housing at an affordable price from the state housing funds in accordance with the norms stipulated by law.

Article 26

Citizens of the Republic of Kazakhstan may privately own any legally acquired property.

Property, including the right of inheritance, shall be guaranteed by law.

No one may be deprived of his property unless otherwise stipulated by a court decision. Forcible alienation of property for the public use in extraordinary cases stipulated by law may be exercised on condition of its equivalent compensation.

Everyone shall have the right to freedom of entrepreneurial activity, and free use of his property for any legal entrepreneurial activity. Monopolistic activity shall be regulated and limited by law. Unfair competition shall be prohibited.

Article 27

1. Marriage and family, motherhood, fatherhood and childhood shall be under the protection of the state.
2. Care of children and their upbringing shall be a natural right and responsibility of parents.
3. Able-bodied children of age must take care of their disabled parents.

Article 28

A citizen of the Republic of Kazakhstan shall be guaranteed a minimum wage and pension, and guaranteed social security in old age, in case of disease, disability or loss of a breadwinner and other legal grounds.

Voluntary social insurance, creation of additional forms of social security, and charity shall be encouraged.

Article 29

1. Citizens of the Republic of Kazakhstan shall have the right to protection of health.
2. Citizens of the Republic shall be entitled to free, guaranteed, extensive medical assistance established by law.
3. Paid medical treatment shall be provided by state and private medical institutions as well as by persons engaged in private medical practice on the terms and according to the procedures stipulated by law.

Article 30

The citizens shall be guaranteed free secondary education in state educational establishments. Secondary education shall be obligatory.

A citizen shall have the right to receive on a competitive basis a higher education in a state higher educational establishment.

The citizens shall have the right to pay and receive an education in private educational establishments on the basis and terms established by law.

The state shall set uniform compulsory standards in education. The activity of any educational establishment must comply with these standards.

Article 31

1. The state shall set an objective to protect the environment favorable for the life and health of the person.
2. Officials shall be held accountable for the concealment of facts and circumstances endangering the life and health of the people in accordance with law.

Article 32

Citizens of the Republic of Kazakhstan shall have the right to peacefully and without arms assemble, hold meetings, rallies and demonstrations, street processions and pickets. The use of this right may be restricted by law in the interests of state security, public order, protection of health, rights and freedoms of other persons.

Article 33

Citizens of the Republic of Kazakhstan shall have the right to participate in the government of the state's affairs directly and through their representatives, to address personally as well as to direct individual and collective appeals to public and local self-administrative bodies.

Citizens of the Republic shall have the right to elect and be elected into public and local self-administrations as well as to participate in an all-nation referendum.

The right to elect and be elected, to participate in the all-nation referendum shall not extend to the citizens judged incapable by a court as well as those held in places of confinement on a court's sentence.

Citizens of the Republic shall have the equal right to serve in a public office. The requirements for candidates for public offices shall be conditioned only by the character of the office duties and shall be established by law.

Article 34

1. Everyone must observe the Constitution, legislation of the Republic of Kazakhstan and respect the rights, freedoms, honor and dignity of other persons.
2. Everyone must respect the state symbols of the Republic.

Article 35

Payment of legally established taxes, fees and other obligatory payments shall be a duty and responsibility of everyone.

Article 36

1. Defence of the Republic of Kazakhstan shall be a sacred duty and responsibility of its every citizen.
2. Citizens of the Republic shall perform military service according to the procedure and in the forms established by law.

Article 37

Citizens of the Republic of Kazakhstan must care for the protection of historical and cultural heritage, and preserve monuments of history and culture.

Article 38

Citizens of the Republic of Kazakhstan must preserve nature and protect natural resources.

Article 39

Rights and freedoms of an individual and citizen may be limited only by laws and only to the extent necessary for protection of the constitutional system, defense of the public order, human rights and freedoms, health and morality of the population.

Any actions capable of upsetting interethnic concord shall be deemed unconstitutional.

Any form of restrictions to the rights and freedoms of the citizens on political grounds shall not be permitted. Rights and freedoms stipulated by articles 10-11; 13-15 paragraph 1 of article 16; article 17; article 19; article 22; paragraph 2 of article 26 of the Constitution shall not be restricted in any event.

SECTION III
THE PRESIDENT

Article 40

1. The President of the Republic of Kazakhstan shall be the head of state, its highest official determining the main directions of the domestic and foreign policy of the state and representing Kazakhstan within the country and in international relations.
2. The President of the Republic shall be the symbol and guarantor of the unity of the people and the state power, inviolability of the Constitution, rights and freedoms of an individual and citizen.
3. The President of the Republic shall ensure by his arbitration concerted functioning of all branches of state power and responsibility of the institutions of power before the people.

Article 41

1. The President of the Republic shall be elected by universal, equal and direct suffrage under a secret ballot for a seven-year term in accordance with the constitutional law by the citizens of the Republic who have come of age.

2. A citizen of the Republic shall be eligible for the office of the President of the Republic of Kazakhstan if he is by birth not younger than forty and has a perfect command of the state language and has lived in Kazakhstan for not less than fifteen years.
3. Regular elections of the President of the Republic shall be held on the first Sunday of December and shall not coincide with the election of a new Parliament of the Republic.
4. The candidate who receives more than 50 percent of the votes of the constituents that took part in the election shall be deemed elected. If none of the candidates receives the above number of votes, a second round of elections shall be held between the two candidates who obtained the largest number of votes. The candidate who receives the larger number of votes of the constituents who take part in the second round of elections shall be deemed elected.

Article 42

The President of the Republic of Kazakhstan shall take office from the moment of swearing to the people the following oath: "I solemnly swear that I will faithfully serve the people of Kazakhstan, strictly observe the Constitution and the laws of the Republic of Kazakhstan, guarantee the rights and freedoms of the citizens, honestly perform the high duties of the President of the Republic of Kazakhstan entrusted to me."

The oath shall be taken on the second Wednesday of January in a ceremonial atmosphere in the presence of the deputies of Parliament, the members of the Constitutional Council, the judges of the Supreme Court as well as all former Presidents of the Republic. In case, stipulated by Article 48 of the Constitution, the oath shall be taken by a person who has taken the powers of the President of the Republic of Kazakhstan within one month since taking the powers of the President of the Republic.

The powers of the President of the Republic shall terminate from the moment the newly elected President of the Republic takes office as well as in the case of premature release from office, resignation or death. All former Presidents of the Republic except those who were discharged from office shall have the title of ex-President of the Republic of Kazakhstan.

One and the same person may not be elected the President of the Republic more than two times in a row.

Article 43

1. The President of the Republic of Kazakhstan shall not have the right to be a deputy of a representative body, hold other paid offices and engage in entrepreneurial-activity.
2. The President of the Republic shall suspend activity in any political party for the period he exercises his powers.

Article 44

1. The President of the Republic of Kazakhstan shall:
annually address the people of Kazakhstan with a message on the state of the country and main directions of the domestic and foreign policy of the Republic of Kazakhstan; appoint regular and extraordinary elections to the Parliament of the Republic; convene the first session of Parliament and accept the oath of its members to the people of Kazakhstan; call extraordinary joint sessions of the Chambers of Parliament; sign laws submitted by the Senate of Parliament within fifteen working days, promulgate the law or return the law or its separate articles for a second discussion and vote; appoint a Prime Minister of the Republic with the Parliament's consent; release him from office; determine the structure of the Government of the Republic at the proposal of the Prime Minister, appoint to and release from office its members, as well as form, abolish and reorganise central executive bodies of the Republic which are not included into the Government; accept the oath of the members of the Government; preside at the meetings of the Government on especially important issues; charge the Government with bringing a bill into the *Majilis* of Parliament; annul or suspend completely or partially the effect of the Government's acts and those of the *akims* of the oblasts, major cities and the capital; appoint the Chairperson of the National Bank of the Republic of Kazakhstan with the Parliament's consent; release him from office; appoint the Procurator General and Chairperson of the (committee of National Security of the Republic with the consent of the Senate of Parliament; release them from office; appoint and recall heads of diplomatic representative offices of the Republic; appoint the Chairperson and two members of the Estimation Committee for control over Implementation of the Republican Budget for a five year term; approve state programs of the Republic; approve a unified system of financing and labor payment for all bodies financed by the state budget of the Republic at the proposal of the Prime Minister of the Republic; adopt a resolution on conducting the all-nation referendum; conduct negotiations and sign international treaties of the Republic; sign ratification instruments; receive letters of credentials and recall from diplomatic and other representatives of foreign states accredited to him; act as the Commander-in-Chief of the Armed Forces of the Republic, appoint and replace the highest command of the Armed Forces; award state decorations of the Republic and confer-honorary, highest military and other ranks, ranked positions, diplomatic ranks and qualification degrees; resolve issues of citizenship of the Republic, and political asylum; exercise pardon of citizens; in the event of a serious and immediate threat to the democratic institutions of the Republic, its independence and territorial integrity, political stability of the Republic, security of its citizens and the disruption of normal functioning of the

Constitutional bodies of the state, the President snail have official consultation with Prime Minister and Chairpersons of the Parliamentary Chambers of the Republic and take measures, caused by a state of emergency on the entire territory or in particular areas of Kazakhstan, and immediately inform the Parliament of the use of the Armed Forces of the Republic; in the case of aggression against the Republic or immediate external threat to its security, the President shall impose martial law on the entire territory of the Republic or in particular areas, declare a partial or total mobilisation and immediately inform the Parliament of the Republic to the effect; form the Republican Guard as well as the Presidential Guard subordinated to the President; appoint to and release from office the State Secretary of the Republic of Kazakhstan, define his status and powers; form the administration of the President of the Republic; form the Security Council, the Higher Judicial Council and other consultative and advisory bodies; exercise other powers in accordance with the Constitution and the laws of the Republic.

Article 45

The President of the Republic of Kazakhstan, on the basis of and with the exercise of the Constitution and the laws, shall issue decrees and resolutions which are binding on the entire territory of the Republic.

In the case envisioned by subparagraph 4 of Article 53 of the Constitution the President of the Republic shall issue laws, and in the case envisioned by subparagraph 2 of Article 61 of the Constitution,—the President or the Republic shall issue decrees having the force of laws in the Republic.

The acts of Parliament signed by the President of the Republic as well as the acts of the President issued on the initiative of the Government shall be preliminary signed respectively by the Chairperson of each Parliaments Chambers or the Prime Minister on whom bear juridical responsibility for the legality of these acts.

Article 46

The President of the Republic of Kazakhstan, his honour and dignity shall be inviolable.

Provision, service, and guard of the President of the Republic and his family shall be carried out at the state's expense.

The provisions of this article shall extend to ex-Presidents of the Republic.

Article 47

1. The President of the Republic of Kazakhstan may be prematurely released from office in the case of continued incapacity to perform his duties due to illness. In this case the Parliament shall form a commission consisting of equal numbers of deputies from each Chamber and specialists of the respective areas of medicine. The decision of premature release based on

the conclusion of the commission and that of the Constitutional Council confirming observance of the established constitutional procedures shall be adopted at a joint sitting of the Parliament's Chambers by the majority of no less than three-fourths from the total number of deputies of each Chamber.

2. The President of the Republic shall bear responsibility for the actions performed while exercising his duties and only in the case of high treason may be discharged from office by Parliament. The decision to bring an accusation and conduct its investigation may be adopted by the majority of the deputies of the *Majilis* at the initiative of no less than one-third of the total number of its deputies. Investigation of the accusation shall be organised by the Senate and by the majority of votes of the total number of the deputies of the Senate its results are transferred for consideration at a joint session of the Parliament's Chambers. The final decision of this issue shall be adopted at a joint session of the Parliament's Chambers by the majority of no less than three-fourths of the total number of the deputies of each Chamber, provided the Supreme Court concludes the validity of the accusation and conclusion by the Constitutional Council that the established constitutional procedures were observed. The failure to arrive at a final decision within two months from the moment of the accusation shall result in the recognition that the accusation against the President of the Republic is rejected. Rejection of the accusation of the President of the Republic in perpetration of high treason at any stage shall result in premature termination of the powers of the deputies of the *Majilis* who initiated the consideration of this issue.
3. The issue of discharge of the President of the Republic from office may not be initiated in the period when the President is considering premature termination of the powers of the Parliament of the Republic.

Article 48

In case of premature release or discharge of the President of the Republic of Kazakhstan from office as well as in case of his death the powers of the President of the Republic shall be transmitted to the Chairperson of the Senate of the Parliament for the rest of the term; if the Chairperson of the Senate is unable to assume the powers of the President they shall be transmitted to the Chairperson of the *Majilis* of the Parliament; if the Chairperson of the *Majilis* is unable to assume the powers of the President they shall be transmitted to the Prime Minister of the Republic. A person who has taken the powers of the President of the Republic shall correspondingly withdraw his powers of the Chairperson of the Senate, the *Majilis*, the Prime Minister. In this case filling of those state positions shall be carried out in the order, stipulated by the Constitution.

A person who has taken the powers of the President of the Republic of Kazakhstan, on the basis and in the order stipulated by Paragraph 1 of the present

Article, has no right to initiate amendments and additions to the Constitution of the Republic of Kazakhstan.

SECTION IV
PARLIAMENT

Article 49

1. Parliament of the Republic of Kazakhstan is the highest representative body of the Republic performing legislative functions.
2. Parliament's powers shall begin from the opening of its first session and terminate with the first session of a new convocation.
3. The powers of Parliament may be prematurely terminated in cases and according to the procedure stipulated by the Constitution.
4. The organisation and activities of Parliament, the legal status of its deputies shall be determined by constitutional law.

Article 50

Parliament shall consist of two Chambers acting on a permanent basis: the Senate and the *Majilis.*

The Senate shall be composed of deputies elected in twos from each oblast, major city and the capital of the Republic of Kazakhstan, at a joint session of the deputies of all representative bodies of the respectively oblast, major city and the capital of the Republic. Seven deputies of the Senate shall be appointed by the President of the Republic for the term of the Senate.

The *Majilis* shall consist of seventy-seven deputies. Sixty-seven deputies shall be elected in constituencies having one mandate and formed according to the administrative-territorial division of the Republic with an approximately equal number of constituents. Ten deputies shall be elected on the basis of the Party Lists according to the system of proportional representation and in the territory of a unified national constituency.

A deputy of Parliament may not be a member of both Chambers simultaneously.

Term of the powers of Senate deputies shall be six years, term of the powers of the *Majilis* deputies shall be five years.

Article 51

1. Elections of the deputies of the *Majilis* shall be carried out on the basis of the universal, equal and direct right under secret ballot. Regular elections of the deputies of the *Majilis* shall be held no later than two months before the termination of the powers of current Parliament.
2. The elections of the deputies of the Senate shall be carried out on the basis of indirect electoral right under secret ballot. Half of the elected deputies of the Senate shall be re-elected every three years. In this case, their regular

elections shall be held no later than two months before the end of their term in office.

3. Extraordinary elections of the deputies of Parliament shall be held within two months from the moment of premature termination of Parliament's powers.
4. A deputy of the Senate may be a citizen of the Republic of Kazakhstan who has been a citizen of the Republic for not less than five years and who has reached thirty years of age, has a higher education and length of service of not less than five years, and has been a permanent resident for not less than three years on the territory of the respective oblast, major city or the capital of the Republic. A deputy of the *Majilis* may be a citizen of the Republic of Kazakhstan who has reached twenty-five years of age.
5. A candidate shall be deemed elected if he receives more than fifty percent of the votes of constituents or electors who took part in the voting in a constituency having one mandate, at the joint session of deputies of all the representative bodies correspondingly of the oblasts, the city of republican significance and the capital of the Republic. If none of the candidates receives the aforementioned number of votes, a second round of voting shall be held between the two candidates who obtained the largest number of votes. The candidate who receives the larger number of votes of the constituents or electors who took part in voting shall be deemed elected. Only those political parties which received not less than seven percent of votes of constituents who took part in the elections, shall be admitted to distribution of deputy mandates in accordance with the results of elections to the *Majilis* on the basis of Party Lists. Elections to the Senate shall be deemed valid in case more than fifty percent of electors took part in the voting. Procedure of elections of the deputies of the Parliament of the Republic shall be determined by constitutional law.
6. A deputy shall take an oath before the people of Kazakhstan.

Article 52

A deputy of Parliament shall not be bound by any imperative mandate.

The deputies of Parliament must take part in its work. The deputies shall only vote in person in Parliament. Absence of a deputy at sittings of the Chambers and their bodies without a good reason for more than three times as well as transferring the right to vote shall cause the imposition of penalties established by law.

A deputy of Parliament shall have no right to be a deputy of another representative body, hold other paid offices, except teaching, research and creative activities, engage in entrepreneurial activity, enter a managing body or a supervisory board of a commercial organisation. Violation of this rule shall result in the termination of a deputy's powers.

A deputy of Parliament during the term of his office may not be arrested, subject to detention, measures of administrative punishment imposed by a court of law, arraigned on a criminal charge without the consent of a respective Chamber except for the cases of being apprehended on the scene of a crime or committing grave crimes.

The powers of the deputies of Parliament shall be terminated in cases of resignation, being recognised as incapable, dissolution of Parliament and in other cases stipulated by the Constitution. A deputy of Parliament shall be deprived of his mandate in cases being duly convicted in a court of law, establishing permanent residency beyond the boundaries of the Republic of Kazakhstan.

Preparation of questions concerning the imposition of penalties on the deputies, their observance of the requirements of paragraph 3 of this article, principles of the deputies' ethics, as well as termination of the deputies' powers and deprivation of their powers and deputy immunity, shall be delegated to the Central Election Commission of the Republic of Kazakhstan.

Source: The Constitution of the Republic of Kazakhstan, 1993.

Appendix-2

The Constitution of the Republic of Kazakhstan (1995)

Decree of the President of the Republic of Kazakhstan

On the Constitution of the Republic of Kazakhstan The President of the Republic of Kazakhstan proposed, and the people of Kazakhstan, at the republican referendum on August 30, 1995, adopted the New Constitution of the Republic of Kazakhstan. In view of the results of the republican referendum having been officially published, and the New Constitution having come into force since September 5, 1995, I RESOLVE:

1. To publish the Constitution of the Republic of Kazakhstan.
2. To stipulate that the original text of the Constitution of the Republic of Kazakhstan, adopted at the republican referendum on August 30, 1995, shall be kept by the President of the Republic of Kazakhstan.
3. The original text of the Constitution of the Republic of Kazakhstan, adopted at the ninth session of the Supreme Soviet of the Republic of Kazakhstan of the twelfth convocation on January 28, 1993, shall be placed for eternal custody with the Central State Archives of the Republic of Kazakhstan.
4. The present Decree comes into effect on the day it is published.

The President of the Republic of Kazakhstan N. NAZARBAYEV

Almaty, September 6, 1995

We, the people of Kazakhstan, united by a common historic fate, creating a state on the indigenous Kazakh land, considering ourselves a peace loving and civil society, dedicated to the ideals of freedom, equality and concord, wishing to take a worthy place in the world community, realising our high responsibility before the present and future generations, proceeding from our sovereign right, accept this Constitution.

SECTION I
GENERAL PROVISIONS

Article 1

1. The Republic of Kazakhstan proclaims itself a democratic, secular, legal and social state whose highest values are an individual, his life, rights and freedoms.
2. The fundamental principles of the activity of the Republic are public concord

and political stability; economic development for the benefit of all the nation; Kazakhstan patriotism and resolution of the most important issues of the affairs of state by democratic methods including voting at an all-nation referendum or in the Parliament.

Article 2

1. The Republic of Kazakhstan is a unitary state with a Presidential form of government.
2. The sovereignty of the Republic extends to its entire territory. The state ensures the integrity, inviolability and inalienability of its territory.
3. The administrative-territorial division of the Republic of Kazakhstan, location and status of its capital are determined by law.
4. The names "Republic of Kazakhstan" and "Kazakhstan" have the same meaning.

Article 3

1. The people shall be the only source of state power.
2. The people shall exercise power directly through an all-nation referendum and free elections as well as delegate the execution of their power to state institutions.
3. Nobody shall have the right to appropriate power in the Republic of Kazakhstan. Appropriation of power shall be persecuted by law. The right to act on behalf of the people and the state shall belong to the President as well as to Parliament of the Republic within the limits of the constitutional powers. The government and other state bodies shall act on behalf of the state only within the limits of their delegated authorities.
4. The state power in the Republic of Kazakhstan is unified and executed on the basis of the Constitution and laws in accordance with the principle of its division into the legislative, executive and judicial branches and a system of checks and balances that governs their interaction.

Article 4

1. The provisions of the Constitution, the laws corresponding to it, other regulatory legal acts, international treaty and other commitments of the Republic as well as regulatory resolutions of Constitutional Council and the Supreme Court of the Republic shall be the functioning law in the Republic of Kazakhstan.
2. The Constitution shall have the highest juridical force and direct effect on the entire territory of the Republic.
3. International treaties ratified by the Republic shall have priority over its laws and be directly implemented except in cases when the application of an international treaty shall require the promulgation of a law.
4. All laws, international treaties of which the Republic is a party shall be published. Official publication of regulatory legal acts dealing with the rights,

freedoms and responsibilities of citizens shall be a necessary condition for their application.

Article 5

1. The Republic of Kazakhstan shall recognise ideological and political diversity. The merging of public and state institutions, and the formation of political party organisations in state bodies shall not be permitted.
2. Public associations shall be equal before the law. Illegal interference of the state in the affairs of public associations and of public associations in the affairs of the state, imposing the functions of state institutions on public associations, and financing of public associations by the state shall not be permitted.
3. Formation and functioning of public associations pursuing the goals or actions directed toward a violent change of the constitutional system, violation of the integrity of the Republic, undermining the security of the state, inciting social, racial, national, religious, class and tribal enmity, as well as formation of unauthorized paramilitary units shall be prohibited.
4. Activities of political parties and trade unions of other states, religious parties as well as financing political parties and trade unions by foreign legal entities and citizens, foreign states and international organisations shall not be permitted in the Republic.
5. Activities of foreign religious associations on the territory of the Republic as well as appointment of heads of religious associations in the Republic by foreign religious centers shall be carried out in coordination with the respective state institutions of the Republic.

Article 6

The Republic of Kazakhstan shall recognise and by the same token protect state and private property.

Property shall impose obligations, and its use must simultaneously benefit the society. Subjects and objects of ownership, the scope and limits of the rights of proprietors, and guarantees of their protection shall be determined by law.

The land and underground resources, waters, flora and fauna, other natural resources shall be owned by the state. The land may also be privately owned on terms, conditions and within the limits established by legislation.

Article 7

1. The state language of the Republic of Kazakhstan shall be the Kazakh language.
2. In state institutions and local self-administrative bodies the Russian language shall be officially used on equal grounds along with the Kazakh language.
3. The state shall promote conditions for the study and development of the languages of the people of Kazakhstan.

Article 8

The Republic of Kazakhstan shall respect principles and norms of international law, pursue the policy of cooperation and good-neighborly relations between states, their equality and non-interference in each other's domestic affairs, peaceful settlement of international disputes and renounce the first use of the military force.

Article 9

The Republic of Kazakhstan shall have its state symbols—the flag, emblem and anthem. Their description and order of official use shall be established by the constitutional law.

SECTION II
THE INDIVIDUAL AND CITIZEN

Article 10

Citizenship of the Republic of Kazakhstan shall be acquired and terminated as prescribed by law, shall be indivisible and equal regardless of the grounds of its acquisition.

A citizen of the Republic of Kazakhstan under no circumstances may be deprived of citizenship of the right to change his citizenship, and may not be exiled from the territory of Kazakhstan.

Foreign citizenship of a citizen of the Republic shall not be recognised.

Article 11

1. A citizen of the Republic of Kazakhstan may not be extradited to a foreign state unless otherwise stipulated by international treaties of the Republic.
2. The Republic shall guarantee its citizens protection and patronage outside its boundaries.

Article 12

1. Human rights and freedoms in the Republic of Kazakhstan shall be recognised and guaranteed in accordance with this Constitution.
2. Human rights and freedoms shall belong to everyone by virtue of birth, be recognised as absolute and inalienable, and define the contents and implementation of laws and other regulatory legal acts.
3. Every citizen of the Republic shall have rights and bear responsibilities owing to his citizenship.
4. Foreigners and stateless persons in the Republic shall enjoy rights and freedoms as well as bear responsibilities established for the citizens unless otherwise stipulated by the Constitution, laws and international treaties.
5. Exercise of a citizen's human rights and freedoms must not violate rights and freedoms of other persons, infringe on the constitutional system and public morals.

Article 13

1. Everyone shall have the right to be recognised as subject of the law and protect his rights and freedoms with all means not contradicting the law including self-defense.
2. Everyone shall have the right to judicial defense of his rights and freedoms.
3. Everyone shall have the right to qualified legal assistance. In cases stipulated by law, legal assistance shall be provided free of charge.

Article 14

1. Everyone shall be equal before the law and court.
2. No one shall be subject to any discrimination for reasons of origin, social, property status, occupation, sex, race, nationality, language, attitude towards religion, convictions, place of residence or any other circumstances.

Article 15

1. Everyone shall have the right to life.
2. No one shall have the right to arbitrarily deprive a person of life. The law shall establish the death penalty as an extraordinary measure of punishment for especially grave crimes and grant the sentenced person the right to appeal for pardon.

Article 16

1. Everyone shall have the right to personal freedom.
2. Arrest and detention shall be allowed only in cases stipulated by law and only with the sanction of a court or prosecutor of law. The detained person shall be provided with the right to appeal. Without the sanction of a procurator, a person may be detained for a period no more than seventy-two hours.
3. Every person detained, arrested and accused of committing a crime shall have the right to the assistance of a defense lawyer (defender) from the moment of detention, arrest or accusation.

Article 17

1. A person's dignity shall be inviolable.
2. No one must be subject to torture, violence or other treatment and punishment that is cruel or humiliating to human dignity.

Article 18

1. Everyone shall have the right to inviolability of private life, personal or family secrets, protection of honor and dignity.
2. Everyone shall have the right to confidentiality of personal deposits and savings, correspondence, telephone conversations, postal, telegraph and other messages. Limitation of this right shall be permitted only in the cases and according to the procedure directly established by law.
3. State bodies, public associations, officials, and the mass media must provide

every citizen with the possibility to obtain access to documents, decisions and other sources of information concerning his rights and interests.

Article 19

1. Everyone shall have the right to determine and indicate or not to indicate his national, party and religious affiliation.
2. Everyone shall have the right to use his native language and culture, to freely choose the language of communication, education, instruction and creative activities.

Article 20

1. The freedom of speech and creative activities shall be guaranteed. Censorship shall be prohibited.
2. Everyone shall have the right to freely receive and disseminate information by any means not prohibited by law. The list of items constituting state secrets of the Republic of Kazakhstan shall be determined by law.
3. Propaganda of or agitation for the forcible change of the constitutional system, violation of the integrity of the Republic, undermining of state security, and advocating war, social, racial, national, religious, class and clannish superiority as well as the cult of cruelty and violence shall not be allowed.

Article 21

1. Everyone who has a legal right to stay on the territory of the Republic of Kazakhstan shall have the right to freely move about its territory and freely choose a place of residence except in cases stipulated by law.
2. Everyone shall have the right to leave the territory of the Republic. Citizens of the Republic shall have the right to freely return to the Republic.

Article 22

1. Everyone shall have the right to freedom of conscience.
2. The right to freedom of conscience must not specify or limit universal human and civil rights and responsibilities before the state.

Article 23

1. Citizens of the Republic of Kazakhstan shall have the right to freedom of forming associations. The activities of public associations shall be regulated by law.
2. The military, employees of national security, law-enforcement bodies and judges must abstain from membership in political parties, trade unions, and actions in support of any political party.

Article 24

1. Everyone shall have the right to freedom of labour, and the free choice of occupation and profession. Involuntary labor shall be permitted only on a sentence of court or in the conditions of a state of emergency or martial law.

2. Everyone shall have the right to safe and hygienic working conditions, to just remuneration for labour without discrimination, as well as to social protection against unemployment.
3. The right to individual and collective labour disputes with the use of methods for resolving them, stipulated by law including the right to strike, shall be recognised.
4. Everyone shall have the right to rest. Working labor agreements stipulating the length of working time, days-off and holidays, and paid annual leave shall be guaranteed by law.

Article 25

1. Housing shall be inviolable. Deprivation of housing shall not be permitted unless otherwise stipulated by a court decision. Penetration into housing, its inspection and search shall be permitted only in cases and according to the procedure stipulated by law.
2. Conditions shall be created in the Republic of Kazakhstan to provide citizens with housing. Citizens in need of housing shall be categorized in a manner to be prescribed by law and provided with housing at an affordable price from the state housing funds in accordance with the norms stipulated by law.

Article 26

1. Citizens of the Republic of Kazakhstan may privately own any legally acquired property.
2. Property, including the right of inheritance, shall be guaranteed by law.
3. No one may be deprived of his property unless otherwise stipulated by a court decision. Forcible alienation of property for the public use in extraordinary cases stipulated by law may be exercised on condition of its equivalent compensation.
4. Everyone shall have the right to freedom of entrepreneurial activity, and free use of his property for any legal entrepreneurial activity. Monopolistic activity shall be regulated and limited by law. Unfair competition shall be prohibited.

Article 27

1. Marriage and family, motherhood, fatherhood and childhood shall be under the protection of the state.
2. Care of children and their upbringing shall be a natural right and responsibility of parents.
3. Able-bodied children of age must take care of their disabled parents.

Article 28

1. A citizen of the Republic of Kazakhstan shall be guaranteed a minimum wage and pension, and guaranteed social security in old age, in case of disease, disability or loss of a breadwinner and other legal grounds.

2. Voluntary social insurance, creation of additional forms of social security, and charity shall be encouraged.

Article 29

1. Citizens of the Republic of Kazakhstan shall have the right to protection of health.
2. Citizens of the Republic shall be entitled to free, guaranteed, extensive medical assistance established by law.
3. Paid medical treatment shall be provided by state and private medical institutions as well as by persons engaged in private medical practice on the terms and according to the procedures stipulated by law.

Article 30

1. The citizens shall be guaranteed free secondary education in state educational establishments. Secondary education shall be obligatory.
2. A citizen shall have the right to receive on a competitive basis a higher education in a state higher educational establishment.
3. The citizens shall have the right to pay and receive an education in private educational establishments on the basis and terms established by law.
4. The state shall set uniform compulsory standards in education. The activity of any educational establishment must comply with these standards.

Article 31

1. The state shall set an objective to protect the environment favorable for the life and health of the person.
2. Officials shall be held accountable for the concealment of facts and circumstances endangering the life and health of the people in accordance with law.

Article 32

Citizens of the Republic of Kazakhstan shall have the right to peacefully and without arms assemble, hold meetings, rallies and demonstrations, street processions and pickets. The use of this right may be restricted by law in the interests of state security, public order, protection of health, rights and freedoms of other persons.

Article 33

1. Citizens of the Republic of Kazakhstan shall have the right to participate in the government of the state's affairs directly and through their representatives, to address personally as well as to direct individual and collective appeals to public and local self-administrative bodies.
2. Citizens of the Republic shall have the right to elect and be elected into public and local self-administrations as well as to participate in an all-nation referendum.
3. The right to elect and be elected, to participate in the all-nation referendum

shall not extend to the citizens judged incapable by a court as well as those held in places of confinement on a court's sentence.

4. Citizens of the Republic shall have the equal right to serve in a public office. The requirements for candidates for public offices shall be conditioned only by the character of the office duties and shall be established by law'. *Paragraph 4 of Article 33 is given in a wording of the Law of the Republic of Kazakhstan of October 7, 1998 [1]284-1 of LRK.*

Article 34

1. Everyone must observe the Constitution, legislation of the Republic of Kazakhstan and respect the rights, freedoms, honour and dignity of other persons.
2. Everyone must respect the state symbols of the Republic.

Article 35

Payment of legally established taxes, fees and other obligatory payments shall be a duty and responsibility of everyone.

Article 36

1. Defense of the Republic of Kazakhstan shall be a sacred duty and responsibility of its every citizen.
2. Citizens of the Republic shall perform military service according to the procedure and in the forms established by law.

Article 37

Citizens of the Republic of Kazakhstan must care for the protection of historical and cultural heritage, and preserve monuments of history and culture.

Article 38

Citizens of the Republic of Kazakhstan must preserve nature and protect natural resources.

Article 39

1. Rights and freedoms of an individual and citizen may be limited only by laws and only to the extent necessary for protection of the constitutional system, defense of the public order, human rights and freedoms, health and morality of the population.
2. Any actions capable of upsetting interethnic concord shall be deemed unconstitutional.
3. Any form of restrictions to the rights and freedoms of the citizens on political grounds shall not be permitted. Rights and freedoms stipulated by articles 10-11; 13-15 paragraph 1 of article 16; article 17; article 19; article 22; paragraph 2 of article 26 of the Constitution shall not be restricted in any event.

SECTION III
THE PRESIDENT

Article 40

1. The President of the Republic of Kazakhstan shall be the head of state, its highest official determining the main directions of the domestic and foreign policy of the state and representing Kazakhstan within the country and in international relations.
2. The President of the Republic shall be the symbol and guarantor of the unity of the people and the state power, inviolability of the Constitution, rights and freedoms of an individual and citizen.
3. The President of the Republic shall ensure by his arbitration concerted functioning of all branches of state power and responsibility of the institutions of power before the people.

Article 41

1. The President of the Republic shall be elected by universal, equal and direct suffrage under a secret ballot for a seven-year term in accordance with the constitutional law by the citizens of the Republic who have come of age.
2. A citizen of the Republic shall be eligible for the office of the President of the Republic of Kazakhstan if he is by birth not younger than forty and has a perfect command of the state language and has lived in Kazakhstan for not less than fifteen years.
3. Regular elections of the President of the Republic shall be held on the first Sunday of December and shall not coincide with the election of a new Parliament of the Republic.
4. Excluded.
5. The candidate who receives more than 50 percent of the votes of the constituents that took part in the election shall be deemed elected. If none of the candidates receives the above number of votes, a second round of elections shall be held between the two candidates who obtained the largest number of votes. The candidate who receives the larger number of votes of the constituents who take part in the second round of elections shall be deemed elected'.

Article 42

1. The President of the Republic of Kazakhstan shall take office from the moment of swearing to the people the following oath: "I solemnly swear that I will faithfully serve the people of Kazakhstan, strictly observe the Constitution and the laws of the Republic of Kazakhstan, guarantee the rights and freedoms of the citizens, honestly perform the high duties of the President of the Republic of Kazakhstan entrusted to me."
2. The oath shall be taken on the second Wednesday of January in a ceremonial atmosphere in the presence of the deputies of Parliament, the members of the Constitutional Council, the judges of the Supreme Court as well as all

former Presidents of the Republic. In case, stipulated by Article 48 of the Constitution, the oath shall be taken by a person who has taken the powers of the President of the Republic of Kazakhstan within one month since taking the powers of the President of the Republic.

3. The powers of the President of the Republic shall terminate from the moment the newly elected President of the Republic takes office as well as in the case of premature release from office, resignation or death. All former Presidents of the Republic except those who were discharged from office shall have the title of ex-President of the Republic of Kazakhstan.
4. Excluded.
   Paragraphs 2, 4, 5 of Article 41, paragraphs 2 and 4 of Article 42 are given in a wording of the Law of the Republic of Kazakhstan of October 7, 1998 N" 284-1 of LRK.
5. One and the same person may not be elected the President of the Republic more than two times in a row.

Article 43

1. The President of the Republic of Kazakhstan shall not have the right to be a deputy of a representative body, hold other paid offices and engage in entrepreneurial-activity.
2. The President of the Republic shall suspend activity in any political party for the period he exercises his powers.

Article 44

The President of the Republic of Kazakhstan shall:

1) annually address the people of Kazakhstan with a message on the state of the country and main directions of the domestic and foreign policy of the Republic of Kazakhstan;
2) appoint regular and extraordinary elections to the Parliament of the Republic; convene the first session of Parliament and accept the oath of its members to the people of Kazakhstan; call extraordinary joint sessions of the Chambers of Parliament; sign laws submitted by the Senate of Parliament within fifteen working days, promulgate the law or return the law or its separate articles for a second discussion and vote;
3) appoint a Prime Minister of the Republic with the Parliament's consent; release him from office; determine the structure of the Government of the Republic at the proposal of the Prime Minister, appoint to and release from office its members, as well as form, abolish and reorganise central executive bodies of the Republic which are not included into the Government; accept the oath of the members of the Government; preside at the meetings of the Government on especially important issues; charge the Government with bringing a bill into the *Majilis* of Parliament; annul or suspend

completely or partially the effect of the Government's acts and those of the *Akims* of the oblasts, major cities and the capital;

4) appoint the Chairperson of the National Bank of the Republic of Kazakhstan with the Parliament's consent; release him from office;
5) appoint the Procurator General and Chairperson of the Committee of National Security of the Republic with the consent of the Senate of Parliament; release them from office;
6) appoint and recall heads of diplomatic representative offices of the Republic;
7) appoint the Chairperson and two members of the Estimation Committee for control over Implementation of the Republican Budget for a five-year term;
8) approve state programs of the Republic;
9) approve a unified system of financing and labor payment for all bodies financed by the state budget of the Republic at the proposal of the Prime Minister of the Republic;
10) adopt a resolution on conducting the all-nation referendum;
11) conduct negotiations and sign international treaties of the Republic; sign ratification instruments; receive letters of credentials and recall from diplomatic and other representatives of foreign states accredited to him;
12) act as the Commander-in-Chief of the Armed Forces of the Republic, appoint and replace the highest command of the Armed Forces;
13) award state decorations of the Republic and confer-honorary, highest military and other ranks, ranked positions, diplomatic ranks and qualification degrees;
14) resolve issues of citizenship of the Republic, and political asylum;
15) exercise pardon of citizens;
16) in the event of a serious and immediate threat to the democratic institutions of the Republic, its independence and territorial integrity, political stability of the Republic, security of its citizens and the disruption of normal functioning of the Constitutional bodies of the state, the President snail have official consultation with Prime Minister and Chairpersons of the Parliamentary Chambers of the Republic and take measures, caused by a state of emergency on the entire territory or in particular areas of Kazakhstan, and immediately inform the Parliament of the use of the Armed Forces of the Republic;
17) in the case of aggression against the Republic or immediate external threat to its security, the President shall impose martial law on the entire territory of the Republic or in particular areas, declare a partial

or total mobilisation and immediately inform the Parliament of the Republic to the effect;

18) form the Republican Guard as well as the Presidential Guard subordinated to the President;
19) appoint to and release from office the State Secretary of the Republic of Kazakhstan, define his status and powers; form the administration of the President of the Republic;
20) form the Security Council, the Higher Judicial Council and other consultative and advisory bodies;
21) exercise other powers in accordance with the Constitution and the laws of the Republic'.

Article 45

1. The President of the Republic of Kazakhstan, on the basis of and with the exercise of the Constitution and the laws, shall issue decrees and resolutions which are binding on the entire territory of the Republic.
2. In the case envisioned by subparagraph 4 of Article 53 of the Constitution the President of the Republic shall issue laws, and in the case envisioned by subparagraph 2 of Article 61 of the Constitution,—the President or the Republic shall issue decrees having the force of laws in the Republic
3. The acts of Parliament signed by the President of the Republic as well as the acts of the President issued on the initiative of the Government shall be preliminary signed respectively by the Chairperson of each Parliaments Chambers or the Prime Minister on whom bear juridical responsibility for the legality of these acts.

Article 46

1. The President of the Republic of Kazakhstan, his honour and dignity shall be inviolable.
2. Provision, service, and guard of the President of the Republic and his family shall be carried out at the state's expense.
3. The provisions of this article shall extend to ex-Presidents of the Republic. *Subparagraph (7) of Article 44 is given in a wording of the Law of the Republic of Kazakhstan of October 7, 1998 N° 284-1 of LRK.*

Article 47

1. The President of the Republic of Kazakhstan may be prematurely released from office in the case of continued incapacity to perform his duties due to illness. In this case the Parliament shall form a commission consisting of equal numbers of deputies from each Chamber and specialists of the respective areas of medicine. The decision of premature release based on the conclusion of the commission and that of the Constitutional Council confirming observance of the established constitutional procedures shall be adopted at a joint sitting of the Parliament's Chambers by the majority of

no less than three-fourths from the total number of deputies of each Chamber.

2. The President of the Republic shall bear responsibility for the actions performed while exercising his duties and only in the case of high treason may be discharged from office by Parliament. The decision to bring an accusation and conduct its investigation may be adopted by the majority of the deputies of the *Majilis* at the initiative of no less than one-third of the total number of its deputies. Investigation of the accusation shall be organised by the Senate and by the majority of votes of the total number of the deputies of the Senate its results are transferred for consideration at a joint session of the Parliament's Chambers. The final decision of this issue shall be adopted at a joint session of the Parliament's Chambers by the majority of no less than three-fourths of the total number of the deputies of each Chamber, provided the Supreme Court concludes the validity of the accusation and conclusion by the Constitutional Council that the established constitutional procedures were observed. The failure to arrive at a final decision within two months from the moment of the accusation shall result in the recognition that the accusation against the President of the Republic is rejected. Rejection of the accusation of the President of the Republic in perpetration of high treason at any stage shall result in premature termination of the powers of the deputies of the *Majilis* who initiated the consideration of this issue.
3. The issue of discharge of the President of the Republic from office may not be initiated in the period when the President is considering premature termination of the powers of the Parliament of the Republic.

Article 48

1. In case of premature release or discharge of the President of the Republic of Kazakstan from office as well as in case of his death the powers of the President of the Republic shall be transmitted to the Chairperson of the Senate of the Parliament for the rest of the term; if the Chairperson of the Senate is unable to assume the powers of the President they shall be transmitted to the Chairperson of the *Majilis* of the Parliament; if the Chairperson of the *Majilis* is unable to assume the powers of the President they shall be transmitted to the Prime Minister of the Republic. A person who has taken the powers of the President of the Republic shall correspondingly withdraw his powers of the Chairperson of the Senate, the *Majilis*, the Prime Minister. In this case filling of those state positions shall be carried out in the order, stipulated by the Constitution. 2. A person who has taken the powers of the President of the Republic of Kazakhstan, on the basis and in the order stipulated by Paragraph 1 of the present Article, has no right to initiate amendments and additions to the Constitution of the Republic of Kazakhstan'.

SECTION IV
PARLIAMENT

Article 49

1. Parliament of the Republic of Kazakhstan is the highest representative body of the Republic performing legislative functions.
2. Parliament's powers shall begin from the opening of its first session and terminate with the first session of a new convocation.
3. The powers of Parliament may be prematurely terminated in cases and according to the procedure stipulated by the Constitution.
4. The organisation and activities of Parliament, the legal status of its deputies shall be determined by constitutional law2.

Article 50

1. Parliament shall consist of two Chambers acting on a permanent basis: the Senate and the *Majilis*.
2. The Senate shall be composed of deputies elected in twos from each oblast, major city and the capital of the Republic of Kazakhstan, at a joint session of the deputies of all representative bodies of, correspondingly, the oblast, major city and the capital of the Republic. Seven deputies of the Senate shall be appointed by the President of the Republic for the term of the Senate.
3. The *Majilis* shall consist of seventy-seven deputies. Sixty-seven deputies shall be elected in constituencies having one mandate and formed according to the administrative-territorial division of the Republic with an approximately equal number of constituents. Ten deputies shall be elected on the basis of the Party Lists according to the system of proportional representation and in the territory of a unified national constituency.
4. A deputy of Parliament may not be a member of both Chambers simultaneously.
5. Term of the powers of Senate deputies shall be six years, term of the powers of the *Majilis* deputies shall be five years'.

Article 51

1. Elections of the deputies of the *Majilis* shall be carried out on the basis of the universal, equal and direct right under secret ballot. Regular elections of the deputies of the *Majilis* shall be held no later than two months before the termination of the powers of current Parliament.

   'Article 48 is given in a wording of the Law of the Republic of Kazakhstan of October 7, 1998 1 284-1 of LRK.

   'Paragraph 2 of Article 49 is given in a wording of the Law of the Republic of Kazakhstan of October 7, 1998 1 284-1 of LRK.

   Paragraphs 2,3,5 of Article 50 are given in a wording of the Law of the Republic of Kazakhstan of October 7, 1998 1 284-1 of LRK.
2. The elections of the deputies of the Senate shall be carried out on the basis of indirect electoral right under secret ballot. Half of the elected deputies of

the Senate shall be re-elected every three years. In this case, their regular elections shall be held no later than two months before the end of their term in office.

3. Extraordinary elections of the deputies of Parliament shall be held within two months from the moment of premature termination of Parliament's powers.
4. A deputy of the Senate may be a citizen of the Republic of Kazakhstan who has been a citizen of the Republic for not less than five years and who has reached thirty years of age, has a higher education and length of service of not less than five years, and has been a permanent resident for not less than three years on the territory of the respective oblast, major city or the capital of the Republic. A deputy of the *Majilis* may be a citizen of the Republic of Kazakhstan who has reached twenty-five years of age.
5. A candidate shall be deemed elected if he receives more than fifty percent of the votes of constituents or electors who took part in the voting in a constituency having one mandate, at the joint session of deputies of all the representative bodies correspondingly of the oblasts, the city of republican significance and the capital of the Republic. If none of the candidates receives the above numbers of votes, a second round of elections shall be held between the two candidates who obtained the largest number of votes. The candidate who receives the larger number of votes of the constituents or electors who took part in the second round of elections shall be deemed elected. Only those political parties which received not less than seven percent of votes of constituents who took part in the elections, shall be admitted to distribution of deputy mandates in accordance with the results of elections to the *Majilis* on the basis of Party Lists. Elections to the Senate shall be deemed valid in case more than fifty percent of electors took part in the voting. Procedure of elections of the deputies of the Parliament of the Republic shall be determined by constitutional law.
6. A deputy shall take an oath before the people of Kazakhstan'.

Article 52

1. A deputy of Parliament shall not be bound by any imperative mandate.
2. The deputies of Parliament must take part in its work. The deputies shall only vote in person in Parliament. Absence of a deputy at sittings of the Chambers and their bodies without a good reason for more than three times as well as transferring the right to vote shall cause the imposition of penalties established by law.
3. A deputy of Parliament shall have no right to be a deputy of another representative body, hold other paid offices, except teaching, research and creative activities, engage in entrepreneurial activity, enter a managing body or a supervisory board of a commercial organisation. Violation of this rule shall result in the termination of a deputy's powers.

Paragraphs 2 and 5 of Article 51 are given in a wording of the Law of the Republic of Kazakhstan of October 7, 1998 No 284-1 of LRK.

4. A deputy of Parliament during the term of his office may not be arrested, subject to detention, measures of administrative punishment imposed by a court of law, arraigned on a criminal charge without the consent of a respective Chamber except for the cases of being apprehended on the scene of a crime or committing grave crimes.
5. The powers of the deputies of Parliament shall be terminated in cases of resignation, being recognised as incapable, dissolution of Parliament and in other cases stipulated by the Constitution. A deputy of Parliament shall be deprived of his mandate in cases being duly convicted in a court of law, establishing permanent residency beyond the boundaries of the Republic of Kazakhstan.
6. Preparation of questions concerning the imposition of penalties on the deputies, their observance of the requirements of paragraph 3 of this article, principles of the deputies' ethics, as well as termination of the deputies' powers and deprivation of their powers and deputy immunity, shall be delegated to the Central Election Commission of the Republic of Kazakhstan.'

Article 53

Parliament at a joint session of the Chambers shall:

1) introduce amendments and make additions to the Constitution; adopt constitutional laws, introduce amendments and make additions to the Constitution at the proposal of the President of the Republic of Kazakhstan;
2) approve the republican budget, the reports of the Government, and Estimation Committee about its implementation, and introduce changes into the budget;
3) conduct a second round of discussion and voting on the laws or articles of the law that caused objections of the President of the Republic within a month's term from the moment the objections were presented. Non-observance of this term denotes the acceptance of the President's objections. If Parliament by the majority of two-thirds of votes from the total number of deputies from each Chamber confirms the decision adopted earlier, the President shall sign the law within seven days. If the President's objections are not overruled, the law shall be deemed not adopted or adopted in the version proposed by the President;
4) have the right to delegate legislative Powers for a term not exceeding one year to the President by two-thirds of the votes from the total number of deputies of each Chamber at the initiative of the President;

5) give consent to the appointment of the Prime Minister of the Republic and the Chairperson of the National Bank of the Republic by the President of the Republic;
6) hear the report of the Prime Minister on the Government's program and approve or reject the program. A second rejection of the program brought about by the majority of two-thirds of votes from the total number of deputies of each Chamber denotes a vote of no confidence in the Government. The absence of such a majority implies the approval of the Government's program;
7) express a vote of no confidence in the Government by the majority of two-thirds of votes from the total number of deputies of each Chamber at the initiative of no less than one-fifth of the total number of the Parliament's deputies and in cases established by this Constitution; *'Paragraph 3 of Article 52 is given in a wording of the Law of the Republic of Kazakhstan of October 7, 1998 [1] 284-1 of LRK.*
8) decide issues of war and peace;
9) adopt a decision concerning the use of the Armed Forces of the Republic to fulfill international obligations in support of peace and security at the proposal of the President of the Republic;
10) put forward an initiative calling for an all-nation referendum;
11) hear annual messages of the Constitutional Council of the Republic on the state of the constitutional legality in the Republic;
12) form joint commissions of the Chambers; elect and release from office their chairpersons; hear reports on the activity of the commissions;
13) exercise other powers assigned to Parliament by the Constitution.

Article 54

Parliament at separate sessions of the Chambers through consecutive consideration of issues first in the *Majilis* and then in the Senate shall:

1) adopt laws;
2) discuss the republican budget and reports about its implementation, changes and additions in the budget, establish and annul state taxes and fees;
3) establish the procedure for resolving the issues of the administrative-territorial division of the Republic of Kazakhstan;
4) establish state awards, honorary, military and other titles, ranked positions, diplomatic ranks of the Republic of Kazakhstan, and define state symbols of the Republic;
5) decide issues of state loans and rendering of economic and other assistance by the Republic;
6) issue acts of amnesty to citizens;

7) ratify and denounce international treaties of the Republic.

Article 55

The following shall belong to exclusive jurisdiction of the Senate:

1) election and discharge from office, the Chairperson of the Supreme Court, the Chairpersons of the Collegium of Justice, and judges of the Supreme Court of the Republic at the proposal of the President of the Republic of Kazakhstan, and swearing them into office;
2) approval of the appointment of the Procurator General and the Chairperson of the Committee of National Security by the President of the Republic of Kazakhstan;
3) deprivation of inviolability of the Procurator General, the Chairperson and judges of the Supreme Court of the Republic;
4) premature termination of the powers of local representative administrative bodies in accordance with the legislation of the Republic;
5) delegation of two deputies to the Highest Judicial Council of the Republic of Kazakhstan;
6) consideration of the issue raised by the *Majilis* about the discharge from office of the President of the Republic and submitting the results for consideration at a joint session of the Chambers.

Article 56

The following belongs to exclusive jurisdiction of the *Majilis*:

1) accepting drafts of laws for consideration and consideration of the drafts of laws;
2) preparation of suggestions concerning the objections of the President of the Republic of Kazakhstan to laws adopted by Parliament of the Republic;
3) election and discharge from office of the Chairperson, Deputy Chairperson, Secretary and members of the Central Election Commission of the Republic at the proposal of the President of the Republic of Kazakhstan;
4) announcing regular elections of the President of the Republic;
5) delegation of two deputies to the Qualification Collegium of Justice;
6) bringing an accusation of high treason against the President of the Republic'.

Article 57

Each Chamber of the Parliament independently, without participation of the other Chamber shall:

1) appoint three members for a five-year term to the Estimation Committee for control over implementation of the republican budget;
2) delegate half of the members of the commission formed by Parliament in the case envisaged by paragraph I of article 47 of the Constitution;

3) elect half of the members of joint commissions of the Chambers;
4) terminate powers of the deputies of the Chambers, as well as resolve the issues of depriving deputies of their deputy immunity at the proposal of the Procurator General of the Republic of Kazakhstan;
5) hold Parliamentary hearings on the issues of its jurisdiction;
6) have the right to hear reports of the members of the Government of the Republic on the issues of their activities, at the initiative of no less than one-third from the total number of the deputies of the Chambers, and adopt an appeal by a majority of two-thirds of the total number of the deputies of the Chambers to the President of the Republic of Kazakhstan to discharge a member of the Government from office in the case of nonobservance of the laws of the Republic, if the President of the Republic refuses such appeal, then the deputies, by majority of not less than two-thirds of votes of the total number of deputies of the Chamber, shall possess the right to put a question to the President anew on release from the position of a member of the Government on expiration of six months since the first appeal. In this case the President of the Republic shall release from the position of a member of the Government.
7) form coordinating and working bodies of the Chambers;
8) adopt procedural orders of their activities and other decisions on the issues connected with organisation and the internal routine of the Chambers".

'Subparagraph 4) of Article 56 is given in a wording of the Law of the Republic of Kazakhstan of October 7, 1998 1 284-1 of LRK. " Subparagraphs 1) and 6) of Article 57 are given in a wording of the Law of the Republic of Kazakhstan of October 7, 1998 1 284-1 of LRK.

Article 58

1. The Chambers shall be headed by their chairpersons who are elected by the Senate and the *Majilis* from among the deputies who have a perfect command of the state language, under secret ballot by a majority of votes from the total number of the deputies of the Chambers. The candidacy for the Chairperson of the Senate shall be nominated by the President of the Republic of Kazakhstan. The candidacy for the Chairperson of the *Majilis* shall be nominated by the deputies of the Chamber.
2. The Chairpersons of the Chambers may be recalled from office and also have the right to submit their resignation if the majority of the total number of the deputies of the Chambers have voted against them.
3. The Chairpersons of Parliament's Chambers shall:
   a) convene sessions of the Chambers and preside over them;
   b) exercise general supervision in preparation of the issues under consideration by the Chambers;
   c) nominate the candidacies of Deputy Chairpersons to the Chambers;

   d) ensure the observance of the procedural orders in the activities of the Chambers;
   e) supervise the activities of the coordinating bodies of the Chambers;
   f) sign acts issued by the Chambers;
   g) each appoint two members to the Constitutional Council of the Republic of Kazakhstan;
   h) fulfill other duties assigned to them by the procedural orders of Parliament.
4. The Chairperson of the *Majilis* shall:
   a) open sessions of Parliament;
   b) convene regular joint sessions of the Chambers, preside at regular and extraordinary joint sessions of the Chambers.
   c) The chairpersons of the Chambers shall issue instructions on the items of their jurisdiction.

Article 59

1. Parliament's sessions shall proceed in the form of joint and separate sessions of its chambers.
2. The first session of Parliament shall be convened by the President of the Republic of Kazakhstan no later than thirty days from the day of publishing of the election results.
3. Regular sessions of the Parliament shall be held once a year from the first working day of September to the last working day of June.
4. Session of Parliament shall be opened by the President of the Republic and closed at joint sessions of the Senate and *Majilis*. In the period between Parliament's sessions, the President of the Republic of Kazakhstan may call an extraordinary joint session of the Chambers on his own initiative, at the suggestion of the chairpersons of the Chambers or no less than one-third from the total number of the deputies of Parliament. Only the issues that were the reason for convocation shall be reviewed at this session.
5. Joint and separate sessions of the Chambers shall be held on condition that no less than two-thirds from the total number of the deputies of each Chamber are present.
6. Joint and separate sessions of the Chambers shall be open. In cases stipulated by the procedural orders, sessions may be closed. The President of the Republic, the Prime Minister and members of the Government, the Chairperson of National Bank, the Procurator General, the Chairperson of the Committee of National Security shall have the right to be present at any session and be heard.

Article 60

1. The Chambers shall form standing committees, the number of which shall not exceed seven in each Chamber.
2. The Senate and *Majilis* shall have the right to form joint commissions on

a parity basis for solution of issues dealing with the joint activity of the Chambers.

3. The committees and commissions shall issue resolutions on items of their jurisdictions.
4. The procedure of formation, the powers and organisation of the activities of the committees and commissions shall be determined by law.

Article 61

1. The right of a legislative initiative shall belong to the deputies of Parliament of the Republic of Kazakhstan, the Government of the Republic and shall be realised exclusively in the *Majilis.*
2. The President of the Republic of Kazakhstan shall have the right to determine priority consideration of draft of laws as well as to declare consideration of a draft of law urgent signifying that Parliament must consider this draft within a month from the day of its submission. If the Parliament does not meet this requirement, the President of the Republic shall have the right to issue a decree having the force of law which shall be. in effect until Parliament adopts a new law as established by the Constitution.
3. Parliament shall have the right to issue laws that regulate the most important public relations, establish fundamental principles and standards dealing with:
   a) legal capacity of individuals and legal entities, civil freedoms and rights, obligations and responsibility of individuals and legal entities;
   b) conditions of ownership and other rights of property; foundations of organisation and activity of state bodies and bodies of local self-administration, state and military service; taxation, establishment and levying of duties and other obligatory payments; the republican budget;
   c) issues of the judicial system and legal proceedings;
   d) education, health care and social provision;
   e) privatisation of enterprises and their property;
   f) environmental protection;
   g) administrative-territorial structure of the Republic;
   h) ensuring defense and security of the state. All other relations shall be regulated by legislative acts.
4. A draft of law considered and approved by the majority of votes from the total number of the deputies of the *Majilis* shall be transmitted to the Senate where it shall be considered for no more than sixty days. A draft of law approved by the majority of votes of the total number of deputies of the Senate shall become the law and shall be submitted to the President to be signed within ten days. A draft of law rejected as a whole by the majority of votes from the total number of the Senate's deputies shall be returned to the *Majilis*. If the *Majilis* approves the draft of law again by the majority of two-thirds of votes from the total number of its deputies, it shall be transferred to the Senate for a second discussion and voting. A twice-rejected draft may not be submitted again during the same session.

5. Amendments and additions to a draft of law proposed by the majority of votes from the total number of the Senate's deputies shall be sent to the *Majilis*. If the *Majilis* by the majority of votes from the total number of its deputies agrees with the proposed amendments and additions, the law shall be deemed to be adopted. If the *Majilis* by the same majority of votes objects to the amendments and additions proposed by the Senate, the disagreement between the Chambers shall be resolved through conciliatory procedures.
6. Drafts of law envisioning reduction of state revenues or increase in state expenditures may be submitted only when supplied with the positive resolution of the Government of the Republic.
7. In the case when of a draft of law submitted by the Government is not adopted, the Prime Minister shall have the right to raise an issue of no-confidence in the Government at a joint session of the Chambers. Voting on this issue shall be held not earlier than within forty-eight hours from the moment of calling for a vote of confidence. If the call for a vote of no confidence does not receive the necessary number of votes established by this Constitution, a draft of law shall be deemed adopted without voting. However, the Government may not use this right more than twice a year.

Article 62

1. The Parliament shall adopt legislative acts in the form of laws of the Republic of Kazakhstan, resolutions of the Parliament, resolutions of the Senate and the *Majilis* having obligatory force on the entire territory of the Republic.
2. Laws of the Republic shall come into effect after they are signed by the President of the Republic.
3. Amendments and additions to the Constitution shall be introduced by the majority of no less than three-fourths of votes from the total number of the deputies of each chamber.
4. Constitutional laws shall be adopted on the issues stipulated by the Constitution by the majority of no less than two-thirds of votes from the total number of the deputies of each Chamber.
5. Legislative acts of the Parliament and its Chambers shall be adopted by the majority of votes from the total number of the deputies of the Chambers unless otherwise stipulated by the Constitution.
6. No less than two readings introducing amendments and additions to the Constitution, adopting constitutional laws or introducing of changes and additions into them shall be obligatory.
7. Laws of the Republic, resolutions of the Parliament and its Chambers must not contradict the Constitution. Resolutions of the Parliament and its Chambers must not contradict laws.
8. The procedure for development, submission, discussion, bringing into effect and promulgation of legislative and other regulatory legal acts of the Republic shall be regulated by a special law and the procedural orders of Parliament and its Chambers.

Article 63

1. The President of the Republic of Kazakhstan may dissolve Parliament in cases: expressing by Parliament of a vote of no confidence in the Government, twice refusal of Parliament to give consent to the appointment of the Prime Minister, political crisis resulting from of insurmountable differences between the Chambers of Parliament or Parliament and other branches of state power.
2. The Parliament may not be dissolved in the period of a state of emergency or martial law, during the last six months of the President's term, as well as within a year after a previous dissolution.

SECTION V
GOVERNMENT

Article 64

1. The Government shall implement the executive power of the Republic of Kazakhstan, head the system of executive bodies and exercise supervision of their activity.
2. The Government in its entire activity shall be responsible before the President of the Republic as well as accountable to the Parliament of the Republic in the case stipulated by paragraph 6 of article 53 of the Constitution.
3. Members of the Government shall be accountable to the Chambers of Parliament in the case stipulated by paragraph 6 of Article 57 of the Constitution.
4. The jurisdiction, the procedure of organisation and activity of the Government shall be determined by constitutional law.

Article 65

1. The Government shall be formed by the President of the Republic of Kazakhstan according to the procedure stipulated by this Constitution.
2. Suggestions about the structure and composition of the Government shall be submitted to the President of the Republic of Kazakhstan by the Prime Minister of the Republic within ten days after his appointment.
3. The members of the Government shall take an oath to the people and President of Kazakhstan.

Article 66

The Government shall:

1) develop the main directions of the social-economic policy of the state, its defence capability, security, guarantee of public order and organise their realisation;
2) present to the Parliament the republican budget and a report about its performance, ensure implementation of the budget;
3) introduce draft of laws into the *Majilis* and ensure enforcement of laws;
4) organise management of state property;

5) develop measures for the conduct of the foreign policy of the Republic of Kazakhstan;
6) manage the activity of ministries, state committees, other central and local executive bodies;
7) annul or suspend completely or partially, the effect of acts of ministries, state committees, other central and local executive bodies of the Republic;
8) appoint to and release from office heads of central executive bodies not encompassed by the Government;
9) excluded;
10) perform other functions assigned to it by this Constitution, laws and acts of the President'.

Article 67

The Prime Minister of the Republic of Kazakhstan shall:

1) organise and supervise the work of the Government, personally answer for its work;
2) within a month after his appointment, present to the Parliament a report about the Programme of the Government and in the event of its rejection, present a new report about the Programme within two months;
3) sign resolutions of the Government;
4) report the main directions of the Government's activity and all of its important decisions to the President;
5) perform other functions connected with organisation and supervision of the Government's activity.

Article 68

1. Members of the Government shall be independent in making decisions within their competence and bear personal responsibility before the Prime Minister for the activity of bodies subordinated to them. A member of the Government who does not agree with the policy, pursued by the Government, or who does not pursue it shall resign or subjected to release from his office
2. Members of the Government shall not have right to be deputies of a representative body, hold other paid offices except teaching, scientific and other creative activities, engage in entrepreneurial activity, enter governing body or a supervisory board of a commercial organisation.

Article 69

1. The Government of the Republic of Kazakhstan shall issue resolutions on the items of its jurisdiction having obligatory force on the entire territory of the Republic.
2. The Prime Minister of the Republic shall issue directions having mandatory force on the entire territory of the Republic.

   Subparagraphs 2) and 9) of Article 66 are given in a wording of the Law of the Republic of Kazakhstan of October 7, 1998 N° 284-1 of LRK. 2 Paragraph

1 of Article 68 is given in a wording of the Law of the Republic of Kazakhstan of October 7, 1998 N" 284-1 of LRK.

3. Resolutions of the Government and directions of the Prime Minister must not contradict the Constitution, legislative acts, decrees and resolutions of the President of the Republic.

Article 70

1. The Government shall resign its powers to the newly elected President of the Republic of Kazakhstan.
2. The Government and any of its members shall have the right to submit a resignation to the President of the Republic of Kazakhstan if they consider further performance of the functions assigned to them to be impossible.
3. The Government shall submit its resignation to the President of the Republic of Kazakhstan in the event that Parliament passes a vote of no confidence in the Government.
4. The President of the Republic within a period often days shall consider the issue of accepting or declining the resignation.
5. Acceptance of the resignation shall denote the termination of the powers of the Government or a respective member. Acceptance of the resignation of the Prime Minister shall denote the termination of the powers of the entire Government.
6. In the event that the resignation of the Government or its member is declined, the President shall charge the Government or its member with continued performance of their responsibilities. In the event that the resignation of the Government owing to the passage of a vote of no confidence is declined, the President shall have the right to dissolve Parliament.
7. The President of the Republic shall have the right on his own initiative to adopt a decision to terminate the powers of the Government and to release any of its members from their offices. The release of the Prime Minister from office shall denote the termination of the powers of the entire Government.

SECTION VI
THE CONSTITUTIONAL COUNCIL

Article 71

1. The Constitutional Council of the Republic of Kazakhstan shall consist of seven members whose powers shall last for six years. The ex-Presidents of the Republic shall have the right to be life-long members of the Constitutional Council.
2. The Chairperson of the Constitutional Council shall be appointed by the President of the Republic, and in case the votes are equally divided, his vote shall be decisive.

3. Two members of the Constitutional Council shall be appointed by the President of the Republic, two—by the Chairperson of Senate, and two—by the Chairperson of the *Majilis*. Half of the members of the Constitutional Council shall be renewed every three years.
4. The Chairperson and members of the Constitutional Council shall not be deputies, hold paid offices except teaching, scientific or other creative activities, engage in entrepreneurial activity, enter a governing body or a supervisory board of a commercial organisation.
5. The Chairperson and members of the Constitutional Council during their term in office may not be arrested, subject to detention, measures of administrative punishment imposed by a court of law, arraigned on a criminal charge without the consent of Parliament, except in cases of being apprehended on the scene of a crime or committing grave crimes.
6. Organisation and activity of the Constitutional Council shall be regulated by Constitutional Law.

Article 72

1. The Constitutional Council by appeal of the President of the Republic of Kazakhstan, the Chairperson of the Senate, the Chairperson of *Majilis*, not less than one-fifth of the total number of deputies of Parliament, the Prime Minister shall:
   a) decide on the correctness of conducting the elections of the President of the Republic, deputies of Parliament, and conducting an all-nation referendum in case of dispute;
   b) consider the laws adopted by Parliament with respect to their compliance with the Constitution of the Republic, before they are signed by the President; consider the international treaties of the Republic with respect to their compliance with the constitution, before they are ratified;
   c) officially interpret the standards of the Constitution;
   d) conclude in cases stipulated by paragraphs 1 and 2 of Article 47 of the Constitution.
2. The Constitutional Council shall consider the appeals of courts of law in cases stipulated by Article 78 of the Constitution.

Article 73

1. The inauguration of the President, registration of the elected deputies of Parliament or results of all-nation referendum shall be suspended in cases of appeal to the Constitutional Council on issues mentioned in subparagraph 1) of paragraph 1 of Article 72 of the Constitution.
2. The term of signing or ratifying of the corresponding acts shall be suspended in case of appeal to the Constitutional Council on issues mentioned in subparagraphs 2 and 3 of paragraph 1 of Article 72 of the Constitution.
3. The constitutional Council shall pass a resolution within one month from the day of appeal. This period of time, at the demand of the President or

the Republic, may be shortened by 10 days if the issue is urgent.

4. The President of the Republic may object, as a whole or in part to the resolutions of the Constitutional Council. These objections shall be overruled by two-thirds of the votes of the total number of the members of the Constitutional Council. If the objections of the President are not overruled, the resolution of the Constitutional Council shall be considered not adopted.

Article 74

1. Laws and international treaties recognised not to be in compliance with the Constitution of the Republic of Kazakhstan, may not be signed or, accordingly, ratified and brought into effect.
2. Laws and other regulatory legal acts, recognised as infringing on the rights and freedoms of an individual and citizen secured by the Constitution, shall be cancelled and shall not be in effect.
3. Resolutions of the Constitutional Council shall come into effect from the day they are adopted, shall be binding on the entire territory of the Republic, final and not subject to appeal.

SECTION VII
COURT AND JUSTICE

Article 75

1. Justice in the Republic of Kazakhstan shall be exercised only by the court.
2. Judicial power shall be exercised through the constitutional, civil, administrative, criminal and other forms of judicial procedure as established by law. In cases, stipulated by law, criminal procedure shall be carried out with participation of jurymen.
3. The courts of the Republic shall be the Supreme Court of the Republic and local courts of the Republic established by law.
4. The judicial system of the Republic shall be established by the Constitution of the Republic and the constitutional law. The establishment of special and extraordinary courts under any name shall not be allowed'.

Article 76

1. Judicial power shall be exercised on behalf of the Republic of Kazakhstan and shall be intended to protect the rights, freedoms, and legal interests of the citizens and organisations for ensuring the observance of the Constitution, laws, other regulatory legal acts, and shall ensure international treaties of the Republic.
2. Judicial power shall be extended to all cases and disputes arising on the basis of this Constitution, laws, other regulatory legal acts, international treaties of the Republic.
3. Decisions, sentences and other judgments of courts shall have an obligatory force in the entire territory of the Republic.

Article 77

1. A judge when executing justice shall be independent and subordinate only to the Constitution and the law.
2. Any interference in the activity of the court in the exercise of justice shall be inadmissible and accountable by the law. Judges shall not be held accountable with regard to specific cases.
3. In application of law a judge must be guided by the following principles:
   a) a person shall be considered to be innocent of committing a crime until his guilt is established by a court's sentence that has come into force;
   b) no one may be subject twice to criminal or administrative prosecution for one and the same offense;
   c) no one may have his jurisdiction, as stipulated by law changed without his consent;
   d) everyone shall have the right to be heard in court;

   Paragraph 2 of Article 75 is given in a wording of the Law of the Republic of Kazakhstan of October 1, 1998 ¹ 284-1 of LRK.'

   e) the laws establishing or intensifying liability, imposing new responsibilities on the citizens or deteriorating their conditions shall have no retroactive force. If after the commitment of an offense accountability for it is canceled by law or reduced, the new law shall be applied;
   f) the accused shall not be obligated to prove his innocence; 7) no person shall be compelled to give testimony against oneself, one's spouse and close relatives whose circle is determined by law. The clergy shall not be obligated to testify against those who confided in them with some information at a confession;
   g) any doubts of a person's guilt shall be interpreted in the favour of the accused;
   h) evidence obtained by illegal means shall have no juridical force. No person may be sentenced on the basis of his own admission of guilt;
   i) application of the criminal law by analogy shall not be allowed.
4. The principles of justice established by the Constitution shall be common and uniform for all courts and judges in the Republic.

Article 78

The courts shall have no right to apply laws and other regulatory legal acts infringing on the rights and liberties of an individual and a citizen established by the Constitution. If a court finds that a law or other regulatory legal act subject to application infringes on the rights and liberties of an individual and a citizen it shall suspend legal proceedings and address the Constitutional Council with a proposal to declare that law unconstitutional.

Article 79

1. Courts shall consist of permanent judges whose independence shall be protected by the Constitution and law. A judge's powers may be terminated

or suspended exclusively on the grounds established by law.

2. A judge may not be arrested, subject to detention, measures of administrative punishment, imposed by a court of law, arraigned on a criminal charge without the consent of the President of the Republic of Kazakhstan based on a conclusion of the Highest Judicial Council of the Republic or in a case stipulated by paragraph 3 of Article 55 of the Constitution; without the consent of Senate except for the cases of being apprehended on the scene of a crime or committing grave crimes.
3. Judges may be citizens of the Republic who have reached twenty-five years of age, have a higher juridical education, length of service of not less than two years in the legal profession and who have passed a qualification examination. Additional requirements to the judges of the courts of the Republic may be established by law.
4. The office of a judge shall be incompatible with a deputy's mandate, holding other paid offices except teaching, research or other creative activity engaging in other entrepreneurial activity, or being a member of a managing body or supervisory board of a commercial enterprise.

Article 80

Financing of courts, provision of judges with housing shall be performed from the republican budget and must ensure the possibility of complete and free exercise of justice.

Article 81

The Supreme Court of the Republic of Kazakhstan shall be the highest judicial body for civil, criminal and other cases which are under the courts of general jurisdiction; exercises the supervision over their activities in the forms of juridical procedure stipulated by law, and provide interpretation on the issues of judicial practice.

Article 82

1. The Chairperson of the Supreme Court, the Chair-persons of the Collegiums and judges of the Supreme Court of the Republic of Kazakhstan shall be elected by the Senate at the proposal of the President of the Republic based on a recommendation of the Highest Judicial Council of the Republic.
2. The Chairpersons of oblast and equivalent courts, the Chairpersons of the Collegiums and judges of the oblast and equivalent courts shall be appointed by the President of the Republic at the recommendation of the Highest Judicial Court of the Republic.
3. The Chairperson and judges of other courts of the Republic shall be appointed by the President of the Republic at the proposal of the Minister of Justice based on a recommendation of the Qualification Collegium of Justice.
4. The Highest Judicial Council shall be headed by the Chairperson who is appointed by the President of the Republic and consist of the Chairperson

of the Constitutional Council, the Chairperson of the Supreme Court, the Procurator General, the Minister of Justice, deputies of the Senate, judges and other persons appointed by the President of the Republic. The Qualification Collegium of Justice shall be an autonomous, independent institution formed from deputies of the *Majilis*, judges, public prosecutors, teachers and scholars of law and workers of the bodies of justice.

5. The status of the Highest Judicial Council and the Qualification Collegium of Justice, and their procedure of formation and organisation of their work shall be determined by law'.

Article 83

1. The procurator's office on behalf of the state shall exercise the highest supervision over exact and uniform application of law, the decrees of the President of the Republic of Kazakhstan and other regulatory legal acts on the territory of the Republic, legality of preliminary investigation, inquest and inspection, administrative and executive legal procedure; and take measures for exposure and elimination of any violations of the law, the independence of courts as well as the appeal of laws and other regulatory legal acts contradicting the Constitution and laws of the Republic. The Procurator's office of the Republic shall represent interest of the state in court as well as conduct criminal prosecution in cases using procedures and within the limits, stipulated by law.
   Paragraph 4 of Article 82 is given in a wording of the Law of the Republic of Kazakhstan of October 7, 1998 N° 284-1 of LRK.
2. The procurator's office of the Republic shall be a unified centralized system with subordination of junior procurators to their seniors and the Procurator General of the Republic. It shall exercise its authorities independently of other state bodies and officials and be accountable only to the President of the Republic.
3. The Procurator General of the Republic during the term of his office may not be arrested, subject to detention, measures of administrative punishment imposed by a court of law, arraigned on a criminal charge without the consent of the Senate except for the cases of being apprehended on the scene of a crime or committing grave crimes. The term of the Procurator General shall be five years.
4. The jurisdiction, organisation and procedure of the activity of the procurator's office of the Republic shall be determined by law.

Article 84

1. Inquiry and preliminary investigation of criminal cases shall be carried out by special bodies and be separated from the court and the procurator's office.
2. The powers, organisation and procedure of the activity of the inquest and investigation bodies, other questions of preliminary investigation in the Republic of Kazakhstan shall be regulated by law.

SECTION VIII
LOCAL PUBLIC ADMINISTRATION AND SELF-ADMINISTRATION

Article 85

Local public administration shall be exercised by local representative and executive bodies which are responsible for the state of affairs of the respective territory.

Article 86

1. Local representative bodies—*Maslikhats*—shall express the will of the population of corresponding administrative-territorial units and with regard to the common public interests shall determine the measures needed for its realisation, and control their implementation.
2. *Maslikhats* shall be elected by the population on the basis of universal, equal suffrage under secret ballot for a four—year term.
3. A deputy of a *Maslikhat* may be a citizen of the Republic of Kazakhstan who has reached twenty years of age. A citizen of the Republic may be a deputy of only one *Maslikhat.*
4. The jurisdiction of *Maslikhats* shall include:
    a) approval of plans, economic and social programs for development of the territory, local budget and reports of their performance;
    b) decision of issues of local administrative-territorial organisation in their jurisdiction; consideration of reports by heads of local executive bodies on the issues delegated by law to the jurisdiction of a *Maslikhat*;
    c) formation of standing commissions and other working bodies of a *Maslikhat*, nearing reports about their activity, decision of other issues connected with organisation of the work of a *Maslikhat*;
    d) exercise other authorities for insuring of the rights and legitimate interests of citizens in accordance with the legislation of the Republic.
5. The powers of a *Maslikhat* shall be prematurely terminated by the Senate on the grounds and according to the procedure established by law as well as in the case of adoption of a decision about self-dissolution.
6. The jurisdiction of *Maslikhats*, procedure of their organisation and activity, and legal status of their deputies shall be established by law.

Article 87

1. Local executive bodies shall be a part of a unified system of the executive bodies of the Republic of Kazakhstan, and ensure conduct of the general state policy of the executive power in conjunction with the interests and development needs of the corresponding territory.
2. The jurisdiction of local executive bodies shall include:
    1) development of drafts of plans, economic and social programs for development of the territory, local budget and provision of their realisation;
    2) management of public property;

3) appointment to and release from office the heads of local executive bodies, resolution of other issues connected with organisation of the work of local executive bodies;
4) exercise other powers delegated to local executive bodies by the legislation of the Republic in the interests of local public administration.

3. A local executive body shall be headed by an *Akim* of the corresponding administrative-territorial unit who is a representative of the President and the Government of the Republic.
4. *Akims* of the oblasts, the major city and the capital shall be appointed to office by the President of the Republic on the recommendation of the Prime Minister. *Akims* of other administrative-territorial units shall be appointed or elected to office in the order, determined by the President of the Republic of Kazakhstan. The President of the Republic shall have the right to release *akims* from office at his own discretion.
5. A *Maslikhat* shall have the right by two-thirds of votes from the total number of its deputies to express non-confidence in the *akim* and raise the issue of his release from office correspondingly before the President of the Republic or a senior *akim*. The powers of *akims* of the oblasts, the major cities and the capital shall terminate when a newly elected President assumes office.
6. The jurisdiction of local executive bodies, organisation and procedure of their activity shall be established by law'.

Article 88

1. *Maslikhats* shall adopt decisions on the issues of their jurisdiction, *akims* shall adopt decisions and resolutions which are binding on the territory of the corresponding administrative-territorial unit.
   Paragraph 4 of Article 87 is given in a wording of the Law of the Republic of Kazakhstan of October 7, 1998 1 284-1 of LRK.
2. Drafts of decisions of *Maslikhats* envisioning a reduction of local budgetary revenues or an increase of local budgetary expenditures may be submitted for consideration only with a positive resolution of the *Akim*.
3. Decisions of *Maslikhats* not corresponding to the Constitution and the laws of the Republic of Kazakhstan may be annulled by a legal process.
4. Decisions and resolutions of *Akims* may be correspondingly annulled by the President, the Government of the Republic of Kazakhstan or a senior *akim*, as well as by a legal process.

Article 89

1. In the Republic of Kazakhstan, local self-administration which ensures that the issues of local significance shall be resolved independently by the population, shall be recognised.
2. Local self-administration shall be exercised by the population directly through elections as well as through elective and other bodies of local self-

administration in rural and urban local communities covering the territories on which groups of the population live compactly.

3. The procedure or organisation and activity of the bodies of local self-administration shall be determined by citizens themselves within the limits of their powers established by law.
4. The independence of the bodies of local self-administration shall be guaranteed within the limits of their powers established by law.

SECTION IX
CONCLUDING AND TRANSITIONAL PROVISIONS

Article 90

1. The Constitution of the Republic of Kazakhstan adopted at an all-nation referendum shall come into effect from the day of official publication of the results of the referendum with the simultaneous termination of the functioning of the previously adopted Constitution of the Republic of Kazakhstan.
2. The day of adoption of the Constitution at the all-nation referendum shall be proclaimed a national holiday—the Constitution Day of the Republic of Kazakhstan.

Article 91

1. Amendments and additions to the Constitution of the Republic of Kazakhstan may be introduced only by an all-nation referendum held by the decision of the President of the Republic made on his own initiative, at the recommendation of Parliament or the Government. The draft of amendments and additions to the Constitution shall not be submitted to an all-nation referendum if the President decides to pass it to the consideration of Parliament. In this case, Parliament's decision shall be adopted according to the procedure established by this Constitution. In case the President of the Republic refuses the proposal of the Parliament on submission of amendments and additions to the Constitution for the consideration of the Republican referendum, the Parliament has the right by majority of not less than four-fifths of votes of the total number of deputies of each Chamber of the Parliament to adopt the law on making of these amendments and additions to the Constitution. In such case the President of the Republic shall sign this law or submit it for the consideration of the Republican referendum which shall be deemed valid if more than half of the Republican citizens, possessing the right to participate in the Republican referendum, take part in it. Amendments and additions to the Constitution, which are submitted for the consideration of the Republican referendum, shall be deemed adopted, if more than half of citizens, taking part in it, vote for it.

2. The unitary status and territorial integrity of the Republic, the forms of government may not be changed'.

Article 92

1. The constitutional laws must be adopted within a year from the day of enactment of the Constitution. If the laws called constitutional in the Constitution or the acts having the force thereof have been adopted by the moment of enactment of the Constitution, they are brought into accordance with the Constitution and deemed to be the constitutional laws of the Republic of Kazakhstan.
2. Other laws named in the Constitution must be adopted according to the procedure and within the terms determined by the Parliament but no later than two years after the enactment of the Constitution.
3. The decrees of the President of the Republic published within the term of his exercise of additional powers in accordance with the law of the Republic of Kazakhstan from December 10, 1993 "0n Temporary Delegation of Additional Powers to the President of the Republic of Kazakhstan and Heads of Local Administration and having the force of law shall attain the force of law and may be altered, amended or annulled according to the procedure stipulated for alteration, amendment or annulment of the laws of the Republic. The decrees of the President of the Republic published within a term he exercises additional powers on the issues stipulated by paragraphs 12-15, 18 and 20 of article 64 of the Constitution of the Republic of Kazakhstan adopted on January 28, 1993 shall not be subject to approval by Parliament of the Republic.
4. The legislation of the Republic of Kazakhstan functioning at the moment of enactment of this Constitution shall be applied in the part that does not contradict it and within two years from the day of the adoption of the Constitution must be brought into accordance with it.

Article 93

With the purpose of implementation of article 7 of the Constitution, the Government, local representative and executive bodies must create all necessary organisational, material and technical conditions for fluent and free-of-charge mastery of the state language by all citizens of the Republic of Kazakhstan in accordance with a special law.

Paragraph 1 of Article 91 is given in a wording of the Law of the Republic of Kazakhstan of October 7, 1998 [1] 284-1 of LRK.

Article 94

1. The President of the Republic of Kazakhstan elected in accordance with the legislation of the Republic of Kazakhstan functioning at the moment of enactment of this Constitution shall acquire the powers of the President of the Republic of Kazakhstan stipulated by it and exercise them during

the term established by the decision adopted at the all-nation referendum of April 29, 1995. By consent of the President of the Republic of Kazakhstan the present term of the powers of the President of the Republic may be reduced by resolution of the Parliament of the Republic, adopted at the joint session of its Chambers by the majority of votes of the total number of deputies of each Chamber. In such case the *Majilis* of the Parliament within one month shall order elections of the President of the Republic of Kazakhstan. The President of the Republic, elected according to the results of these elections, shall take the oath within one month since the day of publication of the results of elections and exercise his duties before taking office of the President of the Republic, elected in regular Presidential elections, which shall be held after the expiration of a seven-year term on the first Sunday of December.

2. The Vice-President of the Republic of Kazakhstan elected in accordance with the legislation of the Republic of Kazakhstan functioning at the moment of enactment this Constitution shall preserve his powers until the expiration of the term for which he was elected'.

Article 95

One half of the deputies of the Senate of the first con vocation shall be elected for a four-year term, the other half of the deputies shall be elected for a two-year term in the procedure, established by Constitutional Law. 2. Provisions of the Constitution of the Republic of Kazakhstan on elections of deputies of the *Majilis* of the Parliament on the basis of Party Lists shall be applied from the beginning of elections of deputies of the *Majilis* of the Parliament of the second convocation.

Article 96

The Cabinet of Ministers of the Republic of Kazakhstan from the day of enactment of this Constitution shall acquire the rights, obligations and responsibility of the Government of the Republic of Kazakhstan.

Article 97

The first composition of the Constitutional Council of the Republic of Kazakhstan shall be formed in the following manner: the President of the Republic, the Chairperson of the Senate of Parliament, the Chairperson of the *Majilis* of Parliament shall each appoint one member to the Constitutional Council for a three-year term and shall each appoint one member to the Constitutional Council for a six-year term. The Chairperson of the Constitutional Council shall be appointed by the President of the Republic for a six-year term.

Paragraph 1 of Article 94 is given in a wording of the Law of the Republic of Kazakhstan of October 7, 1998 [1] 284-1 of LRK.
Paragraph 2 of Article 95 is given in a wording of the Law of the Republic of Kazakhstan of October 7, 1998 [1] 284-1 of LRK.

Article 98

1. The justice and investigation bodies stipulated by this Constitution shall be formed according to the procedure and within the terms stipulated by the respective laws. The functioning juridical and inquiry bodies shall retain their powers until new bodies are formed.
2. Judges of the Supreme Court and the Highest Arbitration Court and local courts of the Republic of Kazakhstan shall retain their powers until the formation of courts, as stipulated by the Constitution. Vacant offices of judges shall be filled according to the procedure, established by the Constitution.

Sources: The Constitution of the Republic of Kazakhstan, 1995

Appendix-3

New Stage in Kazakhstan Democratisation: Speedy Development of Democratic Society

Republic of Kazakhstan President Nursultan Nazarbayev's speech at the joint chambers' session in Parliament (16 May 2007)

This day is historical for Kazakhstan democracy. Draft law on changes and amendments to the Republic's Constitution is submitted for your approval. This document is a logical completion of the scaled work on National program of political reforms, deep changes on our country's political space.

Proclaiming the course for accelerated development of free democratic society we turn thereby a new page in our political history.

Our economic progress, rise of every Kazakhstanian's living standards and the necessary address support have built up a sound basis for the new stage in Kazakhstan's democratic development.

On this basis we are consistently building an open, democratic and prosperous society of free people and a legal state, harmoniously combining in itself:

First, achievements of developed democracies;

Second, best traditions of our multi-national and multi-confessional society.

We realize that to speed up democratisation we need stability, legal-based state and public accord.

World experience shows democracy cannot be built where law and constitutional order are not observed, where economic and social chaos are present, where fundamental rights of an individual are not guaranteed.

Our main task is non-admission of chaos in our country.

I believe, strengthening of social stability, supremacy of law, inter-national and inter-confessional accord and the new geopolitical role and responsibility of Kazakhstan—that's the pledge and gauge of democratic reforms' efficiency.

Dear deputies! We should bear in mind that political modernisation in our country has been going on consistently, step by step, along with building up the required economic conditions, from the very moment we won independence.

And we are following our own, Kazakhstan's way of development. Having studied the world practice we opted for this very evolutionary way. We are against forced implantation of democracy, especially from outside. We are not copying anyone's experience, but are doing what is good for our country and our people. And we succeed in it.

We have passed several stages on this way.

On the first stage—1991-1995—we focused on copying with disintegration processes, building up the basis for Kazakhstan statehood, transition from dictate of one-party system to political pluralism, creation of foundations for democratic development.

That was the most trying time in our life.

On that stage of statehood formation, when drastic, anti-crisis measures were necessary we made an objective choice in favor of concentration of powers on the vertical of executive power. This approach was absolutely justified under the existing internal conditions and in the context of external situation.

We have derived good lessons from this period, the main being realisation that without stable and strong economy, political development is a painful process that can breed public discontent and destabilisation.

Such cataclysms are taking place in our friendly states.

Our principle is—first economy, then politics—has fully justified itself.

It is scientifically proved that authentic democracies at GDP per capita lower than three thousand dollars do not last long. If this index is over six thousand dollars the democracy is viable. I hope this will be our case.

On the second stage—1995-2000 our main concern was creation and consolidation of modern democratic institutes, formation of new political culture basing on the Constitution adopted at the national referendum in 1995.

The Constitution has enabled our progress, not only in terms of deep economic, but political changes too. The proof to it is the new national legislature of the sovereign Kazakhstan. Through it we have created a sound basis for making Kazakhstan the country, where real democratic institutes are a fact, where civil rights and freedoms are guaranteed.

It was all going on amid the hardships, when we had to cope with inertia of post-soviet syndrome and aftermath of Asian financial crisis.

But we succeeded, largely thanks to Kazakhstan 2030 strategy.

Opting for the model of Presidential republic we steered the country out of the post-soviet economic and political chaos. Political stability made our economy attractive to the foreign investors, at that time the main source of capital, necessary to develop the home industry.

Economy was rising, new infrastructure—shaping up and agriculture—developing. New working places and middle class were gradually forming.

Concurrent to it we ensured sustainability of international positions, showed to the world our peaceful policy.

These achievements enabled further democratic development in Kazakhstan, creating conditions for political pluralism, media diversity, civil rights and freedoms, wider public involvement in political changes, creation of thousands of NGO.

Third stage—2001-2006 proved our strategy was right. In this lapse we have ensured a socioeconomic breakthrough to become a regional leader. Our statehood became a fact too.

In the recent years active national dialogue has been going on to work out more effective ways for furthering democratic reforms.

More responsible tasks are on the agenda. Modern threats and challenges demand a more dynamic modernisation of the entire system of socioeconomic and sociopolitical relations. And we have taken up this challenge.

In these years steps have been undertaken to enhance local bodies' powers, delineate competencies between state management levels.

Parliament has adopted the practice of discussing nominations to Government at the core commissions' meetings. Local power (*Akims'*) accounts to the population have been initiated.

Election legislature and practice have improved. In-depth administrative reform is going on, pursing creation of good-quality state services, rise of executive power's accountability and transparence.

In this period recommendations have been worked out on legislature improvement, political parties, media, distinction of powers between state management levels, improvement of judiciary system and judges' status.

All that has been accomplished in the frames of National program for political reforms.

National program for political reforms gave a start to nationwide discussion on further social democratisation.

State commission for democratic reforms development was formed, comprised of members of Parliament, Government, political parties, statesmen. I thank the commission for the work accomplished.

Conception for civil society development in Kazakhstan in 2006-2011 was worked out.

The main thing is that fulfilling the National political reforms' programs helped us achieve a wide public consensus on baseline values of Kazakhstan's democratisation and political modernisation.

Basing on wide public discussion and consultations with main political forces the state commission gave answers to main questions in democratic development on the new stage. Resolutions have been prepared, touching upon:

Effectiveness, transparency and accountability of the executive power and fighting corruption. Decentralisation of state management and local self-management development.

Improvement of the election legislature

Enhancement of Parliament's responsibility

Development of judiciary system in harmony with advanced world standards, judges' independence

Political parties' bigger involvement in the country's life

NGO's growing part in public life

guaranteed civil rights and freedoms

The main result of the state commission's work was practical recommendations on main directions in political modernisation.

It was subsequently resolved to establish a working group comprised of leading lawyers to colligate motions of the Commission for democratic reforms development in Kazakhstan and formulate articles corresponding to the Constitution and the laws.

The upshot of this work was draft amendments to RK Constitution, offered today for your consideration.

It is time to lay down the legislative basis, cementing success of the liberal reforms, already undertaken, expected to lead to a new balance of social and state interests, development of new checks and balances system.

As for the concrete offers on the changes in the Constitution the offered novelties can be grouped in several directions.

First, Re-distribution of powers and responsibilities, rise of Parliament's part.

One of the debated points in national discussion was transfer of certain state leader's powers to Parliament.

The state commission has unanimously supported keeping Presidential form of government on this stage.

Necessity to start building Kazakhstan statehood and market economy from scratch, develop liberal political system demanded decisive social consolidation. That is why I shouldered the responsibility for everything going on in the country. That was absolutely necessary.

But now that all the important parameters in modernisation process are shaped and we realize the process is irreversible it is deemed expedient to re-distribute some duties and responsibilities between President and Parliament.

I offer to follow the way of such amendments to the Constitution, when the republic remains Presidential, but with substantial extension of Parliament's powers.

It practically transforms the model of our republic from Presidential into Presidential-parliamentary.

In keeping with the current Constitution President is the symbol and guarantor of people's unity and state power, inviolability of the Constitution, human and civil rights and freedoms. This principle remains topical in our political system's modernisation and should remain unshakable, as most people in Kazakhstan think, on the new stage of democratic reforms in our country.

I am inclined to believe that President's term in office should be reduced from 7 to 5 years. This reform will be introduced after the year 2012.

The state commission offers to elect half the deputies on majority and another half—on proportional system. But we should go further. I studied international experience and weighing all the pros and cons offer election of *Majilis* deputies on proportional system, which will ensure representation reckoning with our specifics.

The new form of election in Kazakhstan is supposed to provide to all political parties additional opportunities of strengthening their role in the country's political system.

An offer was accepted from the state commission to increase Senate membership through rise of Presidential quota, now from 7 to 15 deputies. Part of them will be appointed following consultations with Kazakhstan peoples' Assembly.

It is offered to endow Senate with such power as adoption of laws at the time of *Majilis* temporary absence, in case of its pre-term termination of powers.

It is offered to coordinate nomination of National bank chair with the Senate.

Next offer is to raise *Majilis* membership up to 107 deputies, 98 elected on proportional system and 9 nominated by Kazakhstan peoples' Assembly.

Thereby the number of deputies in Parliament will grow by 38 members to make up 154 deputies, a normal proportion for our 15-mln population.

The number of joint chambers' sessions will drop considerably. They are to be convened on most important issues only.

It is offered to exclude from the Constitution the provision, saying that the Parliament deputy is not bound by any imperative mandate. Besides, *Majilis* deputies can be dispossessed of their mandate at withdrawal or expulsion from the political party, or at the party's dissolution, whereas this rule does not concern senators.

It is offered to establish the Government's responsibility not only to the state leader, but to Parliament too.

It is offered to enhance Parliament's powers for effective control of the Government's work.

To impeach the Government, *Majilis* will simply need the majority of deputies' votes, not two-third, like before.

At the same time it is offered to retain in the Constitution two cases—the whole Parliament's impeachment to Government. It may concern the Government's report on budget execution. It is also offered to simplify procedure of Parliament's impeachment to a minister.

First, both chambers must be entitled for it.

Second, to express impeachment suffice it to have a simple, not qualified majority of deputies' voices in the chamber in question.

Following the State commission's recommendations the formation scheme is changed for Constitutional Council, Central election commission.

It is offered to form them on a more democratic basis with equal participation of both Parliament chambers.

The part of the Constitution concerning the Government is subject to changes too. The most debated point in this respect is order of Government's formation. The Commission and the opposition offer that Prime minister is elected upon consultations with political parties' factions and on consent of *Majilis* deputies' majority.

The key point at that is creation of new rules for the Government's formation and functioning on the basis of parliamentary majority. From now on *Majilis* part is crucial in approval of the nomination for the Prime minister and consequently the government.

Constitutional duty of PM to bring up in the newly elected *Majilis* the question of credibility to government is another new factor deciding the government's fate.

The Cabinet is formed on Prime minister's offer.

Second, strengthening political parties' role.

Election of *Majilis* deputies on proportional system is a historically important step. Besides PM will represent the party, enjoying majority in Parliament.

This approach will:

In the first place raise political parties' role in forming the government;

secondly, it will make the majority party more responsible for the government's formation and subsequent work.

It is also offered to give up constitutional ban on public organisations' state funding.

It is deemed expedient to work out practical mechanisms for political parties' partial funding from republican budget to support multi-party system in the country.

It is offered to form a legal basis for rise of political factions' part for them to become main tools in political goals fulfillment.

Third, local self-government development.

Fundamental changes are offered in the Constitution in this part. *Maslihats* are to become the backbone in local self-government, elected by the local population to address local-scale tasks.

Five-year term is offered for *Majilis* powers. Oblast, capital's and republic-scale towns' *Akims* will be appointed on corresponding *Maslihts'* consent, like other *Akims*.

Impeachment procedures by *Maslihats* to *Akims* will be simplified. Decision on it will be taken by simple majority of votes.

Offers are made to enter on the Constitution an article on our capital—Astana.

Fourth, Judiciary system improvement

To strengthen judicial power in 2006 on my decree executive power was deprived of the last lever of influence on judicial system—function of court activity control was transferred from RK ministry of justice to Committee for judiciary administering under RK Supreme Court.

From 1 January 2007 jury trial started working in the republic. Specialized courts—administrative and economic—are being developed in the country. Juvenile courts will be created in future.

Draft on court-sanctioned arrest will be adopted. In compliance with State commission's recommendation Qualification justice collegium will be simplified. Its functions are transferred to Supreme Court council to enhance its role as independent body in judges' appointment, responsible for judges' resources quality in the republic.

Fifth, inter-national accord and strengthening of RK peoples' Assembly

Another important condition of Kazakhstan political modernisation is public stability, inter-national accord and friendship.

Activity of RK peoples' Assembly, established in 1995 is aimed at solution of the important task. It has become a unique institute, implementing national policy, basing on equality of all people, irrespective of their nationality and confession.

Provision on the Assembly's formation is entered on the Constitution. RK peoples' Assembly must be given a constitutional status of the organisation, providing representation of various ethnic groups in RK sociopolitical life.

The Assembly's representation in Senate and *Majilis* will increase its role and strengthen peace and accord in the country.

Sixth, further development of civil institutes.

Political liberalisation is impossible without civil society development. Civil initiative development is unthinkable without strong NGO network and TUs.

Measures on civil institutes' support will be taken. To involve RK NGOs in solution of socially important problems laws "On state social order" and "On social partnership in RK" have been adopted. They are to form new model of relations in social policy and effective relations between the state and social sector.

Political modernisation implies rise of media role, independence of media policy and protection of journalists' rights.

At the same time media need to understand their part in democratisation process and their responsibility to society. Similar approaches are supported by the state, elaborating and adopting laws on informational policy.

At present there are many private media in RK: that is the result of our democratic intentions. Strengthening media freedoms one should remember: a word can make creative work, unite people for solution of topical problems and strengthen stability in the republic. But it can also destabilize the situation. That is why freedom of media in any democratic state means not uncontrolled, but responsible media.

Seventh, strengthening of human rights' protection system.

Human rights and freedoms will be widened in the republic. Ombudsman institute has been created in Kazakhstan. Commission for human rights is functioning under RK President. Their role in public life must be raised.

In the frames of acting constitutional field issues on simplification of law enforcement bodies' functions have been solved. Pre-trial detention facilities and citizens' documentation functions were transmitted to criminal-executive system of RK ministry of justice.

Provision on arrest sanctioning by court will be introduced. Implementation of the following offer will lead to abolition of death penalty in the republic. At present it is used for especially grave offences. But in fact the penalty has not been used in the republic for four years in view of the announced moratorium.

Death penalty is applied to terrorist acts, causing human losses and especially grave offences, committed in the time of hostilities. Kazakhstan is becoming a country where death penalty is not practiced.

Dear deputies!

Program for political changes and elaboration of constitutional reforms are among priorities of our advance.

To provide stability and observance of RK Constitution we need to complicate order of amendments to the main law. As it is known to adopt amendments over 50% of voters must support them. We offer to change the order: 2/3 of oblast and town population will support the amendments.

Our way to political reforms was gradual. All the offers have been studied and analyzed. We consulted political parties, scientists, experts and Kazakhstan people. All the offered amendments were widely discussed in media.

I think it is possible to consider the draft law on amendments to RK Constitution within a week. After the amendments' adoption I will offer for your approval a range of constitutional laws, aimed at the novelties' implementation.

I am sure it is high time to make amendments to RK Constitution and start a new stage of RK development. I rely on active Parliament work.

Your resolutions will play a significant part in the republic's fate. They will give a new impetus to RK development and help keep the state stability.

I am sure the deputy corps will do their best to adopt the draft, vital to the state.

I wish you fruitful work.

ASTANA

Source: Kazakhstanskaya Pravda, 17 May 2007

Bibliography

Primary Sources

Akiner Shirin, *Kazakhstan: An Overview*, UNHCR Emergency & Security Service, Council of the European Union, June 2002.

Brezhnev, L.I., *On the Draft Constitution of the USSR*, Moscow, 1977, CPSU: Reports.

27th CPSU Congress: *Documents, Records and Resolutions* (New Delhi, Patriot Publications, 1986).

28th CPSU Congress: *Documents, Records and Resolutions* (Moscow, Novosti Press Agency, 1990).

Closing Speeches by Mikhail Gorbachev, General Secretary of the CPSU, Central Committee at the 27lh CPSU Congress (New Delhi, *Soviet Review*, Vol. 20, No. 12) 17 March 1986.

Commission on Security and Cooperation in Europe *Report on Kazakhstan's Presidential Election*, Washington DC: Organisation for Security and Cooperation in Europe, 10 January 1999.

Constitution (Fundamental Law) of the Russian Socialist Federative Soviet Republic approved on 11 May 1925, *Selected from USSR: Sixty Years of the Union 1922-1982 (*Moscow, 1982).

Constitution (Fundamental Law) of the Russian Soviet Federative Socialist Republic (RSFSR), adopted by the Fifth All Russian Congress of Soviets, 10 July 1918, Selected from *USSR: Sixty years of the Union 1922-1982* (Progress Publishers, Moscow, 1982).

Constitution (Fundamental Law) of the Russian Soviet Federative Socialist Republic adopted by the Extraordinary 17th All Russian Congress of Soviets on 21 January 1937, Selected from *USSR: Sixty Years of the Union 1922-1982* (Moscow, 1982).

Constitution (Fundamental Laws) of the Union of Soviet Socialist Republics, Approved by the Second Congress of Soviets of the USSR on 31 January 1924, Selected from *USSR: Sixty Years of the Union 1922-1982* (Moscow, 1982).

Constitution (Fundamental Laws) of the Union of Soviet Socialist Republics, adopted by the extraordinary 8th Congress of Soviets of the USSR on

5 December 1936, *Selected from USSR: Sixty Years of the Union 1922-1982* (Moscow, 1982).

Constitution (Fundamental Laws) of the Union of Soviet Socialist Republics, adopted at the Seventh (special) session of the Supreme Soviet of the USSR, Ninth Convocation on 7 October 1977 (Novosti Press Agency Publishing House, Moscow, 1982).

Cultural Construction in the USSR: A Statistical Compilation (Moscow, TsSU, 1956).

Current Digest of the Post Soviet Press (Washington) (1985-1991).

Daily Review of the Soviet Press (Moscow).

Economist Intelligence Unit (EIU) Country Reports on Kazakhstan (1997-2000).

Europe World Year-Book (London).

European Commission (EC), *Kazakhstan Economic Trends, 1998,* 4 Vols. (Brussels, 1998).

Facts-on-File (New York).

Gazeti SSSR, *Ethnic Composition of the USSR Population* (Finansy i Statiska, Moscow, 1991).

Gazeti SSSR (1917-1960): *Newspapers of the USSR; A Bibliographical Handbook,* 3 vols. (Moscow: Kniga, 1970).

Gorbachev, Mikhail, S., *Speeches and Writings* (Oxford, Pergamon Press, 1986).

Human Rights Watch Report, "Kazakhstan: Freedom of the Media and Political Freedoms in the Prelude to the 1999 Elections", Vol. 1, No. 11, October 1999.

IMF, *Republic of Kazakhstan—Background Paper and Statistical Appendix (1995).*

IMF, *International Financial Statistics: Supplement on Countries of the Former Soviet Union* (1995-1997 and 1999).

IMF, *Kazakhstan, Economic Review* (various issues).

IMF, *Republic of Kazakhstan—Recent Economic Developments* (1998).

Kazakhstan. Official Government Website accessed on 26 September 2003. <www.president.kz>.

Keesing's Record of World Events (New Jersey).

Lenin, V.I., *Critical Remarks on the National Question, the Right of Nations to Self Determination* (Moscow, 1975).

Lenin, V.I., *On Soviet Socialist Democracy* (Moscow, 1972).

Lenin, V.I., *State and Revolution* (Moscow, 1978).

National Economy of the USSR: Statistical Survey (Statistika, Moscow, 1990).

Nazarbaev, Nursultan. Adiletting aq zholy. Almaty, "Qazaqstan," 1991.

Nazarbayev N., *Address to the 8th Session of Assembly of Kazakhstan's Nations* (Almaty, 2001).

Nazarbayev, N., *Kazakhstan 2030 - Message to the People of Kazakhstan* (Almaty, October 1997).

Nazarbayev, Nursultan, "On the Situation in the Country and Major Directions of Domestic and Foreign Policy: Democratisation, Economic and Political Reform for the New Century", Address to the Nation delivered on 30 September 1998.

Nazarbayev, Nursultan. "The Ideological Consolidation of Society as a Condition of Kazakhstan's Progress", *Kazakhstanskaia Pravda*, 9 October 1993. As translated in *FBIS Daily Report USR-94-003*, 12 January 1994.

Organization for Security and Co-operation in Europe (OSCE) Report, Almaty: 1998.

Summary of World Broadcasts, BBC (Soviet Union) (1985-2000).

The Russian Federal Migration Service (RFMS) and the State Statistics Committee's Data, 1989-1993.

The Soviet Union: 50 Years Statistical returns (Moscow, TsSu, 1969). *The Times Concise Atlas of World History, 5th* edition, (London, 1994).

UN - *Statistical Yearbook*, 1997.

UNDP, *Kazakhstan—Human Development Report* (1995 to 2001).

US Department of State's *Kazakhstan Country Report on Human Rights Practices for 1998*. Washington DC: Bureau of Democracy, Human Rights and Labor 26 February 1999.

United Nation Development Report, Almaty, 1995.

World Bank - *Kazakhstan: The Transition to a Market Economy*, 1995.

World Bank – *Statistical Handbook: States of the Former USSR*, 1997.

Secondary Sources

Books

Abishev, Adel E. (ed.), *Kazakhstan in Focus: Ten Years of Independence,* (Almaty, Centre for Foreign Policy and Analysis: 2002).

Aitken Jonathan, *Nazarbayev and the Making of Kazakhstan*, Continnum, London, 2009.

Akiner, Shirin (ed.), Cultural *Change and Continuity in Central Asia* (London, Kegan Paul: 1991).

Akiner Shirin, Kazakhstan: An Overview, *UNHCR Emergency & Security Service*, Council of the European Union, June 2002.

Alimov, Kadir Z., *Prospects for Development of Institution* (Washington, Central Asia Institute, School of Advanced International Studies, John Hopkins University: 1995)

Allworth, Edward (ed.), *Central Asia: A Century of Russian Rule*, (New York, Columbia University Press, 1967).

Allworth, Edward (ed.), *Soviet Nationality Problems*, (New York, Columbia University Press, 1971).

Allworth, Edward (ed.), The Nationalities Question in Soviet Central Asia, (New York, Praeger, 1973).

Arblaster, Anthony, *Democracy* (Buckingham, Open University Press, 1994).

Armstrong, John A., *Ideology Politics and Government in the Soviet Union, An Introduction* (New York Praeger, 1967).

Azar, Edward E., *The Management of Protracted Social, Conflict* (Brookfield, V.T. Gower: 1990).

Azreal, Jeremy.R., Soviet *Nationalities Policies and Practices* (New York, Praeger, 1978).

Bacon, Elizabeth E, *Central Asia under Russian Rule: A Study in Cultural Change* (New York, Cornell University Press, 1996).

Banuazizi, A. and Weiven, M. (eds.), *The New Geopolitics of Central Asia and its Borderlands* (Bloomington, Indiana University Press: 1994).

Baykov, Alexander; *The Development of the Soviet Economic System*, (Cambridge, Cambridge University Press, 1947).

Beauclerk, J. and Heap, S. "Civil Society-State Relationships: Models and Actualities', Background Paper for INTRAC's 10th Anniversary Conference, *Changing Expectations? The Concept and Practice of Civil Society in International Development,* (Balliol College, Oxford, 13-15 Dec, 2001).

Beissinger, Mark and Lumbomyr Hajda (eds.), *The Nationalities Factor in Soviet Politics and Society* (Boulder. Co., Westview Press: 1990).

Bennigsen, A. and Broxup, Marie, *The Islamic Threat to the Soviet State* (London; Croom Helw, 1983).

Boersner, Demetrio, *The Bolsheviks and the National and Colonial Question*, (Paris, Libraries Minard, 1957).

Bremmer, Ian and Ray, Taras (eds.), *Nations and Politics in the Soviet Successor States* (Cambridge, Cambridge University Press: 1993).

Brezezinski, Zabagniev (ed.), *Dilemmas of Change in Soviet Politics*, (Columbia University Press, 1969).

Bromley, Y., *Major Ethno-Social Trends in the USSR* (Moscow, Progress: 1988).

Carlton, David and Ingram Paul (eds.), *The Search for Stability in Russia and the Former Soviet Bloc* (USA, Ashgate Publishing Ltd: 1997).

Carrere D. 'Encausse, Helene, *The End of Soviet Empire - The Triumph of Nations* (New York, New Republic: 1993).

Carrere D. 'Encausse, Helene, The *Great Challenge: Nationalities and the Bolshevik State, 1917-1930* (New York and London, Holmes and Meier: 1991).

Carrere D. 'Encausse, Helene, *The Nationality Question in the Soviet Union and Russia* (Norwegian Nobel Institute Lecture Series, Oslo, Scandinavian University Press: 1995).

Chandhoke, Neera, *State and Civil Society: Exploration in Political Theory* (New Delhi: Sage Publication, 1995).

Churchward, L.G., *Contemporary Soviet Government* (London, Routledge Kegan Paul, 1968).

Coats, W.P. and Zeida, K., Soviets *in Central Asia* (London, Lawrence and Wishant, 1951).

Cohen Ariel, *Kazakhstan: The Road to Independence* Inergy Policy and the Birth of a Nation (Monogrph) Central Asia-Caucasus Institute&Silk Road Studies Programme Joint Center, Washington 2008.

Comings, Sally. N., *Power and Change in Central Asia* (Routledge, London and New York, 2002).

Conquest, Robert, *The Nation Killers: The Soviet Deportations of Nationalities* (London, McMillan: 1960).

Conquest, Robert, *Power and Policy in the USSR* (London: Macmillan, 1961).

Curtis, Glenn E., *Kazakhstan: A Country Study* (Washington, Federal Research Division, Library of Congress. 1996).

Dallin, Alexander and Rice, C., *The Gorbachev Era* (California, Stanford, 1987).

Daniels, Robert, V., *Is Russia Reformable? Change and Resistance from Stalin to Gorbachev* (Boulder; West View Press, 1990).

Davisha, Karen and Parrott, Bruce, *Russia and the New States of Eurasia* (London, Cambridge University Press: 1994).

Dawson, C., (ed) *The Mongol Mission* (New York, 1995)

Demko, G.J., *The Russian Colonization of Kazakhstan: 1896-1916* (Bloomington, University of Indiana Press, 1969).

Derbyshire J. Denis and Derbyshire, Ian, *Political System of the World* (London, Helicon Publication,1996).

Diamond, Larry and Marc F. Plattner (eds.), *Nationalism, Ethnic Conflict and Democracy* (Baltimore and London, John Hopkins University Press: 1994).

Diamond, Larry and Platter, Marc (eds), *The Global Resurgence of Democracy.* 2nd ed. (Baltimore, The John Hopkins University Press, 1996

Dunlop, John, *The Faces of Contemporary Russian Nationalism* (Princeton, Princeton University Press: 1993).

Dunlop, John, *The New Russian Nationalism* (New York, Praeger: 1985).

Dunn, John (ed.), *Democracy: The Unfinished Journey*, (Oxford, Oxford University Press,1992).

Elazar, Daniel J. (ed.), *Constitutional Design and Power Sharing in the Post-Modern Epoch* (Lanham, University Press of America: 1991).

Fainsod, Merle, *How Russia is Ruled?* (Cambridge:Harvard University Press, 1953).

Feldbrugge, F.J.M., *The Constitutions of the USSR and the Union Republics Analysis* (Texts Reports, Netherlands, 1979)

Fierman, William, *Soviet Central Asia: The Failed Transformation* (Boulder, Westview Press: 1991).

Fowkes, Ben, *The Disintegration of the Soviet Union* (London, McMillan Press Ltd: 1997).

Garbutt, Anne and Heap, Simon, *Growing Civil Society in Central Asia* (Almaty, INTRAC's First Central Asian Regional Conference13-14th June 2002, Occasional Papers Series 39.)

Gerasimov, I.P. (ed.), *Kazakhstan* (Moscow, Nauka: 1969).

Gidadhubli, R.G., *Social-Economic Transformation of Soviet Central Asia* (New Delhi: Patriot Publishers, 1987).

Glebov, Oleg and John Crowfoot (eds.), *The Soviet Empire: Its Nations Speak out* (London, Harvard Academic Publishers: 1989).

Goldhagen, E. (ed.), *Ethnic Minorities in the Soviet Union* (New York, Praeger, 1968).

Goor, Lusvan de (ed.), *Between Development and Destruction: An Inquiry into the Causes of Conflicts in Post-Colonial States* (London, Macmillan, 1996).

Graham, Smith (ed.), *The Nationalities Question in the Soviet Union* (London, Longman, 1990).

Greenfeld, Liah, *Nationalism: Five Roads to Modernity* (Cambridge, Harvard University Press; 1992).

Guenther, Hans (ed.), *The Culture of the Stalin Period* (New York, St. Martin's Press: 1990).

Haghayeghi, Mehrdad, *Islam and Politics in Central Asia* (New York, St. Martin's Press: 1995).

Hajda, Lubmyr, and Mark, Beissinger (eds.) *The Nationalities Factors in Soviet Politics and Society* (Boulder. Western Press: 1990).

Harper, Samuel and Thomson, Ronald, *The Soviet Government* (New York, Van Nostrand Co, 1949)

Hazard, John. N., *The Soviet System of Government* (Chicago, University of Chicago Press, 1970)

Hiro, Dilip, *Between Marx and Muhammad: The Changing Face of Central Asia*, (London, Harper Collins, 1994).

Hopkirk, Peter, *The Great Game in Central Asia* (New York: Kondasha Internationals, 1992).

Hobswawn, Eric, *Nation and Nationalism since 1780: Programmes,, Myth, Reality* (Cambridge: Cambridge University Press, 1992).

Huntigton, Samuel, *The Third Wave: Democratisation in the Late Twentieth Century* (Norman and London; University of Oklahoma Press 1991).

Huntington, S., *Political Order in Changing Societies* (New Haven, Yale University Press: 1968).

Huttenbach, Henry R., *Soviet Nationality Policy: Ruling Ethnic Groups in the USSR* (London, Marsell: 1990).

Jalalzai, Musa Khan, *Central Asia: Political Situation and Economic Opportunities* (Lahore, The Frontier Post Publications: 1994).

James, R., *Power and Partnership? Experiences of NGO Capacity-Building* (Oxford: INTRAC, 2001)

Johnson, Lena and Esenov, Murad (ed.), *Political Islam and Conflict in Russia and Central Asia* (Stockholm, The Swedish Institute of International Affairs: 1999).

Johnson, S.M. (ed.), *Central Asia: Regional Cooperation for Peace and Development* (Rawalpindi, A Friend's Publication: 1998).

Kaiser, Robert J., *The Geography of Nationalism in Russia and the USSR* (Princeton, Princeton University Press: 1994).

Karklins, Rasma, *Ethnic Relations in the USSR: The Perspective from Below* (London, Allen Unwin: 1986).

Katz, Zev, Rogers, Rosemaire and Harned, Frederick, (eds), *Handbook of Major Soviet Nationalities* (New York, Free Press: 1975).

Kaushik, Devendra, *Central Asia in Modern Times* (Moscow, Progress: 1970).

Kautsky, John H., *Political Change in Underdeveloped Countries: Nationalism and Communism* (New York and London, Wiley: 1982).

Kaviraj, Sudipta and Khilnani, Sunil, (eds) *Civil Society, History and Possibilities* (New Delhi, Foundation Books,2002)

Kazakhstan, "Country Reports on Human Rights Practices" (*Bureau of Democracy, Human Rights, and Labor*), February 25, 2004.

Kolste, Paul, *Russians in Former Soviet Republics* (London, Hurst: 1995).

Kozlov, Viktor L., *The Peoples of the Soviet Union* (Bloomington, Indiana University Press: 1988).

Kremenyuk, Victor A., *Conflicts in and Around Russia: Nation Building in Difficult Times* (Westport. Ct., Greenwood Press: 1994).

Kulchik Yuriy, Fadin, Andrey and Scrgeev, Victor, *Central Asia after the Empire* (London, Pluto Press: 1996).

Lane, David, *Politics and Society in the USSR* (London, Weidenfeld and Nicholson: 1970).

Lapidus, Gail W., Zaslavasky, V. and Goldman. P. (ed.), *From the Union to Commonwealth: Nationalism and Separatism in the Soviet Republics* (Montreal, Cambridge University Press: 1992).

Lijphart, Arendt, *Democracy in Plural Societies* (New Haven, Yale University Press: 1977).

Manz, Beatrice F. (ed.), *Central Asia in Historical Perspective* (Colorado,Westview Press: 1996).

Melville, Anderi and Lapidus, G. (ed.), *The Glasnost Papers* (Colorado, Westview Press: 1990).

Millar, James R., and Wolchik, Sharon L. (eds.), *The Social Legacy of Communism* (Cambridge, Cambridge University Press: 1994).

Mendelbaum, Michael, *Central Asia and the World: Kazakhstan, Uzbekistan, Tajikistan, Kyrgyzstan and Turkmenistan* (New York, Foreign Relation Press, 1994)

Montville, Joseph V. (ed.), *Conflict and Peacemaking in Multiethnic Societies* (Toronto, Lexington Books: 1990).

Motyl, Alexander J. (ed.), *Sovietology, Rationality, Nationality: Coming to Grips with Nationalism in the USSR* (New York, Columbia University Press: 1992).

Nahaylo, B. and Swohboda, V., *Soviet Disunion: A History of the Nationalities Problem in the USSR* (London, Hawish Hamilton, 1990).

Naumkin, Vitaly, State, Religion and Society in Central Asia (London, Ithaca: 1993).

Nazarbayev, Nursultan, *The Kazakhstan Way,* Stacey International, (London, 2008).

Nysanbaev A., E. Arynov, B.Yesekeyev, *Republic of Kazakhstan: Five Years of Independent Development.* (Almaty, Edition of Institute of Philosophy, 1996).

Olcott, Martha Brill, *Kazakhstan Unfulfilled Promise* (Washington DC, Carnegie Endowment for International Peace, 2002).

Olcott, Martha Brill, *The Kazakhs* (Standford. C.A., Hoover University Press: 1987).

Olcott, Martha Brill, "Democratisation and the Growth of Political Participation in Kazakhstan," in Karen Dawisha & Bruce Parrot (eds.), *Conflict, Cleavage, and Change in Central Asia and the Caucasus* (Cambridge, 1997).

Orlovsky, Daniel (ed.), *Beyond Soviet Studies* (Washington, Woodrow Wilson Centre Press: 1995).

Page, S.W., *The Formation of the Political States in Soviet Union* (Harvard, Harvard University Press: 1959).

Paksoy, H.B. (ed.), *Central Asia Reader: The Rediscovery of History* (New York, M.E. Sharpe: 1994).

Patnaik, Ajay (ed.), *Commonwealth of Independent States; Problem and Prospects,* (New Delhi, Konark Publishers: 1995).

Pierce, R.A., *Russian Central Asia* (Berkeley, California University Press: 1960).

Piper, Richard, *The Formation of the Soviet Union Communism and Nationalism 1917-1923* (Cambridge, Harvard University Press: 1984).

Pomfret, Richard, *The Economies of Central Asia* (New Jersey, Princeton University Press: 1995).

Ramet, Pedro (ed.), Religion *and Nationalism in Soviet and East European Politics* (Durham, UK, Duke University Press: 1984).

Rashid, Ahmed, *The Resurgence of Central Asia: Islam or Nationalism* (Karachi, Oxford University Press: 1994).

Roeder, Philip G., *Red Sunset: The Failure of Soviet Politics* (Princeton, Princeton University Press: 1993).

Roi, Yaacov (ed.), *Muslim Eurasia: Conflicting Legacies* (London; Frank Cass: 1995).

Rubin, Barnett R. and Snyder, Jack (eds.), *Post-Soviet Political Order: Conflict and State Building* (London and New York, Routledge: 1998).

Ruffin, M. Hott and Waugh, Daniel (eds), *Civil Society in Central Asia* (Seattle and London: Centre for Civil Society International, Central Asia-Caucasus Institute, John Hopkins University, 1999.)

Rywkin, Michael, *Moscow's Muslim Challenges: Soviet Central Asia* (London, C. Hurst and Company, 1982).

Sacks, Paul and Pankurst, J.S. (ed.), *Understanding Soviet Society* (Boston, Unwin and Hyman: 1988).

Sakwa, Richard, *Gorbachev and His Reforms* (Hertfordshire, Philip Allan: 1990).

Sakwa, Richard, Russian *Politics and Society* (London and NY, Routledge: 1993).

Shams-ud-Din (ed.), *Nationalism in Russia and Central Asian Republics: Unfinished Democratic Revolution* (New Delhi, Lancer Books: 1999).

Shams-ud-Din (ed.), *Perestroika and the Nationality Question in the USSR* (New Delhi, Vikas: 1990).

Shapiro, Leonard, *The Government and Politics of Soviet Union* (Hutchison, London, 1965).

Sharma Jitendra, *New Soviet Constitution: An Indian Assessment* (Bombay, Madras, Calcutta, Bangalore, New Delhi. 1978)

Simon, Gerhard, *Nationalism and Policy towards the Nationalities in the Soviet Union: From Totalitarian Dictatorship to Post-Stalinist Society* (Boulder, Westview Press: 1991).

Smith, Graham (ed.), *The Nationalities Question in the Soviet Union* (London, Longman: 1990).

Smith, Graham; Law, Vivein and Wilson, Andrew, *Nation Building in Post-Soviet Borderlands—The Politics of National Identities* (London, Oxford University Press: 1998).

Snyder, Jed C., *After Empire: The Emerging Geopolitics of Central Asia* (Washington DC, National Defence University Press: 1995).

Soucek, Svat, *A History of Inner Asia* (Cambridge, Cambridge University Press: 2000).

Stobdan, P., *India and Kazakhstan: Civilizational Explorations* (Delhi, Heritage Publishers, 2003).

Sultanov, B.K. (ed), *Kazakhstan Today*, The Kazakhstan Institute for Strategic Studies under the President of Republic of Kazakhstan (Almaty. 2010).

Sunny, Ronald Grigor, *The Revenge of the Past: Nationalism, Revolution and the Collapse of the Soviet Union* (Stanford, Stanford University Press: 1993).

Teribilov, Vladimir (Translator M. Salfulin), *The Soviet Court* (Delhi, Central Book Ltd, 1986).

Thompson, Richard H., *Theories of Ethnicity: A Critical Appraisal* (Westport, CT. Greenwood Press: 1989).

Tishkov, Valery, *Ethnicity, Nationalism and Conflict in and after the Soviet Union: The Mind Aflame* (London, Sage Publications: 1997).

Triska, J.F. (ed.), *Constitution of the Communist Party States* (Hoover Institution Publication, 1970).

Tursunov, H.T., *On National Delimitation in Central Asia* (Tashkent: 1957).

Vaidyanath, R., *The Formation of the Soviet Central Asian Republics: A Study in Soviet Nationalities Policy* (New Delhi, People's Publishing House: 1967).

Vineeth, T.K., *Kazakhstan—Commemorating 10 Years of Independence* (New Delhi, Embassy of Kazakhstan: 2001).

Warikoo, K., *Central Asia and China: The Geopolitical Imperatives*, in Shams-ud-din (ed.) *Geopolitics and Energy Resources in Central Asia and Caspian Sea Region* (New Delhi, Lancer Books: 2000).

Warikoo, K. and Dawa Norbu (eds.), *Ethnicity and Politics in Central Asia* (New Delhi, South Asian Publishers: 1992).

Warikoo, K. (ed.), *Central Asia: Emerging New Order* (Delhi, Har Anand Publication: 1995).

Warikoo, K. & Mahavir Singh, *Central Asia: Since Independence.* (Delhi: Shipra Publication, 2004).

Wheeler, Geoffrey, *The Modern History of Soviet Central Asia* (New York, Preager, 1964).

Zakaria, Fareed, *The Future of Freedom: Illiberal Democracy at Home and Abroad* (New York, W.W. Norton and Company Inc, 2003)

Zhovtis, E.A., Freedom of Association and its Realization in Kazakhstan, in M.H.Ruffin, and D.Waugh (eds), Civil Society in Central Asia, Seattle:University of Washington Press,1999

Articles

Abazov, Rafis, 1998, Central Asian Republics: Search for a Model of Development (Central Asia in Transition, No.61). Hokkaido: Slavic Research Center.

Abazov, Rafis, "The Presidential Elections in Kazakhstan: Winner Takes All?" *Contemporary Central Asia*: Vol-3, No-2 1999.

Abbas, Najam, "Executive-Legislature Reunion in Kazakhstan", *Eurasian* Studies, vol. 3, no. 2. Summer 1996.

Afanasyev, Yuri, "Why the Empire Should Crumble," *Time,* 12 March 1990.

Afanasyev, Yuri, "Povedenie izbirateleil elektoralnaia politika v Rossii." *Polis*, No. 3, 1995

Ahmed, Salim, "Kazakhstan: Roots of Democracy," *News,* 25 April 1995.

Ahmed, Salim, "Kazakhstan Strengthens its Democracy", *News,* 4 April 1995

Ahmed, Samina, "The Political Implications of Ethnicity in Central Asia," *Regional Studies,* vol. 13, no.2, spring 1995.

Ahrari, M.E., "Dynamics of Changes in Muslim Central Asia", *Central Asian Survey*, vol. 13, no. 4, 1994.

Aitumukhambetov, A.T., "Five Years of Kazakhstan Independence," *The Muslim,* Islamabad 21 October 1996.

Akataeva, Alia, "Kazakhstan-China Trade and Economic Relations", *Himalayan and Central Asian Studies*, vol. 10, no. 4, October-December 2006.

Akbarzadeh, Shahram, "Political Shape of Central Asia", *Central Asian Survey*, vol. 16, no. 4, December 1997.

Akiner, Shirin, "Islam, State and Ethnicity in Central Asia in Historical Perspective", *Russia and Muslim World,* no. 4 (58), 1997.

Algar, H., "The Naqshabandi Order: A Preliminary Survey of Its History and Significance," *Studia Islamica*, 1976.

Algis, Prazauskas, "Ethnopolitical Issues and Emergence of Nation-State in Central

Asia' in Zhang, Youngjin and Azizian Rouben (ed.), *Ethnic Challenges beyond Borders: Chinese and Russian Perspectives of the Central Asian Conundrum* (St. Anthony's College, Oxford: 1998

Ali, Salamat, "Terrain of Tension," *Far Eastern Economic Review,* 12 August 1993

Anderson, John, "Constitutional Development in Central Asia", *Central Asian Survey,* vol.16, no-3 1997 pp. 301-320.

Armstrong, John A., "Nationalism in the Former Soviet Empire", *Problems of Communism,* vol. 41, nos. 1-2, January-April 1992.

Bagrauov, E., "The Development of Soviet Nationalities", *The Current Digest of Soviet Press,* vol. 24, no. 25, 17 July 1972.

Baizakova, Kuralay, "Democratisation and Political Stability in Kazakhstan", *Himalayan and Central Asian Studies,* vol. 10, no. 4, October-December 2006.

Banerjie, Indranil, "Nazarbayev Emerges Stronger after Polls", *Himalayan and Central Asian Studies,* vol. 10, no. 4, October-December 2006.

Bennigsen, A., "Islam in Retrospect", *Central Asian Survey,* vol. 13, no. 2, 1989.

Beteille, Andre, "Civil Society and Good Society" (*Sociological Bulletin, Journal of the Indian Sociological Society,* vol 50, no 2, 2001).

Blank, Stephen, "Kazakhstan's Foreign Policy in a Time of Turmoil", *A Eurasia Net Commentary* 27th April 2005.

Blank, Stephen, "Ethnic and Party Politics in Soviet Kazakhstan, 1920-1924", *Central Asian Survey,* vol. 10, no. 3, 1991.

Bowyer, Anthony Clive, 2008. 'Parliament and Political Parties in Kazakhstan', Silk Road Paper, John Hopkins University-SAIS. Washington DC.

Bremmer, Ian and Welt Cory, "The Trouble with Democracy in Kazakhstan", *Central Asian Survey,* vol. 15, no. 2, June 1996.

Brown, Bess, "The Public Role in Perestroika in Central Asia," *Central Asian Survey,* vol. 9, no.1, 1990.

Brubaker, Rogers, "Nationhood and the National Question in the Soviet Union and Post Soviet Eurasia: An Institutionalist Account," *Theory and Society,* vol. 23, no. 1, 1994.

Brusina, O.I., "The Russians in Central Asia: An Ethnic Minority with-an Elder Brother's Past," *Russia and the Muslim World,* no. 2, 1993.

Brzezinski, Zbigniew, "Post Communist Nationalism", *Foreign Affairs,* vol. 68, no. 5, winter 1989-90.

Carother, Thomas, 1997. ' Democracy without Illusions', Foreign Affairs, January-February, p.17. Eurasia Daily Monitor, 2005. 'A Victory in Presidential Election', vol.2, no.226.

Confield, Robert, "Restructuring in Greater Central Asia: Changing Political Configuration", *Asian Survey,* vol. 32, no. 10, October 1992.

Dave, Bhavna, "National Revival in Kazakhstan: Language Shift and Identity Change", *Post Soviet Affairs,* vol. 12, no. l, 1996.

Diamond Larry, "Thinking About Hybrid Regimes," *Journal of Democracy,* 2002.

Eden, Naby, "Ethnicity and Islam in Central Asia," *Central Asian Survey,* vol. 12, no.2, 1993.

Fiermann, William, "Religion and Nationalism in Soviet Central Asia," *Problems of Communism,* vol. 38, July-August 1989.

Ford, Bryan, 15 May 2002. 'Delegative Democracy', htpp//www.brynosaurus.com

Fuller, G.E., "Emergence of Central Asia", *Foreign Policy*, vol. 78, Spring 1990.

Galyamova, D. "Division of Powers in Kazakhstan: Constitutional Experience of Independent Development", *Contemporary Central Asia*, vol. 11, no. 3, December 1998.

Garbutt, Anne, and Simon Heap (eds), "Growing Civil Society in Central Asia", *INTRAC*'s First Central Asia Regional Conference, Almaty, Kazakhstan, 13-14 June 2002.

Gleason Gregory, "Asian Values and the Democratic Transition in Central Asia," For a discussion of Central Asia's flawed democratic process" (Harvard *Asia Quarterly* May 2001).

Gleason. Gregory, "Independent Muslim Republics in Central Asia: Legacy of the Past, Shape of the Future", *Journal of Institute of Muslim Minorities Affairs,* vol. 12, no. 2, July 1991.

Glenn, E. Curties, 1996, Kazakhstan: A Country Study, Washington: Library of Congress.

Haghayeghi, Mehradad, "Politics of Privatization in Kazakhstan", *Central Asian Survey,* vol. 16, no. 3, September 1997.

Halbachev, Owe, "World Politics and Indigenous Development in Central Asia," *Aussen Politik,* vol. 43, no. 4, 1992.

Hiro, Dilip, "Islamist Strengths and Weaknesses in Central Asia", *Middle East Journal*, 5 February 1993.

Hunter, Shirin, "Islam in Post-Independence Central Asia: Internal and External Dimensions", *Journal of Islamic Studies,* vol. 7, no. 2, January 1996.

Human Rights Watch, 2004, 'Political Freedom in Kazakhstan', 5 April, http//www.hrw.org/en/node/12147/section/4. Accessed on 14 December 2008.

H.B. Paksoy, (ed), *Central Asia Reader: The Rediscovery of History* (M.E. Sharpe, New York: 1994),p.33.

Hyman, Anthony, "Power and Politics in Central Asia's New Republics", *Conflict Studies*, vol. 27, no. 3, August 1994.

IHFHR, 1999, 'Annual Report', International Helsinki Federation for Human Rights, Italy.

Janusz Bugajski, Event Summary The Future of Kazakhstan after the Presidential Election May 12, 2011, Carnegie Endowment for International Peace, Washington, DC 20036.

Kazakhstan's Record on Human Rights, Democratisation and Fulfilling its OSCE Chairmanship Commitments Executive Summary, 10 June 2008, www.freedomhouse.org. Accessed in 2007.

Kazinform, 17 January 2012.

Ragov, Igor, Ivanovich, "Formation and development of the Constitutional control in the Republic of Kazakhstan". www.const council.kz/eng/

Janabel, Jiger, "When National Ambition Conflicts with Reality: Studies on Kazakhstan's Ethnic Relations", *Central Asian Survey,* vol. 15, no. l, 1996.

Kaapcke, Gretchen, "Indigenous Identity Transition in Russia", *Cultural Survival Quarterly,* vol. 18, no. 2-3, summer 1994.

Kagan, Robert; "The New Republic" in *The Washington Post,* 7th July 2003.

Kalsto, Pal. "Anticipating Demographic Superiority; Kazakh Thinking on Integration and Nation Building", *Europe Asia Studies,* vol. 50, no. 1, January 1998.

Karpat, H. Kemal, "The Old and New Central Asia", *Central Asian Survey,* vol. 2, no. 4, 1993.

Kendirday, Gulnar, "National Liberation Movement of the Kazakh Intelligentsia at the Beginning of the 20th Century", *Central Asian Survey,* vol. 16, no. 4, December 1997.

Khan, Ahsan M.M., "Muslims of Central Asia: A Recap", *Journal of Institute of Muslim Minority Affairs,* vol. 13, no. 1, January 1992.

Khazanov, Anatoly M., "The Ethnic Problems of Contemporary Kazakhstan", *Central Asian Survey,* vol. 14, no. 2, 1995.

Keely, Lange, "Do Borders Make a Nation: A New Analysis of Identities with a Focus on Central Asia," Regional Studies, (Islamabad: Autumn 1997), vol. xv, no.4.

Kubicek, Paul, "Regionalism, Nationalism and Realpolitik in Central Asia", *Europe Asia Studies,* vol. 49, no. 4, 1997.

Kukeyeva, Fatima, "Kazakhstan-US Relations: Some Perspective", *Himalayan and Central Asian Studies,* vol.10, no. 4, October-December 2006.

Kuzio, Taras, "Nationalist Riots in Kazakhstan", *Central Asian Survey,* vol. 7, no. 4, 1988.

Kuznetsova, Sofia, "Islam and Nationalism in Central Asia: Survey of Foreign Publications", *Russian and Muslim World,* no. 10 (40), 1995.

Kurganbaeva, G., "The Analysis of the Development of the Agricultural Branch in Kazakhstan." (KazISS October 10, 2002)

Landau, Jacob M., "The Fortunes and Misfortunes of Pan-Turkism", *Central Asian Survey,* vol. 7, no. l, 1998.

Lane, David, "The Gorbachev Revolution: The Role of the Political Elite in Regime Disintegration," *Political Studies,* vol. XLIV, no. 4, 1996.

Lipovsky, Igor P., "Central Asia: In Search of a New Political Identity," *The Middle East Journal,* vol. 50, no. 2, Spring 1996.

Lipovsky, Igor P., "Kazakhstan Alarmed Over Aggressive Secessionism," *The News,* 6 October 1996.

Lipovsky, Igor P., "The Russian Problem in Central Asia," *Orient Quarterly,* vol. 36, no. 3, September 1995.

Macaulay, Alastair, "Civil Disturbance in Alma Ata: A Comment", *Discussion Paper Series,* Russia and Soviet Studies (University of Sussex: 1987).

Makasheva, Klara, "Kazakhstan and the United Nations", *Himalayan and Central Asian Studies*, vol. 10, no. 4, October-December 2006.

Matveeva, Anna, "Democratisation, Legitimacy and Political change in Central Asia", *International Affairs*, vol. 75, no. 1, January 1999.

Micklin, Philip P., "Soviet Water Diversion Plans: Implications for Kazakhstan and Central Asia," *Central Asian Survey*, vol. 1, No. 4, April 1983.

Mirsky, George L., "Central Asia Emergence", *Current History*, vol. 91, no. 567. October 1992.

Nuri Maqsudul Hasan, "Kazakhstan: Challenges of Nation Building", *Regional Studies*, vol. 15, no. 3, Summer 1997.

O'Donnell, G., "Delegative Democracy", *Journal of Democracy*, vol. 5, no. 1 (January 1994), pp 55-69.

Olcott, Martha Brill, "Central Asia: The Calculus of Independence", *Current History*, vol. 94, no. 5, October 1995.

Olcott, Martha Brill, "Central Asia; Post Empire Politics", *Orbis*, vol. 36, no. 2, spring 1993.

Olcott, Martha Brill, "Kazakhstan," in Collier *Encyclopedia* (New York: Macmillan, vol. 14, 1993.

Olcott, Martha Brill, "Central Asia's Catapult to Independence", *Foreign Affairs*, vol. 71, no. 3, 1992.

Otarbaeva, Bakhytnur, "Evolution of Ethnic Identity of Kazakh People", *Eurasian Studies*, Ankara, no. 13, Spring 1998.

Ovcharenko,Vsevolod, "The State-Civil Society Relationship in Kazakhstan: Mechanisms of Cooperation and Support" in *The International Journal of Not-for-Profit Law*, vol. 6, no. 3, June 2004.

Palat, Madhavan K., "Emergence of Central Asia", *Indian Historical Review*, vol. 18, nos. 1-2, 1991.

Prazauskas, Algis, "Ethnic Conflicts in the Context of Democratizing Political Systems", *Theory and Society*, vol. 20, no. 5, October 1991.

Rashid, Ahmed, "Proxy State", *Far Eastern Economic Review*, 31 March 1994.

Rashid, Ahmed, "Points of Conflict," *Far Eastern Economic Review*, 3 June 1993.

Rashid, Ahmed, "Caught in a Cleft," *Far Eastern Economic Review*, 19 Nov. 1992.

Rashid, Ahmed, "President Nazarbayev Still Faces Major Problems", *Nation*, 24 October 1992.

Rashid, Ahmed, "Ethnic Tensions Simmer in Stalin's Dumping Ground", *Independent*, London, 7 June 1990.

Rashid, Ahmed, "Bless Perestroika and Send Korans", *Independent*, 4 June 1990.

Rashid, Ahmed, "Picking Up Pieces", *Far Eastern Economic Review*, 9 January 1992

Remnick, David, "Kazakhstan: A Republic Rebels", *Washington Post*, Nov. 1990.

Remnick, David, "Kazakhstan's Off Limits Hero", *Washington Post*, 29 Dec. 1990.

Roeder, Philip G., "Soviet Federalism and Ethnic Mobilization", *World Politics*, vol. 43, no. 2, January 1991.

Rumer, Boris Z., "The Gathering Storm in Central Asia," *Orbis,* vol. 37, Winter 1993.

Rywkin, M., "The Impact of Socio-Economic Change and Demographic Growth on National Identity and Socialization", *Central Asian Survey,* vol. 9, no. 2, 1990.

Rywkin, M., "Islam and the New Soviet Man: 70 Years of Evolution", *Central Asian Survey,* vol. 6, no. 4, 1987.

Sabol, Steven, "The Creation of Soviet Central Asia: the 1924 National Delimitation", *Central Asian Survey*, vol. 14, no. 2, 1996.

Sapanov, E., "Elections in Kazakhstan", *Himalayan and Central Asian Studies*, vol. 10, no. 4, October-December 2006.

Sarsembayev, Azamat, "Imagined Communities: Kazakh Nationalism and Kazakification in the 1990's", *Central Asian Survey,* vol. 18, no. 3, 1999.

Schatz, Edward A.D., "Framing Strategies and Non-Conflicts in Multi-Ethnic Kazakhstan", *Nationalism and Ethnic Politics,* vol. 6, no. 2, summer 2000.

Sengupta, Anita, "Minorities and Nationalizing States in Central Asia", *International Studies,* vol. 34, no. 3, 1997.

Shams-ud-Din., "Soviet Languages Policy", *Studies in Islam,* New Delhi, vol. 19, no. 3, July 1982.

Shomanov, Askar Z., "Social Modernization of Kazakh Society," *Contemporary Central Asia,* New Delhi, vol. 1, no. 1, 1997.

Simes, Dimitri, "The Return of Russian History", *Foreign Affairs,* vol. 73, no. 1, January-February 1994.

Soni, Sharad K., "Changing Image of a Capital City: Relevance of OSCE Summit for Astana's International Recognition," in Materials of the Fourth Annual International Scientific Conference on Independence of the State and Capital of the Country: Connotation of Meanings (Astana: Elorda, 2011), pp. 39-45.

Soni, Sharad K., "Kazakhstan OSCE Chairmanship and Regional Security," in Materials of International Scientific—Theoretic Conference on World Politics and Kazakhstan: Problems and Perspectives (Almaty, 2011), pp. 51-58.

Starr Frederic, "Democratisation in Central Asia: the public's view," *Central Asia Institute Briefing Paper*, The Paul H. Nitsze School of Advanced International Studies, 1997.

Stobadan, P., "Looking Towards Central Asia", *Strategic Analysis,* vol. 16, no. 18, November 1993.

Stobdan, P., "Islamic Reawakening in Central Asia: Towards Stability or Conflict," *Strategic Analysis*, vol. 15, no. 6, September 1992.

Sylie, K., "Kazakh Pleads Russia's Cause", *Guardian Weekly,* 27 September 1992.

Soucek, Svat, "A History of Inner Asia" (Cambridge University Press, London: 2000), p. 46.

Szporluk, Roman, "Dilemmas of Russian Nationalism", *Problems of Communism,* vol. 38, no. 4, July-August 1989.

Tazmini, Ghoncheh, "The Islamic Revival in Central Asia: A Potent Force or a Misconception", *Central Asian Survey*, vol. 20, no. 1, 2001.

Tishkov, Valery, "Perspectives on Ethnic Accord in Post-Soviet Space", *Cultural Survival Quarterly*, vol. 18, nos. 2-3, Summer 1994.

Tishkov, Valery, "Post-Soviet Ethnography—Not a Crisis but Something More Serious," *Anthropology and Archeology of Eurasia: A Journal of Translations*, vol. 33, no. 3, Winter 1994-95.

Tishkov, Valery, "The Soviet Empire Before and After Perestroika", *Theory and Society*, vol. 20, no. 5, October 1991.

Tolipov, Farkhod, "Nationalism as a Geopolitical Phenomenon: The Central Asian Case", *Central Asian Survey*, vol. 20, no. 2, 2001.

Unal, Ceviokoz, "A Brief Account of the Economic Situation in the Former Soviet Republics of Central Asia", *Central Asian Survey*, vol. 13, no. l, 1994.

Utegenova, Ailuna, "OSCE Activities in Central Asia", *Himalayan and Central Asian Studies*, vol. 10, No. 4, October-December 2006.

Warikoo, K., "Dynamics of Change in Soviet Central Asia", *World Affairs*, vol. 3, June 1991.

Warikoo, K., "The Resurgence of Central Asia", *Strategic Analysis*, vol. 15, no. 6, September 1992.

Warikoo, K., "Central Asian Resurgence", *Seminar*, no. 393, May 1992.

Warikoo, K., and Mahavir Singh, Central Asia: Since Independence (Delhi: Shipra Publication, 2004).

Warikoo, K., "Russia's Policy towards Kazakhstan during Yeltsin Period", *Himalayan and Central Asian Studies*, vol. 10, no. 4, October-December 2006.

Weidemann, Diethelm, "The Asian Dimension of the Dissolution of the USSR: The Central Asian Conflict Constellation-Origin, Structure, Complexity and Specificity", *Strategic Studies*, vol. 16, no. 3, Spring 1994.

Wolczuk, K., "Presidentialism in Ukraine: A Mid-Term Review of the Second Presidency", *Democratisation*, vol. 4, no.3, 1997, pp.152-171.

Zaslavsky, Victor, "Nationalism and Democratic Transition in Post Communist Societies", *Daedalus*, vol. 25, 1950.

Zhangazy, Ruslan, *About the Main Tendencies of Language Policy*, Institute for Strategic Studies under the President of the Republic of Kazakhstan, July 12, 2006.

Journals and Periodicals

Asian Survey.

Central Asia Monitor (Fairhaven, Vermont).

Central Asian Review (London).

Central Asian Survey (London).

Central Asiatic Journal (Wiesbaden).

Contemporary Central Asia (New Delhi).

Current History.

Europe Asia Studies (Glasgow).
Foreign Affairs (New York).
Harvard Journal of Asiatic Studies (Cambridge).
Himalayan and Central Asian Studies (New Delhi).
International Affairs (Moscow).
Journal of Asian History (Wiesbaden).
Kazakhstan (Alma Aty).
Kazakhstan Paradise of Central Asia: 15 years of Progress 1991-2006, (India).
Post-Soviet Geography (Wiesbaden).
Regional Studies (Islamabad).
Soviet Studies (Glasgow).
World Focus (New Delhi).

Newspapers
Central Asian Post (Bishkek).
Ekspress-K (Alma Aty).
Globe (Alma Aty).
Indian Express (New Delhi).
Kazakhstanskaya Pravda (Alma Aty).
Moscow News (Moscow).
New York Times (New York).
Pravda (Moscow).
The Asian Age (New Delhi).
The Hindu (New Delhi).
The Times (London).

Websites
www.statson.edu/departments
www.lib.uchicago.edu
www.udel.edu
www.paurus.com
www.hrw.org/reports
www.osce.org
www.kisi.kz
www.missions.itu.int
http://www.kazelection2004.org/thecec.htm
www.iwpr.net
www.president.kz
missions.itu.int
www.unm.edu/gleasong
http://www.keston.org
www.upinfo.call
www.heritagenet.unesco.kz/kz/hn-english/history_en.htm

www.president.kz/articles

www.heritagenet.unesco.kz/kz/hn-english/history

http//www.state.gov/g/drl/rls/irf/2001, Human Rights and Labor: 2001, (online: web)URL

http://www.eurasianet.org/departments/insight/articles/eav042705.shtml

http://www.photius.com/countries/kazakhstan/society/kazakhstan_society_religion.html. *Sources:* The Library of Congress Country Studies; CIA World Factbook

http://news.bbc.co.uk/1/hi/world/asia-pacific/country_profiles/1298071.stm

NationinTransit,2004 unpan1.un.org/intradoc/groups/public/documents/nispacee/unpan016578.pdf

www.unpanl:un.org/intradoc/groups/public/documents/apcityunpano 18210.pdf

Index